FREE INDIRECT

LITERATURE NOW

LITERATURE NOW

Matthew Hart, David James, and Rebecca L. Walkowitz, Series Editors

Literature Now offers a distinct vision of late-twentieth- and early-twenty-first-century literary culture. Addressing contemporary literature and the ways we understand its meaning, the series includes books that are comparative and transnational in scope as well as those that focus on national and regional literary cultures.

Caren Irr, *Toward the Geopolitical Novel: U.S. Fiction in the Twenty-First Century*

Heather Houser, *Ecosickness in Contemporary U.S. Fiction: Environment and Affect*

Mrinalini Chakravorty, *In Stereotype: South Asia in the Global Literary Imaginary*

Héctor Hoyos, *Beyond Bolaño: The Global Latin American Novel*

Rebecca L. Walkowitz, *Born Translated: The Contemporary Novel in an Age of World Literature*

Carol Jacobs, *Sebald's Vision*

Sarah Phillips Casteel, *Calypso Jews: Jewishness in the Caribbean Literary Imagination*

Jeremy Rosen, *Minor Characters Have Their Day: Genre and the Contemporary Literary Marketplace*

Jesse Matz, *Lasting Impressions: The Legacies of Impressionism in Contemporary Culture*

Ashley T. Shelden, *Unmaking Love: The Contemporary Novel and the Impossibility of Union*

Theodore Martin, *Contemporary Drift: Genre, Historicism, and the Problem of the Present*

Zara Dinnen, *The Digital Banal: New Media and American Literature and Culture*

Gloria Fisk, *Orhan Pamuk and the Good of World Literature*

Peter Morey, *Islamophobia and the Novel*

Sarah Chihaya, Merve Emre, Katherine Hill, and Jill Richards, *The Ferrante Letters: An Experiment in Collective Criticism*

Christy Wampole, *Degenerative Realism: Novel and Nation in Twenty-First-Century France*

Heather Houser, *Infowhelm: Environmental Art and Literature in an Age of Data*

Jessica Pressman, *Bookishness: Loving Books in a Digital Age*

Sunny Xiang, *Tonal Intelligence: The Aesthetics of Asian Inscrutability During the Long Cold War*

Thomas Heise, *The Gentrification Plot: New York and the Postindustrial Crime Novel*

Ellen C. Jones, *Literature in Motion: Translating Multilingualism Across the Americas*

Free Indirect

THE NOVEL IN A POSTFICTIONAL AGE

Timothy Bewes

Columbia University Press
New York

Columbia University Press
Publishers Since 1893
New York   Chichester, West Sussex
cup.columbia.edu
Copyright © 2022 Columbia University Press

Library of Congress Cataloging-in-Publication Data
Names: Bewes, Timothy, author.
Title: Free indirect : the novel in a postfictional age / Timothy Bewes.
Description: New York : Columbia University Press, 2022. | Series: Literature now |
Includes bibliographical references and index.
Identifiers: LCCN 2021054788 (print) | LCCN 2021054789 (ebook) | ISBN 9780231191609
(hardback) | ISBN 9780231192972 (trade paperback) | ISBN 9780231549479 (ebook)
Subjects: LCSH: Fiction—History and criticism. | Fiction genres—Philosophy. |
Postmodernism (Literature)
Classification: LCC PN3347 .B49 2022 (print) | LCC PN3347 (ebook) |
DDC 809.3—dc23/eng/20211117
LC record available at https://lccn.loc.gov/2021054788
LC ebook record available at https://lccn.loc.gov/2021054789

Cover design: Elliott S. Cairns
Cover image: Private collection. Photo © Christie's Images /
Bridgeman Images. © 2021 C. Herscovici /
Artists Rights Society (ARS), New York.

For t.

The bottom has dropped out.

—J. M. COETZEE

The modern fact is that we no longer believe in this world. We do not even believe in the events which happen to us, love, death, as if they only half concerned us. . . . The link between man and the world is broken.

—GILLES DELEUZE

CONTENTS

ACKNOWLEDGMENTS xiii

LIST OF ABBREVIATIONS xvii

Introduction
Unthinking Connections 1

PART I. The Novel Form and Its Limits

Chapter One
The Problem of Form 17
The Novel Thinks 17
The Meaning of Novelistic Form 20
Absolute Relationality 29
Free Indirect Discourse and the Free Indirect 34

Chapter Two
Against Exemplarity: W. G. Sebald 39
Instance and Example 39
Exemplarity and the Novel 50

Principles of Narration   56
The Pure Look   58
The Struggle of Austerlitz   60

PART II. The Emergence of Postfictional Aesthetics

Chapter Three
The Instantiation Relation   71
The Contemporary Critical Predicament   71
The Bridge (the Problem of the Opening)   74
The Rhetoric of Contemporary Criticism   80
The Instantiation Relation in Literary Criticism   85
All Views Are Partial: Reading Zadie Smith   89

Chapter Four
The Postfictional Hypothesis   96
Degree-Zero Connection   96
From Representation to Instantiation: Forster's Howards End   100
Collapse of Narrative Standpoint   105
Instantiation as a Question of Language: Possible Objections   113

Chapter Five
The Logic of Disconnection   121
Chronotopes of Interpretation: Foucault with Bakhtin   121
The "Novelistic Element": Free Indirect Discourse   128
A Theory of "Discontinuous Systematicities"?   134
Is Disconnection Also a Chronotope?   141

Interlude
Fictional Discourse as Event: On Jesse Ball   155

PART III. The Free Indirect

Chapter Six
How Does Immanence Show Itself?   163
The Sense of Sense   163
A Theory of the Contemporary Novel?   171
Resolution as "Deflection": Lukács with Cora Diamond   173
Instantiation and the Literary Regime   188

Chapter Seven
What Is a Sensorimotor Break? Deleuze on Cinema   195
The Possibility of Thinking   195
The Historical Argument   201
The Any-Instant-Whatever, the Out-of-Field, the Interstice   207
Heautonomy   214
Disconnecting the Sides: Free Indirect Subjective   217

Interlude
Profiling   228

Chapter Eight
Rancière: Toward Nonregime Thinking   231
The Aesthetic Regime   231
Hitchcock: Cinema of Completion   241
The Interstice: Realist Form or Crystals of Time?   243
Penultimacy   248
The Primacy of Relation: Samuel Beckett   251

Conclusion
The Indeterminate Thought of the Free Indirect   255

NOTES   261

INDEX   303

ACKNOWLEDGMENTS

The writing of this book was made possible by the intellectual and scholarly environment of Brown University, my professional home for almost two decades. I would like to thank two successive English department chairs, Philip Gould and Richard Rambuss, for their kindness, interest, and support during the period of its completion. A faculty fellowship at the Cogut Institute for the Humanities in 2015 enabled me to present an early version of chapter 3. I have enjoyed extraordinary levels of support from my university administration, including the granting of sabbatical semesters in 2014 and 2018.

Many friends and colleagues have talked with me about this project. Branka Arsić, Rita Barnard, Rey Chow, Ellen Rooney, Leonard Tennenhouse, and Rebecca Walkowitz encouraged its first inklings. Nancy Armstrong has been a continual sounding board, reader, and collaborator over many years. Amanda Anderson, Stuart Burrows, David Cunningham, John Marx, Adi Ophir, Ben Parker, and Marc Redfield offered engaged and often challenging feedback on specific sections: huge thanks to them for their influence on this work. Joanna Howard is my primary interlocutor for contemporary fiction and introduced me to much of the writing that has informed the argument. Conversations with Ariella Azoulay, Réda Bensmaïa, John Cayley, Michelle Clayton, Merve Emre, Julia Jordan, Jacques Khalip, Rolland Murray, and Ada Smailbegović have sent me toward sources

I might not otherwise have found. Elizabeth Weed's claims of nonunderstanding always felt like the most profound understanding. A cotaught seminar on Mikhail Bakhtin at Brown with Paja Faudree in 2019 was revelatory and illuminating. I would like to thank the participants in that class, as well as those in an earlier seminar on Bakhtin in fall 2017.

I'm grateful for many invitations to speak that proved to be workshops for the argument. Fabio Durão's gracious hospitality at the State University of Campinas, São Paulo, in June 2012 provided the occasion for the first airing of the hypothesis. Hu Jihua's kind invitation to visit Beijing International Studies University in June 2014 enabled a further development of the thesis. Thanks to Sarah Winter, Eleni Coundouriotis, and the participants in the Human Rights seminar at University of Connecticut; to Raji Vallury at the University of New Mexico; to Adam Spanos at New York University and Philip Tsang at the University of Pennsylvania; to Caitlin Charos and Javier Padilla for invitations to Princeton in 2013 and 2015 (and Zahid Chaudhary for his close engagement); and to Doug Haynes and Charlotte Terrell for invitations to the University of Sussex in 2012 and 2017. Thanks to Eric Hayot for inviting me to Penn State in 2015. For panel invitations at crucial moments I would like to thank Toral Gajarawala, Liz Anker, and Chris Holmes, as well as Tom Eyers, Emilio Sauri, and Ellen Rooney and Khachig Tölölyan. I'm grateful to the participants in "Novel Marxisms" at Stanford University in 2016 (Jasper Bernes, Joshua Clover, Benjamin Kohlmann, Anna Kornbluh, Annie McClanahan, Mark McGurl, Sianne Ngai, Michael Szalay) and to Mark for the invitation. Thanks to Political Concepts—Ann Stoler, Emily Apter, Susan Buck-Morss, Jacques Lezra, Stathis Gourgouris, Jay Bernstein, and Adi Ophir—for their invitation and engagement in 2015 and beyond. Mathias Nilges has done me the honor of numerous conversations and invitations over the past few years, including at the Marxist Literary Group Institute on Culture and Society in 2010, a Modern Language Association convention panel in 2012, and Johannes Gutenberg University of Mainz in 2019, with Tim Lanzendörfer. I thank him profusely.

Deidre Lynch and Yoon Sun Lee hosted me at the Novel Theory seminar at the Mahindra Humanities Center at Harvard for a conversation with Sianne Ngai in February 2021; thanks to them and to Sianne and the other attendees for a very engaging and helpful session. Thanks to Gabriel Rockhill and participants for a penetrating conversation and seminar at the

Atélier de Théorie Critique summer school in June 2020. Thanks to Arthur Bueno, Simon Gurisch, and others for conversations on Lukács at the University of Frankfurt in spring 2021.

I'm indebted to Columbia University Press, especially Philip Leventhal, senior editor, whose patient but rigorous questions vastly improved the manuscript, and the editorial team of Literature Now—Rebecca Walkowitz, Matt Hart, and especially David James—for their early enthusiasm, their feedback at numerous junctures, and their encouragement and advice. Two anonymous readers provided two rounds of reports that shaped the project in its early stages and in the final straight. I can't thank them enough for their generosity and scrupulousness.

An early version of chapter 2 was published in *Contemporary Literature* 55, no. 1 (2014). Thanks to the University of Wisconsin Press and the journal's editors.

This book is for Thangam Ravindranathan, with whom I have the great fortune to share days, evenings, meals, tea, books, writing, students (occasionally), extended families, vague dogs, and a horse with a pouch. She (perhaps) agrees with nothing in it, least of all (perhaps) the author's belief in a form of writing that barely tolerates agreement. Nonetheless, it has benefited, immeasurably and irrecompensably, from her linguistic precision and textual attentiveness, her equal attunement to the light and the shadows, and the force of her intellectual generosity, which is to say, her refusal to shut out that which would shut her out.

"Only error individualizes," writes Bakhtin in *Problems of Dostoevsky's Poetics*. In a sense that goes beyond the rhetoric of professional modesty, everything that is erroneous in this book is mine. It is even more the case that what is mine is erroneous.

ABBREVIATIONS

ATP   Gilles Deleuze and Félix Guattari, *A Thousand Plateaus*, trans. Brian Massumi (Minneapolis: University of Minnesota Press, 1987)

C1   Gilles Deleuze, *Cinema 1: The Movement-Image*, trans. Hugh Tomlinson and Barbara Habberjam (London: Athlone, 1986)

C2   Gilles Deleuze, *Cinema 2: The Time-Image*, trans. Hugh Tomlinson and Robert Galeta (London: Athlone, 1989)

FF   Jacques Rancière, *Film Fables*, trans. Emiliano Battista (Oxford: Berg, 2006)

MPL   V. N. Vološinov, *Marxism and the Philosophy of Language*, trans. Ladislav Matejka and I. R. Titunik (Cambridge, MA: Harvard University Press, 1986)

PL   Jacques Rancière, *The Politics of Literature*, trans. Julie Rose (Cambridge: Polity, 2011)

SER   Georg Lukács, *Studies in European Realism*, trans. Edith Bone (New York: Howard Fertig, 2002)

TN   Georg Lukács, *The Theory of the Novel: A Historico-Philosophical Essay on the Forms of Great Epic Literature*, trans. Anna Bostock (Cambridge, MA: MIT Press, 1971)

FREE INDIRECT

INTRODUCTION
Unthinking Connections

What might the novelist Rachel Cusk mean when she says, in an interview about her latest work in a critically acclaimed trilogy, "I'm not interested in character because I don't think character exists anymore"?[1] Pressed to explain her statement, she opines that character may have nothing to do with how people actually live, that character "probably" operates in a person's life "to create . . . a dysfunction," and that how we live and how we communicate "seem to be eroding the old idea of character." In an earlier work in the author's trilogy, a first-person narrator declares that "what other people thought was no longer of any help to me," since "those thoughts only existed within certain structures, and I had definitively left those structures."[2] What structures are these, and what kind of "thought" is only possible outside them?

In another interview, the writer W. G. Sebald describes modes of certainty in contemporary fictional narration as "unacceptable": "I . . . think that we largely delude ourselves with the knowledge that we think we possess, that we make it up as we go along, that we make it fit our desires and anxieties and that we invent a straight line of a trail in order to calm ourselves down." To be subjected as a reader "to the rules and laws of fiction" is, he says, "tedious."[3] And yet, speaking of his own work, he does not disavow the premises of fiction. His narrators simply avoid or are incapable of the "omniscience" of an older period and even the unified perspective from which its narratives emerged. What kind of shift has taken place when a register of narrative certainty gives way to one of crisis and disorientation, in which the authenticity not only of the account but also of the experience falls into doubt? "My rational mind is . . . unable to lay the ghosts of repetition that haunt me with ever greater frequency," says one of Sebald's narrators. "Like a gramophone repeatedly playing the same sequence of notes," such experiences have "less to do with damage to the machine itself than with an irreparable defect in its programme."[4]

The crisis is not biographical, confined to the body and mind of the narrating subject, for biographical crises are perfectly compatible with fictional narratives. One might even say they are necessary to the novel as a "state of imbalance" that is "destined to be objectively righted" by the work's end.[5] What has become fragile is rather the "programme," the formal principles and qualities of the work, including the presumption of a directionality to the plot, the cycles of suspense and revelation, the "expressive" element, and even the structure of the sentence. Why else has writing become a prominent and intrusive element in the consciousness of so many fictional protagonists, such that moments of perception or reflection are perpetually doubled, subverted, by an awareness of their literary or formal quality—an awareness that renders indeterminate the distinction between reality and fiction? After repeatedly forgetting the four-digit code for his bank card at an ATM, the narrator-protagonist of a 2011 novel set in New York City experiences his nervous reaction "as though I had become a minor character in a Jane Austen novel." He reflects: "Such sudden mental weakness . . . was from a simplified version of the self, an area of simplicity where things had once been more robust."[6]

Another writer, Renee Gladman, reflecting on her creative practice, describes thoughts, impulses, and memories as mental "energies" that have a very different "architecture and sense of time" than the sentence:

> When we move from our minds into language, from something that must be multilayered, full of fragments, full of complete feelings, like novels that exist in the shape of an instant, what are we doing? . . . How do we put the complex shape of our interiority . . . into the straight line of the sentence? I think particularly of the English sentence, which forces one to begin with a

subject, a kind of encapsulated self or other that speaks, sees, knows, or, in the case of objects, a subjectivity that presumes grasp-ability.[7]

With her literary career well under way, Gladman begins a practice of "drawing" that she considers to be continuous with her writing practice. More precisely, her writing takes on a self-disavowing quality as a material documentation, in language, of the decision not to write: "I wasn't writing. I was decidedly not-writing; even as I held this pen in my hand, I swore I wouldn't write. I didn't." At the same time, the writing continues by means of a transformation in the relation between its material and immaterial aspects. Gladman cites a statement about drawing by an installation artist, which she reapplies to writing: "Drawing is a process of thought which is conducted by the hand." Writing thereby acquires a manual, *nonrepresentational* relation to thought. It is a writing with no more direct access and no higher resolution with respect to thought than drawing. "I made a line; it couldn't be read, but I felt the story in my body. It was as experimental as everything else. I made the line while talking in my head, which was what I did while I wrote. So I was writing, but it was drawing that had accumulated."[8]

In moments like these—when a "dysfunction" is asserted in place of a character, when a protagonist identifies "structures" of thought in which she no longer resides, when a narrator doubts the authenticity of the experiences he is narrating and another narrator finds even his mental frailty reminiscent of a "simplified version of the self," when a writer considers her work's "thought" to be more directly accessed through movements of the hand than of the mind—a category or space of meaning is being invoked not as a distinct contribution of the work to a larger project of understanding or a transmissible series of insights but, on the contrary, as a problem.

There may be no more fundamental question in literary studies than what a work means, whose thought it is voicing, what it is really saying. But one might also claim, as this book will do, that this question has a special significance in the literature of our own era, that there is no historical period in which the question of thought comes more directly into focus as a problem and no period in which it is more difficult to address. When the thought of the work is seen as fundamentally eluding "the straight line of the sentence" or the "straight line of a trail," how can it become the object of a critical study? How is literary exposition possible?

In asking such questions, one is positing the existence of something that has been highly contested within the field of novel theory: a project or an aspect to the work that is not derivable from the novel's representational apparatus and that cannot be paraphrased—something, in other words, that alludes to the singularity of the novel form. One ascribes a quality to the novel that is impossible to substantiate. This, perhaps, is why the question of thought is rarely addressed directly in critical studies other than in terms that deflect it onto some other dimension of the work or refuse it altogether.

In the argument of this book, however, deflections, refusals, even failures and incapacities will be precisely as important to the story of the novel's thought as insights, revelations, intuitions, and enigmas—or more so. For there is a thought in the contemporary novel that eludes the two modes of literary thinking for which we have established critical approaches and vocabularies: (1) a *direct*, grammatically self-evident mode of representation, associated with traditions of rhetoric, fine writing, and public discourse, and (2) an *indirect*, veiled, or otherwise coded thinking peculiar to modern aesthetic works, where what is being said is a matter of almost endless deliberation, a mode that emerges, historically, alongside a discourse of literary "interpretation" and the figure of the critic. Both modes, or "regimes" (to use Jacques Rancière's term), assume that there is a *subject* of the work, a thinking entity who is responsible for it and whom the reading might be supposed to reconstruct. Both assume, therefore, the presence of an *expressive* element—an idea, however enigmatic, whose ultimate point of reference and origin is that same subject. Both assume the existence of a *form* in which the expressive element is embodied or transfigured and that is in principle legible or penetrable.

These assumptions, taken together, amount to a belief in the work's connection to the world, a connection that is dramatized by the concept of "fiction" as well as by the technologies of interpretation that literary critics bring to bear on the work. That basis of connection and intelligibility is explicit in Rancière's term "regime." Artistic regimes, according to Rancière, are "modes of relating thought, language, and world." In an artistic regime, "thought represents its own content in the exteriority of a figure."[9] A regime of the arts, writes one commentator, "operates on the basis of a certain understanding of language and meaning, and their links to reality."[10]

This understanding is important to the present work, but precisely as the institutional and disciplinary limit *beyond which* it seeks to ground a conception of the novel as a mode of thought. For my argument will converge on the claim that the thought of the novel—as opposed to the thought of its author, narrator, readers, characters, social world, historical context, etc.—is not part of any established or emergent artistic regime. If an artistic regime forges a link with reality, the link constituted by the thought of the novel is neither "direct" nor "indirect." The proposition of this book is that it might rather be conceived as *free indirect*, after the "style" of represented speech and thought that the modern novel is widely reckoned to have invented. However, in distinction from free indirect "style" or "discourse" as it is described in prevailing accounts, the thought that I will call "free indirect" is not localizable in an "encapsulated self or other" (a character or narrator); it does not take the form of speaking, seeing, or knowing; and its content is not graspable as an object.

There are two further aspects of this claim that exist in historical tension. First, while this capacity for thought is a constant in the historical formation of the novel, it has not been examined nor even acknowledged in the main traditions of novel theory, which talk about the novel's thought only in terms that reinscribe—that may even have helped establish—the central aesthetic ideologies of our world: the ideology of *form* (the existence of nameable ideas that are given legible or sensuous manifestation in art and literature), the ideology of the *expressive subject* (individuals as the principal subjects or envelopes of thought), and the ideology of *fiction* (a fundamental separation between two registers of writing based on the writer's intentions with respect to the real). This book will identify these aesthetic ideologies as modes of "instantiation" and their ontological presuppositions as "instantiation relations." Novel thought takes place as an unthinking of those relations, which is to say (to quote one of the great theorists of Marxist aesthetics), a thinking of its own "internal distantiation" from them.[11]

Second—and despite the consistency of its presence in the history of the novel—this mode of thought is blazingly evident in English-language fiction during the period with which this book is primarily concerned, the two decades since the publication of J. M. Coetzee's novel *Elizabeth Costello* (2003). *Elizabeth Costello* does not inaugurate this mode of thought, nor does it bear any responsibility for it. Coetzee's novel is simply one of the works from our own period that illustrates it most clearly, for *Elizabeth*

Costello features, as content, a number of ethical and philosophical problems of our time: the question of animal rights, the problem of the humanities (their ethnocentrism and Eurocentrism), the "problem of evil" in a secular age (the simultaneous impossibility and necessity of designating it as such), the "problem of realism," etc. *Elizabeth Costello*, I will argue, enacts a failure of the novel to address these questions in any applicable way. This "failure" cannot be explained in terms of the author's objectives; it is not being "staged" for artistic or intellectual purposes. What registers as failure in *Elizabeth Costello* is a noninstrumental, nonsubjectively inhabitable, nontransferable and therefore nonideological thought specific to the novel, a thought that takes place at the limits of the novel's formal qualities. Whereas novel *criticism* has been defined by the effort to forge *interpretive* links between the content of the work and the world, and whereas novel *theory* proposes *theoretical* explanations for the same relation, what the novel of our time does unceasingly—in works by Jesse Ball, Teju Cole, Dennis Cooper, Rachel Cusk, Renee Gladman, James Kelman, Ben Lerner, Tao Lin, Valeria Luiselli, Patrick Modiano, W. G. Sebald, Ali Smith, Zadie Smith (to mention only the few writers touched on in this work)—is effect the *dissolution* of all such links. A twenty-first-century theory of the novel must acknowledge and do justice to this enigmatic, little-studied, in fact barely noticed, technically untheorizable, yet insistent quality of the literature of our period: a quality of not only refusing to connect the work and the world but of thinking, inhabiting, even forging the space of their disconnection.

The liberal critical tradition has, for the most part, been interested in ideas in works of literature only as aesthetic or historical features; the question of their plausibility is not its concern. Even Aristotle's distinction between the "universal truths" that poetry is capable of and the "particular statements" that are proper to history is a distinction between literary effects.[12] "Only the very foolish would think of attempting to verify" poetic statements, wrote I. A. Richards in 1924. For this reason, Richards goes on, the "falsity" of ideas we encounter in literature "is no defect," and "their truth, when they are true, is no merit."[13] Three decades later, Ian Watt's *The Rise of the Novel* (1957) tasks itself with identifying the "basic congruity" between literary forms and the social structures and belief systems that pertain in the world of those forms. Watt thereby dissolves the possibility of approaching the thought of the novel as anything other than an ideological reflection. Thus, for Watt, in the age of the novel there is no significant gap or slippage among the "literary, the philosophical and the social spheres," insofar as all three are delimited by a "modern field of vision . . . mainly occupied by the discrete particular, the directly apprehended sensum, and the autonomous individual."[14] One might make the same sort of claim of critics such as Northrop Frye, whose *Anatomy of Criticism* (published the same year as *The Rise of the Novel*) deals with the question of thought under the heading of "theme" (*dianoia*), derived from an Aristotelian dramatic framework according to which the work's thought is precisely as discoverable as its plot,[15] or Wayne C. Booth, whose *The Rhetoric of Fiction* (1961) is framed as a consideration of the "rhetorical resources" available to the writer "as he tries, consciously or unconsciously, to impose his fictional world upon the reader."[16]

It is really only with the Marxist tradition that the question of thought is introduced into the study of the novel, albeit negatively, in the form of its foreclosure. Writing fifteen years after Watt and Frye, Fredric Jameson articulates the paradoxical quality of this foreclosure in a penetrating discussion of a body of work that has arguably contributed the most to a systematic Marxist approach to literature (and the novel in particular): that of Georg Lukács. According to Jameson, what makes a full engagement with Lukács's work (and historical materialism in general) impossible for a "Western" readership is its "denial of the autonomy of thought itself," that is, "its insistence, itself a thought, on the way in which pure thought functions as a disguised mode of social behavior."[17] That subordinate clause, "itself a thought," is crucial to the power of Jameson's analysis and to its suggestiveness for my purposes here. Marxism too, Jameson implies, is a "cultural object," which is to say "a spiritual commodity," one that, as such, "devalues" and "ruins" itself in its insistence on "the social determination of thought." Thus, the very "thought" that denies the autonomy of thought is itself "irreducible to pure reason or to contemplation." The long paragraph in which Jameson unfolds this reflexive logic ends on a devastating note, to the effect that the structure of historical materialism "refuses us in the very moment in which we imagine ourselves to be refusing it." What Jameson doesn't say is that this logic of refusal applies *whether we refuse it or embrace it*. Historical materialism requires us to acknowledge that its acceptance, no less than its "refusal," fails to apprehend its critical project to the very degree that it is subjectively inhabited—to the degree that it is "thought" at all.

Jameson's observation is, in an important sense, the point of departure of the present work. For that denial of "pure thought" at the heart of the "very structure of historical materialism"—a denial on the grounds of "the unity of thinking and action, or . . . the social determination of thought"—is also, as Jameson is aware, a thought, although one that in its pure (unacknowledgeable, unparaphrasable) form *cannot be ours*. Where, then, might we possibly locate the Marxist "thought" that turns away from its subjective apprehension? This book proposes a radical answer to that question: in the novel, at the limit of its formal elements.

Each of the book's three parts is devoted to one of three central claims. First, *the question of thought in the novel can and must be approached separately from that of the novel's* representation *of thoughts*. Part 1, "The Novel Form and Its Limits," outlines the case against a conception of the novel limited to or defined by form. Such a conception, which is the point of departure of all existing theories of the novel, rules out of consideration, at the outset, the very element that the present work insists is fundamental: the novel's own capacity for thought. Chapter 1, "The Problem of Form," outlines this case theoretically, through an analysis of the ways explicit and implicit meaning ("content") is already present in most conceptions of novelistic form. Approaching the novel as a form thus restricts one's sense of the novel to such embedded (instantiated) meanings. By contrast, this chapter presents a rationale for identifying a noninstantiated, noninstantiable thought at the limits of the work's form. Chapter 2, "Against Exemplarity," enlarges this case by way of a critical study of the German-English writer W. G. Sebald. Like all novelistic writing, Sebald's work is concerned with the question of "connection," a question that comes into focus here through the figure of the example. The presence of examples, whether as instructional models or simply as members of epistemological sets or categories, is one of the primary ways that novels establish their social relevance and legibility. However, in Sebald's work exemplarity is not a project or an aspiration but a problem, one that comes to appear to his narrators as a betrayal of experience. As the formal qualities of Sebald's writing begin to resemble those of conventional novels (with the presence of fictional characters, the structuration of plots as quest narratives, the sustained exploration of "themes"), the prospect of those elements cohering into connections and acquiring a normative value introduces a formal discrepancy into Sebald's work. In its permanently unresolved relation to exemplarity, Sebald's project is thus located at an important juncture in the trajectory of the novel that has occasioned the present study.

Part 2, "The Emergence of Postfictional Aesthetics," examines the second major proposition of the book, that *an evolution of the novel is under way that involves a replacement of the forms of fiction and fictionality by formally ambiguous modes of writing, with ontological implications that extend beyond the practice of literature.* The chapters introduce this proposition by way of three "logics" that have lately become graspable on the basis of recent tendencies in literary production: "instantiation," "postfiction," and "disconnection." However, to call them "logics" rather than, say, "forms" is to insist that they should not be considered formal or generic features of contemporary literature. Rather, they are critical formations that, in the case of the "instantiation relation," are imposed on the work by interpretive protocols that eclipse the novel's thought, referring what takes place in the novel to structures of knowledge, behavior, or identification. Chapter 3 introduces the concept of instantiation through the work of the analytic philosopher David Armstrong and the literary critic Dorothy J. Hale. Whereas Armstrong's work on the "ontology of states of affairs" reveals the idealist underpinnings of all instantiation relations, Hale is responsible for introducing "instantiation" as a term that captures the centrality of point of view to the formal evolution of the modern novel. In a critical essay, the British writer Zadie Smith calls this element "the watermark of self that runs through everything you do." Indeed, Smith is an important figure for Hale's project to reestablish terms for an ethical grounding of the novel in its capacity for alterity, "rooted in the modernist notion of narrative form." Yet Zadie Smith's literary works, I claim, for all their formal conventionality, spill out of any normative reading governed by the "watermark of self," even one that hangs a conception of ethical value on the novel's "nonconflictual multiperspectivalism."[18] There is an absoluteness to the dialogicality of Smith's work that exceeds and thus unthinks the very virtues of positionality and alterity even as it also "thinks" them.

By contrast with the instantiation relation, the "postfictional hypothesis" opens up an awareness of something that takes place in the novel but outside the interpretive protocols one might bring to it. Postfiction extends a certain principle of fictional discourse identified by various thinkers, including Ann Banfield and Mikhail Bakhtin: that there is no formal (as opposed to circumstantial) criterion with which to differentiate a piece of fiction from a piece of nonfictional writing, nothing, therefore, that *formally* guarantees that the nonfiction writing I am reading at any moment is not operating as fiction, that the ideas or viewpoints I am responding to directly, in earnest absorption, are not, in fact, the discourse of a fictional character. What this suggests is that the principle of fiction is precisely that: not a form but a principle that exists in tension with the genre category. For, as a principle and a practice, fiction is capable of consuming—enveloping in its logic—every attempt to differentiate it in formal terms. We can state this proposition more programmatically: As a principle that is latent within any writing that connects a subject and an object—any truth claim, any statement of point of view, any assertion of commitment to a cause or struggle, any avowal of solidarity, any confession of guilt or claim of innocence, any interpretive or theoretical proposition—fiction is capable of hollowing it out, of breaking the connection in the very act of making it. That capability is what I am calling "postfiction": an element in the practice of fiction that unthinks or deauthorizes the very claims made by the work, whether direct or indirect, rhetorical or aesthetic, forceful or subtle, overt or implicit, conscious or unconscious. One of the claims of chapter 4, "The Postfictional Hypothesis," is that this principle is increasingly making itself felt outside the practice of fiction, in discourses and rhetorical practices that we habitually think of as critical or expository.

Chapter 5, "The Logic of Disconnection," begins the task that will be developed in part 3: that of addressing directly, in a theoretical register, the nature or "status" of this disconnection and deauthorization. The chapter revisits accounts by Mikhail Bakhtin and Benedict Anderson of how the novel form coheres as a spatiotemporal unity: a "chronotope," in Bakhtin's formulation, or an "imagined community," in Anderson's. Both concepts put forward an image of spatiotemporal continuity that operates as the sole principle of coherence—a "degree zero" order of connection without the need of a perceiving character or narrator to make the connection explicit. The *sufficiency* of these principles is also the source of their ideological force. For chronotopes inherently carry an "evaluating aspect," Bakhtin points out, just as, for Anderson, the "calendrical coincidence" shared by characters in an imagined community binds them together even without their mutual acquaintance. In both cases, explicit commentary would undermine the power of the formation by destroying its artistic "wholeness." The concrete achievement of the novel is to produce a quality of "living artistic perception," a thinking of time and space in their inseparability.[19] The ideological force of the chronotope is precisely that of the instantiation relation: a connection that need never be put into words.

But in thinking chronotopically, the novel also thinks the limits of the chronotope. If the classical novel is chronotopic, it brushes up against a world and a thought that do not function chronotopically, where the laws of causality, narrative purpose, and individual motivation—the great inventions of the novel—are unreliable or fall desperately short. The chapter turns to Michel Foucault, who in "The Order of Discourse," his inaugural lecture of 1970, called for a method that could acknowledge the limits of these spatial thematizations of discourse, a method founded on precisely the "discontinuity" between different formal and discursive practices. Foucault's proposed method has never been realized in the critical and social sciences, for the simple reason that its very logic is propositional, not instantiable. Chapter 5 concludes by exploring two novelists, James Kelman and Patrick Modiano, both of whom write at the limits of the novel's chronotopic organization and who thus underwrite the case for the novel as the proper domain for the practice of Foucault's theory of "discontinuous systematicities," precisely in its exit from the instantiation relation.

Third, *if there is a thought of the contemporary novel, it is not thinkable by us.* In part 3, "The Free Indirect," I argue that Gilles Deleuze's two books on cinema provide the most promising theoretical basis for understanding the decentering and deauthorization of literary discourse that I am calling the "free indirect." In a philosophically ambitious, far-reaching attempt to reframe the problem of expression by relocating it outside the subject, Deleuze identifies a noncentered model of thought in the cinematic image. However, I argue that this reframing is made possible not only because of the revolutionary technology of the cinema but also by qualities in the novel already set forth in the work of Bakhtin and that of his colleague Valentin Vološinov. This link between Deleuze and Bakhtin introduces a circular dimension to my claims of a transformation in the terms and conditions of the critical reading of the novel.

The question that titles chapter 6, "How Does Immanence Show Itself?" attempts to dramatize both the central undertaking of literary criticism as a practice and its transformation into an unresolvable quandary in the contemporary period. The chapter opens with the philosophical articulation of this quandary in Gilles Deleuze's 1969 book *The Logic of Sense*, where its abyssal nature is addressed and explored using the paradoxical formulation "the sense of sense." The discussion traces the evolution of this question from its appearance, early in the twentieth century, as a founding predicament of the theory of the novel as a field to its current importance, both acknowledged and unacknowledged, in the work of several active and prominent philosophers and critics of the novel. This chapter also functions as a further elaboration of the concept of instantiation and its implications for literary analysis.

Chapter 7, "What Is a Sensorimotor Break? Deleuze on Cinema," addresses the historicity of Deleuze's claim of a "sensorimotor collapse" in modern cinema, a shift that anticipates—but also in a sense repeats—the transition that is central to the argument of this book: from a world in which the instantiation relation is able to account for the thought of the novel to one in which it isn't. Deleuze identifies in cinema a thought of the "interstice," a thought that resists the "resolution" that Lukács attributes to novelistic form, a thought that is irreducible to its linguistic or conceptual embodiment but that is nevertheless actualized in the images of movement and time.

This claim for cinema's capacity to think is audacious, not least in its insistence (in the face of a tradition of modern philosophical and political critique that has long maintained the opposite) that thought is possible. But the radical terms and conditions of this possibility, I argue, are shared by the novel: that cinematic thought is not centered in the human subject, that it has no need of "theory" (least of all a theory of cinema or a theory of the novel), and that what enables it is not the creative or imaginative power of an artist or writer but a technological quality—in the case of cinema, the cinematic apparatus; in the case of the novel, the spatiotemporal processes of writing, composition, transcription, revision, editing, etc. In this regard, both cinema and the novel bring into being a distinct mode of subjectivity that the film director Pier Paolo Pasolini calls a "free indirect subjective." Pasolini's provocation, considered alongside the work of Bakhtin and

Vološinov, makes possible a long-overdue correction in how we critically understand the novel's most famous formal discovery, free indirect discourse.

Chapter 8, "Rancière: Toward Nonregime Thinking," examines Jacques Rancière's critique of Deleuze's work on cinema in the name of what Rancière calls the "aesthetic regime." In rejecting Deleuze's category of a sensorimotor break, Rancière's project also poses a significant challenge to the periodizing argument of this book. However, in a detailed engagement with Rancière's schema I demonstrate that the differences Rancière is concerned to establish between Deleuze's project and his own are not verifiable in any conclusive sense. Rancière's real significance may be in undertaking an even more complete exit from the logic of instantiation than Deleuze, one that takes place *outside of its own theoretical register*. This discussion returns us to the postfictional hypothesis outlined in part 1, for, without saying so, Rancière's project asks that we extend the "dialogical" qualities that Bakhtin attributes to the novel to our own critical procedures—and I argue, does so itself.

None of these three major claims can be historically substantiated or verified. Each would be easy to "debunk" by citing one or another novelistic work in which opposed tendencies to the ones identified in this book could be discerned or by invoking the many formal or syntactical elements in the works under discussion that imply a contrary significance to those suggested here. But this book is not about objective, formal developments in the novel or about a historical or philosophical stage to which the novel has brought us. It is about a logic of novel thinking that reaches its fullest realization in the continual emergence of a thought that is *not* verifiable or falsifiable, a thought that barely registers at the formal level, a thought that may not even be subjectively inhabitable but in which *the novel's refusal of prevailing ideologies is located*.

For our world is one in which ideology no longer operates primarily at the level of ideas (i.e., "content") but at the level of instantiation (i.e., "form"). Any idea is acceptable to the dominant order as long as it can be identified, named, located, and attributed, thus attached to a subject. For novel theory to be content to operate on the level of what is spoken in the work—or, indeed, left unspoken—is for it to remain wholly within this ideology of form. This work of theory, then, distinguishes itself by its attempt to tell the story of the novel not from some point of special critical insight or author-ity derived from its situatedness in the present but *from the hypotheti-cal perspective of the novel's fullest realization*, that is, from the world of absolute dialogicality that the novel is continually bringing into existence.

PART I

The Novel Form and Its Limits

Chapter One

THE PROBLEM OF FORM

Maybe politeness is the same as sarcasm. Someone should write that book.

—TAO LIN

THE NOVEL THINKS

Not since the emergence in Europe of "literature" or "aesthetics" in the eighteenth century has it been possible to take what is spoken by a narrator or character to be what the work itself says or thinks. This does not mean, of course, that the latter is inaccessible or nonexistent. Forms that become enigmatic in the transition from a "representational" to an "aesthetic" mode attain a new basis of legibility that amounts to a new form of expression, one that is not imitable, teachable, or demonstrable. That even the artist may not understand "how his ideas . . . arise and meet in his mind" is the principle of his or her "genius," according to Immanuel Kant.[1] Following the Kantian logic, Jacques Rancière refers to the "mute speech" of literature: an "art that speaks without speaking, that claims to speak without speaking."[2]

But in the last few decades the paradoxical conditions of enunciation and reception under which the novel speaks "without speaking" have themselves been so fundamentally transformed that the work is no longer interpretable using conventional literary-critical methods. Such methods presuppose the stability of the novel as an object of analysis, the existence of clear boundaries around the work, the discreteness of literary discourse as against other modes of writing and speaking (including literary criticism, economic analysis, or historiography), the transcendentality of the writing subject with respect to that discourse, and a relationship of mutuality and complementarity between fiction and the world. With the dissolution of these premises, critical discourse finds itself unable to access the work or its thought.

Faced with this redoubled "muteness," a muteness that may be materially indistinguishable from the work's eloquence, it is tempting to conclude instead that the work's thought has risen to the surface, that contemporary fiction is discovering the pleasures of existing in harmonious alignment with its idea, that readers can dispense with the labor of locating, identifying, reproducing, and interrogating a thought that belongs to the work as distinct from its characters, authors, or narrators. To do so, however, is to ignore the novel's unique access to a thought that, in its essence, *refuses the ideological formations of our world*, a thought that, in doing so, operates at the limits of critical intelligibility.

Thus, critics who celebrate a new "honesty" or "directness of expression" in twenty-first-century fiction, or call for a return to literary "realism" as an antidote to the mystifications of political discourse, or look to the power of the novel to make "connections" in a world of increasing fragmentation and alienation misunderstand both the ideological quality of contemporary notions such as the inherent value of connectedness and self-expression and the nature of the novel's recent trajectory. Such propositions assume that the ethical or political substance of the novel continues to be located in its manifest, formal elements and that such identifiable elements operate critically or ideologically in the same way as other rhetorical forms.

Perhaps novels functioned like this in the past. When the narrator of Dickens's *Bleak House* (1853) declaims, upon the death of poor Jo the crossing sweeper, "Dead, your Majesty. Dead, my lords and gentlemen. Dead, Right Reverends and Wrong Reverends of every order. Dead, men and women, born with Heavenly compassion in your hearts. And dying thus around us, every day," it is plausible to assume that the moral center of the work coincides with the implied positionality of Dickens's narrator.[3] Similarly, when Huck Finn utters the "awful words" in chapter 31 of *The Adventures of Huckleberry Finn* (1884) as he destroys the letter revealing the whereabouts of Jim—"All right, then, I'll *go* to hell"—the critical tradition confidently locates the moral subjectivity of the work in the person of Huck himself or in the author's indulgence toward his character.[4] Huck's conviction that he has sinned is accepted as the all-too-legible "subterfuge" of Twain's novel, as Leslie Fiedler puts it—a formal dissemblance "typical of our classic novelists."[5]

Many critics, of course, continue to read works from all periods and traditions in this way. But recent developments in novelistic fiction are enabling a conception of the novel form in which what is most important and singular to the novel—its thought—takes place, rather, at the limits of formal identification. Such developments include the appearance of a number of novelistic practices located "on the very edge of fiction," as one American writer has put it.[6]

This book attempts an encounter with these developments that is informed by an approach to the novel *as itself a mode of thought*. Such an approach is at odds with an understanding of the novel as a form; indeed, I will argue that the novel's own thought is obscured even by so intuitive and "natural" a critical operation as that of taking the work as an object of analysis.[7]

The case put forward in *Free Indirect* is, first, that the unstable boundaries of the contemporary novel are consistent with the novel's historical evolution over the last century or more. Second, and more important, the meaning of this instability cannot be grasped as long as we think of it in negative terms: as a deficit of thought, a betrayal of "facts," or the imperiling of "critique." On the contrary, the space that has opened up on the borders of the novel is the site of a thinking that resists the imperatives of an increasingly "interconnected," networked, economically administered society.

The two propositions implicit here may be stated more provocatively and directly as follows. First: what is most timely and urgent in the contemporary novel *exceeds its character as a form*. Second: *the novel thinks*. The meaning of the word "thinks" in this sentence is identical to that in Martin Heidegger's "shocking statement" (in *What Is Called Thinking?*): "Science does not think."[8] The novel thinks in exactly the sense in which science, for Heidegger, doesn't. That science has the "good fortune" not to be thinking, says Heidegger, is guaranteed by the fact that it has "the assurance of its own appointed course." Thus it is the lack of an "appointed course" for the novel that makes it of particular importance and significance in a technocratic era where all possible options for thought—data-linked to income, postcode, employment, demographic reporting, patterns of behavior—seem to have been anticipated and laid out in advance, where the task of thinking has become more challenging than ever before and the nature of thought itself more difficult to grasp.

THE MEANING OF NOVELISTIC FORM

When we talk about form, it is important to observe that a complex relation between the material and its meaning is part of the formal qualities of the novel. The Soviet-era Russian linguist V. N. Vološinov states this principle clearly, using the example of sculpture:

> By virtue of its significance [form] exceeds the material. The meaning, the import of form has to do not with the material but with the content. So, for instance, the form of a statue may be said to be not the form of the marble but the form of the human body, with the added qualification that the form "heroicizes" the human depicted or "dotes upon" him or, perhaps, denigrates him (the caricature style in the plastic arts); that is, *the form expresses some specific evaluation of the object depicted*.[9]

Content, even unspecified content, is intrinsic to form. This principle has a special significance in the case of the novel, since one thing we have long known about the novel is that its "specific evaluation of the object depicted" does not require direct expression in the work.

Arguably, the critic who established this principle as a foundation of the modern novel was Percy Lubbock, an English academic writing in the early part of the twentieth century. In *The Craft of Fiction* (1921), Lubbock takes the subject of Flaubert's *Madame Bovary* to be "absolutely fixed and determined," a quality that makes it "a good point of departure for an examination of the methods of fiction."[10] According to Lubbock, Flaubert's subject is not Emma Bovary but "the history of a woman like her in just such a world as hers, a foolish woman in narrow circumstances; so that the provincial scene, acting upon her, making her what she becomes, is as essential as she is herself" (80). The work's subject, then, is both an "evaluation" ("a foolish woman") and an explanation (the "making" of her). Both aspects are implicit. Each is revealed by the work "little by little, page by page" but is also "withdrawn as fast as it is revealed" (3). This is the paradox of novelistic form, and Flaubert's work is its perfect embodiment. Lubbock writes:

> Flaubert never has an instant's illusion, he always knows [Emma] to be worthless. . . . He knows it without asserting it, needless to say; his valuation of her is only implied; it is in his tone—never in his words, which invariably

respect her own estimate of herself. His irony, none the less, is close at hand and indispensable. . . . [It] gives him perfect freedom to supersede Emma's limited version whenever he pleases.

(89–90)

This paradox is not only peculiar to the novel; it is the specific form of linkage that enables the work to cohere ideologically. Internally—that is, diegetically—it connects Emma Bovary to her environment, suggesting a sociological explanation of the kind that has long underpinned the literary structure known as "realism." Externally—that is, interpretatively—the same paradox connects the work to both the world in which the work is produced and the world in which it is read (these worlds may, of course, be spatially and/or temporally different). This connection suggests the operation of a logic whereby the work's meaning (a second-level order of reference) is determinable despite not being specified by the work itself. In both cases, what is presupposed is an objective state of affairs, one that Georg Lukács, in a staunch defense of novelistic realism in 1938, sums up as "man in the whole range of his relations to the real world."[11]

Each of these two contexts—internal-diegetic, external-interpretative—has its dedicated, twentieth-century slogan: "Only connect . . ." and "Always historicize!"[12] The first, by the novelist E. M. Forster, is an injunction to the work—to its characters, narrators, and authors: to draw connections and nothing more. The second, by Fredric Jameson, is an injunction to the critic: to make good the discursive gap that is immanent to the form of the novel, thus completing the work. As Jameson puts it, "Texts come before us as the always-already-read; we apprehend them through sedimented layers of previous interpretations" (9). "Always historicize!" directs attention to "the interpretations through which we attempt to confront and to appropriate" the work (9–10). The object is the formal structures, historical formations, and prevailing interpretive codes in which a work is enabled to mean—contexts that are implicit in the work itself and that have their ultimate point of reference, for Jameson, in the "untranscendable horizon" of a Marxian social totality, however abstract (10).

The form of the novel, then, includes a connective element that is minimally figured in the work. This element, and its minimal figuration, is the basis of the importance accorded to terms such as "realism," "ethics," and "irony" in the field of novel theory. Along with more recent formulations such as "social indexicality" and "social formalism," these terms represent possible answers to a question that almost every theorist of the novel articulates, at some point, as the central motivation of his or her work: how to understand the relation between the manifest elements in the work and the unnarrated, assumed, or imputed ones. Mikhail Bakhtin, Vološinov's close associate, phrases the question as follows: "How are the heroes' worlds, and the ideas that lie at their base, united with the world of the author, that is, with the world of the novel?"[13] For the sociologist Pierre Bourdieu, writing in the early 1990s, the question must be addressed to the nature of novelistic discourse itself: "What indeed is this discourse which speaks of the social or psychological world *as if it did not speak of it*; which *cannot speak* of this world except on condition that it only speak of it as if it did not speak of it, that is, in a *form* which performs, for the author and the reader, a *denegation* (in the Freudian sense of *Verneinung*) of what it expresses?"[14] In the words of Jacques Rancière, writing a decade later: "If the whole is not the assembly of the parts, it must be the substance immanent in the units. But how is this immanence to show itself?"[15]

Realism—Ethics—Irony

The most substantial and enduring answer that literary criticism gives to this question goes by the name "realism." For Lukács, its greatest theorist, the proper concern and object of the authentically realist work is "those elements which endure over long periods and which constitute the objective human tendencies of society and indeed of mankind as a whole" ("Realism in the Balance," 47). Such elements are never named or delineated directly, for at the moment of the work's composition they "only exist incipiently" (48). No "determination" or "conviction" on the part of the writer can ensure his ability to capture such tendencies adequately. What is necessary is only that he has "a living relationship to the cultural heritage," which means "being a son of the people, borne along by the current of the people's development" (54). Realism presupposes both a sense of the work—and of society itself—as a "whole" and the identifiability of the writer's place in it. Individual elements are significant only as particular "angles" upon, and thus entrances to, a "profound and accurate grasp of constant and typical manifestations of human life" (56). The truth of the authentic realist work has no subjective component. The perspective of the aristocrat Balzac may be just as illuminating as those of the bourgeois Gorky and Stendhal, for the defining element of the realist novel is not ideological content but connection:

> In the works of a great realist everything is linked up with everything else. Each phenomenon shows the polyphony of many components, the intertwinement of the individual and social, of the physical and the psychical, of private interest and public affairs. . . . The great realists always regard society from the viewpoint of a living and moving centre and this centre is present, visibly or invisibly, in every phenomenon.[16]

The critic Barbara Foley expounds this logic as that of typicality, which she defines as "the notion that fictional characters and events embody in microcosm the dialectics of the historical moment portrayed in a given text." Typicality has "functioned centrally," she observes, in all Marxist literary criticism predicated upon the "truth-telling capacities of works of fiction."[17] It is therefore only in a "mediated" sense, by registering "key features of historical actuality," that works of fiction may be said to make "assertions." Even a text as ideologically compromised as Margaret Mitchell's *Gone with the Wind*, Foley suggests, may be "a source of truth without, strictly speaking, telling the truth" (97).

Other theorists of the novel have imagined the conceptual whole of the work in ethical terms. Invoking Lukács's early work *The Theory of the Novel*, Thomas Pavel, for example, proposes that the central quandary of the novel is a concern about "the individual's connections with the life of the community," a concern expressed in the question of "whether moral ideals do or do not belong to the human world."[18] Its ethical expression takes the form of the "difference between what human beings *ought to do* and what they *do*." Thus the main character types of the novel may be identified according to how they reconcile this difference, that is, on whether the moral ideal is "part of their world and resonates, so to speak, outside and around them"; whether they merely "aspire"—not always successfully—"to act in accordance with moral ideals"; or whether they are denied "access to their own innermost recesses"—in which case their moral self-understanding becomes "blurred" and the characters themselves remain "enigmatic." In the progression through these character types, Pavel sees the historical development of the novel from Greek antiquity to the European sentimental novel in the eighteenth and nineteenth centuries to realism and modernity.

In *The Theory of the Novel* Lukács identifies "irony" as the connecting term. Irony, he writes—opening a fascinating twenty-page reflection—signals

> an interior diversion of the normatively creative subject into a subjectivity as interiority, which opposes power complexes that are alien to it and which strives to imprint the contents of its longing upon the alien world, and a subjectivity which sees through the abstract and, therefore, limited nature of the mutually alien worlds of subject and object, understands these worlds by seeing their limitations as necessary conditions of their existence and, by thus seeing through them, allows the duality of the world to subsist.[19]

As such, irony—and the glimpse of subjective understanding it affords—remains a "purely formal" response to what Lukács calls the world's "fragility" (75). The connecting term here is the self-observing individual who, as the seat of the work's irony, "transforms itself into a purely receptive subject." In the novel's irony, that is to say, the work's minimally figured connections are resolved in a form that is familiar from the denouements of practically every novel we have read. A work's lines of thematic and narrative tension achieve a point of relative closure in what Lukács describes as

> a fanciful yet well-ordered round of misunderstandings and cross-purposes, within which everything is seen as many-sided, within which things appear as isolated and yet connected, as full of value and yet totally devoid of it, as abstract fragments and as concrete autonomous life, as flowering and as decaying, as the infliction of suffering and as suffering itself.
> (75)

What Lukács is intuiting here, five years before his turn to Marx, is that novelistic ideology is formally coherent and complete to the degree that, at the level of content, it "excludes completeness" (73). This intuition also enables him to say, a few pages later, that irony is "the objectivity of the novel" (90), a claim that we may take to be synonymous with the idea that irony—no less than realism and ethics—is a form from which the novel's real thought is foreclosed.[20]

That thought is never named in positive terms in *The Theory of the Novel*—certainly not as "thought." However, the claim that it nevertheless informs Lukács's thesis in *The Theory of the Novel* (as "fragility," "the possibility of the ultimate nothingness of man," "absurdity"—terms that withhold from it the status of form) is important to the argument of this book.[21] If irony, for Lukács here, is the "objectivity" of the novel, the subjectivity of the novel has no formal manifestation whatsoever.

This book identifies a logic common to these formal resolutions of the complexity of the novel and proposes new terms with which to designate them: instantiation and "the instantiation relation." As an element intrinsic to novelistic form, instantiation will refer to an idea (a connective relation) whose presence is signaled in the work without being articulated and on the basis of which a claim is made, implicitly or explicitly, for the work's social significance. Just as the color red or green, a quality or attribute, is not named but instantiated by the presence of an apple in a bowl, and just as the "musicality" of a man named Coriscus or the "whiteness" of a man named Callias need not be spoken to be evident to people who encounter them,[22] so ideas in novels have no need of being espoused by a speaker within the work to transport their normative power to the outside. Indeed, the stronger and truer claim is that for ideas to enjoy such power outside the work they *must not* be so named or expressed, for by being so they become an object of representation and are thus relativized, tied to a particular subject position and diegetical situation, their portability curtailed.

Catherine Gallagher has offered one of the clearest contemporary analyses of this logic, which she associates with the emergence of fiction as a conceptual category in eighteenth-century Britain.[23] In Gallagher's understanding, fiction is a paradoxical form of referentiality that is distinct from both truth, on one side, and lying, on the other. "The founding claim of the form," she writes,

> was a nonreferentiality that could be seen as a greater referentiality. What distinguished the new writers of fiction [from the subjects of earlier questionable discourses such as lies and libels] was the insistence that the human referent of the text was a generalization about and not an extratextual, embodied instance of a "species." Certainly the novel provided imaginary instances, but it renounced reference to individual examples in the world. The fictionality defining the novel inhered in the creation of instances, rather than their mere selection, to illustrate a class of persons.
>
> (342)

Gallagher's phrase "a nonreferentiality that could be seen as a greater ref-erentiality" defines the instantiation relation of the work of literature in a nutshell, and it applies to the work's ideas just as it does to its characters. In the era of "literature" or "aesthetics," no reader can mistake an idea or utterance of a character for the idea or utterance of the work, yet no atten-tive reader can fail to extrapolate from the "nonreferentiality" of the first to the "greater referentiality" of the second. Both are part of the novel's form.

To read the novel for what is unnamed, for the social types instantiated by the work's characters, or for the underlying ideas and propositional strains that are "shown" rather than "told" (Lubbock, 62) is to limit one's critical attention to the work's formal-ideological aspects. To approach the novel as a work of moral complexity, with sometimes self-subverting strands of argument that remain irresolvable as they play out in the minds of char-acters and thus of readers—to conceptualize the work's subject matter in terms of the philosophical quandaries that it opens up and leaves us mull-ing over—even such attentive, critical reading does nothing other than resolve the novel's inherent paradoxicality, facilitating its expressive dimen-sion and completing its ideological operation. Deep into his realist phase Lukács made the following observation: "Chekhov said quite rightly, in con-nection with Tolstoy, that putting a question correctly is one thing and finding the answer to it something quite different; the artist absolutely needs to do only the first" (*SER*, 146). But the "correctly formulated" ques-tion and the withheld answer are not so different when seen in the light of the instantiation relation; the minimal space between them is inscribed in the formal conventions of the novel.[24] Asking the question ("showing") and finding the answer ("telling")—that is to say, instantiation and representation—both fall short of the novel's thought.

Legibility—the legibility of what is unstated—is intrinsic to the appara-tus of literature. Jacques Rancière calls this formation the "aesthetic regime," and he names *Madame Bovary* as its foundational and most emblematic work. In Rancière's account, we intuit the incipient love between the young Charles and Emma not through any declaration by one to the other but from the evocative atmosphere as they sit together in a parlor. The only description we need is that of their silence as a piece of dust is blown along the stone floor by a draft of air. It is a minimally figured connection because it contains the least information necessary to communicate the idea of Charles's and Emma's mutual attraction.[25] According to Rancière, the

narrative mode of the aesthetic regime is the "paratactical linking of simple perceptions," a connectedness from which the linking term is absent
(124). Its first great theorist in the modern period is Kant: "If forms do not
constitute the exhibition of a given concept itself, but are only supplemen-
tary presentations of the imagination, expressing the concept's implications and its kinship with other concepts, then they are called (aesthetic)
attributes of an object, an object whose concept is a rational idea and hence
cannot be exhibited adequately."[26] There is nothing unrepresentable,
according to Rancière—even when it comes to such definitively "modern"
experiences as the camps, or the bombs at Hiroshima and Nagasaki, or
colonial violence. Instead there is a general mode of aesthetic representation, the structure of which Rancière describes as paratactical but that we
might equally formulate in terms of instantiation: the use of particular
images, persons, and situations in order to invoke a generality that has no
need (or possibility) of being named "in its own appropriate language"
(126).

The question addressed in the present work is *not*, then, how to understand the instantiation relation, for the instantiation relation is the basic
organizational principle of every novelistic work, and its understanding has
been the achievement of the great analysts of bourgeois aesthetic ideology,
including Kant, Lukács, Bourdieu, Jameson, and Rancière. The question is
how to understand the very different relationality that exists at the borders
of the novel's form, a relationality that takes place not out of some merely
formal possibility and not as an artistic response to, say, the penetration of
the logic of capital into the intimacy of the subject—for it is obvious that
no such response could guarantee its immunity to that logic. It comes about,
rather, with the collapse of the categories of knowledge that literary forms
are able to bring forth (directly or indirectly) in the realm of thought. The
collapse is manifest not as a subjective incredulity on the part of the work's
authors, narrators, or characters but as a crisis of legibility of the work itself.

How, then, to understand that relationality without producing yet
another "theory of the novel" that would only deliver it over to the knowable
and the conceptualizable? How to avoid thereby ruining the experience of
those readers who are drawn to precisely what in the novel resists theoretical explanation? How to read what is illegible in the novel? For increasingly, it seems, only what is illegible in the work can sustain the "utopic
element" that Theodor Adorno, half a century ago, continued to identify as

the defining quality of artworks, even as he saw the space it occupied being squeezed to extinction.[27] Only through what is unintentional, indeed involuntary, is the work able to escape that "subjective impoverishment" that, under the "neoliberal" organization of the economy, takes the form of expressed subjectivity itself.[28] Once art becomes "completely 'integrated' into the market," writes Maurizio Lazzarato, it no longer retains "the promise of emancipation"; its occasion is nothing but "a new technique for the government of subjectivity" (152, 154). In Lazzarato's analysis, the artist Marcel Duchamp appears as one of the earliest diagnosticians and casualties of this predicament, in which the practice of art is implicated in an almost irresistible "command to occupy a place, a role, and an identity with one's body and soul." Duchamp, writes Lazzarato, made the art world as such the object of his "permanent and categorical refusal." By refusing "the injunction to be an artist" while continuing to adhere to "artistic practices, protocols, and procedures," Duchamp located himself "neither outside nor inside art as an institution, but at its limit, at its borders" (154–55).

But for all the historical importance of Duchamp's gesture, no such heroic narrative is necessary when it comes to the novel, nor is such a stance even possible; for while the novel effortlessly accommodates artists' programs, manifestos and statements of intent, even those emerging from a despair toward or disavowal of the novel form, in hosting such statements the novel cannot help dissociating itself from them. "It is precisely as ideologemes," writes Mikhail Bakhtin, "that discourse becomes the object of representation in the novel."[29] Ideas in the novel are neutralized as "a particular way of viewing the world" precisely by the fullness and detail of their treatment.

The other side of the novel's ideological hospitality, then, is its conflicted relation to its very legibility. This conflictedness is present in all novels, even works of the utmost conventionality and "realism," even works whose formal self-awareness appears to acknowledge the space of ambiguity at their limits, even works produced at the dawn of capitalism rather than at its catastrophic apogee.

As long as we approach the novel primarily as a form, we fail to think or experience the extraordinary possibility of a thought that exists outside form or that consists in thinking the limits of form. We fail, that is, to give critical significance to those elements of the work that are untroubled by the logic of representation and that of instantiation. Gallagher is attentive to such a possibility when she writes of the "elation of a unitary unbound-edness" that accompanies the reader's encounter with the incompleteness of a fictional character "forever tethered to the abstraction of type" and of thus discovering the lovely sensation of living a life "without textuality, meaningfulness, or any other excuse for existing" (361).

If we limit our critical engagement with the novel to its formal qualities, it is possible to imagine that the canonical history of American literature has been, as Toni Morrison puts it, "free of, uninformed, and unshaped by the four-hundred-year-old presence of, first, Africans and then African-Americans in the United States."[30] It is possible—indeed necessary—to denounce, with Amitav Ghosh, the "collusion" or "complicity" of modern writers and artists for having "remained just as unaware of the [environ-mental] crisis on our doorstep as the population at large."[31] Such formal deficits in the history of the novel are undeniable. To identify and repair them has been, and will continue to be, a necessary activity of literary pro-duction and scholarship. But again, in undertaking such activity we restrict our attention to the novel's ideological qualities, ensuring that only those elements in the work with an "excuse for existing" carry critical significance. Thus we separate novel criticism from that thought that, outside the instan-tiation relation, quietly dismantles the certainty, solidity, and knowability of the world being depicted.

ABSOLUTE RELATIONALITY

If—as the narrator of Robert Walser's 1907 novel *The Tanners* puts it—"a painter thinks in colors, a musician in notes, a sculptor in stone, a baker in flour, a poet in words, and a farmer in patches of land," while a bank direc-tor thinks "in money,"[32] a novel thinks in relations. But there is no analogy between the novel's relationality and the musician's notes or the sculptor's stone, for the relationality of the novel is absolute: it persists despite any for-mal (ethical or linguistic) operation with which we, or the novel itself, might seek to resolve it. In a March 1949 letter to the art critic and historian Georges Duthuit, Samuel Beckett talks of refusing "the state of being in rela-tion as such" and of the tantalizing possibility of an "expression in the absence of relations *of any kind*."[33] Beckett is attributing this possibility to the work of a painter of his and Duthuit's acquaintance, Bram van Velde. But Beckett's letter, and the short momentous text that resulted from it,

Three Dialogues, should be read as a statement of creative aspiration, one that took place during the period of Beckett's most consequential struggle with the limits of the novel form. Three weeks after the March 9 letter, Beckett would begin writing *The Unnamable*, the last in the three-book series that began with *Molloy* and *Malone Dies* (*Letters*, 163n5). Van Velde, says Beckett to Duthuit,

> is brave enough . . . to grasp that the break with the outside world entails the break with the inside world, *that there are no replacement relations for naive relations*, that what are called outside and inside are one and the same. I am not saying that he makes no attempt to reconnect. What matters is that he does not succeed. His painting is, if you will, the impossibility of reconnecting. There is, if you like, refusal and refusal to accept refusal. That perhaps is what makes this painting possible.

But, as Beckett subsequently tells Duthuit, his attempt to evoke, in van Velde, an absence of relationality fails. "Whatever I say, I shall seem to be locking him back into a relation" (140).

The attempt is taken up again more than thirty years later in another work on visual forms, when the philosopher Gilles Deleuze organizes his two-volume study of cinema around the proposition of a historical break in the nature of the cinematographic image. In Deleuze's account, a "classical" cinema in which the relations between the image and thought are "well defined" gives way, over several decades, to a "modern" cinema in which the various terms of those relations collapse: the concept of a "whole" that stands outside the image as the object of its interrogation, the notion of a thought that subsists beneath and in the absence of its conscious forms, and the notion of a world of action whose meaning is determined by the interests (however understood) of the actors.[34] The three modes corresponding to these forms of relation—"critical thought, hypnotic thought, action-thought," as Deleuze summarizes them—do not survive the break in the cinematographic image. In the "new relations with thought" that appear in modern cinema, the power of thought is replaced by "an unthought in thought" or "an irrational proper to thought" (181). The whole, outside the image, is replaced by a new "point of outside [*dehors*] beyond the outside world [*monde extérieur*]" that enters each image and displaces its connection to the whole, and the unity posited by a human action together with its motivations, causes, and intentions is replaced by a nondetermined, acentered, and decentered perception located in the cinema apparatus itself. It is with this development, Deleuze says, that cinema attains "the particular powers of the novel" (187).

To think in relations is to think outside the forms that would put an end to relationality: the form of innocence, the form of criminality, the form of property, the forms of sanity and insanity, the form of senility, the form of justice, the form of expression, the form of plagiarism, the form of genius, the form of idiocy, the form of sarcasm, the form of politeness, the form of experience, the form of race, the form of sex, the form of gender, the forms of debt and indebtedness, the form of society, the form of the economy, the forms of development and of progress, the form of the ideal, the forms of the unity of time and of space, the forms of literature and art, the form of narrative, the form of form, the form of formlessness. The novel, one might say, is "intersectional" in its essence, for intersectionality "resists static representations of people's identities and social locations."[35] To think outside such forms is to identify the power of thought not with the positive connection of forms but with the spaces of "fragility" or discontinuity at their borders (or, what amounts to the same thing, to recategorize such connections as interruptions). When Morrison speculates that the "major" themes of the literature of the United States—"individualism, masculinity, social engagement versus historical isolation; acute and ambiguous moral problematics; the thematics of innocence coupled with an obsession with figurations of death and hell"—look radically different when considered from the perspective of "a dark, abiding, signing Africanist presence" that hovers "at the margins of the literary imagination" (*Playing*, 5–6), she is registering the intersectionality of the novel as the site of a thought that happens irrespective of an author's intentions or a critic's interpretive schemas: a thought that, without being able to say so, "explode[s] and undermine[s]" all overt or submerged themes and treatments (16). When Morrison names that site "blackness" or "Africanism" (6–7), these names are provisional, for race and blackness, too, are "invented" and "fabricated" forms (6), the effect of which has been to condemn African American artists and scholars to the "old and sad routine . . . of defending, forever defending, their right to exist—a tedious battle, so unoriginal, so enervating it left no time and no strength for the real work of artists and scholars, which is to refine its own creation and go about their own business."[36] If there is a subject of thought named "intersectionality," it inhabits a space between positive terms; no identity is attributable to it. This, also, is why the thought of the novel is beyond the reach of theoretical discourse—increasingly so. Theory, or what Morrison calls "criticism as a form of knowledge" (*Playing*, 9), is concerned with making connections. The novel itself, even as its characters and narrators incessantly draw connections or outsource the work of doing so to its readers and critics, is becoming ever more attuned to the need and the capacity to vacate them.

Of course, many novelistic works are produced that fail to achieve or to sustain this "essence," interrupting the novel's intersectionality by affirming one or another conceptual form as the defining one. Such interruption is a condition, no doubt, of bringing any work of fiction to closure. Some works do so from the outset, cohering an entire theme and plot around an idea as simple as, for example, "the possibility and efficacity of good deeds" (as Lukács summarizes the central proposition of many of Tolstoy's stories) (*SER*, 167) or as crude as "the anterior bad luck of being sexually unattractive" (as the male protagonist understands a girlfriend's misfortunes in an inexplicably celebrated mid-twentieth-century work of English comic fiction).[37] What is more usual, as Lukács also observes of Tolstoy, is when the novel's normative propositions have no need of being stated directly. Tolstoy's works are marked not by revelations of the "immediate link between exploiter and exploited" but by a "dazzling mass of brilliantly observed small detail" (*SER*, 177, 171), which enables the "true existential interconnections" to emerge:

> In individual traits which on the surface seem to have nothing to do with exploitation—in what his characters think of the most abstract problems, in the fashions in which they make love and in many other such things, Tolstoy demonstrates with admirable realist artistry . . . the link between such traits in his characters and the parasitic nature of their existence.
> (177)

A recent work suggests a contemporary variation on this framework. A successful neurosurgeon named Henry, well advanced in his career, reflects on the persistence of his belief in the "invisible folds and kinks of character, written in code, at the level of molecules" that seem to determine the abilities, vulnerabilities, and hence destinies of the various struggling and impoverished people in his environment. (Such people include a man in the early stages of Huntington's disease who has invaded Henry's home, threatened his family, and been subsequently overpowered by the neurosurgeon and his teenage son.) Henry speculates that one consequence of this proposition is that "no amount of social justice will cure or disperse" them, yet the seeming normativity of this conclusion is tempered by the character's self-caricature as a "professional reductionist," by his acknowledgment that "he is no social theorist," by his ability to recognize and ironize the discourses that frame and arrange his thoughts, and by intimations of his own finitude and mortality.[38] Ian McEwan's novel is just as susceptible to conventional ideological critique as the most ethically inflected moments in Tolstoy. Such a critique might locate the work's "inexorable truthfulness"—as Lukács puts it in relation to Tolstoy (*SER*, 167)—not in Henry's casual neurobiologism but in the very gulf separating the character's consciousness from a real understanding of the social inequities that surround him and the possibility of their remediation. But Lukács's earlier work *The Theory of the Novel* opens up a more fundamental critical assessment of this work in its discussion of irony (mentioned earlier). The question at issue is not whether McEwan's novel endorses Henry's conservative views about neurobiology and social justice but how the novel resolves the mutual incomprehension and incompatibility between those views and the ethical and aesthetic values of the other characters. What, then, is the form of linkage peculiar to this work? Lukács writes:

> The writer's irony is a negative mysticism to be found in times without a god. It is an attitude of *docta ignorantia* towards meaning . . . ; in it there is the deep certainty, expressible only in form-giving, that through not-desiring-to-know and not-being-able-to-know [the writer] has truly encountered, glimpsed and grasped the ultimate, true substance, the present, non-existent God.
> (90)

In the contemporary period, in other words, the most effective way to interrupt or foreclose the novel's intersectionality is to transform it into pluralism, a whole that may be collectively instantiated by a variety of incommensurable, self-identical, discursive, and existential forms.[39] Thus, a narrator-protagonist's failure to comprehend the ethical commitments, professional vocabularies, or standards of expertise of other characters is accompanied by tolerance, even admiration, for the various forms of virtuosity they embody. McEwan's *Saturday* is a lesson in what is perhaps the dominant aesthetic ideology of our age: a belief in "form-giving"— disciplinary practices, technical idioms, artistic mastery, even cultural traits and attributes—as marking the limit of thought.[40]

Such themes and structures (Tolstoy's ethical denunciations, Amis's chauvinism, McEwan's ideological pluralism) may be *generically* recognizable as novelistic. For what reading of a novel does not turn on the explicatory qualities of some such subjective revelation? What plot can evolve without the discovery of someone's criminality, virtue, wrongedness, psychological transformation, or capacity for self-expression? However, these formal elements do not exhaust or account for the novel, and they are not essential to it. Connections, whether external (sociological, philosophical, ethical) or internal (narrative, subjective, ironic), whether intended (part of the artist's plan) or unintended (part of the work's ideology), whether "represented" (named and established) or "instantiated" (unnamed and unspecified), *are not the primary work of the novel.* They are not its endpoint, nor do they participate in the event of the work.

On the contrary. The novel is evolving toward a thought that is neither speakable nor instantiable; a thought whose "subjectivity" is located outside the novel's representational economy; a thought that does not abide by the logics of authorship and expression; a point of view from which the work's narrative, characters, plot developments, and philosophical themes and motifs appear not as *carriers* of meaning but as *distractions* from it and that is consequently immune to their explanatory power. Such a thought does not enter the work either as an object of representation or a subject of enunciation. It cannot be paraphrased or inhabited by any critic or theorist, no matter how steeped in the history of the novel and no matter how tortuous or complex his or her theoretical system or nomenclature, for its endpoint is not a "congruity" (Ian Watt) but an incongruity.

FREE INDIRECT DISCOURSE AND THE FREE INDIRECT

The possibility of such a thought has come into view at certain moments in the history of philosophy and the theory of the novel. Rarely, if ever, in these scholarly discourses has it taken a conceptual form or enjoyed critical or philosophical advocacy. Indeed, this study has been undertaken in the awareness that any such conceptualization or advocacy, far from opening up a new front of scholarship in the theory of the novel, would place the idea it sought to produce further beyond the reach of critical discourse.

Nevertheless, a figural complement to this thought may be found in a central feature of the modern novel, one that many critics have asserted to be the novel's unique discovery and invention: the stylistic mode known as "free indirect discourse." Since its identification by linguists and literary critics at the end of the nineteenth century (of course, novelists and other writers had long been using it), free indirect discourse has been conceptualized as a technique for the representation of a character's speech or thought that avoids the conventional framing syntax of indirect speech (the words "he said" or "she thought") in favor of a kind of immediate access.[41] Thus (to take a well-known example), the first sentence of James Joyce's story "The Dead"—"Lily, the caretaker's daughter, was literally run off her feet"— achieves, as Vološinov puts it, "the identification of the narrator with his character" (since the reporting verb "she thought," the vehicle of their differentiation, is omitted) while maintaining, in the same syntactical formulation, the narrator's "independent position" (by means of the retention of "pronouns appropriate to indirect discourse").[42] This combination of contradictory effects has been described by different theorists of free indirect discourse using analogous pairs of terms, for example "empathy" and "irony," "emotions" and "distance," "omniscience" and "partiality."[43]

Among critics and narratologists, the nature of free indirect discourse has been fervently debated. On one side, free indirect discourse is imagined to be (in the words of Franco Moretti) "a sort of stylistic Panopticon." "Respeaking a character's thoughts or speeches," writes D. A. Miller, "the narration simultaneously subverts their authority and secures its own."[44] We are enabled to see not only into the "mind" of the character but beyond it, into the "hidden recesses of self-consciousness," as Peter Boxall has written of Jane Austen's *Emma*, "to see what she herself cannot."[45] It is on such grounds that the novelist Henry Green abandoned the technique toward the end of his career. "Do we know, in life, what other people are really like?" he said in 1950. "I very much doubt it. We certainly do not know what other people are thinking and feeling. How then can the novelist be so sure?"[46] On the other side, free indirect discourse is understood as a liberation of fictional characters from the judgments that authors, or their narrators, may presume to offload upon them. Hans Robert Jauss notes that readers of *Madame Bovary* are under no obligation to accept the verdict that Flaubert seemed to be issuing upon Emma Bovary. That *Madame Bovary* offers no condemnation of its protagonist's "lasciviousness," a fault for which the work's nineteenth-century prosecutors condemned it, is the very reason why the modern literary-critical universe celebrates it.[47] Adopting a version of this position, Anne-Lise François claims that free indirect style frees characters from the "burdens" that other representational forms subject them to, such as that of "having 'thoughts that rise to the level of the express-ible'" or of "having to signal 'deep' or unfathomable emotion." Characters are freed, in other words, "from the work of speaking for themselves, giving accounts, and making themselves legible to others."[48]

The fact that such opposed critical perspectives on a particular narrative technique can exist and for there to be no sure way of adjudicating between them is, of course, remarkable in and of itself. Summarizing the opposition, Moretti proposes a third possibility, one that he claims is all but indisputable when it comes to *Madame Bovary*. When "character and narrator lose their distinctiveness," he writes, they "are replaced (almost) everywhere by the abstract voice of current ideology. The emotional tone, the lexicon, the shape of the sentence—all the elements on which we rely to extricate the subjective from the objective side of free indirect style—are now amalgamated in the . . .'"objective" impersonality' of the *idée reçue.*"

To insist on identifying the "focalization" (the point of view) of free indirect discourse, whether characterologically or ideologically, is understandable, of course, if one is a literary critic.[49] However, such identification rarely suffices as an account of the work's perspective in any particular case; its identifiability can only be insisted upon in the abstract. To do so is to preserve the sense of free indirect discourse as nothing more troubling or complicated than a technique for representing one subjective interiority from the perspective of another. The various critical positions outlined in this chapter assume that nothing is more natural to the practice of literature, nothing more politically innocuous—or politically productive—than to subject a fictional character, in the fullness and interiority of its being, to the ear and gaze of an authority external to it. Each position (with the possible exception of that of Anne-Lise François) assumes that the theoretical problem of free indirect discourse is fully comprehended by the question of *whose* thoughts are being represented, *with what* framing intentions, and *to what* rhetorical or aesthetic ends. Each, in other words, retains what Vološinov calls the "ideologeme" of the "inner subjective personality, with all its subjective intentions and all its inner depths" as the primary, basic unit of thought (*MPL*, 152–53).

This book begins from a different premise: that when it comes to the novel, the question of the identity of the speaker or thinker and the substance of its thought—a political question, as much as a critical one—*cannot be settled theoretically without fundamental changes in our critical assumptions and procedures.* That is, the question of the novel's thought cannot be addressed successfully in a critical discourse that presumes a unity of the speaking subject, a corresponding unity of the spoken utterance, and the fact of the work as a translation or transposition of thoughts or events that preexist it as its ultimate point of reference.

Despite the main title of this book, episodes of free indirect discourse are not especially privileged in the following chapters; this is not a study of free indirect *style* or *discourse*. Such episodes merely stand as the most visible markers of the formal limits that have been evoked in the course of this opening chapter. Nevertheless, Vološinov's account of free indirect discourse is one of those "moments" in the history of philosophy where the possibility of an uninstantiated thought of the novel comes into view. "What we have in quasi-direct discourse," Vološinov writes (using Gertraud Lerch's term) "is not a simple mechanical mixture or arithmetical sum of two forms but a completely new, positive tendency in active reception of another person's utterance, a special direction in which the dynamics of the interrelationship between reporting and reported speech moves" (*MPL*, 142).

Fiction understands this without having to be told. Writers of fiction in the present period are addressing the problem of thought—which is to say, the problem of point of view—by giving up any claim to the representation or the democratizing of perspectives. What we are seeing in contemporary writing is the appearance of what Bakhtin called a "zone of maximally close contact between the represented object and contemporary reality in all its inconclusiveness" (*Dialogic Imagination*, 31). Literature, in other words, has reached the point of bringing into being—inventing—*a thought that cannot be inhabited subjectively.*

In this book, the term "free indirect," liberated from its use as a modifier in the technical concepts of "free indirect style" and "free indirect discourse," will give expression to a decentering and deauthorization of

literary discourse, to the possibility of a thought (a point of view) no longer saddled by affiliation—or even antipathy—to the novelistic "forms"
enumerated earlier or to the concepts on which the critical practices of
commentary, interpretation, and theorization depend: voice and subject,
character and type, story and world, fiction and reality.

The central hypotheses of this book, therefore, may be summarized as
follows:

1. Instantiation, a logical relation that is as old as philosophy itself, is also the
organizational and ideological structure of the novel. Nothing in the *form* of the
novel, nothing the novel *says* or *does*, is possible outside this structure, which is
inseparable from the novel's critical legibility.

2. Coexisting with this truth about the novel, however, is an alternative
understanding of the novel that is at odds with its formal qualities. The impossibility of arriving at a formal definition of the novel, an impossibility established
by Bakhtin,[50] does not mean that the novel does not exist. It means, quite simply,
that what defines the novel exceeds its form—exceeds, that is, the structure that
has organized almost all professional literary criticism since the novel's inception.
This structure presupposes that a thought is always instantiated in a form. Of
course, such instantiated thoughts are present everywhere in the novel, but they
are not the thought of the novel, which consists, rather, in a noninstantiated, noninstantiable idea. In dispensing with the instantiation relation, the contemporary
novel makes visible and overcomes the predominant aesthetic ideology of the
postindustrial, "neoliberal" world.

3. Even in its pedestrian and least interesting forms, literature undertakes this
exit from the instantiation relation more successfully and completely than the
most rigorous and systematic as well as the most experimental and unconventional
"theoretical" work.

4. The "free indirect," understood not as a "style" or "discourse" but as a nonanchored, noncentered perspective, is the means by which the novel escapes the
claims of ideology itself. Insofar as this principle is generalizable outside the practices of writers of literature, it represents the most promising avenue for a rediscovery of the possibility of thought in our time, when a thought without interest
has seemingly become inconceivable.

Chapter Two

AGAINST EXEMPLARITY

W. G. Sebald

In a world reduced to a multiplicity of chaos, it is only the formal structure of the work of art, insofar as it does not refer to anything else, that can serve as unity.

—GILLES DELEUZE, *PROUST AND SIGNS*

INSTANCE AND EXAMPLE

Exemplarity is a conceptual relationship in which the parts of a work are linked to a whole. The "whole" in this formulation is not just the whole of the work but that of a world of which the work is a part and to which the work and the exemplary instances within it are tied by the work's claim to relevance and to legibility. Exemplarity is the fabric of connectivity in which the literary work has its being. It is the always unstated logic according to which readers identify with the characters of a work or by which they may search in it for indications of how to live. Exemplarity is a bridge between the world *about* which we read and the world *in* which we read. It links the sensuous and the conceptual. By its means, as Alain Badiou says in *Logics of Worlds*, "we simultaneously think the multiplicity of worlds and the invariance of the truths that appear at distinct points in this multiplicity."[1] Badiou is evoking a continuity between the painted horses in the ancient cave of Chauvet and the horses in Picasso's work, a continuity that assumes a relation in common. Exemplarity presupposes the existence of a conceptual whole (for example, Horseness), its divisibility (or exemplification), and our dwelling "not only amid things, or bodies" but "in the transport of the True, in which it sometimes happens we are required to partake" (20).

Exemplarity borders on, indeed substantially overlaps with, the primary conceptual relation that organizes this book: the logic of instantiation.

Other thinkers have taken steps to differentiate these ways of conceiving the relationality that is inherent in the work. Agustín Zarzosa, addressing Deleuze's film theory, distinguishes six possible "relations that films may entertain with concepts." He names these "instance," "allusion," "example," "illustration," "exception," and "case"—the last being the privileged "monadic" form that comprehends all the others (and, according to Zarzosa, escapes the metaphoricity with which they straddle the universal and the particular).[2] Case is for Zarzosa a relation in which concept is not "internalized" by the image but exists in "proximity" to it: "both are monads expressing the world from their point of view" (50). The most important distinction Zarzosa makes, for my purposes, is one he derives from Kant's *Metaphysics of Morals*: between an instance and an example.[3] An instance, says, Zarzosa, merely "unif[ies] various particulars by expressing their common properties," whereas an example "prov[es] its force by acting upon [such] particulars" (41). What Zarzosa is getting at is the difference between a cognitive or ontological relation and a moral or instructional one. In a 2007 introduction to a special issue of *Critical Inquiry*, Lauren Berlant also privileges "case," although she situates the term differently with respect to the Kantian distinction. Case, she says, is an "actuarial" relation, rather than a "gestural" one: "To ask the question of what makes something a case, and not a merely gestural instance, illustration, or example, is to query the adequacy of an object to bear the weight of an explanation worthy of attending to and taking a lesson from."[4]

In this discussion, exemplarity will be used to denote both what Zarzosa calls an "instance" and what Berlant calls a "case." In an aesthetic context, it is not necessary to make a theoretical distinction between a "merely gestural" and an "actuarial" example, for an instance "act[s] on particulars" simply by making an appearance. In the aesthetic regime, in other words, the quotient of added significance necessary to turn a gestural example into an actuarial one is zero. In the aesthetic regime, to use Jacques Rancière's formulation, the gestural and the actuarial are "part and parcel of [*appartiennent à*] the same mechanism."[5]

This is not to say that instance and example are identical. Adapting Kant's usage, "instance" here signals nothing more than the invocation or appearance of the term in question, while "example" denotes the meaningful, normative connection that accumulates around it or is attributed to it. Some theorists, such as Toril Moi, have attempted to redeem exemplarity from the normative violence of representation by glossing it as a "nonexclusionary" relation to the idea. Examples, suggests Moi, are not implicated in the "boundedness" of abstract concepts; they are simply ways to "think seriously about the particular case, about the ordinary, the common and the low."[6] Examples are by definition "concrete": they arise in everyday conversation and remain tied to the "particular case." They do not require that what is said about them must hold "for every conceivable example" (92). Moi's discussion adheres to Ludwig Wittgenstein's insistence that concepts have "blurred edges" and are usable only on that basis. Concepts cohere not on the basis of qualities that every instance has in common but on the basis, rather, of "family resemblances."[7] Both Wittgenstein and Moi are, in their way, resisting the logic of the instantiation relation while seeking to preserve the practical utility of the example. Philosophy begins, says Moi, "when we realize that your examples vie with mine"—that two modes of experience may be incommensurable. The gap between experiences is also, then, the gap between one person's example and its concept. In a discursive or readerly situation, the appearance of an example should be considered not as an "order" (an element in a discursive regime) but an invitation to dialogue and an "appeal to the other's freedom" (Moi, 92).

In her references to "philosophy" and "freedom" Moi is tacitly invoking Kant's faculty of judgment. According to Kant, judgment, as opposed to (say) the application of rules or the following of instruction, enjoys "no directions or precepts," for judgment is the exercise of "so-called mother wit," a "gift of nature" the want of which, he says further, "no scholastic discipline can compensate."[8] Judgment, unlike "understanding," exists in the gap between subjects, which is to say, in the gap between the "form" and the "content" of cognition (114), between the rule and its application, between theory and practice. Deficiency of judgment is a failure to occupy, subjectively, the space opened up by the inherent imperfection of the example. For examples, says Kant, "seldom adequately fulfil the conditions of the rule" (115). Thus, a physician, judge, or politician may frequently "blunder" in the application of the principles he possesses in his head. "Whilst he can comprehend the general *in abstracto*," a lack of judgment will prevent him from being able to determine "whether a particular case *in concreto* ought to rank under the former" (115). Judgment is a structure in which what is revealed is not truth or cognition but a point of view. When such a point of view elicits a degree of consensus it may be recognized or celebrated for its faculty of judgment. Judgment—or "philosophy," as Moi has it—is then a place of resolution, a "form," no less, that holds at bay the world's "fragility" for as long as the form remains intact.

When literary works are used as examples, they too are positioned in that space of resolution, a function to which (in some sense) they are ideally suited. Writing about the use of literary texts as examples in the context of moral philosophy, the British philosopher Onora O'Neill writes that abandoning the general for the particular—in the manner of Wittgensteinian philosophers interested in "thinking through examples"—merely suppresses the shared cultural context implied in any moral discourse that takes place on the basis of examples. Attempts, says O'Neill (citing the British Wittgensteinian philosopher Peter Winch), to transfer the burden of exemplarity from general rules of action to the "pivot" of the particular example, and thus treat the example in isolation from its concept, "must presuppose sufficient community of moral views—an ethical tradition, perhaps, or a shared ideology—for there to be something which 'we' . . . do want to say about a given example."[9]

It is precisely the disappearance of such a notion of community and the dissolution of the form of judgment that seems to be the ground, or occasion, of a refusal of the "force" of exemplarity in contemporary works of fiction, a refusal that I will explore here in the work of the late German-English writer W. G. Sebald. In Sebald, connection seems possible only on the basis of a suspension of exemplarity, whether intradiegetic or extradiegetic. This suspension is instigated with two evident premises of Sebald's project: that logical connections themselves are a matter of uncertainty and that fiction is no longer a form that can sustain—or that requires—an identifiable whole to authenticate it. This suspension explains the "enigmatic" quality of Sebald's writing. In the absence of exemplarity (which, strictly speaking, is not an absence but the unavailability of an interpretive structure), the enigmaticalness is experienced as a situation of impasse or inertia: the equal presence of the desire for connection and its impossibility.

This formal inertia is maintained consistently across the four prose literary works that Sebald published before his death. In the earliest of these, *Vertigo* (*Schwindel*) (1990), Sebald's narrator, disembarking from a train that has just pulled into Milan, experiences a sense of abandonment as two of his fellow passengers disappear into the city:

What connection could there be, I then wondered and now wonder again, between those two beautiful female readers and this immense railway terminus which, when it was built in 1932, outdid all other train stations in Europe; and what relation was there between the so-called monuments of the past and the vague longing, propagated through our bodies, to people the dust-blown expanses and tidal plains of the future.[10]

What connection could there be . . . ? The question is a perennial one in Sebald: it is asked repeatedly, such that the question of connection, the problem of connection, might be said to be the central preoccupation of his writing.

It makes no sense, therefore, to complain about the forced or "strained" connections in Sebald's works,[11] for connection in Sebald is not a site of resolution but of the posing of a question. Connections are never established other than provisionally. Nor is it especially meaningful to assert, as some critics have done, that Sebald's is a world of "interconnectedness," that—as Mark R. McCulloh puts it—his fiction is guided by the principle of "the interconnectedness of all things."[12] For interconnectedness in Sebald is only ever an abstract proposition.[13] Answers to the question of connection are never offered except insofar as a new connection is constituted by the work itself. The only kind of connection affirmed by Sebald's texts is an immanent one, forged at the moment of the text's composition, in the pages of the very book we are reading. "I sat at a table near the open terrace door," writes Sebald's narrator from a bar in Limone, "drawing connections between events that lay far apart but which seemed to me to be of the same order. I wrote with an ease that astonished me. Line by line I filled the pages of the ruled notepad I had brought with me from home" (*Vertigo*, 94). What is he writing? What connections is he making? He is writing, of course, nothing other than the words we are reading. The connections drawn "between events that lay far apart" are the ones constituted by these words, and they endure no longer than the moment of writing itself. I sat . . . I wrote . . . I filled . . . These simple formulations are as enigmatic as anything in Sebald, for they come from a postfictional universe in which it is no longer possible to distinguish the person writing from the person represented, the actions described from the act of description. In the universe of Sebald's writing, the fictional conceit has collapsed.

The implications of this collapse are illustrated most clearly by contrast with the works of Charles Dickens. We cannot not think of the following moment in *Bleak House*: "What connexion can there be, between the place in Lincolnshire, the house in town, the Mercury in powder, and the whereabout of Jo the outlaw with the broom. . . . What connexion can there have been between many people in the innumerable histories of this world, who, from opposite sides of great gulfs, have, nevertheless, been very curiously brought together!"[14] In Dickens, the conceit is intact; fiction is a fully operative category. Consequently, the connections are nailed down: they are found in exploitation and social inequality, in the vanities and inhibitions of class distinctions, and in the greed and laziness of every class faction except those at the very bottom.

What has happened since Dickens was writing such that the kinds of social, economic, and ethical connections presupposed in Dickens's works are no longer possible? How, that is, do we explain the always suspect nature of connection in Sebald? Implicit in these questions is that we have passed from a historical situation in which connections (of causality, of influence, of determination) were intact to one in which such connections have become generally implausible. This implication raises methodological issues crucial to the approach of this book. It would be easy to argue, for example, that disconnection (or even the uncertainty of connections) is not a generalizable phenomenon, that Sebald's ambiguous relation to connection is a matter of aesthetic choice or temperament, with no claim to the status of a cultural or historical logic. Might the crisis of connection—if such a tendency were observable in contemporary culture—be better understood as a symptom, a failure of political and intellectual responsibility, of the kind that, in his later work, Georg Lukács detected in the tendency of modernist writers to privilege the contents of consciousness over knowledge of the totality?[15]

Such objections, despite the "materialist" terms in which they are often articulated, fall short of the historico-philosophical approach I will pursue here. "Historico-philosophical," a term that originates in Lukács's *Theory of the Novel*, means an approach that rejects the capacity of subjective categories to explain the formal features of literary works (or anything else). A subjective category is one whose unity is located within the self. In a historico-philosophical approach, entities such as the writer's beliefs or intentions, or the question of his or her complicity in dominant ideologies, or the sense of an underlying political agenda, while no doubt operative in the work's composition, are not derivable from a reading of the work. Nor, therefore, can they be held to have any explanatory privilege regarding its meaning. Likewise, aesthetic values like authenticity or sincerity, and even legal concepts such as plagiarism, do not register at the historico-philosophical level other than as formal phenomena, "resolutions" that depend for their unity on the unverifiable claims of an individual conscious-ness. Historico-philosophically, then, the subjective (conceptual, thematic) dimensions of a work do not coincide with the work's substance, even when such elements expand within the novel form, giving the work an "essayis-tic" quality and seeming to carry a large burden of readerly interest. A work of art takes form from necessity rather than the subjective inclinations of its author. It is important not to confuse "necessity" with destiny or fatal-ity, which, as terms oriented around a definite (temporal or spatial) perspec-tive, are also subjective forms. Nor does necessity imply universality or inevitability, in the sense often associated with Hegel's philosophy of his-tory. Necessity means simply that the work is a solution arrived at provi-sionally and in specific circumstances. Those circumstances—the problem or set of problems to which the work responds—should be understood not in transcendent ("personal" or "political") terms but as rigorously corre-lated with the formal qualities of the work.

The first problem to which the work responds, then, is that of writing, of how to produce a work. In coining the term "historico-philosophical," Lukács noted that any sense of the "failure" or "incompleteness" of a par-ticular work is a result of confusing its substance with its "content" (*TN*, 73). To condemn as subjectivist, incomplete, or confused a work or body of work on the grounds of the unhistorical, subjective quality of the sentiments expressed in it or of the confusion and alienation experienced by its fictional characters is itself unhistorical and subjectivizing. To take the content of a work for its substance, to accept the utterances in a novelistic work or the conceptual terms thematized by it as the key to its meaning, or to explain its formal qualities (say, Sebald's "ambiguous relation to connection") directly by reference to socio-historical forces and conditions is, in differ-ent ways, to limit one's understanding of the work to the view from the sub-jective bridge, the vantage point of exemplarity. It is to presuppose the unity of the work's individual elements, their representability, and thus an isomorphic relation between the work and the world outside it.[16]

It is also to preserve the inviolability of the position of the critic with respect to the "crisis" that has befallen the writer. By contrast, the historico-philosophical approach is itself born of the crisis of exemplarity, for Lukács's innovation in *The Theory of the Novel* might be seen as the discovery of a principle of form whose corresponding "content" is, for the first time, no longer identifiable. What is at issue in the problem of connection in W. G. Sebald's work is not simply the dominant modes of literary representation and comprehension but the resources of critical intellection itself. Exemplarity names the structure of instantiation that holds together the category of fiction and its viability as an object of study. The differences between Sebald's writing and that of Dickens register not simply a subjective dissolution of that structure but a historical one. Sebald's works are part of a crisis or refusal of the structure of exemplarity. The crisis is not unique to Sebald's work; however, Sebald is a singular, illuminating occasion of it. Since exemplarity is part of the logic of fiction, its refusal is also a renegotiation or clarification of the terms on which fiction, as a practice, remains possible.

Note on Terminology

One of the peculiarities of exemplarity is that there is no readily available technical vocabulary with which to talk about the structure of the example and, as we have seen, little agreement over its political effects. The complexity involved in thinking about the function of examples in literary works is revealed as soon as we start to think about how the relation between the different elements in the structure of exemplarity has been conceptualized.

For Giorgio Agamben, writing in *The Coming Community* (1990), the example is an ambiguous formation. Far from being simply a form of category thinking or the substrate of an ethics, the example "escapes" the neutrality of mere linguistic being, "the antinomy of the individual and the universal,"[17] but it does so because of, rather than despite, its normative (ethical or identitarian) status. The example stands as "one singularity among others," yet, insofar as it "exerts its force," it is elevated into another order of existence. The example, this is to say, is defined by its instantiation. The only property common to the category of the example is that of "being-called": "not being-red, but being-*called*-red; not being-Jakob, but being-*called*-Jakob." The example "is a singular object that presents itself as such, that *shows* its singularity" (10). But in showing its singularity, the example also destroys it.[18]

For the literary critic Saidiya Hartman, exemplarity is implicated in an ethnological regime of looking that subjects archival material to a structure of interpretation limited to preexisting categories of knowledge. Thus exemplarity is the great temptation and pitfall of the archival historian. The scholar whose work begins from a rejection of such knowledge categories, for whom the archive is "a death sentence, a tomb, a display of the violated body, an inventory of property,"[19] will be drawn to precisely those parts of the archive where the record is less complete. In *Wayward Lives, Beautiful Experiments*, Hartman is interested in the lives of young African American women living in Philadelphia and New York at the turn of the twentieth century, several generations after the end of slavery—existences whose sole traces consist of photographs discovered in municipal archives, in published anthologies, in documentary accounts of slums and urban communities and other sources.[20] The images Hartman assembles include formal portraits, news pictures, film stills, amateur snapshots, police mugshots, stylized "artistic" depictions, as well as photographs "taken by social reformers and charity organizations" (18). Her study is organized around elements in such images that suggest a refusal by those depicted of "the terms of visibility imposed on them": averted eyes, turned backs, fleeting movements at the edge of the frame, rigid postures that belie any salacious intent in the arrangement, opaque expressions and gazes that "assume nothing shared between the one compelled to appear and those looking" (18, 25). The fact that they evade "capture" is the very reason they are important to Hartman's project; for "young women not in desperate need, not saddled with children, and old enough to say *Hell no* and *Get out of my face*" (19) represent the possibility of an exit from all sociological regimes and orders of thought—an exit through the doors of the archive. *Wayward Lives, Beautiful Experiments* wants to do justice to the "lovely silhouettes and dark shadows" in the photographs Hartman discovers and, at the same time, to register the difficulty of the enterprise, for such fugitive elements are "impossible to force into the grid of naturalist description or the taxonomy of slum pictures" (18). Hartman is interested in the very details of these women's lives that escape even her own gestures of "annotation"—the aspiration that her words may act as a "shield" to "protect" her subjects, to "deflect" the ethnographic gaze upon them (26). Her method involves, as she puts it, the search for a "latent image capable of articulating another kind of existence" than the officially approved one—for instance, "a runaway image that conveys the riot inside" (30) or, as she says at the end of *Wayward Lives*, "a glimpse of the earth not owned by anyone" (349).

The predicament of Hartman's project (just as it is the predicament of the study of the novel for Lukács) is that there is no way to fend off the appropriating, exemplifying gaze, even with a self-consciously "experimental" approach. The "riot inside" the mind, for example, once it makes an appearance in her text, cannot guarantee its nonsociological status. Like a novel, *Wayward Lives, Beautiful Experiments* is unable to accommodate the theoretical misgivings and yearnings that have brought Hartman to the point of composing the book, for even as she laments the coercion of her subjects into visibility by the attentions of ethnographers and social reformers (21), her work imposes upon them new "terms of visibility," a new, unholy alliance between liberation and appropriation. The singular image that opens the book, a small albumen print from around 1882 of a young girl posed on a horsehair sofa, nude like an odalisque—a girl whose body is "exposed" but who nonetheless "withholds everything" (27)—acquires narrative extension through a fictional conceit: that the girl is not one but many, linked through descriptive features (such as a "longing in [the] eyes") that function narratively and proleptically to connect anonymous existences across time and space (35, 81). In the end, says Hartman, the girl's story becomes "a serial biography of a generation, a portrait of the chorus, a moving picture of the wayward" (31). "In my search for her," she continues, "I soon encountered all the others hovering about her—the sociologist, housing reformer, probation officer, club woman, social worker, vice investigator, journalist, and psychiatrist—all of them insisting their view of her was the truth. One of them was always there, standing in my way, blocking my path whenever I encountered her" (33–34). Hartman's book is caught on the quandary that defines the novel, according to Lukács: that the novel is always trying, and failing, to get out of the way of *its own* gaze.

J. M. Coetzee dramatizes this quandary in *The Master of Petersburg*, a novel that features a fictionalized Dostoevsky in 1869 struggling to complete his work *Demons*. As represented by Coetzee, what torments the novelist is that his writing is not a matter of "fidelity" to his material but a matter of "betrayal," that the terms of visibility that Dostoevsky's work extends to his subjects—his landlady, her young daughter, his own deceased son—are "to be turned to another use, to be gripped to him and fall with him."[21] Lukács describes the quandary of the novel form as its "'bad' infinity," an inherent lack of limits that forces the novel to have "recourse to the biographical form" in order to cohere (*TN*, 81). The danger, however, is that "only a subjective aspect of the totality" will be given form—that the novel's sense of totality is no longer organized by what is "existent" but by what is exemplary (74). "I had to be mindful not to do damage of my own," writes Hartman (34). The paradox of Hartman's project, as it is the paradox of the novel, is that the work's success is measured by the degree to which its subjects escape its gaze. "Only when God is silent does God speak," writes Coetzee in *The Master of Petersburg*. "When God seems to speak God does not speak" (237).

In order to register these difficulties and ambiguities of exemplarity, I will make provisional use of the terminology that I. A. Richards developed in order to theorize the metaphor; that is, I will use "vehicle" to talk about the exemplifying term—the example—and "tenor" to talk about the category, concept, or set of which the exemplifying term is an instance.[22] Unlike the mathematical language of *term* and *series*, *case* and *set*, or *one* and *multiple*—a relation Agamben designates with the mathematical sign ε, "belonging to"—this borrowing of Richards's terminology is an attempt to acknowledge that the example always "exerts its force," that, as Agamben observes, "the proper place of the example is always beside itself" (10); that—*pace* Massumi and Moi—the example carries with it something of what it exemplifies. The pure mathematicity of the relation between particular and universal is destroyed by the instantiation of the example.[23] Exemplarity thus endangers the mode of relationality that Agamben names and attempts to safeguard with the phrase "whatever being" (*l'essere qualunque*).[24] "Whatever being" signifies a mode of allusion in which the object is "reclaimed" from its properties, which is to say, from its quality of "belonging to this or that set, to this or that class (the reds, the French, the Muslims)"—reclaimed "not for another class nor for the simple generic absence of any belonging, but for its being-*such*, for belonging itself" (1–2). "Whatever being" is a conception of being that is anterior (which is to say, indifferent) to all relations of exemplarity. "Whatever being" is an attempt at conceptualizing a notion of being that is outside (prior to) instantiation, and for Agamben it is this idea of a noninstantiated being that will define the "coming politics": a "co-belonging without any condition of belonging" (Agamben, 86).

EXEMPLARITY AND THE NOVEL

The element of exemplarity in fiction has never been straightforward. According to Catherine Gallagher, the possibility of truth in fiction takes the form of an equation in which particularity is exchanged for generality. The novel "could be judged generally true," she writes, "even though all of its particulars are merely imaginary."[25] The structure of the example consists precisely in that exchange. "Novelists' characterizations," Gallagher notes, "could only have referential value by pointing to what [Henry] Fielding calls a 'species.'" This structure, however, is not a stable one. For Gallagher, a "gulf" opens up "between type and instance" in the novel (361), a gulf that is bridged by the proper name, the novel's "key mode of nonreferentiality" (341), which is irreducible to exemplarity. "Novelistic personae," she writes, "even when invented on purpose to exemplify classes of persons, quickly proved too specific to cover all the cases in a 'species.' The excessive and irrelevant detail of any individualized instance tended to obscure the view of its supposed class" (343). Exemplarity, this is to say, is always under pressure in the novel; exemplary relations never demonstrably exhaust the elements of the work, even while exemplarity ensures a level of semantic stratification without which every novel would be meaningless, unreadable.

For these reasons, the burden of my argument here will fall more heavily on the negative claim (the rejection of exemplarity in contemporary fiction) than on the positive one (that exemplarity is constitutive of the novel). And yet, if Sebald is a special case of the former, Dickens is a special case of the latter. In illustrating social connections—in existing in order to illustrate them—characters in Dickens are nothing if not exemplary. It is to the unambiguous, typological connections in Dickens's works that we can attribute their "fabular" quality, in Thomas Keenan's sense of that term. By fabular, what Keenan means is their dependence upon and reiteration of the logic of exemplarity.[26]

In the fable, as Keenan makes clear, two functions or levels of exemplarity are brought into the open: the semantic (narrative) and the rhetorical (ethical). The relation between these two functions is a site of ambiguity in every novelistic work, an ambiguity that diminishes as one moves toward the fabular pole and increases as one moves toward the realist one. "The promise of the 'and,'" writes Keenan—meaning the double register of rhetoric *and* narrative—"which guides us through text to value, whether ethical or semantic, is also a threat: the threat of example's excess, its iteration rather than its graceful self-effacement" (46–47).[27]

In the novel, and in modern aesthetics in general, the narrative and the ethical functions enter into a semiotic economy predicated on the explicitness of the former and the implicitness (the unspeakability) of the latter. In *The Theory of the Novel*, Lukács explains this economy as a relation between the "parts" of the work (the various entities that exist as individualities: characters, objects, descriptions, encounters, utterances, events) and the "whole," the work's entirety, its significance. The novel, he notes, marks a historical shift from a world that is "homogeneously organic and stable," in which parts are fully "justified by their mere presence," to one that is "heterogeneously contingent and discrete," in which only a structure of global meaning can justify the presence of individual elements. The transition is from the world of the epic—where (in the terms of the present discussion) there is no semiotic economy, no "exemplarity"—to that of the novel, the work that is differentiated and organized only in respect of a larger whole, whether or not this whole is specified in the work itself. "In contrast to the epic," writes Lukács, the individualities of the novel "must have a strict compositional and architectural significance, whether this takes the form of contrasting lights thrown upon the central problem . . . or of the introduction, by way of a prelude, of hidden motifs which are to be decisive at the end" (76). The "compositional and architectural significance" of the parts depends on the extrapolation of a larger order of significance to the work, and thus (although Lukács doesn't use the word) on the exemplary quality of the parts. What Lukács calls the "compositional tact" of the novel (77) is the veiling or withholding of this logic of exemplarity. Without this tact, the novel is, for Lukács, nothing more than an "entertainment novel" (73). In detective fiction, for example, the relation between part (clue) and whole (solution) is opened up, solved, and exhausted, all within the frame of the work.

Before discussing Sebald's work in more detail, it will be helpful to look briefly at two other texts in which the problem of exemplarity is articulated in different terms and with correspondingly different solutions: the opening chapter of Coetzee's *Elizabeth Costello* and V. S. Naipaul's *An Area of Darkness.*

Counterexamples

In *Elizabeth Costello*, Elizabeth, an elderly, distinguished writer, on a visit to a college in Pennsylvania to receive a literary award and give a lecture, has a private conversation after the event with her son John, her companion on the trip. Elizabeth is surprised at the absence of any "heavyweight" faculty members at her talk. "The heavyweights," John tells her, "don't involve themselves in this kind of show. The heavyweights are wrestling with the heavyweight problems." Elizabeth is peeved:

> "I am not heavyweight enough for them?"
>
> "No, you're heavyweight all right. Your handicap is that you're not a problem. What you write hasn't yet been demonstrated to be a problem. Once you offer yourself as a problem, you might be shifted over into their court. But for the present you're not a problem, just an example."
>
> "An example of what?"
>
> "An example of writing. An example of how someone of your station and your generation and your origins writes. An instance."[28]

This distinction between an "example" and a "problem" maps approximately onto Lukács's distinction between an entertainment novel—which posits and solves its "problematic" entirely within the frame of the work—and the novel proper, in which problematicity is constitutive and unresolvable (72–73). In *Elizabeth Costello* the literature professors we meet—Elizabeth thinks of them as "goldfish" (6)—treat Elizabeth's work as "entertainment novels," which is to say that the professors seem preoccupied with exemplarity, determined to wrest Elizabeth's work into the realm of identity (underpinned by categories such as intention, reference, and representation).[29] In an interview she gives during the visit, Elizabeth is asked whether in her novel based on Joyce's *Ulysses* Molly Bloom's refusal to have sex with her husband is a message that "until men have worked out a new, post-patriarchal identity, women should hold themselves apart" (10–11). The suggestion is treated by Elizabeth with derision. The question assumes that fictional characters exist to transmit recognizable identity positions, moral quandaries, and solutions to the reader, who, in carrying such entities away from the text, consumes it—assumptions that are easily mocked. In *Elizabeth Costello*, however, the professors—the absent "heavyweights" no less than the present "goldfish"—are exemplary. Thus, the message that the approach of the "goldfish" is inadequate depends for its transmission on the very mode of reading that, with the distinction between the heavyweights and the goldfish, the text seems be militating against.

These exchanges illustrate one form in which the problem of exemplarity has entered the imagination of contemporary writers of fiction: as a predicament in which, whichever way one turns, one is always exemplifying in one direction or another. In Sebald, the problem of exemplarity has none of this sense of inevitability—in part because the problem is articulated differently. For Sebald the question is not primarily one of literary reception—the conflict between writing and criticism—but of production. Sebald is not interested in how a writer can avoid being read as exemplary (of one's "station," one's "generation," or one's "origins"), or how a writer might frame his or her works in such a way that they evade all modes of identitarian interpretation. For Sebald the question is how a writer can avoid *writing* or even *seeing* in such terms. How can one avoid producing a text that reiterates, or simply participates in, the logic of exemplarity?

In his nonfiction work *An Area of Darkness* (1964), V. S. Naipaul constructs an entire logic of India and Indianness, the effect of which is to justify his procedure of reducing everyone he meets to the level of an example. The book opens, however, with a powerful denunciation of exemplary modes of perception. For the visitor to India, writes Naipaul,

to see its poverty is to make an observation of no value; a thousand newcomers to the country before you have seen and said as you. And not only newcomers. Our own sons and daughters, when they return from Europe and America, have spoken in your very words. Do not think that your anger and contempt are marks of your sensitivity. You might have seen more; the smiles on the faces of the begging children, that domestic group among the pavement sleepers waking in the cool Bombay morning, father, mother and baby in a trinity of love, so self-contained that they are as private as if walls had separated them from you: it is your gaze that violates them, your sense of outrage that outrages them. You might have seen the boy sweeping his area of pavement, spreading his mat, lying down; exhaustion and undernourishment are in his tiny body and shrunken face, but lying flat on his back, oblivious of you and the thousands who walk past in the lane between sleepers' mats and house walls bright with advertisements and election slogans, oblivious of the warm, over-breathed air, he plays with fatigued concentration with a tiny pistol in blue plastic. It is your surprise, your anger that denies him humanity. But wait. Stay six months. The winter will bring fresh visitors. Their talk will also be of poverty; they too will show their anger. You will agree; but deep down there will be annoyance; it will seem to you then, too, that they are seeing only the obvious; and it will not please you to find your sensibility so accurately parodied.[30]

The passage is almost Dickensian in its moral relentlessness, its pitilessness toward the outraged spectator of India's poverty, and its willingness to elevate a certain pitch of rhetorical condemnation to the limits of readerly tolerance.

However, for all its moral fervency, crucial differences are apparent between the context in which Naipaul is writing and that of Dickens. Even as he implicates his own situatedness in the critique, Naipaul is constructing a logic of India, one that is intrinsic to it and that allows him to insert everyone he meets into a frame of exemplarity. In a world in which the exemplary relation is collapsing—in which the kind of forensic social anatomization that we find in Dickens is increasingly difficult to sustain—Naipaul relocates it in an *elsewhere*: a zone that is spatially removed from the one in which he observes and writes. At several moments Naipaul comes close to acknowledging the dishonesty of this operation. "To define," he writes, "is to begin to separate oneself, to assure oneself of one's position, to be withdrawn from the chaos that India always threatens" (47). Yet instead of refusing the seduction of separation, Naipaul is progressively taken over by it, such that *An Area of Darkness* is finally less about India than about India's to-be-looked-at-ness. In *An Area of Darkness* the tenor of the exemplary term is always twofold: each character we meet is exemplary both of a certain social *type*, extendable in principle across the nation, and of the *logic* according to which India and Indians are condemned to exemplarity. "A knowledge of degree," writes Naipaul, "is in the bones and no Indian is far from his origins" (55). The logic is traced to the Bhagavad Gita, from which Naipaul quotes frequently: "And do *thy* duty, even if it be humble, rather than another's even if it be great. To die in one's duty is life: to live in another's is death" (47). With this invocation of the *Gita*, the responsibility for looking at India in terms of exemplarity is detached from Naipaul's person and shunted onto the object of his vision. The logic is contradictory; Naipaul rails against the very structure that permits him to look as he does, but the contradiction is invisible to Naipaul because his own thinking disarticulates *being* from *seeing*, the object of the gaze from the nature of the gaze itself.

Gandhi is an important figure in Naipaul's analysis, as an outsider who was able to see India in a way that it had never been seen before: in all its filth, dishonesty, and degradation. By implication, Naipaul's own perception too is of this quality. Liberated by his outsider status from the "knowledge of degree" that prevents Indians from seeing themselves but does not protect them from the logic of being (exemplarity) that enables Naipaul to see them, Naipaul presents us with a number of quasi-fictional characters whose presence in his text is justified precisely by their exemplarity and who disappear from the narrative almost as soon as they are introduced.[31] They are types, defined solely by their occupation or social class, but they are also exemplary of the logic that for Naipaul functions in India more naturally than anywhere else and that supplies a substrate of readymade significance to every fleeting encounter. It is this logic of exemplarity that Edward Said is referring to when he writes of Naipaul's "reliance on a European tradition of supposedly direct observation."[32] In Naipaul, the distinction between "entities that see" and "entities that are seen" is impregnable. Naipaul exemplifies, in short, *because he is not himself part of what he is looking at.*

The ethical claims of Sebald's writing rest almost entirely on the rejection of this logic. Naipaul's work asks to be taken as a form of travelogue—a project that reports on a series of perceptions or encounters while problematizing or reflecting upon them. In such a form, the question of exemplarity easily migrates toward the question of ethical representation more generally. How, asks Naipaul, is it possible to engage with the world and report on that engagement without reducing the object of our encounter to an "instance"? How to see without referring the object of one's gaze to categories of thought that cannot help but pre-form that object? The quandary is unresolvable. For Naipaul, no visitor to India can escape this logic.

The great interest of critics in the ethical valences of Sebald's work seems to involve the idea that his writing, too, addresses such quandaries.[33] Yet Sebald's writing resists the extraction and reapplication of such questions from the work to the situation of a generalized "ethical" perception. In an important sense, Sebald's work rejects the hypothesis of a seat of perception where the kind of connections that might authorize an ethical reading would be contemplated and processed. The most powerful and distinctive features of Sebald's works include, first, their refusal of any hierarchical distinction between entities that *see* and entities that *are seen* and, second, their reluctance to invoke categories that, by the weighing of significance, threaten the "equal and undiminished right" of everything to exist (*Vertigo*, 73). If there are ethical lessons to be drawn from Sebald's work they depend not on the quality of the narrative eye it casts upon the objects it encounters but on a certain technological quality to his enterprise, by which the question of perception is obviated. The use of photography in the body of Sebald's narratives is one element of this. The ethical substance of Sebald's writing consists in the degree to which it achieves a form of perception that, to quote Roland Barthes writing about the photograph, "could never be repeated existentially"—that is, could never be replicated by a human being.[34]

PRINCIPLES OF NARRATION

We can see the principles of composition and narration of Sebald's texts being established at the start of the second chapter of Sebald's 1992 book *The Emigrants*, about a schoolteacher named Paul Bereyter. The narrative begins with Paul's recent suicide, told from the perspective of Sebald's narrator, a pupil of Paul's in the 1950s. We learn that Paul had been prevented from teaching under the Third Reich, years before the narrator had him as a teacher; that in recent years Paul had become reclusive and increasingly eccentric; and that he later killed himself on the railway line outside the town of S, where Sebald's narrator grew up. In the opening pages the narrator describes his preparations to write Paul's story:

> Belatedly, I tried to get closer to him, to imagine what his life was like in that spacious apartment on the top floor of Lerchenmüller's old house, which had once stood where the present block of flats is now. . . . I imagined him lying in the open air on his balcony where he would often sleep in the summer, his face canopied by the hosts of the stars. I imagined him skating in winter, alone on the fish ponds at Moosbach; and I imagined him stretched out on

the track. As I pictured him, he had taken off his spectacles and put them on the ballast stones by his side. The gleaming bands of steel, the crossbars of the sleepers, the spruce trees on the hillside above the village of Altstädten, the arc of the mountains he knew so well, were a blur before his short-sighted eyes, smudged out in the gathering dusk. At the last, as the thunderous sound approached, all he saw was a darkening greyness and, in the midst of it, needle-sharp, the snow-white silhouettes of three mountains: the Kratzer, the Trettach and the Himmelsschrofen.

(29)

But this fictionalizing approach is abandoned. Sebald explains: "Such endeavours to imagine his life and death did not . . . bring me any closer to Paul, except at best for brief emotional moments of the kind that seemed presumptuous to me. It is in order to avoid this sort of wrongful trespass that I have written down what I know of Paul Bereyter." What is so unacceptable about the approach that Sebald takes initially and then rejects? What is the difference between what Sebald avoids doing—in his writing of the narrative of Paul Bereyter and elsewhere—and what he does?

When Sebald resumes the story of Paul Bereyter, he provides us with two successive narratives, the first by Sebald's first-person narrator (29–41), the second by Paul's companion in the last twelve years of his life, Lucy Landau (42–63). Both narratives, which comprise the remainder of the chapter, avoid simply taking Paul as their object. The narrative by the first-person narrator tells of the narrator's first encounter with Paul on entering the school as a new pupil, of his friendship with a fellow pupil named Fritz, and of Paul's inspiring teaching, which replaced pedagogical authority with direct, sensuous experience. Sebald's text follows this same principle, favoring embodied visual and auditory experience over disembodied pontification or speculation. When the narrative focus shifts from the first-person narrator to Lucy, again it is not Paul's story that Lucy tells but her own; in fact, the narrative begins not in Lucy's voice but with the narrator's *own* story of meeting Lucy, followed by Lucy's narration to him of her upbringing, before she finally tells of her own first encounter and friendship with Paul.

The same principle characterizes the treatment of emotion. When Sebald rejects his first attempt at the story, he mentions the presumptuousness of the "brief emotional moments" by means of which he had seemed to get closer to Paul but only by a "sort of wrongful trespass" (29). In the two completed narratives, by contrast, moments of emotion are rendered purely visually; emotions themselves are never identified. When a visiting violinist performs in Paul's schoolroom, we read that Paul, "far from being able to hide the emotion that young Brandeis's playing produced in him, had to remove his glasses because his eyes had filled with tears. As I remember it, he even turned away in order to conceal from us the sob that rose in him" (41). Later, at a moment of heightened emotion during Lucy's narrative, Sebald neither names nor ventriloquizes Lucy's emotion but simply reports her words: "I do not find it surprising . . . not in the slightest, that you were unaware of the meanness and treachery that a family like the Bereyters were exposed to in a miserable hole such as S then was, and such as it still is despite all the so-called progress; it does not surprise me at all, since that is inherent in the logic of the whole wretched sequence of events." Sebald describes this, retrospectively, as a "little outburst" (50) but avoids commenting upon or characterizing it in a way that would invest authority in the narrator.

THE PURE LOOK

An indication of how Sebald himself might have thought about the differences between the abandoned beginning of "Paul Bereyter" and the two completed narratives is found in the presence of photographs in Sebald's texts and in the way Sebald speaks about them. In an interview several years before he died, Sebald describes the photographs in his texts in the following way: "I think they do tell their own story within the prose narrative and do establish a second level of discourse that is mute. It would be an ambition of mine to produce the kind of prose which has a degree of mutedness about it. The photographs do, in a sense, help you along this route."[35]

In an essay on Kafka dating from 1997, Sebald makes reference to something like a logic of the photograph that he detects in Kafka's writing. Sebald's essay is full of droll contempt for the academic industry of Kafka studies, devoted as it has been to wresting "meanings" out of Kafka's "difficulty."[36] Kafka's works, for Sebald, demand interpretive "restraint, keeping to the facts alone and refusing to indulge in attempts at elucidation" (153). Certain moments in Kafka, he says, resemble the experience of looking at photographs—he mentions Kafka's 1911 obsession with a Jewish actress called Frau Tschissik, in the course of which Kafka makes numerous visual notes.[37] Sebald comments:

> In passages like these and many others, where the observer . . . is absorbed in the individual, isolated aspects of a physicality beyond his reach, for instance the "faint white of the low neck of a blouse" . . . the erotic aura of such pictures—snapshots taken, so to speak, without permission—is due to their proximity to death. For the very reason that looking at one's fellow men with so pitiless a gaze is forbidden, one has to look again and again. The all-revealing, all-penetrating gaze is subject to compulsive repetition, always wanting to reassure itself that it really did see what it saw. Nothing is left but looking [*das reine Schauen*—"the pure look"]. . . . The dead, the living, and the still unborn come together on the same plane.[38]
>
> (156–57)

What Sebald is responding to is the purely optical quality of such passages, in which an image is apparently resurrected, preserved in the face of "real time." As Barthes observes in *Camera Lucida*, "what I see [in a photograph] is not a memory, an imagination, a reconstitution, a piece of Maya . . . but reality in a past state: *at once the past and the real*" (82).

In a comparable passage, the narrator of Sebald's *Vertigo* describes his fascination with the work of the Italian Renaissance painter Pisanello:

> It is many years now since the paintings of Pisanello instilled in me the desire to forfeit everything except my sense of vision. What appealed to me was not only the highly developed realism of his art, extraordinary for the time, but also the way in which he succeeded in creating the effect of the real, without suggesting a depth dimension, upon an essentially flat surface, in which every feature, the principals and the extras alike, the birds in the sky, the green forest and every single leaf of it, are all granted an equal and undiminished right to exist.
>
> (72–73)

What would it mean to generate a mode of writing in which, as in photographs, "nothing is left but looking . . ." (that is to say, no "tenor," no concept pre-forming the image); in which "the dead, the living, and the still unborn come together on the same plane"; in which every feature is granted "an equal and undiminished right to exist"? If Sebald's works don't realize such an ambition, they at least dramatize it. His writings do not transmit a mode of looking or perception that preexists them or takes place outside them. There is no "perspective" in Sebald's works, or, rather, they are perpetually overcoming or annulling every point of perspective. This is what distinguishes him from Naipaul and from what Said calls the "European tradition of supposedly direct observation." It is what imperils the status of the example in Sebald's work and what lends the work of Pisanello such resonance for his project. To "forfeit everything except my sense of vision" means to forfeit *the very place from which one regards the object*, to forfeit, then, the category of expression, the "tenor" of the exemplary relation. It is also to forfeit the place of the subject. There is no primary, nonobjectifying gaze that precedes the writing, no holy gaze located in the brain of Sebald himself, who would, in such a reading, be elevated into a kind of saint of perception. If there is a nonobjectifying, nonexemplifying gaze in Sebald, it is achieved only in and through the writing.

THE STRUGGLE OF *AUSTERLITZ*

Sebald's last prose narrative, *Austerlitz,* is both the most interesting and the most difficult text of Sebald's in which to address these issues. One reason has to do with its thematic concerns. *Austerlitz* appears to converge on the theme of the Holocaust, and the Holocaust stages the problem of exemplarity like nothing else. For on one hand, the Holocaust cannot serve as an example. If reduced to the status of a generic theme or trope, it responds by crying "obscenity." This is the meaning behind every stricture on the impossibility or inappropriateness of art after Auschwitz. On the other hand, that very quality makes it the supreme example of the category of experience known variously as the unrepeatable, the intolerable, the unrepresentable. In an axiomatic formulation of Georges Didi-Huberman's, the Holocaust is "the invisible and unthinkable object par excellence," the exemplary nonexemplary event.[39]

A second reason has to do with the fact that *Austerlitz* is the most novel-like of Sebald's texts and thus the work whose departures from novelistic conventions are the most significant. Of his four works in prose, only *Austerlitz* centers on a character who is unambiguously fictional. The inner form of the novel, writes Lukács, "has been understood as the process of the problematic individual's journeying towards himself, the road from dull captivity within a merely present reality—a reality that is heterogeneous in itself and meaningless to the individual—towards clear self-recognition" (*TN*, 80). The passage seems to describe the narrative of Austerlitz, a character whose deep unhappiness is expressed as an inability to form close relationships, a discomfort with linear temporality, periodic crises in his capacity to read and write, and thoughts of suicide—symptoms, arguably, which find their explanation in the story of his origins, as revealed during the course of the narrative. But what makes Lukács's *Theory of the Novel* fascinating for understanding Sebald's *Austerlitz* is its explanation for the biographical form: the underlying "'bad' infinity" of possible content. For Lukács there is nothing that, in principle, may not become part of the novel's content, a condition for which the novel compensates by rigorously relating each separate element of the work "to the central character and the problem symbolized by the story of his life" (*TN*, 81).

With its biographical organization, then, the story of Austerlitz risks sliding into the kind of symbolic and illustrative writing that, in the chapter on Paul Bereyter, Sebald embarks upon and then aborts. The biographical form threatens to take over the work, transforming it into an imaginatively gratifying, moral exercise. Such a form cannot help but invoke categories of experience; it proceeds by inserting its characters into sets: trauma sufferers, melancholics, Holocaust victims. Such a shift would involve drawing an etiological or symptomatological connection between, say, Austerlitz's various eccentricities and crises (his relation to writing, to reading, to intimacy, to time) in the first half of the novel and his childhood displacement and orphanhood, as revealed in the book's second half.

And yet, despite the suggestions of exemplarity throughout Sebald's work, the connections that would confirm them are never articulated from any privileged narrative standpoint, nor is any ethical nostrum that might be derived from them. The story of Austerlitz's quest for and discovery of his origins, revealed to Sebald's narrator by Austerlitz over the last 170 pages of the novel in an almost continuous narration,[40] begins with a personal crisis, in the form of a nervous breakdown:

> If language may be regarded as an old city full of streets and squares, nooks and crannies, with some quarters dating from far back in time while others have been torn down, cleaned up, and rebuilt ... then I was like a man who

has been abroad a long time and cannot find his way through this urban sprawl anymore, no longer knows what a bus stop is for, or what a back yard is, or a street junction, an avenue or a bridge. The entire structure of language, the syntactical arrangement of parts of speech, punctuation, conjunctions, and finally even the nouns denoting ordinary objects were all enveloped in impenetrable fog. I could not even understand what I myself had written in the past—perhaps I could understand that least of all. All I could think was that such a sentence only appears to mean something, but in truth is at best a makeshift expedient, a kind of unhealthy growth issuing from our ignorance, something which we use, in the same way as many sea plants and animals use their tentacles, to grope blindly through the darkness enveloping us. The very thing which may usually convey a sense of purposeful intelligence—the exposition of an idea by means of a certain stylistic facility—now seemed to me nothing but an entirely arbitrary or deluded enterprise. I could see no connections anymore, the sentences resolved themselves into a series of separate words, the words into random sets of letters, the letters into disjointed signs, and those signs into a blue-gray trail gleaming silver here and there, excreted and left behind it by some crawling creature, and the sight of it increasingly filled me with feelings of horror and shame.

(123–24)

Austerlitz's breakdown amounts to a crisis in the very connections between part and whole, "vehicle" and "tenor" that exemplarity (and thus the very legibility of the work) depends upon. The relation of Sebald's novel *Austerlitz* to exemplarity might thus be seen as the precise inverse of Naipaul's *An Area of Darkness*. Just as, with the conceit of India's to-be-looked-at-ness, Naipaul projects the exemplarity onto his object of study, so, with the becoming-biographical of the narrative of *Austerlitz*, Sebald transfers the *crisis* of exemplarity, the *failure* of exemplarity, onto *his* object of study: Austerlitz himself. If the connection between Austerlitz's "crisis of connection" and his biography could be established as the centerpiece of the narrative, the story would become representative, comprehensible, and containable. The experience would be removed from the narrator and from the author (the two are always indistinguishable in Sebald), who would thereby retreat to the margins of the work, become part of the work's framing apparatus. Simultaneously, the story would become an object of contemplation for the reader, who would similarly be expelled to the work's edge, its exterior—the position that Naipaul occupies with respect to India. The work would become spatially organized by this identification of a biographical center of convergence. All consistency of feature, all equality of the right to exist, would be erased.[41]

However, this is not ultimately what happens in Sebald's works—not even *Austerlitz*, in which Sebald's gestures toward a conventional narrative framework are more concerted than anywhere else. Austerlitz's narration of his writing crisis cannot be separated from earlier moments in Sebald's work where his writer-narrators both experience and resolve the problem of connection in the same instant of writing. Austerlitz's description of the impossibility of writing, a description as eloquent as the experience is devastating, is as perfectly "crystalline," therefore, as the episode of fervid note taking in the hotel bar in Limone. In Sebald—by contrast with Dickens— connections are aleatory. They exist, but they might equally not have existed. In an interview from 2001, Sebald made the following remark about his own origins: "I was born in May 1944 in a place the war didn't get to. . . . Then you find out it was the same month when Kafka's sister was deported to Auschwitz. It's bizarre; you're pushed in a pram through the flowering meadows, and a few hundred miles to the east these horrendous things are happening. It's the chronological contiguity that makes you think it is something to do with you."[42] Sebald's last book jeopardizes this principle of "chronological contiguity" by the presence of the protagonist, whose story threatens to impose an economy of significance, a principle of striation, upon every element in the book. For example, the series of chance encounters between Austerlitz and the narrator at the beginning of the book become inflected in a manner that other encounters in Sebald's work, such as the conversations with William Hazel, the gardener at Somerleyton, and with the Dutch businessman Cornelis de Jong, in *The Rings of Saturn*, do not.[43] That is to say, the narrative that ensues depends entirely upon those chance events. The most important of these events are, first, Austerlitz's fortuitous discovery of the disused Ladies' Waiting Room at Liverpool Street train station—the site where, as a small boy, he met for the first time his adoptive parents—and second, the radio program he hears while browsing in an antiquarian bookstore, which tells the story of the wartime *Kindertransport* from Eastern Europe to England, prompting Austerlitz's realization that "these fragments of memory were part of my own life as well" (141).

However, this difference in *Austerlitz* is only apparent by contrast with Sebald's earlier texts. Indeed, one might say that the function of *Austerlitz* in seeming to relegate the principle of "equality of existence" is to make apparent what is so radical in those earlier texts. Despite the revelations about Austerlitz's origins that emerge from his journey to Prague in the second half of the narrative, the book concludes not with a positive image of writing (as revelation) but with a negative one. Austerlitz leaves Paris for the Pyrenees to pursue a lead on the possible fate of his father. Meanwhile, the narrator returns to Antwerp, the location of the Nocturama where the book opens, and to Breendonk, the fortress that was used as a prison by the Nazis. On the banks of the fortress moat he reads from Dan Jacobson's *Heshel's Kingdom*, a book about Jacobson's search for the story of his grandfather Heshel, a rabbi who died in Lithuania in 1919. The final image is taken from the prologue to Jacobson's book. The opening to the vast diamond mines at Kimberley in South Africa, to where Jacobson's family had emigrated after Heshel's death, appears to the author as a "chasm into which no ray of light could penetrate." The image signifies for Jacobson the dividing line between "ordinary life" and its "unimaginable opposite," and thus "the vanished past of his family and his people" (297), even as he undertakes to write that history.[44]

If there is a definitive image of writing in Sebald's work, it is precisely the chasm or fissure. At the beginning of *The Rings of Saturn*, the narrator, from his hospital bed, sees a vapor trail bisecting the space framed by his window. "At the time," he writes, "I took that white trail for a good omen, but now, as I look back, I fear it marked the beginning of a fissure that has since riven my life" (18). Taken alone, the image is enigmatic. However, in a subsequent episode of *The Rings of Saturn*, Sebald's narrator visits the Sailors' Reading Room in Southwold, where he examines the log of the *Southwold*, a patrol ship that was anchored off Southwold pier in 1914. As he reads the record of planes and ships passing through, the image of the trail reappears: "Every time I decipher one of these entries I am astounded that a trail that has long since vanished from the air or the water remains visible here on the paper" (93).

The narrator of *The Rings of Saturn* never draws any connection between the episode in Southwold and the moment (earlier in the narrative but chronologically later) in the hospital. Were he to do so, the connection would be performatively broken in the same instant. For it is the *unstated* connection between the two passages in *The Rings of Saturn* that reveals that "the fissure that has since riven [his] life" is writing. The element that connects the two images is the vehicular trail, the trace of which is visible only in writing, "the mysterious survival of the written word" (*Rings*, 93). Again, the connection remains valid only insofar as it is *not* made by the text, for were Sebald to allude to it, the link between writing and the fissure would be established—and thereby broken. In the course of the long walk through Suffolk, a walk that puts Sebald's narrator in hospital and thus inaugurates the work we are reading, the image of writing is thus transformed from a positive entity, an enterprise of connection and revelation, into a negative one, a "fissure."

This same transformation marks the historical shift between Dickens's writing and Sebald's, as well as the difference between the false beginning of "Paul Bereyter," full of imaginative and creative "presumption," and the story as it comes to be written, in which every possible extrapolation, every exemplary relation, is refused. In each case, connection is transformed from the great achievement of writing into the confirmation of its failure. In Sebald, then, writing is the connection *that connects and breaks simultaneously*. As Austerlitz sits in the Ladies' Waiting Room at Liverpool Street station, experiencing at once "all the hours of [his] past life," he tells us (via the narrator): "I felt something rending within me, and a sense of shame and sorrow, or perhaps something quite different, something inexpressible because we have no words for it" (137).

Modernity, writes Gilles Deleuze in 1983, is a "new state of things where the synsigns disperse and the indices become confused."[45] This situation, says Deleuze, calls for "new signs" or "a new kind of image" that no longer refers to a "globalizing" or "synthetic" state of affairs but to a "dispersive" one. Thus, "ellipsis" is no longer simply a mode of narration but a quality of "the situation itself" (207). This distinction—between ellipsis as a "mode of the tale" and as an element of the situation—is crucial to Deleuze's claim of the existence of a cinematic image in which "the fissure has become primary."[46] But the distinction is difficult to establish with respect to any particular work or image, since in both cases the connective sign is indefinitely withheld from its formal elements.

For Jacques Rancière (whose own project and engagement with Deleuze will be discussed in chapter 8), this breaking of connections should be understood through the historical emergence of literature as a distinct "regime" of meaning in the nineteenth century: "a new way of linking the sayable and the visible, words and things" (*Politics of Literature*, 9). In the new mode, what is said is no longer what is meant or thought, which means that it enters into a relationship with an apparatus of literary-critical (psychoanalytic, Marxist, feminist, deconstructive, ethical, etc.) interpretation that gives expression to that unspoken element. In a recent essay, Rancière applies this same formulation to W. G. Sebald, in whose work, says Rancière, "even the absence of a link sometimes forges the link."[47] But not even Rancière's model quite captures the devastating twist that Sebald's figure of the fissure brings to this formation: that the forging of the link is *dependent* on its absence, that the connection thereby absconds from the work not merely rhetorically or stylistically but constitutively.

For Sebald, speaking in 1997, the difference between his own situation as a writer and Dickensian (or Austenian) exemplarity is primarily historical:

> If you refer to Jane Austen, you refer to a world where there were set standards of propriety which were accepted by everyone. Given that you have a world where the rules are clear and where one knows where trespassing begins, then I think it is legitimate, within that kind of context, to be a narrator who knows what the rules are and who knows the answers to certain questions. But I think these certainties have been taken from us by the course of history, and that we do have to acknowledge our own sense of ignorance and of insufficiency in these matters and therefore to try and write accordingly.
>
> (WOOD, 27)

My argument is not that Sebald's works do not make connections. Connections are made, just as examples are drawn. But the ethical significance of his texts does not lie in the connections they make but in the lack of consequence to those connections, whether historical, epistemological, or indeed ethical. In *Austerlitz*, there is no hierarchy of significance between, say, the objects in the window of the Antikos Bazar in Terezín—the "festive white lace tablecloth" or the "three brass mortars of different sizes" (195–96)—which retain their enigma, and the objects in the Ghetto Museum a few streets away, despite the fact that the latter furnish Austerlitz with "incontrovertible proof" of the system of forced labor operated by the Nazis throughout Europe (198–99). They are accorded the same space and significance in the text. Meanings are made, they take place, but meanings, too, are objects perceived. In Sebald's works, every entity and utterance has an "equal and undiminished right" to exist because no entity or utterance is given explanatory significance over any other. The connections in Sebald's narratives signify only in their happenstance, in their *having been made*—or, to use Agamben's phrase, in their "whatever being."

What is surprising about Sebald's last text *Austerlitz* is that it should come as close as it does to suggesting a unifying principle of the work in the figure of Austerlitz himself, that is, to constructing a protagonist who is emblematic of a dark period in Europe's history and thus positing a personal explanation for the contemporary crisis of meaning. Sebald risks the ethical substance of his project on the tantalizing possibility of a text that will add up. Yet the connections that would confirm the larger lessons of *Austerlitz*, beyond the purely adventitious quest of Austerlitz himself, are not finally established by the text. The ethical power and fascination of the work rest on how close it comes to instantiating them and on its inability or its refusal finally to do so.

PART II

The Emergence of
Postfictional Aesthetics

Chapter Three

THE INSTANTIATION RELATION

> An "age" does not pre-exist the statements which express it,
> nor the visibilities which fill it.
>
> —GILLES DELEUZE

THE CONTEMPORARY CRITICAL PREDICAMENT

The critic of the contemporary period faces a unique predicament. The works that are most directly expressive of the thought of the era do not speak in a voice that is accessible to the critical register. A gap or discrepancy has opened up at the heart of the literary work, between the work's idea and every conceptual entity in the work. This gap is conceivable as a negative relation: between the idea or substance of the work and the logic of the instance. Anything that makes an appearance in the work ensures, thereby, its lack of consequence. The work does not speak its idea. More precisely, the idea survives in the work only in the form of its absence; when it appears, it does so as a negation of its essence. What this means for the practice of criticism is that, in interpreting the work, in attempting to paraphrase or ventriloquize it, the critic establishes his or her exile from the work's true significance.

To begin with such a statement is no doubt to limit one's reception to a readership that is already attuned to a certain taste for speculative thinking within critical theory. On the other hand, to invoke the "era" and its "thought" in this way is to condemn oneself, and the critical discourse one inhabits, to a regime of utterance and utterability from which this opening statement seems to want to liberate the work. Can the era really be characterized in positive terms, as if an epoch were anything other than "the statements which express it,"[1] that take place within it? Do not unitary for-mulations such as "the thought of the era" designate precisely what is *least* expressive of the contemporary period, a period characterized, rather, by a proliferation and multiplicity of perspectives? And, having proposed an order of thought that cannot be given form, is it really possi-ble to make a conceptual distinction between works that express it and those that do not, without establishing one's own discourse in the latter category—without, that is, reintroducing the "logic of the instance" into the reading of literature?

Two subjective logics are here caught in a mutual stranglehold: one pred-icated on communicability (which is to say, the principle of the adequacy of language and conceptualization), the other on the inherent incommu-nicability of the idea and the mistrust of language. Whichever group of works one considers to express the "thought of the era" will depend on whether one's critical temperament is such as to require a closing of the gap, even at the expense of the work's idea, or an attentiveness to the singular-ity of the idea, at the expense of critical clarity and influence. In either case, the critic or theorist condemns his or her own discourse: in the first case, to tautology—to simply restating the manifest themes of the work; in the second case, to accusations of mysticism or, worse, irrelevance.

The merest reflection, however, will reveal that these paired logics of communicability and incommunicability, instantiation and its impossibil-ity, have coexisted at least since the appearance of the novel, the form that is constituted out of the gap between the idea and its embodiment in a char-acter or an image. The difference defines not only the history of the novel but the history of its theorization, for how can one theorize a form whose essence is a disconnection, a disjunction, without thereby negating it? Ques-tions about the origin, nature, history, end, prospects, or constitutive lim-its of the novel posit a unity to the form that is at odds with the fundamen-tal "disunity" that Georg Lukács, arguably the founder of the theory of the novel as a field, finds to be peculiar to it.

Paradoxically, however, Lukács's 1920 book *The Theory of the Novel* is not a theory of the novel. For not only does Lukács not know what a novel is; he finds the very question to be self-defeating.[2] In *The Theory of the Novel*, the novel is considered not as a "closed" (*geschlossen*) art form but as a mode of thought predicated upon a discrepancy—between "the conventionality of the objective world and the interiority of the subjective one" (*TN*, 70). This gap is for Lukács unbridgeable; or, rather, the novel is the expression of the gap. Thus, the novel designates less a form or genre than a condition of thought in which form and content are for the first time radically heterogeneous. "The dissonance special to the novel," he writes,

> the refusal of the immanence of being to enter into empirical life, produces a problem of form whose formal nature is much less obvious than in other kinds of art, and which, because it looks like a problem of content, needs to be approached by both ethical and aesthetic arguments, even more than do problems which are obviously purely formal.
> (71)

What Lukács means by "the refusal of the immanence of being to enter into empirical life" is that the "problematicity" of the novel is not articulable by it but constitutive of it. Lukács makes a distinction between the novel and its "caricatural twin," the "entertainment novel"—a form that is so close to the novel as to be "almost indistinguishable from [it]" (73)—on the basis of their radically different conceptions of the ethical substance of the work, which is to say the nature of the relation between the work and life. The difference summarized by Lukács is between *having a problematic* and *being problematic*. "Having a problematic" suggests a problem-solving, gap-closing quality to the work, the possibility of a convergence, whereas "being problematic" implies that, if the novel resolves the gap, it does so only provisionally or formally—in terms created for that purpose by the work itself.

There is no need to accept Lukács's division between art and entertainment to recognize the distinction between "having a problematic" and "being problematic" as a fault line that runs through the modern novel and its theorization. Retaining Lukács's terms, the "entertainment novel" accepts the existence and limits of the novel as a form. The entertainment novel opens up a "problematic," which may be narrative, ethical, or philosophical, and addresses or deals with it within the work, which is exhausted by it. The entertainment novel reserves all concerns and preoccupations for the work's content; it thereby presupposes an ethical legitimacy to the novel and to the activity of the novelist. When we ask questions of the novel form as such or propose that the "age of the novel" may be over or coming to an end, we limit our concerns to this formally circumscribed conception of the novel.

By contrast, the novel proper, according to Lukács, is predicated on a fundamental uncertainty regarding its own definition, its ethical substance, and the possibility of its making any meaningful utterance whatsoever. The novel "excludes completeness," he writes, but "only so far as content is concerned" (73). "In contrast to other genres whose existence resides within the finished form" (such as epic), the novel "appears as something in process of becoming" (72–73). The world of the novel is one in which an instantiation of the problematic is impossible, for the problem that defines the novel *is the problem of instantiation itself.* In the novel, unlike in other forms, representation (of ideas, characters, or viewpoints) is not a technical problem but an ethical one.

The fact is that only the "entertainment novel," a form premised upon a positive relation between the content of the work and its idea, is theorizable. The theory of the novel is limited to the understanding of entertainment novels or, alternatively, is destined to turn all novels into entertainment novels.[3] Moreover, it is not clear that there is a real distinction between the novel and the entertainment novel. Perhaps the difference is nothing other than that between a work that has been subjected to a theoretical analysis and one that has not or between a work considered and treated as subject to theorization and a work not so considered. To make this proposition is, again, to register the quandary facing literary theory in the contemporary period. For the theory of the novel, in transforming the condition of problematicity into an *attribute,* a "problematic," misapprehends the essence of the novel *in the very act of grasping its formal qualities.*

THE BRIDGE (THE PROBLEM OF THE OPENING)

This paradox is more often alluded to in works of fiction than criticism. Indeed, on a certain reading of contemporary fiction, the noninstantiability of the work's idea looks like the overriding obsession of the twenty-first-century novel. In the opening sentences of J. M. Coetzee's novel *Elizabeth Costello* (2003), the disconnection between the world and the work is established as the very condition of the work's existence:

> There is first of all the problem of the opening, namely, how to get us from where we are, which is, as yet, nowhere, to the far bank. It is a simple bridging problem, a problem of knocking together a bridge. People solve such problems every day. They solve them, and having solved them push on.
>
> Let us assume that, however it may have been done, it is done. Let us take it that the bridge is built and crossed, that we can put it out of our mind. We have left behind the territory in which we were. We are in the far territory, where we want to be.[4]

In Coetzee's conceit, the bridge does not join the two territories; rather, it ensures and maintains their separation. On the near bank is a world constituted by the logic of communicability; from the point of view of the diegesis—the far bank—it is purely abstract, "nowhere." On the other side is the world of the fiction, the novel. Crossing the bridge would imply the possibility of transmission between the two worlds, a connection (the nature of which would remain to be determined) between what goes on in the work and what goes on outside it. In *Elizabeth Costello*, however, the bridge is not crossed, or at least, the crossing of the bridge is not narrated. Rather, the bridge must be "assume[d]" to be "built and crossed," and then "put . . . out of our mind."

The refusal or inability to narrate the crossing of the bridge is not unique to Coetzee's work. In fact, no novel has ever done so and perhaps no theoretical work either. Almost all works of fiction, whether implicitly (Charles Dickens's *Bleak House*, James Joyce's *Dubliners*) or explicitly (Marcel Proust's *À la recherche du temps perdu*, Nadine Gordimer's *Burger's Daughter*), assume, if only formally, the contiguity of the two worlds. And the same goes for criticism, the presupposition of which is a positive connection between the literary work and the activity of the critic. The distinction of *Elizabeth Costello* is in acknowledging the relation as a problem at the outset and presenting it spatially, via the figure of the nontraversable bridge, as a divide that can only be passed over.

In doing so, the character of the work as a conceit, a fiction, is conveyed irreversibly into the diegesis. In *Elizabeth Costello*, not only is the bridge not traversed; the effect of acknowledging its presence (or absence) is that even the "assumed" transposition to the far bank is interrupted. The bridge that is silently traversed in works of fiction that make no mention of it is, in *Elizabeth Costello*, effectively dismantled.[5]

In this way, the opening lines of the book affect everything that subsequently appears in its pages. "Elizabeth is a writer," we read, "born in 1928, which makes her sixty-six years old, going on sixty-seven" (1). The effect of the opening paragraph, combined with Coetzee's narrative use of the present tense, is that even such moments of scene-setting narration are readable as free indirect discourse. To use a distinction made by the critic Ann Banfield, it seems that from this moment on there is no "pure narration" in *Elizabeth Costello*, only "represented speech and thought."[6] "[John] is here, with her, out of love. He cannot imagine her getting through this trial without him at her side. He stands by her because he is her son, her loving son. But he is also on the point of becoming—distasteful word—her trainer" (3). The focalization in this passage is most obviously that of Elizabeth's son John. However, there is a second focalization, another order of diegetic consciousness: that of an unnamed, unpersonified, but embodied subject existing in time and space and—as such—in the process of establishing a fictional conceit. The passage does not "communicate" a thought, therefore, but "performs" one (as D. A. Miller has described Jane Austen's use of free indirect style).[7] The performance is not, primarily, John's but that of a supposed author figure internal to the diegesis. It is not the neutral setting-out of a fictional *mise en scène* but the diegetical staging of a conceit, the performative quality of which will remain in view throughout the work.

In this regard, *Elizabeth Costello* is an event in the history and theory of the novel. However, the event is not inaugurated by *Elizabeth Costello*; rather, *Elizabeth Costello* is the work that makes it legible, thinkable. In its essence, the emergence of the postfictional universe is not an event of literary production. It is less a new idea than a new order of legibility, of thinkability.

As in every work of fiction, the world of *Elizabeth Costello* is one in which ideas are represented. As in every work of fiction, the condition of such representation is a break in the connection with the site of authorship, the place of utterance. Reference, of course, takes place: characters and places are named; thoughts (ideas) and descriptions are attached to them; a biographical history is narrated; relations between characters and with places are specified. But ideas make their way into the work only at the cost of their substance, which is to say, their transmissibility. The bridge in *Elizabeth Costello* is a figure of absolute separation between the conditions of "ordinary" (technical, rhetorical, political, conversational, etc.) language and those of novelistic discourse—and thus of the "fundamental dissonance" that, according to Lukács, structures and organizes the novel form (62). Yet the absoluteness of the separation—the fact that the space of disconnection is not traversed but *passed over*—suggests that there is no way back once the transposition has taken place. The distinction between "ordinary" discourse and "novelistic" discourse is the afterimage of a regime of signification that—from the point of view of the other side, at least—has ceased to operate. In the world into which we are escorted by Coetzee's recent work, the crucial separation is not between "ordinary" and "novelistic" discourse, the "near" bank and the "far," but a separation or difference *within* every manifest or instantiated idea. This nonequivalence with itself is produced, made sensible, only insofar as the idea makes an appearance in the work.

One possible name for this event is the universalization of the principle of free indirect discourse. As a form of "represented speech and thought," free indirect discourse is noninstantiating discourse. Free indirect discourse is third-person narration that, at the level of what is spoken, makes no direct claims on our ideological investments or faculties of intellection, for, as Ann Banfield points out, free indirect discourse "falls outside any framework structured by the communicative relation between *I* and *you*" (141). To "universalize" (or "infinitize")[8] the principle of free indirect discourse means to consider it not as a formal technique but as a secret wish or propensity of all discourse. As such, free indirect discourse is writing or speech that relinquishes its authority, its earnestness, as a condition of its utterance.

Consider the following passage from *Elizabeth Costello*, an interpolation by an unspecified subject, who may be—but may also not be—Elizabeth's son John:

Realism has never been comfortable with ideas. It could not be otherwise: realism is premised on the idea that ideas have no autonomous existence, can exist only in things. So when it needs to debate ideas, as here, realism is driven to invent situations—walks in the countryside, conversations—in which characters give voice to contending ideas and thereby in a certain sense embody them. The notion of *embodying* turns out to be pivotal. In such debates ideas do not and indeed cannot float free: they are tied to the speakers by whom they are enounced, and generated from the matrix of individual interests out of which their speakers act in the world—for instance, the

son's concern that his mother not be treated as a Mickey Mouse post-colonial
writer, or Wheatley's concern not to seem an old-fashioned absolutist.
(9)

The passage is like a pure utterance dropped into the text, a commentary upon the implications of the work's opening conceit, spoken as if from the "near" side of the bridge, a world where the credibility of the statement, the question of its truth or falsity, is still adjudicable. The passage, that is to say, inhabits a critical register. And yet, if a work of fiction cannot, as Stephen Mulhall observes of *Elizabeth Costello*, "contain or embody the problem of the opening as a problem" (177), such a work also cannot theorize the conditions under which an idea can appear in it *without a gap being opened up within the theorization itself*: between its subjective and objective dimensions. No "grammatical evidence" is provided as to the focalization of the passage;[9] indeed, Mulhall casually attributes its sentiments to Coetzee (182). Whatever its attribution, the idea that novelistic ideas "are tied to the speakers by whom they are enounced" does not survive its expression in a novel, other than as what Bakhtin called an "object of representation."[10] It is either the reflection of a character in a narrative situation, in which case it is not an animating idea of the work at all and asks nothing of us, or it is an extradiegetic interpolation by a disembodied narrator, in which case it disproves itself from the other side of the equation. In either case, the expressed idea is incompatible with its instantiation.

The truth of Coetzee's elaborate paradox, however, is that there is no ambiguity of focalization, for what is taking place is not the presentation of an idea but the staging of an impossibility. The challenges of the passage are on a different scale, therefore, from the quandaries of an earlier generation of expository criticism when faced with the ambiguities of focalization regarding, say, the adjectives "stately" and "plump," in the description of Buck Mulligan that opens Joyce's *Ulysses*, or the identity of the voice that, in Forster's *Howards End*, opines that Beethoven's Fifth Symphony is "the most sublime noise that has ever penetrated into the ear of man."[11] Attempts to determine the point of view of such passages presuppose what Wayne C. Booth called a "rhetoric of fiction": a capacity for "communication," the substance of which may be more or less obscured from the reader by an author's "technique" but is understood to be transmissible in principle.[12] For Booth, "the author's judgment is always present, always evident to anyone who knows how to look for it. . . . Though the author can to some extent choose his disguises, he can never choose to disappear" (20). A rhetoric of fiction implies an ultimate point of view (a consciousness) anchored within each work, "purposes" (specifiable or not) that are proper to it, a commitment to the work's discreteness, and an ethics of reading that accepts and respects these conditions (377). What Booth calls the "morality" of technique is a task that impacts as much on the author as the critic; it assumes a connection between the far bank and the near that the work is able to bridge and the critic obliged to reconstruct:

> The artist must . . . be willing to be both a seer and a revelator; though he . . . certainly need not include explicit statement of the norms on which his work is based, he must know how to transform his private vision, made up as it often is of ego-ridden private symbols, into something that is essentially public. . . . In short, the writer should worry less about whether his *narrators* are realistic than about whether the *image he creates of himself,* his implied author, is one that his most intelligent and perceptive readers can admire. (395)[13]

Booth's *The Rhetoric of Fiction* is over fifty years old. Its usefulness here is primarily in helping to define the limits of an approach that does not seem able to respond satisfactorily to a work such as *Elizabeth Costello,* that is, in establishing the terms of a shift from an established aesthetics of the novel to an emergent one. Booth's statements articulate, in a relatively blunt form, what is implicit in every critical approach to the novel that is oblivious to, or simply refuses, the lessons of the nontraversable bridge that Coetzee erects at the threshold of his work.

If there was once a "rhetoric of fiction," the implications of a "universalized" free indirect discourse—a free indirect discourse no longer understood as a "technique" but as the inherent logic of all literary writing—would be that such a rhetoric could no longer confidently be isolated and separated from the views of the characters within the work. Such a development would imply an incipient awareness, perhaps barely acknowledged among writers themselves, that the conditions of speaking and writing, the opportunities and limits of literary expression, have changed irreparably. The proposition would point to the need for a transformation in our understanding of the critic's vocation.

THE RHETORIC OF CONTEMPORARY CRITICISM

There is nothing new about the myth of a nonrhetorical or "pure" art. Such a notion has long been understood to be part of the ideological self-conception of the artist and of art itself. Twentieth-century innovations in criticism—most notably, the ideology critique of the French "structural Marxist" and German Frankfurt School traditions and the sociological analysis of taste in the work of Pierre Bourdieu—are the theoretical formations that wrestled most productively with the contradiction between the claims of art to "autonomy" and its critique.[14]

Booth's insistence on a rhetoric of fiction is another demystification of such notions of a "pure" art. One of the salutary developments within literary studies, for Booth, is the (then recent) appearance of "handbooks about how to write best sellers," where the author is advised to "think of his reader and write accordingly" (90). And it is Booth's line of thinking, with its matter-of-fact separation between writer and critic, rather than the French and German theoretical troubling of that distinction, that has seemed to gain traction among literary critics in the United States over the last decade or two. In *The Program Era* (2009), the critic Mark McGurl writes about the appearance of Booth's work in 1961, after a period in which the New Critical doctrine of "impersonality" held sway, as "part of a widespread return to the idea that a human being might remain present, in some way, in the dead print the reader holds in her hands" (233).[15] McGurl sees his own study, on the creative writing degree program in the United States and its importance for understanding developments in twentieth-century American fiction, as a qualified reassertion of Booth's gesture after the "absurdly one-sided" dominance of poststructuralism in the U.S. academy (233). For McGurl, the discipline of "writing pedagogy" retrospectively appears as a principle of half-century-long resistance to the "Derridean critique of phonocentrism," by virtue of its "structural commitment to the construction—as opposed to deconstruction—of student subjectivity" (233). For McGurl, as for Booth, "fiction emerges in the most literal sense from the experiences of the author" (19). Even when it does not make use of the terms of ideology critique (class interests, false consciousness), the ideological-critical distinction between the form of the work and its meaning, or between the critical subject and the object of study, endures in the procedures of contemporary criticism—except for the strange circumstance that the "ideology" itself remains intact, as I will discuss in what follows.

McGurl states, "You don't have to be a dogmatic historical materialist to believe that a transformation of the institutional context of literary production as fundamental as [the creative writing program] might matter to a reading of postwar American literature" (24). The question of the work's substance, its "ideological" meaning or expressive content, however, is left almost entirely undiscussed in McGurl's book. A few pages later he writes— "in [the] spirit" of Horkheimer's and Adorno's *Dialectic of Enlightenment*— that "we can take for granted that the whole truth of any given instance of art exceeds its membership in some category" (32). The "excess" in question is precisely the gap that is passed over in Coetzee's conceit of the bridge. But McGurl's reference to Adorno and Horkheimer is mostly perfunctory, a demonstration of familiarity with a point of view rather than an allusion to a problematic that will substantially inform his work. For "insofar as the category might help to make that excess visible," he writes, qualifying his own remark, "it is all the more useful." The excess is never made "visible" in *The Program Era* other than in such moments of rhetorical slippage: as an abstraction. *The Program Era* alternates between an acknowledgment of the artificiality of its own procedures and a consistent adherence to the limits of those procedures. In McGurl's account, his book seeks to shift critical attention from the "academic criticism of contemporary literature" to the "actual institutions, technologies, and practices from which postwar fiction emerges" (31). This shift is underpinned, however, by the "aura of literature," an article of faith of many of the writers McGurl discusses. McGurl alludes to it as such, but he does not address it as a problem. On the contrary, literary studies "is probably unthinkable except as built upon a foundation of awe" (10). The principal case of McGurl's book, as a work of criticism, is that the literary output of the program era is remarkable for its extraordinary "quality" (ix): that there is "more excellent fiction being produced now than anyone has time to read" (408, 410). Thus the transcendent character of art does not only survive McGurl's analysis but is upheld by it.

The same might be said of Franco Moretti's work on the evolution of "world literature" and the method of "distant reading."[16] For Moretti, the important question is not how a work speaks, or what it says, but how a literary form evolves, how a field is stratified, how a particular work becomes canonical—which means that in Moretti's work, as in McGurl's, the power of the aura is simply set aside as immaterial. As Moretti points out, the rise of the novel in the European eighteenth century depended not on intensive but "extensive," "distracted," even (using a word of Jan Fergus's) "desultory" reading (174–76). "Taking the novel seriously as an aesthetic object slowed down consumption—while a quickened market for novels discouraged aesthetic concentration" (176).[17]

And it is in accordance with this logic, rather than from any desire to complexify it, that Moretti wants to transfer the critic's attention from texts themselves to the "smaller" and "larger" units, respectively, of "devices" and "genres" (77). Like McGurl, Moretti repeatedly notes the "simplifying," even "brutal" quality of his own procedures. "If we want to understand the system in its entirety," he writes in the flagship essay of his project, "we must accept losing something. We always pay a price for theoretical knowledge: reality is infinitely rich; concepts are abstract, are poor" (49). The significance of the insights generated by Moretti's practice of distant reading are limited, then, to forms (the picaresque, the epistolary novel), devices (stream of consciousness, decodable clues), genres (the Bildungsroman, detective fiction, "captivity narratives"), categories of canonicity ("core" and "periphery," "local" and "foreign"); in short, institutions and objects of "knowledge," each of which is simultaneously assumed to be unitary and acknowledged as an abstraction.

Unlike McGurl, Moretti's conception of the literary system does not subjectivize the work by reference to the author. The stability of Moretti's system has its basis, rather, in an economic model, a relationship of "debt" and "credit" flowing from "core" to "periphery" and back again (46), in which certain formal discoveries are held, in their unity, to have a geographical origin and a field of reception and influence. Within this system, "close" and "distant" reading are caught in a relationship of necessary "compromise" between the parts and the whole, between attention to works and knowledge of "the system in its entirety" (48–49)—or, as Moretti puts it in a retrospective note, between "the abstraction of model-building and the vividness of individual examples" (1–2).[18] The "iron" premise of close reading, as he calls it, is that "only a few [individual texts] really matter" (48). Moretti frames distant reading, by contrast, as democratic—a way of paying attention to the "great unread" (45). In fact, nothing is less egalitarian than to thereby insert the "great unread" into a relation of exemplarity or exceptionality with the simply "great." Moretti calls close reading a "theological exercise" (48), yet the "condition of knowledge" that he wants to put in its place is no less theological. To read in the light of canonicity, even in order to correct or dispute the constitution of the canon, is—as another famous text by Walter Benjamin makes plain—to read from the point of view of the victors.[19]

In thus leaving the "aura" of the literary work intact and in vastly expanding the scale of analysis, contemporary criticism seems to depart from Booth's insistence on a "rhetoric" of fiction; yet in the most important ways such tendencies are continuous with it. Both perspectives emerge as solutions to, but also ways of avoiding, the contemporary predicament with which I began: the enigma of the novelistic utterance, in the form of the disconnection between its instantiated elements and its substance. Both avoid addressing the question of "thought" (expression or meaning) and the more difficult question of whether or how the conditions of novelistic expression might change or be in the process of changing. Finally, both critical formations remain anchored in a subjectivizing perspective. In Booth and McGurl this subjectivism is manifested in the intentionality of the author, whereas for Moretti the sovereignty is located with the reader. Again, this sounds like democracy. But Moretti's reader is not the reader or critic who thinks with (or alongside, or against) the text but the mass consumer, or rather, the mass of consumers, in relation to which Moretti the theorist remains the master—the "global synthesizer," as Jonathan Arac has put it (45). Furthermore, the sovereignty of the theorist is not weakened but paradoxically affirmed and enacted in Moretti's numerous self-corrections and recantations.

In other words, there is an extraordinary, unbridgeable gap in contemporary criticism around the question of expression, in which even those critics who insist that the final point of reference for the critic is the author and his or her intentions are unable, on that basis, to say much else about the work other than to allude to its "excellence" and in which those who locate everything of critical significance away from the author and the text do so on the basis of "a sort of cosmic and inevitable division of labour" (Moretti, 59). There is a "fundamental dissonance," to use Lukács's phrase, in Franco Moretti's conception of the novel, but for Moretti it is locatable *geographically*, not, then, within the utterance of the work (as for Lukács) but *between* the "historical conditions" peculiar to its locality and the foreign imposed "form." The latter, for Moretti, constitutes the limit of the critic's competence, forever dividing the metropolitan reader from the local "material" (57). In both Moretti's and McGurl's writing, form and forms are inadequate and at the same time mark the limit of the critic's penetration of the text.

But what if it were the case that the real thought, the real utterance—what Lukács called the historico-philosophical truth—of the work were not located in some sphere removed from the critic but consisted in that inaccessibility to critical and theoretical discourse? What if the moment of disjunction and disconnection were not a gap to be either bridged or ignored by the critic but precisely where the truth and expression of the work were manifest? What if a "rhetorical" treatment of a work were destined to miss the essence of its thought in the very process of capturing it? What if, in other words, the thought of which literature is capable were no longer of a kind that could be grasped sensuously or conceptually but rather—to paraphrase G. W. F. Hegel—had come to the point of a historical "forsak[ing]" of the possibility of reconciliation in "sensuous" or conceptual form,[20] the point, that is, of leaving the domain of imagination altogether? In that case, the failure and evasiveness of the critical approaches discussed here would be further expressions of our critical-historical predicament. It would mean that the conditions of thought itself in the contemporary period were more closely approximated by the far bank of Coetzee's unbridgeable divide than by the near one.

Thus, even Moretti's critical project would most profitably be read not under the discursive conditions of the near bank, the side of commentary and communication, but as emanating from the far bank, the side of fiction, the diegesis. For all their understanding of themselves as writing in the critical register, one would arrive closer to the historical and philosophical significance of Moretti's or McGurl's work were one to treat what they write as the utterances of a literary character whose discourse is as dubious as the discourse of Dostoevsky's heroes, as unaccommodating of "recognition and affirmation" as even the yearning for acceptance and understanding of the Underground Man is for him.[21] Under those conditions, the absences and apparent failings in the work of Moretti and McGurl could be said to speak to the central quandary addressed in the present work just as eloquently as anything articulated directly in their writing.

Such a case, of course, cannot easily be made from the near bank, the world predicated upon communicability. That is to say that such a case is not of the order of verification. Were it to be verified, the entire case would be disproven, for the case depends on the possibility that the thought of the literary work, or the thought of the era, is a thought that cannot be "instantiated" (for example, verified, falsified, actualized, illustrated, or expressed). The case for uninstantiability is neither verifiable, then, nor falsifiable. And the same must therefore be said of its opposite, the hypothesis of the "rhetoric of fiction," which presupposes that what speaks in the literary work is in every case a limited intentionality; that the thought of the work is, in principle, nameable and identifiable; that the critic need only "[know] how to look for it." We are in a new, postfictional universe once it becomes possible to ask whether the thought of the work might be something it is in principle incapable of making explicit; whether the substance of the work could be found precisely in the *not making explicit*; whether the thought in question could ever be reproduced by a critical reader, no matter how theoretically attuned or sophisticated; whether, finally, these conditions could be extended even to certain nonfictional works, whose capacity for thought might be similarly liberated from the constraints of the "instantiation relation."

THE INSTANTIATION RELATION IN LITERARY CRITICISM

In analytic philosophy, an "instantiation relation" designates a relation between "particulars" and "universals," such that a particular entity can be said to "instantiate" a universal quality. Instantiation therefore presupposes a distinction between "primary" and "secondary" qualities, between *things*, with qualities that are essential to and inseparable from them—the absence of which would fundamentally change the things themselves—and *attributes*. The British philosopher F. H. Bradley writes similarly of a distinction between the "substantive" and the "adjective."[22] Conceived in such terms, the problem of instantiation is the problem of Being. Stephen Mumford articulates the problematic, in the context of the work of the Australian philosopher David Armstrong, as follows: "Where it is the case that the apple is red, what holds the apple and the redness together?"[23]

Is there, in other words, an "instantiation relation"? A significant strand of analytic philosophy has answered this question in the negative. Bradley himself gives his name to "Bradley's regress," a thought experiment used to demonstrate the fallacy of the instantiation relation. The experiment is summarized by David Armstrong as follows:

> Suppose that *a* stands in the relation R to *b*. R is instantiated by the pair *a* and *b*. So a special extra relation of instantiation is needed to weld the ordinary relation R to the two particulars. And if it really is needed, then why is not a still further relation needed to get the special extra relation, and R, and the two particulars together, and so *ad infinitum*?[24]

Following Bradley, Armstrong argues against an ontology of things or substances, on one hand, and qualities or attributes, on the other (that is to say, against an ontology in which particulars can be said to "instantiate" universal qualities). Instead Armstrong proposes an "ontology of states of affairs," in which a state of affairs, comprising always some confluence of universal and particular, can be said to be "fundamental," that is to say, particular. For Armstrong, in other words, there are no uninstantiated universals or any propertyless particulars.[25]

The positive use of the term "instantiation" in the context of literary works therefore implies that the relation between the work and the world is that of a part to a whole, a particular to a universal; that the work is capable of "instantiating" an idea, a character type, a narrative situation, an ethical or practical quandary; that such instantiation can be directly beneficial for the reader's experience and understanding of the world; that the work makes possible a degree of (no doubt imperfect) knowledge or judgment about life and society, philosophy and art, state and political structures, and available modes of resistance to them. The problem of instantiation is also therefore a phenomenological problem, a problem of perception. Instantiation presupposes an economy of perception and expression in which, as Dorothy J. Hale has written, the author is implicitly "constituted . . . as a perspective," a point of view necessarily limited by its "social positionality."[26]

It is almost impossible for a literary critic to avoid making some form of instantiation relation the basis of his or her work, even if he or she seems to be arguing against it. (As a character in Samuel Delany's novel *Trouble on Triton* phrases it, "That's a type too.")[27] Instantiation, perhaps, is nothing more than a link—a bridge between the world and the work—and it can take various forms. When it comes to literary criticism, an instantiation relation amounts to, as Hale puts it, a "belief that the novel can formally both encapsulate and fix a social world."[28] Hale names this belief with the phrase that provides the title of her 1998 book, "social formalism." In her view, instantiation, a term she uses with deliberation, is a "subplot" of the evolution of the theory of the novel through many different methodological stages (15). Her work, that is to say, may be read as an attempt to rewrite "the history of the theory of the novel" (18) as the history of the instantiation relation. Social formalists, writes Hale—a category that includes critics with such different approaches as Henry James, Mikhail Bakhtin, Gérard Genette, Roland Barthes, Henry Louis Gates, and Terry Eagleton— "imagine . . . that the form of the novel can accurately instantiate both the identity of its author and the identity of the subject the author seeks to represent" (8).

The term "instantiation" leaves unspecified the nature of the connection between the work and the world—but in doing so, I will argue, it preserves a kind of degree-zero principle of connection as the very basis of all critical reading. In the work of "recent novel theorists," says Hale, the novel "does not simply represent identity through its content but actually instantiates it through its form" (13). Instantiation is thus for Hale at the heart of any claims the novel might make to ethical significance:

> Social formalism . . . develops from an ethics of altruism—the notion that the novelist spontaneously desires to represent the wonderful other as an interesting subject—to an ethics of linguistic intrinsicality—the notion that the novelist should strive to represent the other in her "own terms" as a speaking subject—to a politics of linguistic diversity—the notion that the novelist can subvert social hegemony by representing the heterogeneousness of individual and social identity, defined as a mediated plurality of ideological "speaking" subjects whose definitive alterity is understood exclusively in linguistic terms.
>
> (126–27)

Putting aside—for the time being—the question of the applicability of the logic of instantiation and the term "social formalism" to such a wide array of thinkers, we can note that Hale's work describes and performs a shift in the conceptualization of the relationship between literature and its significance: from representation to instantiation. Instantiation, for Hale, is a form of connection that remains intact in the face of the many challenges to representation in the modern period. Such challenges arguably define the most decisive shifts in critical method during the twentieth century, which culminate in what Fredric Jameson has called "the necessary failure of art and the aesthetic, the failure of the new, the imprisonment in the past" in postmodernity.[29] Hale's narrative of the recent history of novel theory frees the novel from one logic of connection and reembeds it in another. Indeed, the phrase that Jameson makes central to his analysis of postmodernism, "cultural logic," might be taken as another synonym of instantiation. "This whole global, yet American postmodern culture," writes Jameson, "is the internal and superstructural expression of a whole new wave of American military and economic domination throughout the world: in this sense, as throughout class history, the underside of culture is blood, torture, death, and terror."[30] For Jameson, it remains an obligation of the critic to hold onto the logic of instantiation in the face of a contemporary cultural "depthlessness" and "weakening of historicity" (6). "If we do not achieve some general sense of a cultural dominant," he writes, "then we fall back into a view of present history as sheer heterogeneity, random difference, a coexistence of a host of distinct forces whose effectivity is undecidable" (6). Jameson is clearly a "social formalist" in Hale's meaning of the term.

Since 2007, Hale has been undertaking an analysis of what she calls the "novelistic aesthetics of alterity," a formation that shifts the terrain of her discussion from novel theory to novels and novelists.[31] Hale, however, never gives up her Boothian commitment to the rhetoric of fiction, and she rejects the proposition of a specifically contemporary break with that rhetoric: "From Edith Wharton to Philip Roth and from Joseph Conrad to J. M. Coetzee, novelists have attempted to reconcile the genre's double imperative: to represent the author's particular vision of life through the representation of characters who are not mirrors of authorial identity but autonomous points of view" ("*On Beauty*," 819). What distinguishes the "novelistic aesthetics of alterity" is this double movement: the instantiation of the novelist's "particular vision of life" through the representation of "social subjects different from himself" (821). The irreducible "social embedded[ness]" of a novel's point of view is revealed at moments when stylistic limitations become apparent, such as William Faulkner's abandonment of interior monologue when it comes to telling the story of Dilsey, the Compsons' black servant in *The Sound and the Fury*. What Hale calls the "perspectival economy" of the novel (822) is a field populated by "social positions" that are either accessible to or "resist" novelistic representation. For Hale, it seems, this social positionality signals the discursive limits of the project of literary criticism, limits that reflect those of the novel form itself. The novel instantiates a "particular vision of life," and when it is unable or refuses to do so, that inability or refusal is itself referable to a social positionality that "will not be scrubbed away" (822). What lies behind Faulkner's recourse to lyricism when faced with the challenge of Dilsey is thus "the high school dropout, the autodidact, William Faulkner" (822).

ALL VIEWS ARE PARTIAL: READING ZADIE SMITH

Hale's 2012 essay on Zadie Smith's *On Beauty* further and fascinatingly illustrates the shift from the logic of representation (which is to say, visibility) to a logic of instantiation (invisibility) as it has played out in the scene of criticism. Much of the evidence for Hale's discussion of Smith's novel is derived from three reflective essays that Smith wrote before and shortly after the publication of *On Beauty* and that Hale treats as documents that reliably convey the writer's intentions and hence the aesthetic organization of the work in question.[32] In these pieces, Smith puts forward what Hale describes as "a serious attempt to articulate a theory of the positive value of literature as an ethical discourse" ("*On Beauty*," 826/107). "Fictional truth is a question of perspective, not autobiography," writes Smith. "It is what you can't help tell if you write well; it is the watermark of self that runs through everything you do. It is language as the revelation of a consciousness" ("Fail Better," 6). "One can falsify a description of oneself," paraphrases Hale, "or lie in a statement of belief, but one can't counterfeit the way one sees, the point of view from which one makes sense of the world" (828/108). Smith's own thinking about the ethical possibilities open to the novel thus feeds directly into Hale's idea of an "aesthetics of alterity" specific to the form, according to which the novel "not only gives the reader access to a consciousness other than her own, but also best teaches the reader to appreciate that consciousness as other" (831/110).

Hale compares the aphoristic mode of *On Beauty*—a self-conscious repetition of the style of E. M. Forster's intrusive narrator in *Howards End* (the plot elements of which are also closely followed by Smith's novel)—with Elaine Scarry's philosophical work *On Beauty and Being Just*, an inspiration for Smith's novel (and the source of her title). By inserting some of Scarry's "truth claims" into the mouths of her characters, Smith, says Hale, does not "invalidate" Scarry's philosophical discourse; she "novelizes" it (824/105). "Novelization," a term from Bakhtin's essay "Epic and Novel," here refers not to the liberation of literary discourse from formal stylization but to the translation of the idea into a form that, according to Hale, is distinctive to the novel: "social discourse." Smith's novel "show[s] the novel's power as a genre to dramatize the oppositional but mutually defining nature of these modes of knowing: in the moment of the lived apprehension of truth and beauty, we forget that we see only from a point of view" (826/106).

None of this does anything to dismantle or even complicate the idea of the novel as a medium for the communication of ideas. "Like the philosopher," says Hale, the novelist "writes because she has meaning to convey, beliefs to express, truth to put forward" (824/105). But the mode of this expression is no longer one of direct, or even indirect, representation:

> On the one hand, the vision of life that the author projects through the novel can be said to instantiate the author's constitutive way of seeing: her vision of life is told by the novel, taken as an expressive whole. On the other hand, within the novel itself point of view is formally structured as an ongoing negotiation between interpreting subject and interpreted world. To understand the novel as a whole as the expression of the author's individual point of view is to forget the way the novel itself insists on the social contexts that produce and mediate authorial vision.
>
> (830/109)

Toward the end of her essay, Hale turns her attention to a series of third-person aphoristic interpolations in Smith's narrative that are "presented through or near free indirect discourse" (839/120). Hale selects five passages from scores of possible examples. "When you are guilty, all you can ask for is a deferral of the judgment," says Smith's narrator, apparently commenting directly—extradiegetically—on a protestation by one of her characters. Several chapters later, we read: "Each couple is its own vaudeville act"—referring to the parental couple at the center of the novel—and then, characterizing their own and their friends' awkward responses to the appearance of their son Jerome: "The ill-pitched greetings that compassionate age sings to mysterious youth rang out" (Smith, *On Beauty* 13, 56).[33] In her commentary, Hale outlines three possible understandings of the focalization of such passages. They could be the viewpoint of an omniscient narrator, expressing "opinions that the author has gained through perspicacious living," they may offer the views of a character in the novel "voiced by a helpful narrator," or they might represent "the transcendent insight of the literary author as genius, as seer" (as, for example, in Forster's *Howards End*) ("*On Beauty*," 840/121). The undecidability of these options leads Hale to identify their primary effect as a readerly one: "The multiplication of enunciatory positions staged through the narration of *On Beauty*'s aphorisms demands that the reader inductively locate her own position in relation to the possibilities before her" (841/121–22). In a further nuance, Hale claims that a relativizing qualification of such self-positioning can be attributed to Smith's novel: "Smith's narrativization of the aphorism also performs the ethical and political risk of the wisdom claim: that such generalizations can be shallow and reifying, engaging in the injustice of social stereotyping or the bathetic simplification of individuality" (842/122). What is "instantiated" in *On Beauty*, then, is less an idea or point of view than a dispersed awareness of social positionality, that is to say, an ethic that recognizes even the "shallow[ness]" and "reifying" nature of such recognition. This is, of course, another social positionality and thus both a point of view and an idea.

In this way it is apparent that the shift in the conceptual understanding of the connective tissue of the novel, from representation to instantiation, is a shift from a communicative to an "ethical" mode of criticism, from conceiving the primary substance of the novel in terms of language and signification to conceiving it in terms of "consciousness" and "ways of seeing." Thus, in Hale's conception of the novelistic aesthetics of alterity, the "bridge" that was demolished with the collapse of realism is reconstructed; the respective positions of novelist, character, and reader are stabilized; the ethical valence of the novel form is redefined and consolidated—all while the question of the literary substance is decoupled from representation. The subject position of the author who speaks, the unity of the utterance, its linearity and irreversibility, all survive the shift perfectly intact.

What is never quite entertained by Hale—nor, it seems, by any other professional reader of *On Beauty*—is the possibility that Smith's novel is a work of "postfiction"; that, despite Smith's own remarks about her work and about literature in general, *On Beauty* does not sustain any consistent perspective, *not even a perspective that puts perspective into question*; that *On Beauty* is not a work of the transition from representation to instantiation but—like *Elizabeth Costello*—a work in which the instantiation relation is no longer supportable, in which point of view itself is abandoned. Further, that such abandonment is most evident in the very moments when Smith, or a third-person narrator, inserts herself intrusively into the narrative. For all the apparent conventionality of Smith's fiction, one of the premises of the present argument is that such a "postfictional" reading must be possible in principle, irrespective of whether such a reading is likely to gain adherents in a particular case.

Certainly, Smith's work might and should be read in relation to the conventions of the comic novel in English, a form based, according to Bakhtin, on "the stratification of common language and on the possibilities available for isolating from these strata, to one degree or another, one's own intentions, without ever completely merging with them."[34] In the English comic novel, says Bakhtin, the parodic stylization of languages is often interrupted by the "direct authorial word," in which "the semantic and axiological intentions of the author" are "directly embodie[d]" (301). Such interruptions, we have noted, are common in Smith's work, which seems thus to bear out Bakhtin's sense of the "state of movement and oscillation" that characterizes the relationship of eighteenth-century English comic authors such as Henry Fielding, Tobias Smollett, and Laurence Sterne to demotic language and establishes her continuity with that tradition. At times, says Bakhtin, the "common" language explored in the comic novel is exposed as "inadequate to its object"; at other times, the author "becomes one with it, maintaining an almost imperceptible distance, sometimes even directly forcing it to reverberate with his own 'truth,' which occurs when the author completely merges his own voice with the common view" (302).

Bakhtin's analysis is highly pertinent to both *On Beauty* and Smith's earlier novel *White Teeth*, particularly the importance he assigns to perspective and to what he calls "linguistic consciousness." In Smith's works, everything and everyone is looked *at*; demotic locutions are localized, rendered distinct and individual. Not a single person is introduced without being subjected to a fleeting visual characterization or without his or her language being presented as a unified—what Bakhtin calls a "reified"—entity (299). Nothing and no one is excluded from this objectifying gaze. Nevertheless, the gaze in Smith emanates from the same place as the characters themselves. Every gaze seems to be reversed or multiplied; no one gaze or narrative perspective retains its authority. Like the view from the Bowden living room window, "just below street level," in the earlier novel *White Teeth*, all views in Zadie Smith's fiction, including that of the narrator, are "partial."[35] Both *On Beauty* and *White Teeth* satirize even that order of pluralistic, universal visibility that makes the composition of the work possible. Thus, the benevolent headmaster of Glenard Oak school, whose model of discipline involves seating his charges in a large circle "allowing everybody to express their point and make themselves heard" (*White Teeth*, 248); thus, the music teacher Poppy Burt-Jones, telling her disruptive pupils, "I don't think it is very nice to make fun of somebody else's culture" (129); thus, the horticulturalist Joyce Chalfen, intoxicated by the possibilities of "hybridity" and "cross pollination" that two black teenagers, Millat Iqbal and Irie Jones, represent for her affluent liberal Jewish household (262–71). Indeed, among the "identities" on which each of Smith's works casts its parodic gaze is the organizing perspective of the work.

Bakhtin is under no illusions that proliferations of "speech diversity" in a work of fiction amount to "heteroglossia"—one of several terms with which he denotes the quality of "unfinalizability" that he attributes to the thought of the novel and its capacity to undermine or displace all positions of linguistic authority (308). When languages are subjected to parodic treatment, their internal, "fundamental" dialogicality is denied (327). The heteroglossia of the comic novel remains rhetorical, external, as long as it "does not exceed the boundaries of literary language conceived as a linguistic whole" (308). On the other hand, says Bakhtin, even in the works of Fielding, Smollett, and Sterne we find a stylization that "penetrates the deepest levels of literary and ideological thought itself, resulting in a parody of the logical and expressive structure of any ideological discourse as such (scholarly, moral and rhetorical, poetic) that is almost as radical as the parody we find in Rabelais" (308). When, therefore, the "illuminating" (or parodic) language is precisely as reified as the one "illuminated" (or parodied) (361–62), the normative dimension of the overall structure has vanished entirely; we have instead just another image of a language. Bakhtin elsewhere calls this the principle of "addressivity" in the novel (*Problems*, 251–52).

A postfictional reading of Zadie Smith's work would suggest that the spatializing and territorializing function that Bakhtin attributes to the words of the author, which would "represent and frame another's speech [to] create a perspective for it" ("Discourse in the Novel," 358), is always interrupted in Smith's work by her extension of the principle of stylization to the framing narrative itself. Dialogue in Zadie Smith is not only relative, taking place between linguistic consciousnesses; it is also absolute, determining the very conditions of the evolution and operation of each represented language, including, again, that of the narrator. Taken together, the images of language put forward in the novel are also an image of the novel's "inability to say anything once and for all or to think anything through to its end" (Bakhtin, 365). No instantiation relation, then, only "an indissoluble concrete unity that is contradictory, multi-speeched and heterogeneous." This heterogeneity forms the dialogical background to any truth, authorial consciousness, or ethics of "alterity" that we might try to extract from the work.

To advance such a critical proposition "professionally" risks—more than scandal—irrelevance. For it has long been held that the function of criticism is to articulate the truths that the literary work, for reasons of "tact" or "taste," cannot or will not make explicit; to make the case that the truths that criticism is capable of speaking, or ventriloquizing, are the truths of the work in question; and to form an evaluative assessment of them. Dorothy Hale sustains this critical mission in reading *On Beauty* as a work that inhabits the "novelistic aesthetics of alterity" by instantiating, and thus reproducing, a dispersed awareness of social positionality. The critic Frank Kermode put this more simply, half a century ago, when he claimed that if poets "help us to make sense of our lives," the more modest task of critics is to "mak[e] sense of the ways we try to make sense of our lives."[36] This conception is already predicated on the shift from representation to instantiation.

In the contemporary moment, however, and across a wide range of literary and critical texts, it is apparent that the presumptions of this standard critical enterprise, in all its modesty, are precisely as speculative as the alternative proposition, the "postfictional" hypothesis. As in Smith's novels, the normative claims, expressed sentiments, and character judgments of narrators can no longer confidently be extracted from the body of "represented speech and thoughts." It is only a short step from the claim that the work's relation to its essence is one of instantiation, or that the identity of that essence is perpetually debatable, to that of the fundamental noninstantiability of any such essence in the contemporary novel. At the very least, therefore, it seems that the latter hypothesis, the absence of an instantiation relation between the literary utterance and its meaning, or the existence of an alternative relation, must be explored in greater detail.

Chapter Four

THE POSTFICTIONAL HYPOTHESIS

DEGREE-ZERO CONNECTION

The postfictional hypothesis comes into appearance, initially, as a series of negative possibilities: that the relation between writing and criticism may not be as symbiotic as Frank Kermode's understanding of the role of the critic, or Wayne Booth's, or Fredric Jameson's, or Dorothy Hale's, seems to suggest; that the relation is, rather, an interstice that can never be bridged, an interstice that, as such, has its own order of thought; that the relation is best conceived not as a compact, or even a conflict, but a fissure between two fundamental and irreconcilable presumptions, the presumption of instantiability and that of uninstantiability; that the so-called tact of the writer may be nothing but *an invention of the critic* to justify his or her own activity of producing a work that can speak its truth; that the writer's tact is not a gesture of aesthetic discretion but, on the contrary, an element in the institutionalization of the work, designed to distract the novel from its evolution toward a thought located outside all subjective or conceptual unity, an *internally dialogical* thought that takes place in the crevices between forms, or concepts, or intentions.

What makes the hypothesis of the emergence of a postfictional aesthetics unignorable is that this evolution of the thought of the novel cannot be halted or delayed by attempts to finalize the utterance of the text. Indeed, the dialogical qualities of the work seem to be hastened, rather than averted, with every attempt to instantiate its thought, whether by the work itself or by any other agent, including the author. The interstice, in other words, gapes ever larger the more direct or forthright the effort to close it.

The novelist, writes Booth in a passage quoted in the previous chapter, "need not include explicit statement of the norms on which his work is based." For Booth, remember, the vocation of the critic is to reconstruct such statements in their absence, that is to say, to establish the connection that Coetzee's conceit of the impassable bridge demolishes. In this way, the thesis of the "autonomy of art" is always accompanied by and dependent upon the pedestrian contributions of the critic. But what happens when the writer does exactly what Booth suggests he needn't do: provide "explicit statement" as to the foundations and practical consequences of his or her text, as in the opening chapter of *Elizabeth Costello* or the authorial interpolations in Zadie Smith's *On Beauty*? What happens when the plodding pedestrianism is found on the side of the fiction and the displays of unverifiable, nontransferable, "characterological" invention are located on the side of criticism?[1] Well, what "happens"—in the sense of what is instantiated—is, precisely, nothing. The instantiation relation, which we may begin to understand as a presupposition of the "rhetoric of fiction," is in such moments rendered demonstrably inadequate as a basis for a reading of the work.

Thus, when an unnamed and unspecified voice in *Elizabeth Costello* reflects that, in works of fiction, "ideas do not and indeed cannot float free,"[2] the implications for Coetzee's own work are catastrophic yet also negligible, for the idea in question (the nontransferability of fictional ideas) is proven and disproven in the same instant. The idea holds only if it does not hold *in this particular instance*, and vice versa. So simply is the instantiation relation—on which hangs the novel's direct or indirect purchase on everyday life—dismantled.

Moments like this confirm a truth about the novel that is apparent in Lukács's consideration of its ethical organization: that no work of fiction may interpret itself without that interpretation requiring further interpretation, and so on ad infinitum. Such moments of "self-interpretation" appear as points of special vulnerability in the infrastructure of the "rhetoric of fiction," where the logic of instantiation threatens to give way to a logic of perpetual interpretability, a vertiginous formation that removes any principle of finality from the work. And yet this truth emerges, strangely and paradoxically, at a moment in *The Theory of the Novel* when Lukács seems to be arriving at quite different conclusions.

A Hitherto Unremarked Moment in Lukács's *Theory of the Novel*

According to Lukács, the novel is composed of "the paradoxical fusion of heterogeneous and discrete components into an organic whole which is then abolished over and over again" (84). Every moment of reflection in a novel is also, inevitably, a moment of "form-giving" that cannot help but "deflect" (to use Carrol Clarkson's word)[3] personal responsibility for it, in the emergence of what Lukács calls a "second naïvety" (85). Any reflection that Elizabeth Costello's son John (or the narrator, or Coetzee himself) undertakes within the diegetic frame of the novel is implicated in this structure, which Lukács calls the "deepest melancholy of every great and genuine novel." For through such reflection, "the writer's naïvety suffers extreme violence and is changed into its opposite." What Lukács calls the novel's "tact" is achieved when the reflection is given form—precisely by being made an element of the work's "content"—and the "balance" proper to the novel is established, albeit fleetingly and provisionally. In practice, of course, the moment of reflection and the "ethical self-correction" are simultaneous; the "violence" of reflection and the "second naïvety" of form-giving are inseparable. Thus, the novel is always, for Lukács, an "interaction of two ethical complexes, their duality as to form and their unity in being given form" (84).

In such moments, Lukács seems fully inserted into the logic of instantiation; his thought seems perfectly congruent with the "social formalism" that, for Dorothy Hale, characterizes the dominant theoretical approaches to the novel through the twentieth century. However, what Lukács says next suggests that another dimension of thought is also present in his understanding, a seam of "purely sensuous form-giving" in which there is no "bridge" to be traversed, or left untraversed, or simply passed over; in which no distance between the banks even opens up. The spatiality of Lukács's imaginary is startling: perspective, point of view, plays no part in this speculative dimension at all. The passage in question contains no verbal or grammatical indication that a shift in Lukács's thinking has taken place or that an alternative tradition in the organization of the novel is being proposed:

What happens to an idea in the world of reality need not become an object
of dialectical reflexion in every kind of creation [*Form*] in which an idea is
given form as reality. The relationship between idea and reality may be completely dealt with [*wird . . . erledigt*] by means of purely sensuous form-
giving, and then no empty space or distance is left between the two which
would have to be filled with the author's consciousness and wisdom. Wisdom can be expressed [*erledigen*] before [*vor*] the act of form-giving: it can
conceal itself behind the forms and does not necessarily have to surmount
itself, as irony, in the work.

(84, TRANSLATION MODIFIED)

This line of thinking—of an order of thought ("wisdom") and expression that is inseparable from *and yet at odds with* the logic of form—remains
undeveloped in Lukács's work.[4] Perhaps he loses faith in its viability, yet it
haunts the chronology of *The Theory of the Novel*—from the opening evo-
cation of a world in which "the fire that burns in the sky is of the same essential nature as the stars" to the final imagination of a utopia that is incompatible with any formal depiction of it. A page later, Lukács speaks of the
second naivety as a mere "formal substitute of the first," a melancholy form-
giving that "points eloquently at the sacrifice that has had to be made, at
the paradise forever lost, sought and never found" (85). Lukács is generally
understood here to be referring to the lost world of the epic. In his later
repudiation of the book's "utopianism," Lukács seems to assume this meaning (20). But the true loss here is not the epic of the past but a missed logic
of the present as glimpsed in the earlier paragraph: the logic of a wisdom
that is achieved not *through* but *prior to* the act of form-giving (the 1971 English translation of Lukács's text is misleading here). What Lukács is alluding to is a thought *that is not able to be instantiated at all*, whose essence
consists in the impossibility of its instantiation.

In Lukács, all reflection has a melancholic quality given its insertion into
a spatial back-and-forth between loss and recovery (via the naivety of form).
What Lukács never considers in *The Theory of the Novel* is the kind of paradox we encounter in the passage from *Elizabeth Costello*, as well as in the
two images of a vehicular trail in W. G. Sebald's *The Rings of Saturn* (discussed in chapter 2): a self-reflection that simultaneously renders impossible a tactful entry into "form," that opens up, instead, a pure void—one

that is equally conceptualizable as a plenum. The dimension of self-reading in these works is incapable of being folded into Lukács's second (or some third or fourth) naivety. The real achievement of such self-reflection—indeed of its mere possibility—is in escaping the potentially infinite cycle of naivety and resignation, tact and reflection, and thus carving out an alternative to the profound "melancholy of every great and genuine novel." The idea that such self-reflection, in its absolute uninstantiability, might thereby provide an answer to that melancholy is also, therefore, untracked and unanticipated by Lukács.

FROM REPRESENTATION TO INSTANTIATION: FORSTER'S *HOWARDS END*

Lukács's analysis not only reveals the centrality of the instantiation relation to the novel form but helps us understand what the terms of any interruption of this relation would involve. Coetzee's ingeniously constructed object lesson is not just an aesthetic effect, the repercussions of which would be confined to the experience of reading *Elizabeth Costello* (or to the contemporary predicament of fiction in general). The relation of disconnection that he brings into existence, between the repeatable content of a novelistic reflection and its substance, also functions retroactively. Coetzee's conceit implicates every moment in every novel in which a character has an idea, or imagines a fictional situation, or composes a poem that appears in the work, or experiences a fantasy of any kind, or reflects on the appropriateness or inappropriateness of a word he or she has just used, or indeed offers an explanation of what we are reading. Again, such moments, while always framable in diegetical or perspectival terms (diegesis is the condition for their appearance), are at the same time irreducible to a diegetical logic. Such cases force a rupture of the instantiation relation as well as of the perspectival frame. It is precisely under such conditions that they achieve the status of a mode of thought in themselves.

The "retroactive" consequences of the passage from Coetzee's work may be spelled out by reference to a specific example. The well-known reflection that opens the fifth chapter of E. M. Forster's 1914 novel *Howards End* concerning the "generally admitted" sublimity of Beethoven's Fifth Symphony may be said to posit a certain relation, according to which Beethoven's symphony "instantiates" the universal quality of sublimity.[5] In Forster's sentence—"It will be generally admitted that Beethoven's Fifth Symphony is the most sublime noise that has ever penetrated into the ear of man"—the word "is" is, as David Armstrong puts it, "the 'is' of instantiation," the predicate that links an object (the symphony) and a universal (the sublime).[6] Yet—at least for the twentieth-century critical approaches that can be grouped together using Booth's phrase "the rhetoric of fiction"—a further substance-attribute relation is proposed by the very appearance of this aesthetic assessment within Forster's narrative. An author or narrator—at any rate, a unified consciousness—speaks his (or her) mind; thus (i), a subject position is imagined (which in this case counts as an "object"), together with (ii) a spoken idea (a "universal") and (iii) a world in which that position can express itself and be heard. Faced with this moment, critical opinion that approaches the novel as a medium of communication is limited to certain critical operations: questioning the authority of the sentiment (whether it is really endorsed either by the work or by Forster himself), considering the possible narrative positions from which it is expressed, evaluating the aesthetic failure or success of the conceit, and assessing its implication in the class relations or colonial relations that are also the theme of Forster's work. Thus, the work is considered within an overall economy of signification, based on the effective transmission and reception of information, direct or indirect. All "ideological" criticism (a term that can be extended to cover the full range of approaches demarcated by the "rhetoric of fiction") takes place under these economic and rhetorical assumptions. Thus, ideological criticism *presupposes* the relevance of the instantiation relation to the analysis of literature.

Such considerations can define and delimit our critical activity, however, only if we take the absence of grammatical evidence regarding focalization in the Forster passage as an indicator of the absence of focalization, that is, only if we presuppose, first, that a work, or an utterance within it, is, in however mediated a form, a thought or expression by a nonembodied subject located outside it, the nature of which it is the task of the critic to determine, and, second, that all formal or literary discourse in the novel is best understood as a mediated transmission of that prior thought. Such assumptions find support, of course, in the epigraph to *Howards End*, "only connect," a phrase that is transposed to the title page from the book's twenty-second chapter, where it appears as a fragment of free indirect discourse from the perspective of Margaret Schlegel.

In that chapter, Margaret, we read, is contemplating how best to help her
fiancé, the wealthy and insensitive Henry Wilcox, connect the "prose" and
the "passion" and so become "a man":

> It did not seem so difficult. She need trouble him with no gift of her own.
> She would only point out the salvation that was latent in his own soul, and
> in the soul of every man. Only connect! That was the whole of her sermon.
> Only connect the prose and the passion, and both will be exalted, and human
> love will be seen at its highest. Live in fragments no longer. . . . Nor was the
> message difficult to give. It need not take the form of a "good talking." By
> quiet indications the bridge would be built and span their lives with beauty.
> (187–88)

Only connect, we cannot fail to realize, is the doctrine of instantiation (as
opposed to representation). *Only* connect: the degree zero of connection.
The approach that Margaret is taking with respect to Henry's repair is that
which the critical apparatus of social formalism attributes to the literary
text itself: "quiet indications" rather than forthright representations. By
such means is the bridge "built and crossed."

At this moment in the story, however, the doctrine does not take successfully. For Henry, reflects Margaret, is "obtuse": "He simply did not notice
things" (188). One character's failure to connect is, of course, an occasion
for the connection to be made by another. Henry can't, or won't, see the
connection (in this case, between the economic fate of the bank clerk Leonard Bast and Henry's complacent advice, delivered a few months earlier,
that Leonard "clear out" of his place of employment; 139, 190). Margaret can,
and does. By means of this sequence of events, Forster not only instantiates the doctrine of connection; he names it and bestows further authority
upon it by installing it as an epigraph. The "idea" of *Howards End* is thus
laid bare. When Henry, an Insensitive Character, tells Margaret's furious
sister Helen, "There is no Social Question" (192), Forster is making sure to
tell us, by reliable narrative means, precisely the opposite: There is a Social
Question; that is to say, there is an instantiation relation. Thereby is the connection between literature and life also instantiated. Instantiation is the
relation without which literature has no meaning.

This moment in Forster is a key event in the evolution of novelistic aesthetics in the twentieth century, both because it makes transparent the

centrality of the instantiation relation to the organization of the novel and because, in doing so, it destroys the "balance" that the instantiation relation depends on. Thus *Howards End*, by its failure fully to intuit the terms of the relation, throws them into relief, sharpening our sense of its limitations. In Jacques Rancière's notion of the modern literary (or aesthetic) "regime," connections are made precisely by not being made. "In literature, intentions don't count. If the author has to say what he's doing, that means he hasn't done it."[7] Flaubert's *Madame Bovary*, published half a century before *Howards End*, is for Rancière the crucible in which the "relationship of address, the connection between one active will and another will"—a connection that defines the classical representational universe—is dissolved (14). In Flaubert's works, in which the feelings of characters are expressed by the flowing of a stream, the bending of grasses in the current, and the settling of a "thin-legged insect" on a water lily,[8] "meaning is no longer a relationship of will to will. It is a relationship of sign to sign, a relationship written on mute things and on the body of language itself" (*Politics of Literature*, 15), a relationship, that is to say, no longer of representation but of instantiation. Likewise, Virginia Woolf's *To the Lighthouse*, published in the decade after Forster's novel, "shows us how truth is enclosed in the perfection of the attitudes and gestures of the housewife, Mrs Ramsay. But that truth is mute, unaware of itself. Its expression is torn between two poles."[9] *Howards End* is constructed upon the same degree-zero connection as *Madame Bovary* and *To the Lighthouse*, except that in *Howards End* this order is thematized within the diegesis and reestablished outside it— seeming at once to defer the emergence of the "literary regime" and to dissolve the singular relation at its center: the instantiation relation itself.

Despite the work's staging and championing of the instantiation relation, is it possible, however, that Forster does not believe in it? Or rather, that whatever thought might be attributed to the work (as opposed to its author) is predicated not on the instantiation relation but on its collapse? Clearly, the reader is not trusted—by the author or the work—to make the connections that, in the narrative, only the bourgeois Schlegels are capable of. One could say, perhaps, that the effect of Forster having to name those "quiet indications" of the instantiation relation is to confirm their ineffectiveness—not only intradiegetically, in the form of their restriction to the Schlegels, but extradiegetically. As the principle and assumption of all literary criticism, instantiation depends for its effect on the novel's "social representativeness"—the "belief," as Dorothy Hale puts it, "that the novel can formally both encapsulate and fix a social world" (*Social Formalism*, 5). Perhaps the real thought at the heart of *Howards End*, its secret terror, is conveyed not in the platitudinous incantation "only connect" but in Henry Wilcox's profane utterance: There is no Social Question; that is, there is no instantiation relation. For what is certain is that the instantiation relation (if there is such a thing) does not require naming. Like the moment of self-reading in *Elizabeth Costello*, which proposes the disembodied idea that there are no disembodied ideas in works of fiction—thereby establishing that the first condition of realism is the disappearance of the real—the thematization of connection in *Howards End*, far from ensuring the survival of the instantiation relation, demolishes it.

If, on the other hand, we adopt the manner in which Carrol Clarkson compares the openings of Jane Austen's *Pride and Prejudice* and Coetzee's *Diary of a Bad Year*,[10] it is apparent that however unwilling Forster may have been to trust in the "second naïvety," however doubtful of the novel's capacity to transmit an idea in the absence of an explicit narrative commentary, the reflection on Beethoven and even the doctrine of "connection" are ever open to being framed by the logic of the diegetical utterance—no less so, indeed, than some more explicitly "embodied" fictional idea.

In the light of this set of possibilities, the challenge of reading *Howards End* would be to identify in it that "prophetic element" that Forster, elsewhere, locates in the works of Herman Melville and D. H. Lawrence, novelists whom "it is idle to criticize."[11] When Forster defines the "prophetic" work, it is as something that is *inimical* to instantiation:

> The essential in *Moby Dick*, its prophetic song, flows athwart the action and the surface morality like an undercurrent. It lies outside words. . . . *Moby Dick* is full of meanings; its meaning is a different problem. It is wrong to turn the Delight or the coffin into symbols, because even if the symbolism is correct it silences the book. Nothing can be stated about *Moby Dick* except that it is a contest. The rest is song.
> (*ASPECTS OF THE NOVEL*, 126, 128)

Whatever Forster's own intentions in *Howards End*,[12] perhaps that work, too, is readable with the awareness that, when it comes to the novel form, *there is no instantiation relation*, or, rather, that there is in the novel a logic, a seam of thought that—irrespective of what is represented or takes place in the work—can be expressed "before"—but also as a profound discontinuity with—"the act of form-giving," form-giving considered not merely as literary creation but as instantiation. To say the same thing in different terms: everything in the novel, even an epigraph, has the potential to be read, framed, imagined, as (to use again Banfield's phrase) "represented speech and thought."

But why should the universalization of free indirect discourse—otherwise known as the collapse of the logic of instantiation—be limited to works of fiction? Given that there is nothing to mark off the moment of "deflection" in *Elizabeth Costello*, or in *Howards End*, or indeed in *Pride and Prejudice*, how can the principle of deflection, the principle of the universalizability of free indirect discourse, be prevented from expanding outward, potentially implicating all language use? Where, after *Elizabeth Costello*, can we locate a point of nonfictional, anchored subjectivity from which an interpretation may take place that does not itself require, invite, further interpretation? When, in the reading of a work, does the moment come at which one can definitively say of a particular utterance, This is meant in earnest? After *Elizabeth Costello*, perhaps, nothing in the novel—and nothing outside it either—may ever again, with certainty, be read as "pure narration."

COLLAPSE OF NARRATIVE STANDPOINT

If, as Ann Banfield has said, "to narrate is to speak,"[13] the collapse of narration into "represented speech and thought" would amount to the collapse of the communicative element of the novel, that is to say, the collapse of the narrative standpoint itself. One might continue to claim that, theoretically, no such collapse is possible; that—as Mark McGurl has it—"fiction emerges in the most literal sense from the experiences of the author"; that however "dazzlingly ironized," however creatively condensed or displaced, inverted or transfigured, literary output remains a "conversion of memory into felicitous expression" (*Program Era*, 19). One might say that every work is written from a point of view, that the very disavowal of point of view presupposes a point of view capable of such disavowal. But such claims appear abstract and idealizing when faced with the absence of any "grammatical evidence of a narrator's point of view" in a particular sentence

(Banfield, 189). By taking a strictly grammatical and syntactical approach to the question of focalization—and against writers and critics who understand free indirect discourse to be a "merging" of narrator's and character's points of view, an "intertwining of objective and subjective statement," as one of her interlocutors puts it (185)[14]—Banfield argues that free indirect discourse is effectively "narratorless" (196). This proposition makes Banfield an outlier among literary critics, who seem, as a body, incapable of contemplating any escape on the part of literature—even a momentary one—from the regimes of signification, point of view, and (thus) criticism itself.

Is There a Compositional Unconscious?

Banfield's approach has a great deal to recommend it for anyone interested in exploring the possibility of an end to the schema in which the meaning of the literary text has its ultimate determination in the figure of the expressive (intentional or unintentional) subject. What Banfield's premises make evident is a quality of perception in narrative writing that is singular and therefore unreproducible and untranslatable. To adapt an observation from the work of Walter Benjamin concerning photography, Banfield, we might say, makes it possible to conceive of "another nature that speaks to the [consciousness of the novel] than to the eye: 'other' in the sense that a space informed by human consciousness gives way to a space informed by the unconscious."[15] Like the viewpoint of the camera, the narrative utterance, so considered, is irreducible to a subjective anchoring; it does not reproduce a preexisting perspective and is therefore neither referable to a point of view nor extrapolatable into one.

In coining the term "optical unconscious" to talk about the photographic image, Benjamin is borrowing the word "unconscious" from the discourse of psychoanalysis, but his usage is metaphorical. Unlike the psychic unconscious, the optical unconscious is perfectly visible, but only in the photograph. The optical unconscious is not noticeable, thinkable, before the photograph was taken; it becomes so only in and with the photograph. Benjamin describes it as "the tiny spark of contingency, of the here and now, with which reality has (so to speak) seared the subject" (510). In the case of writing, this "other" nature, similarly, does not precede the appearance of the work and is not conceivable without it. What produces it is the process of composition—in particular, according to Banfield, the technical element of revision, an element that plays an analogous role, in Banfield's theory of narrative, to the fact of the camera in Benjamin's theory of photography. "Only in writing may the process of revision, which is part of the process of composition, vanish in the finished piece, the 'clean copy,' leaving no sign of what the first or any intervening version might have looked like" (272).

This association between literature and photography may seem counter-intuitive. The "spark of contingency" in photography is produced instan-taneously and in the absence of the photographer's intention, whereas in writing, it would seem, a kind of idealized (unknowable, nonsubjective) knowledge is produced in a condition of heightened intentionality, as the narrative is revisited and refined over the duration of the work's composi-tion. In photography it is a matter of the preservation of traces; in writing it is a matter of their erasure. Writing, says Banfield, "makes possible the development of a narrative style where the act of production, of perfor-mance, leaves no trace in linguistic structure" (271). The question at issue, however, is not that of immediacy or intentionality but impersonality:

> The sentence of narration bears witness to the possibility of an objective knowledge—statements without the intervention of a knowing subject. Whatever may be the problematics of attaining such knowledge, its ideal pos-sibility can be envisaged, because language itself contains the objective statement, an abstract objective content is independent of whether a subject can validate it. Such a formal entity can be linguistically realized, even if, in speaking it, the human subject renders it subjective.
> (270)

Banfield herself draws no connections with Benjamin's interest in mechan-ical reproduction. However, she illustrates her idea of narrative as a non-subjective, nonvalidated, hypothetical knowledge by analogy with two mechanical apparatuses that capture, respectively, the objective (narrative) and subjective (consciousness) dimensions of narrative fiction: the clock and the lens. The clock is a model of objective knowledge, and the lens a model of "the representation of consciousness"—of subjective experience. The clock, she writes, like narration, "embodies the fact that time passes and is inherently (re) countable," while the lens "is witness to the fact that representation, even a representation of the mind, need not imply a representing mind" (273). Both mechanisms are "objectivizations": modes of knowing that are not themselves inhabitable. "They are our knowledge," she writes further, "but in ourselves we cannot know them directly." Analogously, what gets invented in narrative is "a knowledge in some sense unknown."

Thus, even a contemporary literary critic like McGurl, who insists on retaining a communicative model of literature, might himself be susceptible to a reading that separates the utterances of his work from the place of authorship that might once have functioned to guarantee the conviction with which they are made. "There is little doubt," writes McGurl in justification of the communicative model,

> that John Irving shares the opinions of his character on the limitations of biographical reading—little doubt that Garp is in general the author's (as they say) mouthpiece. . . . The indeterminacy of the relation between author and character is in this case quite real, a matter of pragmatic fact, but to make it a principle (whether by way of prohibitions against the "biographical fallacy," as the New Critics called it, or in the absurd declarations of the "death of the author" that were heard in the 1960s) is to risk missing one of the most basic dynamics of postwar literary production.
>
> (19–20)

By "one of the most basic dynamics of postwar literary production" McGurl is denoting the "biographical reading of fiction," underpinned by two elements of what McGurl calls the "autopoetic process": creativity and personal experience (19). McGurl quotes the critic Alfred Appel, defending Vladimir Nabokov against "earnest" readers who, on the basis of observed "similarities" between the author and narrator of Lolita, "conclude that *Lolita* is autobiographical in the most literal sense." The author, writes Appel (in McGurl's paraphrase), "is much more sophisticated than that." For McGurl, such "naïve" readers are also "savvy," insofar as fiction does emerge "in the most literal sense" from the experiences of the author. Writing fiction, McGurl goes on, "*is* one of those experiences" (19). "Sophistication" on the part of an author describes, of course, nothing other than the logic of instantiation: the mechanism by which a direct connection is replaced by an indirect one, but the same goes for McGurl's sophisticated *recovery* of readerly "naïvety," which simply restores the representational logic that is suspended by the degree-zero logic of instantiation.

Many elements in this passage, however, suggest that McGurl only sustains this logic of instantiation *by presenting himself as something like a literary character* and the critical principles he seems to be proposing as fictional ideas. "There is little doubt" sounds like the opening of an authoritative utterance. Yet, in itself, there is no grammatical element that prevents us from reading it as a passage of nonfocalized free indirect discourse—like "It is a truth universally acknowledged," "Every account of the origins of the state," or "It will be generally admitted." Such sentences are "unspeakable," in Banfield's sense, unique to written discourse and unreproducible in an oral context. Each, that is to say, is "narratorless." As an instance of "represented speech and thought," each lacks "perspective," which is to say, a normativizing dimension. Syntactically, Banfield might say, and therefore semantically, these opening phrases are "indistinguishable" (258).

There is a further quality to McGurl's prose that might encourage us to read him as a writer in the postfictional mode. When McGurl uses the distancing phrase "as they say" parenthetically to frame the word "mouthpiece," or when he refers to "the absurd declarations of the 'death of the author,'" the buttonholing tone suggests that the place from which they are uttered has no more preexisting unity (a unity preexisting the utterance itself) than, say, that of the narrator of *Howards End*. When McGurl acknowledges that "a restriction to fiction is simply one of the innumerable limitations I have had to accept in order to lend coherence to the critical narrative I want to construct" (28), the category of "fiction" is being massaged into a unity, along with the position of the critic and the "excellence" of the fiction he is discussing. The belief of McGurl himself in these notions is just as doubtful, then, as the belief of E. M. Forster in the "sublimity" of Beethoven's Fifth Symphony. In both cases the sentiments expressed are inseparable from their conditions of representation. In the case of Forster, those conditions involve a work of fiction in which the spoken idea may never, with certainty, be attached to the author. In the case of McGurl, the conditions are historical and involve the composition of a work of criticism in a period in which the so-called death of the author has become so thoroughly absorbed into critical orthodoxy that to argue its "absurdity" no longer risks anything at all, especially not some reversion to a pre-Barthesian era of critical-authorial sovereignty.

The strongest evidence for this reading of McGurl is found at the end of *The Program Era*, when, building toward a conclusion that will seem to endorse the rise of the creative writing program, McGurl asks rhetorically, "Isn't postwar American fiction, after all, unprecedented in its excellence?" He continues: "If I could, I would ask this concluding question with two voices in counterpoint, and only one of them sarcastic" (408). The boasted aim of *The Program Era*—to move the critical conversation decisively away from the conservative tendency to deplore the effect of creative writing programs on literature's supposed autonomy—is justified by McGurl on the basis of the "tedious[ness]" of such approaches, "love of the educational system that has made most of us [McGurl's generation of critics] what we are," and "the fun of it." None of these, of course, is a conventional or plausible "scholarly" rationale; none, therefore, can be confidently or conclusively situated outside the fictional realm. Such mannerisms, I want to suggest, function in the same way as the "word with a loophole" that Mikhail Bakhtin identifies in Dostoevsky's writing, which Bakhtin defines as "the retention for oneself of the possibility for altering the ultimate, final meaning of one's own words."[16]

Once the discourse of literary criticism begins to accommodate such self-distancing rhetorical strategies it can no longer be said to have any subjective unity. Or more precisely, its unity is "a fully realized and thoroughly consistent dialogic position" (Bakhtin, 63). To invoke a distinction made by Gilles Deleuze, perhaps McGurl, like Forster, Coetzee, and Austen, is operating less as an "author" than as an inventor of "assemblages," an approach to writing that, as Gregory Flaxman comments, "annihilates the last vestiges of individuality and interiority."[17] The real thought of McGurl's work would then be located not in anything spoken in the text or instantiated by it but in its interstices (for example, in the gap between the "two voices in counterpoint," one celebrating the rise of the creative writing program, the other deploring it). McGurl's insistence on the continuing viability of the communicative model of literature would then be the form in which the collapse of that model was decisively demonstrated and the status of *The Program Era* as a key register of that event was assured. Following this line of thinking, it may no longer be necessary or appropriate to enter into a professional-dialectical relationship with the work of a critic such as McGurl.

The *Elizabeth Costello* Effect

After *Elizabeth Costello*, then, it becomes possible to read even a book-length argument for the irreducibility of the biographical approach in literary criticism in "characterological" terms—as the work of a fictional persona, conducted not in the discourse of "critical reason" but as an extended exercise in "represented speech and thought." *Elizabeth Costello* stages a difference internal to the grammatical regime that once held in place the terms in which a certain kind of utterance may be understood. But when I say "after" *Elizabeth Costello*, what I really mean is "with" *Elizabeth Costello*. For *Elizabeth Costello* opens up a space of difference *within the speaking subject* and within his or her own discursive utterances, precisely by narrowing the gap between the discourses of narration and "represented speech and thought" *to a point of indiscernibility*. *Elizabeth Costello* thereby corrodes the communicative potential of the scholarly discourse we inhabit as literary critics.

This act of corrosion cannot, strictly speaking, be attributed to *Elizabeth Costello*, for to do so would be to attach qualities of subjectivity and finality to Coetzee's work that are incompatible with the central claims of postfictional aesthetics. Referring to Kafka's story "A Report to an Academy," Elizabeth tells the faculty and students at Altona College: "We don't know and will never know, with certainty, what is really going on in this story: whether it is about a man speaking to men or an ape speaking to apes or an ape speaking to men or a man speaking to apes . . . or even just a parrot speaking to parrots" (19). The point is applicable not just to Kafka's story—a first-person monologue that does not provide us with an extradiscursive point from which to judge the events narrated—but to *Elizabeth Costello* itself, a work narrated, technically, in the third person, but one—as I suggested in chapter 3—whose discursive environment might be described as a universalized free indirect discourse. "The word-mirror has broken," Elizabeth tells her audience, "irreparably, it seems. About what is really going on in the lecture hall your guess is as good as mine. . . . The dictionary that used to stand beside the Bible and the works of Shakespeare above the fireplace . . . has become just one code book among many" (19).

Read literally, this statement is one of the less convincing moments in *Elizabeth Costello*. Coetzee gives Elizabeth's argument a chronological framing that seems inattentive to the conventions of realist narrative. As Ann Banfield puts it, it is fiction itself—rather than any particular development within fiction in, say, the last thirty, fifty, or a hundred years—that "abolishes all distinction between the true and the false" (263). Thus literature has never used language on the basis of fixed, dictionary definitions. Even a sentence of "omniscient" third-person narration is rarely, within the dominant protocols of modern criticism, understood as a statement by an identifiable speaker, referring to objects that could be said to exist outside the text. If the word-mirror has broken, the world in which it was intact is not a *chronologically* different (i.e., earlier) world within the evolution of fiction but a *rhetorically* different, nonfictional one, a world of historiography, scientific research, or philosophy—discourses that, unlike novelistic narrative, are subject to "judgments of truth and falsity" (Banfield, 258). "There used to be a time when we knew," says Elizabeth. But what model of fiction ever proposed that "when the text said, 'On the table stood a glass of water,' there was indeed a table, and a glass of water on it, and we had only to look in the word-mirror of the text to see them"? What differences *within* fiction are being established at this moment in Coetzee's text?

Elizabeth's statement, we must remember, is Elizabeth's, not Coetzee's. Like the earlier claim that realism "has never been comfortable with ideas," the assertion that "the word-mirror is broken" is self-implicating. Either the assertion is true, in which case it must be false in this instance, since the statement is unambiguously uttered by a fictional character, or it stretches the bounds of credibility, in which case the character of Elizabeth must be accepted as an unreliable individual, whose utterances are explicable by means of some psychological category (naivety, curiosity, vanity, madness, criminality, stupidity, etc.) peculiar to her biography. The premises of the work would be thereby established on conventionally novelistic terms. According to Lukács, the disparate forces of the novel—on one hand, a "conceptual system which can never completely capture life"; on the other, "a life complex which can never attain completeness because completeness is immanently utopian"—are "balanced and brought to rest" in the biographical principle. This contrasts with the world of the epic, in which an individual life is "never anything more than an example," a "substratum" of social values, rather than a "vehicle" of them (77). "In the biographical form the balance of both spheres which are unrealised and unrealisable in isolation produces a new and autonomous life that is, however paradoxically, complete in itself and immanently meaningful: the life of the problematic individual" (78).

In the case of *Elizabeth Costello*, however, neither reading is credible. Elizabeth is not a spokesperson for Coetzee, nor is she a "problematic individual." The breaking of the word-mirror consists precisely in the implausibility of both readings—either of which would amount to a way of resituating the claim of the broken word-mirror in another perfectly reflective surface: in Coetzee's intentions, on one hand, or the diegetic closure of a fictional narrative, on the other. In the interstice between two possible readings, the work no longer permits us to consider which is the work's true voice nor even to measure the difference between the thought that is represented in the work and the thought of the work. The mode of fiction in which the word-mirror is broken is one in which the "rhetoric of fiction"— that is to say, any approach to the work that presupposes the function of instantiation—breaks down.

Of course, the discursive worlds of historiography, scientific research, philosophy, and literary criticism (the rhetoric of fiction) continue to function. Naturally, both McGurl's and Coetzee's work attract, even invite, professional readings predicated on the sense of there being something to say and a style or form in which it is said. Nevertheless, a lurking dissatisfaction attends all readings of these works that proceed under those assumptions. Postfictional aesthetics takes seriously the possibility that such "professional readings" fail to touch the thought of which the work is capable. Postfictional aesthetics is under way when methods of elucidating the thought of the work can be said to fail to hit their mark by the very deliberation with which they place it in their sights.

INSTANTIATION AS A QUESTION OF LANGUAGE: POSSIBLE OBJECTIONS

Instantiation, then, is a tendency with which every novelistic work, and perhaps every modern literary form, is in tension. However, an obvious question arises that must now be addressed. If the failure or collapse of the instantiation relation is a quality that is being attributed to the thought of the period and located in its most representative literary works, why is the *relation* between that quality of uninstantiability and the works in question not also an "instantiation relation"? That is to say, why is the "collapse"

of the instantiation relation not itself a historical situation that asks critics
nothing more than to establish a "basic congruity" with its literature—like
that which Ian Watt identifies between the premodern Greeks' "philosophical preference for the universal" and the "non-realist nature of their literary forms" or between the "realist epistemology of the modern period" and
the individualism of the classic novel?[18] Is the contemporary failure or
absence of the instantiation relation an objective fact or a merely subjective one, a perspective that dissolves as soon as it is recapitulated as a new
formal relation?

What, in other words, is the fate of the instantiation relation or its collapse when it itself is instantiated? How can the term "instantiation," the
concept of the "instantiation relation," or the figure of "Bradley's regress"
enter a particular discursive context—say, literary-critical discourse—
*without falling prey to the pitfalls that attend any formalization of a literary-
critical method*? How can the very analysis of the "instantiation relation"
escape the instantiation relation?

These questions also raise the issue of language, for if there is no instantiation relation, how is language—which is predicated upon categories and
sets, statements and terms that refer to those sets, and subjects whose intelligent agency determines the selection and arrangement of those terms—
possible? How can critical or theoretical reflection itself take place without
instantiation? What would language, let alone critical discourse, look like
without instantiation? It is tempting to reply to both questions in strict disciplinary terms, pointing out that the critique of the "instantiation relation" is concerned not with language but with universals (qualities) and particulars (objects); that the hypothesis of a "world of states of affairs"—the
claim that "universals are nothing without particulars" and that "particulars are nothing without universals"[19]—is a claim about ontology, not epistemology or human understanding; that the critique of the instantiation
relation cannot be transferred to language; that there is no contradiction,
therefore, in a literary (or theoretical) work that takes the critique of instantiation relations as its object.

D. M. Armstrong

This, however, is not how David Armstrong addresses the question. For
Armstrong, the question of instantiation in language is opened up by the

idea of synonymity. Synonymous statements can be held to be derivative of a certain true (or false) philosophical "proposition" that underlies them and that may be understood as their "content" (Mumford, 166). Armstrong withholds the instantiation relation from language with his suggestion that (as Mumford paraphrases it) propositions—like all universals—can "exist only in their instances." Extrapolating from Armstrong's understanding, it seems that the question of the ontological existence or nonexistence of an "instantiation relation" has no coherence or meaning (i.e., cannot even be addressed) in the absence of the utterances that make such a proposition apparent. The relationship between the proposition and its content is not one of "mereology"—of a part to the whole—whether we are talking about the claim for the existence or nonexistence of such a relation. For Armstrong, the "non-mereological form of composition" that makes up states of affairs "allows the possibility of having different states of affairs with identical constituents" (*A World of States of Affairs*, 118). Thus, the absence of an instantiation relation presupposes the paradoxical possibility of innumerable "instances" of such a nonrelation, *with no necessary principle of unity between them*. No instantiation relation also means: no *general* absence of an instantiation relation.[20] Therefore, for the two self-consuming passages of artistic reflection discussed earlier—a disembodied reflection about the embodied nature of novelistic ideas in *Elizabeth Costello* and an implied link between the trail of a vessel and the trail of writing in *The Rings of Saturn*—for these two episodes to be taken to speak synonymously of the absence of an instantiation relation does not require us to accept that it is the same absence, or that the historical situation is the same in each case, or even that there is a historical situation to speak of.

V. N. Vološinov

A second approach to the question of language is found in the work of the Russian linguist Valentin Vološinov, whose philosophy of language emerges in direct opposition to Saussurean linguistics. As Ferdinand de Saussure taught us, a linguistic sign does not name a preexisting entity but registers a distinction—both conceptual and phonetic—between two adjacent signs (signifieds or signifiers) in a system of signifying differences with "no positive terms."[21] With the claim that signifier and signified are tied in a relation that is both arbitrary and indissoluble, Saussure might be said to have developed a theory of language outside instantiation, one that forecloses any possible consideration of language as a "mereological" relation. Thus, even the sign "instantiation," in the sense I have been giving it in this book, denotes not a positive object or process but a *conceptual* discrepancy (a difference from, say, representation or expression). The appearance of any such term or concept in a discursive system announces not the appearance of a new "idea" but a semantic opening, that is to say, a new space of (un)thinkability. The term "instantiation," then, may be used to demonstrate that language is not an instantiation relation.

However, Saussure's linguistic model, with its radical separation of the system of language (*langue*) from the speech act (*parole*), also reinscribes an instantiation relation at the point of the utterance. "By distinguishing between the language itself and speech," writes Saussure, "we distinguish at the same time: (1) what is social from what is individual, and (2) what is essential from what is ancillary and more or less accidental" (13–14). Saussurean linguistics posits, on one hand, a "product passively registered by the individual" (the universal system of signifying differences) and, on the other, an "individual act of the will and the intelligence," in which the speaker (or writer) "uses the code provided by the language in order to express his own thought" in a "psycho-physical" process of "externalization" (14). Externalization is another word for instantiation. Indeed, externalization, which presupposes an opposition between inside and outside— the most entrenched and absolute of all Saussure's constitutive dualisms—underpins the hierarchy of language and writing in Saussure, according to which "the sole reason for the existence of the latter is to represent the former" (24).[22]

Vološinov rejects Saussure's separation of the act of speech from the system of language on this basis. The "inert system of self-identical norms," "external to and independent of any individual consciousness," as put forward by Saussure, "does not correspond to any real moment in the historical process of becoming" (*MPL*, 66, 65). "From a truly objective viewpoint . . . language presents the picture of a ceaseless flow of becoming."

Vološinov's understanding suggests an evacuation of any objective viewpoint upon language and thus of any conception of language as an objectively graspable entity. Such an objective conception is an abstraction. It presupposes an approach to language from outside, a "deliberation" upon it;

thus, it removes at the outset the most important characteristic of all language, which is that it is spoken "in [a] particular, concrete context" and
among members of a "particular [language] community" (*MPL*, 66, 67). If
we forget this, says Vološinov—which we do as soon as we take up a historical or philological position with respect to it—"we forfeit the very essence
of the thing we are studying" (46). For the speaker, as opposed to the phi-
lologist, the abstract system of language is irrelevant:

> The speaker's focus of attention is brought about in line with the particular,
> concrete utterance he is making. . . . For him, the center of gravity lies not
> in the identity of the form but in that new and concrete meaning it acquires
> in the particular context. What the speaker values is not that aspect of the
> form which is invariably identical in all instances of its usage, despite the
> nature of those instances, but that aspect of the linguistic form because of
> which it can figure in the given, concrete context, because of which it becomes
> a sign adequate to the conditions of the given, concrete situation.
>
> We can express it in this way: what is important for the speaker about a
> linguistic form is not that it is a stable and always self-equivalent signal, but
> that it is an always changeable and adaptable sign. That is the speaker's point
> of view.
>
> But doesn't the speaker also have to take into account the point of view
> of the listener and understander? Isn't it possible that here, exactly, is where
> the normative identity of a linguistic form comes into force?
>
> This, too, is not quite so. The basic task of understanding does not at all
> amount to recognizing the linguistic form used by the speaker as the famil-
> iar, "that very same," form, the way we distinctly recognize, for instance, a
> signal that we have not quite become used to or a form in a language that we
> do not know very well. No, the task of understanding does not basically
> amount to recognizing the form used, but rather to understanding it in a
> particular, concrete context, to understanding its meaning in a particular
> utterance, i.e., it amounts to understanding its novelty and not to recogniz-
> ing its identity.
> (68)

Not only is language not an instantiation relation; the very operation of
language—"language as such" (69)—takes place as an overcoming of the
instantiation relation. There is no instantiation relation—except as

constructed from a perspective of "abstract objectivism" situated outside language as such. "For a person speaking his native tongue, a word presents itself not as an item of vocabulary but as a word that has been used in a wide variety of utterances by co-speaker A, co-speaker B, co-speaker C and so on, and has been variously used in the speaker's own utterances" (70).

This undeniably theoretical critique of the instantiation relation, of course, suggests a certain objective fact: a relation between subjective consciousness and the experience of language. As Vološinov says, "there is no such thing as experience outside of embodiment in signs" (85). This proposition draws from Vološinov the same rhetorical question that was asked at the beginning of this section: Isn't the absence of an instantiation relation an objective situation that, as such, is prone to instantiation? Or as Vološinov poses it: "Does it follow that this relationship between the subjective consciousness and language as a system of objective, incontestable norms is itself bereft of any objectivity?" (66). Vološinov's answer is immediate and unambiguous: "Of course not. Properly understood, this relationship can be considered an objective fact." Thus, the *absence* of a relation between *langue* and *parole*—that is to say, the nonexistence of language "as a system of incontestable and immutable norms"—may be spoken of in the theoretical mode because, again, the absence of an instantiation relation may only be generalized *in the abstract*. In reality, nothing unites the "instances" of such a nonrelation, which may be instantiated ad infinitum with no consequences for the normative claim of its nonexistence.

The converse and complement of Saussure's abstract system is expression, which is made up of two elements: "that inner something which is expressible, and its outward objectification for others" (Vološinov, 84). Any theory of expression, Vološinov goes on to say,

inevitably presupposes that the expressible is something that can somehow take shape and exist apart from expression; that it exists first in one form and then switches to another form. This would have to be the case; otherwise, if the expressible were to exist from the very start in the form of expression, with quantitative transition between the two elements (in the sense of clarification, differentiation, and the like), the whole theory of expression would collapse. The theory of expression inevitably presupposes a certain dualism between the inner and outer elements and the explicit primacy of the former, since each act of objectification (expression) goes from inside out. Its sources are within.

(84)

A theory of expression or the expressible is always, then, a theory of instantiation. And what we—with Vološinov—are positing in opposition to the instantiation relation is not the absence of a relation between a particular and a universal, the system of language and an enunciation, but the *primary, fundamental* nature of that relation. "There is no individual enunciation," say Gilles Deleuze and Félix Guattari in a text profoundly influenced by Vološinov's work. "There is not even a subject of enunciation."[23] Instantiation is as inappropriate a concept for understanding language as it is for understanding the ontological relation between substances and attributes. There are no terms, no thought, possible that do not presuppose the existence of a collectivity. When I speak, there is no I that is not itself formed by the orientation toward "possible expression" and by "the social orientation of that expression" (Vološinov, 90). "Each and every word," writes Vološinov,

> expresses the "one" in relation to the "other." I give myself verbal shape from another's point of view, ultimately, from the point of view of the community to which I belong. A word is a bridge thrown between myself and another. If one end of the bridge depends on me, then the other depends on my addressee. A word is territory shared by both addresser and addressee, by the speaker and his interlocutor.
>
> (86)

There is, in fact, no need for a bridge, for the bridge is formed in the very imagination of a bridge but equally in the imagination of its absence.

How should we understand the historical situation in which a prominent writer of fiction reimagines the meaning of a work of literature as taking place not on the basis of "territory shared" but as the traversal of a gulf, an abyss of empty space that cannot be navigated but only "assumed" to be crossed? Does such a reimagination introduce the concept of instantiation into literature or does it, on the contrary, signal a rupture with, and thus a liberation from, the instantiation relation? And if such questions cannot be answered without reaffirming the instantiation relation, reestablishing it at the heart of the work, what would it mean to install something else in its place? What conception of literary meaning can we propose in place of the one that a generation of writers seems to be fighting to keep at bay?

Chapter Five

THE LOGIC OF DISCONNECTION

CHRONOTOPES OF INTERPRETATION:
FOUCAULT WITH BAKHTIN

"I wish I could have slipped surreptitiously into this discourse which I must present today, and into the ones I shall have to give here, perhaps for many years to come." At the beginning of "The Order of Discourse," his 1970 inaugural address at the Collège de France, Michel Foucault evokes an image of the impossible "beginning" of discourse and the "longing" not to have to begin, that is, to be already "enveloped by speech, carried away well beyond all possible beginnings." He continues:

> I think a good many people have a similar desire to be freed from the obligation to begin, a similar desire to be on the other side of discourse from the outset, without having to consider from the outside what might be strange, frightening, and perhaps maleficent about it. To this very common wish, the institution's reply is ironic, since it solemnises beginnings, surrounds them with a circle of attention and silence, and imposes ritualised forms on them, as if to make them more easily recognisable from a distance.[1]

It is impossible not to compare the anxiety Foucault is describing with that of Coetzee's narrator at the beginning of *Elizabeth Costello*, faced with the "problem of the opening." In each case the writer is imagining a relation to discourse that would be no relation at all, since the writer or inhabitant of discourse would simply exist within it, neither differentiated from it nor dominated by it, neither preceding nor subject to it. In both cases, however, the exercise has the paradoxical effect of *introducing* a relation to discourse as problematic. Thus fictional discourse, for the narrator of *Elizabeth Costello*, is a matter of bridging—or vaulting—a certain separation between the world of the writer and the world of the fiction. For Foucault, spatial distance is imposed by the categories with which the institution attempts to control and regulate discourse, in a "solemnization" of its boundaries.

There are three main such procedures: *commentary* (which establishes the hierarchy between "fundamental or creative discourses" and those that "repeat, gloss, and comment"), the *author* (the subject, the origin of discourse), and the *disciplines* (the existence of limits, definitions, and conventions, a virtual trajectory of future discovery). These categories are distinct from the prohibitions and conditions that are imposed on the "outside" of discourse, which concern what can and cannot be said, who is and is not recognized as having the power to speak. Foucault is concerned, rather, with the "internal rules," with protocols of reading and reception, classification and distribution, that serve to organize and stratify the functions of discourse. In every case it is a question of spatializing: imposing a separation between discourse and the object or event.

The principle of distance is precisely the principle of instantiation, premised on a distinction between primary and secondary qualities. Accorded a subject (a speaker), an object (an idea or referent), a set of methodological conventions, and the possibility of future, as yet unknowable, discoveries (a discipline), discourse is referred to an entity from which it may be said to originate, another entity that it describes with more or less adequacy, and a realm of future intellectual development to which it may afford an opening. These thematics operate as follows, according to Foucault:

> The commentary-principle limits the chance-element in discourse by the play of an identity which would take the form of repetition and sameness. The author-principle limits this same element of chance by the play of an identity which has the form of individuality and the self. . . . In a discipline, unlike a commentary, what is supposed at the outset is not a meaning to be rediscovered, nor an identity which has to be repeated, but the requisites for

the construction of new statements. For there to be a discipline, there must be the possibility of formulating new propositions, ad infinitum. (59)

Foucault's thinking here bears comparison with some of Bakhtin's reflections on discourse, especially in a section of the 1934–1935 essay "Discourse in the Novel" in which Bakhtin discusses the nature of "authoritative" discourse:

> The authoritative word is located in a distanced zone, organically connected with a past that is felt to be hierarchically higher. It is, so to speak, the word of the fathers. Its authority was already *acknowledged* in the past. It is a *prior* discourse. It is therefore not a question of choosing it from among other possible discourses that are its equal. It is given (it sounds) in lofty spheres, not those of familiar contact. Its language is a special (as it were, hieratic) language. It can be profaned. . . . Authoritative discourse may organize around itself great masses of other types of discourses (which interpret it, praise it, apply it in various ways), but the authoritative discourse itself does not merge with these (by means of, say, gradual transitions); it remains sharply demarcated, compact and inert. . . . Its semantic structure is static and dead, for it is fully complete, it has but a single meaning, the letter is fully sufficient to the sense and calcifies it.
>
> (342, 343)

There are significant differences between Bakhtin's and Foucault's projects. For Bakhtin, authoritative discourse is everything that "novelistic" discourse is not. For Foucault, by contrast, discursive power does not function as a "sharply demarcated" separation but is better grasped, precisely, in the form of "gradual transitions." There is no hard and fast differentiation, he says, but rather "a kind of gradation among discourses" (56, 57). Further, it is not clear that literature, for Foucault, is exempt from the procedures of institutional control, especially since literary works are among those that define the relationship between text and commentary, discourses that "give rise to a certain number of new speech-acts which take them up, transform them or speak of them" (57). The inclusion of "disciplines" in Foucault's typology makes clear that perspective establishes a relation not only to "prior" entities (identities, rediscoveries) but to future ones also (possibilities, imaginings). Temporality is as spatial a concept as distance. Yet what is striking is that both Foucault and Bakhtin align the authority of discourse with distance and the eradication of authority with the eradication of perspective.

Another concept from Bakhtin's theory of the novel throws a different light on the spatialization inherent in Foucault's three procedures for the internal control of discourse. The term "chronotope," coined in the remarkable essay "Forms of Time and of the Chronotope in the Novel," written (for the most part) in 1937–1938, designates "the intrinsic connectedness of temporal and spatial relationships that are artistically expressed in literature."[2] With this concept, Bakhtin makes thinkable the abstraction involved in any attempt to conceive of time and space separately. The chronotope, he says, is "a formally constitutive category of literature" (84); it defines "a literary work's artistic unity in relation to an actual reality" (243). Chronotopes provide "the ground essential for the showing forth, the representability of events" (250). The road, one of the most important chronotopes in literature, is an image in which "time . . . fuses together with space and flows in it (forming the road); this is the source of the rich metaphorical expansion on the image of the road as a course: 'the course of a life,' to set out on a new course,' 'the course of history' and so on" (244). The chronotope is the principle of connectivity of the novel form. The term "chronotope" conceptualizes the modes of connection at the heart of all novelistic representation, but, crucially, it does so without replicating the logic of instantiation, for the concept of the chronotope is a way of thinking the inseparability of time and space in the context of the literary utterance. In a footnote early on in his essay, Bakhtin qualifies Kant's definition of space and time as "transcendental" entities, claiming them, rather, as "forms of the most immediate reality" (85n). As the French philosopher Henri Bergson, who shares this rejection of Kant's framing of the issue of space and time, puts it, "the theory which [Kant] works out in the Transcendental Aesthetic consists in endowing space with an existence independent of its content, in laying down as *de jure* separable what each of us separates *de facto*, and in refusing to regard extensity as an abstraction like the others."[3] By contrast (with Kant), the confluence of space and time in Bakhtin's notion of the chronotope is, in a philosophical sense, fundamental. Just as for the philosopher David Armstrong things are only separable from their attributes *in the abstract*, just as for Vološinov the expressible only exists as expression—an utterance's "concrete" element being that which enables it to function in a given situation, rather than that which is "invariably identical in all instances of its usage" (*MPL*, 68)—so for Bakhtin and for Bergson time is always experienced in space, and vice versa. As Gary Morson and Caryl Emerson, commenting on Bakhtin's notion of the chronotope, observe, "time and space constitute a whole." Time "is always in one way or another *historical* and *biographical*, and space is always *social*."[4] In separating them we imbue them with homogeneity; we make time countable, which is to say abstract—apprehensible only in segments of indirect, nondurational time. It is insofar as we separate time from duration—linearize it, make it countable—that time is instantiated, becomes an abstraction. However, to conceive of this operation in such terms is also inaccurate, for there is no universal or pure time that is *subject to* instantiation. Bergson's concept of duration is thus a rejection of the instantiation relation as applied to time and space; *durée* should be understood not as "pure," transcendental time but, on the contrary, as concrete, lived time.

Similarly, Bakhtin's notion of the chronotope is a rejection of the abstraction that is present in all theories of instantiation, predicated on the universal or transcendental qualities of space and time and on their experience in a particularized or limited form. As Bakhtin says, "*living* artistic perception . . . makes no such divisions and permits no such segmentation" (243); the analogy with Vološinov's critique of "abstract objectivism" is obvious. Chronotopic formations (the chance encounter on the road, the "web of intrigue" in the salon, the mood of "petty-bourgeois" stagnation pervading the provincial town, the moment of crisis at the threshold) constitute "organizing centers for the fundamental narrative events of the novel"— places where "the knots of narrative are tied and untied" (250). In the salons of Stendhal's novels, "historical and socio-public events" are woven together with "the personal and even deeply private side of life, with the secrets of the boudoir." In Balzac, houses are spatialized images of time as "materialized history" (247). In the threshold spaces of Dostoevsky's novels (which include staircases, halls, and corridors, as well as streets and squares), time takes on an "instantaneous" quality, falling outside the "normal course of biographical time." The determining moments in Dostoevsky take place as "crisis events": "falls, resurrections, renewals, epiphanies, decisions that determine the whole life of a man" (248). "Any and every literary image is chronotopic," says Bakhtin; indeed, "language, as a treasure-house of images, is fundamentally chronotopic" (251).

Coetzee's image of the bridge in the opening paragraphs of *Elizabeth Costello*, together with the "abyss" that it spans, would seem to be an exemplary chronotope. However, since it is explicitly present as a metaphor—since it does not have the silent organizing function in the novel that such images do in nineteenth-century realist fiction—its chronotopic quality is also manifest as a larger chronotopic formation in which the fact of authorship is explicitly present in the narrative. When the narrator tells us that we are going to skip the details of a certain scene, that "it is not a good idea to interrupt the narrative too often" but that "unless certain scenes are skipped over we will be here all afternoon,"[5] a chronotopic situation (a place, a time) is being constructed: a scene of *narration and focalization* taking place in a diegetic space that is not Elizabeth's world at all. The organizing chronotope of *Elizabeth Costello*—a work, I suggested earlier, that universalizes the principle of free indirect discourse—involves an interruption of the standard chronotopic formation that connects "a literary work's artistic unity" with "an actual reality." The operating and organizing chronotope of *Elizabeth Costello* is inseparable from the appearance of a noninstantiating, deperspectivizing novelistic discourse.

Arguably, then, even non- or despatializing discourses are chronotopes. Bakhtin's concept of the chronotope has no normative element; chronotopes are neither positive nor negative entities. No decision can be taken to think nonchronotopically, just as no writing may be undertaken in the absence of language. Chronotopes are irreducible, primary. Thus forms of instantiation, too, are chronotopic. Kant's insistence, in *Critique of Pure Reason*, that space "does not represent any property of objects as things in themselves" but is simply "the form of all phenomena of the external sense" and the "subjective condition of the sensibility, under which alone external intuition is possible"; his proposal that time is "nothing else than the form of the internal sense"; and even his careful acknowledgment that the intuitions of space and time have no "shape or form" other than those we "supply . . . by analogies"—for example, by representing the course of time with "a line progressing to infinity," such that "successivity" (time) is made analogous to "co-existence" (space)—viewed with Bakhtin, these principles, which attribute a universality to space and time and condemn form itself as a mere instantiation, are chronotopes.[6] This formula does not work in reverse. Bakhtin's notion of the chronotope is not a mode of instantiation relation, for, as the concept of the chronotope dramatizes concisely, *there are no instantiation relations* other than the ones we impose through interpretive procedures. The formation of an instantiation relation is always a moment of premature, excessive, or incomplete interpretation. And yet, is there any interpretation that is not, by definition, premature, excessive, or incomplete?

The themes of commentary, authorship, and disciplinarity outlined in Foucault's "The Order of Discourse" are chronotopes that establish an instantiation relation insofar as they impose on what Foucault calls "the chance element of discourse" spatial motifs such as the *inner truth* of the utterance, motifs of *individuality* and *expression*, and the proposition of the *future evolution* of knowledge. As such, these themes imply, or construct, a certain spatiotemporal unity and directionality to the discourse in question. Bakhtin himself is well aware that the image of the author is a chronotope and that a chronotopic image "is a created, and not a creating, thing" (i.e., that it never coincides with the author him- or herself or with the processes that underlie the origin of the work) (256).

But the same could be said of the "chance element of discourse" that Foucault opposes to these themes and even of the principle of "discontinuity" that Foucault wants to establish at the heart of discourse. These propositions, too, are chronotopes—which is simply to say that they function as principles of connection, that they qualify as a "thought," just as much as the motifs of authorship or disciplinarity that Foucault wants to displace. As Morson and Emerson remind us, the thought of a literary work is always chronotopic.[7] It is Bakhtin who first noticed and named the presence of chance in the novel as a chronotopic element. The logic of the Greek romance, a genre that flourished between the second and sixth centuries, says Bakhtin, "is one of random *contingency*, which is to say, chance *simultaneity* (meetings) and *chance rupture* (nonmeetings), that is, a logic of random *disjunctions* in time as well. In this random contingency, "earlier" and "later" are crucially, even decisively significant. Should something happen a minute earlier or a minute later, that is, should there be no chance simultaneity or chance disjunctions in time, there would be no plot at all, and nothing to write a novel about" (92).

THE "NOVELISTIC ELEMENT": FREE INDIRECT DISCOURSE

For Foucault, then, literary texts do not escape the spatializing logic of the orders of discourse but are further incarnations of it; this is so even insofar as they put forward a principle of nonspatiality to counterpose to that logic. The name "literature" is for Foucault no mark of privileged discourse but just another principle of classification to be comprehended simply as a term in the gradation of discourses.

And yet, in "The Order of Discourse" Foucault appears to preserve the possibility of an "effacement" of this spatialization or "gradation" of discourse—as long as the site of this effacement refuses (or is refused) the name "literature": "The radical effacement of this gradation can only ever be play, utopia, or anguish" (57). Any such "play" (as in Borges's story "Pierre Menard, Author of the *Quixote*," a work that "effaces" the chronotopic figure of commentary with the image of "a commentary which is nothing but the solemn and expected reappearance word for word of the text that is commented on"),[8] any display of "anguish" (as in Foucault's opening gesture, or its probable discursive model, Samuel Beckett's *The Unnamable*),[9] any utopian image (say, the young Karl Marx's imagination of communism as a revolution of the "senses" involving a relation to the thing "for its own sake")[10] would only "annul one of the terms of the relation each time, and not . . . do away with the relation itself."

The relation in question, of course, is that of instantiation. Even literature cannot be reliably instituted as a vehicle for the effacement of the instantiation relation—the chronotopic connection between entities and attributes, qualities and forms. There is no doing away with the relation *in general*, just as there is no absence of an instantiation relation in general. For Foucault, this is to say, there is no literature *in general*.[11]

The issue then arises of the implication of Foucault's own discourse in the question of the possibility of a momentary despatialization of discourse. Might Foucault's work be one of those in which the terms of the relation— say, the difference between an order of secondary, subordinate speech acts, whose meaning coincides perfectly with their pronouncement, and another whose meaning remains indefinite, to be perpetually puzzled over—is annulled, albeit provisionally, during the moment of its encounter? Could it be said, for example, that in those opening sentences to "The Order of Discourse," Foucault is speaking not in the mode of criticism or commentary but in something like a "novelistic" discourse? That the "I" that Foucault mobilizes in the passage refers not to Foucault—at least, not the proper name Foucault, the writer who puts his name to *The Archaeology of Knowledge* or "The Order of Discourse"—but to an I that will survive "over and above [its] formulation" (57)? The anxieties expressed in these opening sentences would then be instances not of direct (or indirect) discourse—a discourse attributable to a subject who precedes (and endures beyond) it—but of free indirect discourse, otherwise known as "represented speech and thought."

When Bakhtin speaks of the "novelistic element" that can make an appearance even in texts that are not otherwise receivable as novels, what he is referring to is the "artistic representation of another's word" (350), that is to say, free indirect discourse. The presence of such "novelistic" elements in legal texts and ethical tracts, Bakhtin notes, raises irresolvable problems concerning thought, desire, motivation. In a sense, the entire problematic of the postfictional world is summarized in just a few lines in Bakhtin's "Discourse in the Novel":

> All fundamental categories of ethical and legal inquiry and evaluation refer to speaking persons precisely as such: conscience (the "voice of conscience," the "inner word"), repentance (a free admission, a statement of wrongdoing by the person himself), truth and falsehood, being liable and not liable, the right to vote and so on. An independent, responsible and active discourse is the fundamental indicator of an ethical, legal and political human being. Challenges to this discourse, provocations of it, interpretations and assessments of it, the establishing of boundaries and forms for its activity (civil and political rights), the juxtaposing of various wills and discourses and so on—all these acts carry enormous weight in the realms of ethics and the law. (349–50)

Once the element of "represented speech and thought" enters such nonfictional discursive spaces, the stability of those spaces and of their orienting categories is thrown into doubt. Take, for example, the problem of criminal confession in an ethical or legal context or the problem of motivation in a sociological context—as applied to, say, a suicide bomber or a perpetrator of hate crimes. "The problem of *confession*," writes Bakhtin, "has so far been interpreted only at the level of laws, ethics and psychology." As such, the problem is merely legal: a problem of truth or falsity. For the philosophy of language, however, confession is a "problem of a thought, a desire, a motivation that is authentic" (350). That problem is posed most directly, according to Bakhtin, by a writer of fiction: Fyodor Dostoevsky. Everything put forward in Dostoevsky's works concerning the heroes' motivations remains doubtful, for reasons that have to do with those works' navigation of perspective. Bakhtin makes a similar observation in *Problems of Dostoevsky's Poetics*:

> Not only the reality of the hero himself, but even the external world and the everyday life surrounding him are drawn into the process of self-awareness, are transferred from the author's to the hero's field of vision. They no longer lie in a single plane with the hero, alongside him and external to him in the unified world of the author—and for this reason they cannot serve as causal or genetic factors determining the hero, they cannot fulfill in the work any explanatory function.[12]

In Dostoevsky, motivations never take on the status of sociological or otherwise generalizable truths. Such "pragmatic links" are possible only on the basis of characters having "become objects, fixed elements in the author's design" (7). Since Dostoevsky never adopts any perspective on his characters, no such links are posited independently of his characters' own points of view. What holds Dostoevsky's works together, says Bakhtin, are connections of "a different sort entirely."

If it could be hypothesized that Foucault, too, were speaking not in his own voice but in represented speech and thought, that—in an inversion of the structure that prevails in Dostoevsky's fiction—everything framed by Foucault's own voice is in fact a ventriloquy of discourses that surround, condition, facilitate, and infiltrate the thought of Foucault's own texts, then we might begin to envisage Foucault himself as a postfictional thinker, indeed, as one of the founders and originators of the postfictional hypothesis.

Foucault says nothing about free indirect discourse in "The Order of Discourse"; it seems to be the great, unacknowledged category in his essay, indeed in all of his work. Yet perhaps this is because free indirect discourse is precisely a mode that is everywhere present there.[13] One of Foucault's most direct statements on the quality of his own discourse is made during an interview in 1977 in which he is asked to comment on the claim that his writing "strives to depict, before the very eyes of the reader, relations that are abstract and remote"; that, consequently, his analyses have a "dramatic" and "fictive" quality. Foucault replies that he is perfectly aware that he has "never written anything but fictions" but that, at the same time, fictional discourses are able to induce "effects of truth," to "engende[r] or 'manufactur[e]' something that does not as yet exist."[14]

What does this mean for the role Foucault might have in imagining a critical relation to the literary text that would perpetually defer the establishment of a perspective upon it, even in the apparently innocuous form of an interpretive connection? Could this offer an alternative to the critic's obligation to establish an understanding of, and thus connection to, the works under his or her perusal? In Bakhtin's notion of the chronotope, it would seem, there is no space (nor need) for such an alternative, for the chronotope comprehends all such objectives and all conceivable alternatives to them. Alternatives are nothing but further chronotopic formations, further modes of connection.

What distinguishes Foucault from Bakhtin, then, are the hints of a non-chronotopic method haunting Foucault's discourse, a mode of reading that would attempt to affirm "the chance element" as such, that might thereby lead to an "outside in which the speaking subject disappears" ("Maurice Blanchot," 13). Besides the internal rules of discourse examined in "The Order of Discourse" (commentary, authorship, disciplinarity) there remains another possibility that Foucault is unable to name without risking the very pitfalls (instrumentalism, interiority, and subjectivization) that he is presenting as part of the story of the institutionalization of discourse.

Instead of naming it, Foucault recommends three "decisions" that should inform our analytical procedures: to "call into question our will to truth, restore to discourse its character as an event, and lastly, throw off [lever enfin] the sovereignty of the signifier" (66, translation modified). All three take place in that impossible, unconceptualizable space between thought and speech. Underlying these decisions is no "great unsaid" or "unthought" that it would be the task of this method to "articulate or to think at last" (67). Any such unthought or unsaid would by definition imply an instantiation relation, a universal that could not be represented but only instantiated, a further inscription of the distinction between reality, in its unfathomable richness, and mere concepts, the poverty of form. This is also the structure that underpins the ideologies of "tact" and "balance" that organize the aesthetic regime: what I have earlier described as the degree zero of connection. Rather, Foucault's envisaged methodology proceeds on the basis of a principle of "discontinuity": "Discourses must be treated as discontinuous practices, which cross each other, are sometimes juxtaposed with one another, but can just as well exclude or be unaware of each other" (67). In place of the notions inherited and reproduced by traditional practices of scholarship (authorship, expression, consciousness, motivation, causality), Foucault's approach will substitute terms that no longer imply either spatiality or interiority: *event, series, discontinuity, chance, difference.* It is no longer possible, writes Foucault, "to establish links of mechanical causality or of ideal necessity between the elements which constitute them." The challenge becomes to "think the relations between chance and thought" without positing a substantive connection (69). This failure (or abnegation) of theory signals the refusal of all instantiation relations—including, of course, the instantiation relation that would take the form of a *general absence* of an instantiation relation.

If the "discontinuity" asserted in the body of Foucault's text is not a "theory," then what is it? What is its "status," as Foucault puts it? It is not possible to give a straightforward answer to this question, for any answer would amount to gouging a theory out of the absence or impossibility of one. Discontinuity would become, at that moment, a connection, a continuity.

"What status must be given to this discontinuity?" (69). In asking the question, Foucault's essay is perhaps the first attempt to imagine a program or a method that would take place outside the forms of instantiation. This is what Gilles Deleuze means when he acclaims Foucault as a thinker of multiplicity. In Foucault, he says, we encounter "the most decisive step yet taken in the theory-practice of multiplicities."[15] Multiplicity in Deleuze is a principle of resistance to all relations of instantiation. Thus, multiplicity aspires to abjure all conceptuality insofar as concepts allude to something given. There is for Deleuze no multiplicity "in general." Nor is multiplicity a merely dialectical complement to "unity" or the "one." Deleuze's concept of multiplicity derives from Bergson, who distinguishes between a "discrete," spatialized multiplicity (the setting out of objects in a line, which are thereby "externalized" relative to each other) and a pure multiplicity "without quantity" (that is to say, without number)—something like an absolute heterogeneity (*Time and Free Will*, 120–21).

Among the contexts in which multiplicity is liable to be displaced by an instantiated form of itself is temporality. Time, duration, is reconceived as a "homogeneous medium" (123), a divisible whole combined of a succession of separately but simultaneously experienced instants. In the light of Bergson's analysis it becomes apparent that simultaneity, "the intersection of time and space," as Bergson defines it (110), is another chronotopic formation. The same goes for motion. If we try to think of motion "by itself," outside the object that "instantiates" it, as it were, we "extract mobility" from motion (111). The truth—which might have come from the work of David Armstrong as much as from Bergson—is that there is no motion outside mobility, outside the mobile object. Thus, there is no instantiation relation between the universal attribute of motion and the particular object in which it is manifest.

Bergson acknowledges the difficulty of thinking duration or motion in their "original purity" (106). For Bergson we cannot help but think the relations of space and time by dividing up duration into "simultaneities." A simultaneity is a form of measurable time whose measurability depends on its having been already turned into space. A measured second of time, for example, has nothing to do with time considered as duration. What it marks is not duration but only the coincidence of my temporality with yours, with everyone else's. "Duration properly so called has no moments which are identical or external to one another, being essentially heterogeneous, continuous, and with no analogy to number" (120). Like the notion of "pure perception" encountered in the first chapter of Bergson's *Matter and Memory*—"a perception which exists in theory rather than in fact and would be possessed by a being . . . capable . . . of obtaining a vision of matter both immediate and instantaneous"[16]—duration seems to be a hypothetical or speculative entity: something that cannot easily be thought, in its essence, without "finalizing" it (Bakhtin's term), thereby failing to think it. To think outside the chronotope of simultaneity, then, is to think hypothetically. Notions such as pure perception, duration, and multiplicity resist the logic of spatialized time precisely because their proper register is that of speculation. Instantiation relations are affirmed by the invocation or mobilization of the concept *as such*.

On the other hand, duration should not be thought of as noninstantiated time, since for Bergson, no less than for Armstrong, *there is no instantiation relation* except as a "ghost of space haunting the reflective consciousness" (*Time and Free Will*, 99). This is also why Foucault insists on the need to avoid conceptualizing some "vast unlimited discourse, continuous and silent" that is "quelled and repressed" by the rarefying systems that constitute the orders of discourse (Foucault, 67).

A second context in which multiplicity tends to be replaced with an instantiation of itself is subjectivity, in the form of a conception of the individual as an emblem of, or spokesperson for, a universality. Foucault details several themes or motifs in which such a conception takes effect, including that of the "founding subject" and that of "originating experience," ways in which the "reality" of discourse (the chance element) is "elided"—made subject to a generality of which existing discourse is a mere instance (65). With the theme of the founding subject, an individual is attributed the task of "animating the empty forms of language with his [or her] aims" and of grasping "by intuition the meaning lying deposited within" things themselves (65). History is stratified in relation to "horizons of meaning beyond time"; all human activity is conceived in terms of "elucidation." The theme of originating experience, likewise, assumes "a primordial complicity with the world" as the very basis of "our possibility of speaking of it" (65). In speaking, that is to say, we are essentially naming, judging, knowing a world that precedes us *as* experienceable, as potentially significant. Our capacity for experience is only a particular order of the prior capacity of the world to experience itself.

A THEORY OF "DISCONTINUOUS SYSTEMATICITIES"?

The difficulty of deriving critical-practical implications from Foucault's theoretical questions is undeniable. Nevertheless, such implications have begun to be explored in critical discourses that take their lead from what writers of literature are actually doing in their work. In *Born Translated: The Contemporary Novel in an Age of World Literature*, an account of a fundamental transformation in the culture and place of translation in the contemporary literary marketplace, Rebecca Walkowitz identifies two older paradigms in which a relationship of literature to political community is posited in fields such as philosophy, anthropology, and legal theory. Walkowitz calls these "possessive collectivism" (taking the phrase from the work of the anthropologist Richard Handler) and "imagined communities" (after Benedict Anderson's influential work of that name).[17] Walkowitz does not use the term "instantiation," but the structure is apparent in her elaboration of both paradigms. In possessive collectivism, literary works are considered as belonging to the nation "because they are the embodiment of its internal spirit or genius." The logic is tautologous: "we know the nation has a spirit or genius because it has literary works to show for it."[18] Among minorities and colonized subjects, Walkowitz points out, the ideology of possessive collectivism is further reinforced by its role in "validating intellectual labor and justifying political sovereignty" (26).[19] Similarly, in imagined communities, she says, the nation is imagined "as a shared, exclusive collectivity among strangers." Walkowitz comments: "If we can perceive the novel as a container for strangers who act together without knowing it, then we can imagine the nation as a container for us, the readers of that novel, who act together in just the same way—simultaneously. Collectively, and invisibly" (26–27).

Both paradigms, possessive collectivism and imagined community, are versions of what we have earlier described as "social formalism" (Dorothy Hale's term), the "degree zero" of connection. The members of an imagined community, writes Anderson, "can even be described as passing each other on the street, without ever becoming acquainted, and still be connected" (25). The connective logic of this image, of course, is Bakhtin's chronotope. This logic is perfectly able to accommodate chance events, encounters, even nonevents and failed encounters. For both Bakhtin and Anderson it is not necessary that connections are rendered explicit, placed in the mind of an author or character. The substance of the connection is nothing but the possibility of a single viewing position, whether such a position is actually represented in the novel or not: a position from which all that happens *would be* apprehensible, if not comprehensible, and from which time, as a linear succession of countable "simultaneities," is measurable.

Walkowitz's innovation is to posit a historical situation, that of the contemporary Anglophone novel, in which the terms of the two paradigms of "possessive collectivism" and "imagined community" are no longer intact and thus no longer inform novelistic production. The basis of this transformation, however, is social and linguistic, since for Walkowitz the language of the text and that of its readers are no longer the same—not "theoretically" but in actuality. For Walkowitz, there may no longer be an "original language to speak of" (27). This historical situation is informing the appearance of works that are produced already with an eye to their translation. They are "born translated," meaning that translation is not "secondary or incidental" to their production but a "condition" of it (4). Translation has not only entered language but displaced it.

In making this claim, Walkowitz shifts Bakhtin's theoretical intuitions about the heteroglossia (*raznorečie*, literally "multilanguagedness") of the modern European novel in an empirical, i.e., historical direction. "The unity of a literary language," writes Bakhtin, "is not a unity of a single, closed language system, but is rather a highly specific unity of several 'languages' that have established contact and mutual recognition with each other" (*Discourse in the Novel*, 295; quoted in Walkowitz, 24). Bakhtin is talking about the entry of individual dialects into "literary language," at which point they are "deformed and . . . cease to be that which they had been simply as dialects" (294). In Walkowitz's schema, this quality of "multilingualism" operates in the early twenty-first century "at an even greater scale" (24). However, Walkowitz is conceiving heteroglossia not as a *qualitative* dimension of all novelistic language but as a *quantitative* element that pertains, in the first instance, in society, and only secondarily—as a matter of representation—in the novel. Multilingualism is not, for Walkowitz, an absolute quality of novelistic language but a relative, historically evolving one. The decline of the two older paradigms is the basis of the new forms of community that her work sets out to imagine. "Today's born-translated novel," Walkowitz says, "rather than expand belonging, strives to keep belonging in play. It does this," she continues, "by implying that the book we are holding begins in several languages" (25).

No doubt the scalar transformations described in Walkowitz's notion of the "born-translated" novel have taken place. "World-shaped novels feature traveling characters who speak different languages, sometimes within the same national space," argues Walkowitz. "Above all, world-shaped novels explore translation by asking how people, objects, ideas, and even aesthetic styles move across territories, and how that movement alters the meaning and form of collectivity" (122, 123). What happens, however, if we approach the forms of "possessive collectivism" and "imagined community" not, primarily, as configurations of community or identification but as chronotopic formations? Walkowitz provides a rationale for doing so when, early on in *Born Translated*, she suggests that Benedict Anderson's *Imagined Communities* might be read not for its "argument" but as an "example" of world literature. The book's own history of translation and publication, that is to say, is implicated in the constitution of the very "transnational communities" that it subjects to analysis (27–28). "Whereas world literature once referred to a group of 'works,'" comments Walkowitz, "it now refers to a 'network,' a 'system,' a 'republic,' or a 'problem'" (29). It should be clear that the world literary "system" central to the work of critics such as Franco Moretti and Pascale Casanova is a chronotope: an image of connection predicated upon a relation of parts and whole that is implicitly spatiotemporal.[20] As Michael Gardiner summarizes, "the local is linked to the global via the systematic nature of cultural capital, and nations accumulate status, authority and legitimacy via recognition by literary institutions of global reach."[21] The "literary-system" chronotope, as we might call it—like the novelistic chronotopes identified by Bakhtin—is an image of spatiotemporal connection, of time "fus[ing] together" with space.

Chronotopically, however, not much is changed in the proposition of a shift from "nation-shaped" novels to "world-shaped" ones. In both formations, certain connective (chronotopic) structures survive: the principle of *identity* (as implied in the figure of the literary work as the "container" for such identities) and what Erich Auerbach called a "horizontal," that is, "temporal and causal" structure of chronological relation (on which the legibility of themes and narratives such as migration and undocumented labor, humanitarian aid, and the ties between international finance and art depends).[22] In such a shift, the dimensions of the instantiation relation are enlarged, but the relation itself, the categories it presupposes, are the same. Walkowitz draws on an essay by Mariano Siskind to argue for a "double logic of parity and expressivity" in the born-translated novel:

> Parity . . . implies that world literature is a container for different but equivalent traditions. Expressivity has meant that each tradition is imagined to possess specific characteristics that can be communicated and preserved through literary works. Imagining other kinds of containers and other kinds of objects, born-translated novels generate histories of literary production rooted in target rather than source. . . . Emphasizing target . . . becomes a way to reject the principle of diffusion, in which literature begins in one place, typically Europe, and then moves out to other places. Instead of diffusion, these works introduce rival chronologies that place translation at the source of literary history.[23]
>
> (122)

As defined here, "parity" and "expressivity" simply rename the connective principles of simultaneity and identity. Their ideological forms are, respectively, the concept of succession and the "founding subject." Walkowitz's attempt thereby to understand the forms of identification that might cohere on the basis of the absence of an original language, to position the "born-translated" novel as a form that convokes a sense of belonging from the "primacy of translation," and even the introduction of "other kinds of containers" and "rival chronologies" to acknowledge the scalar transformations under way in contemporary writing illustrate the difficulty of construing a theoretical basis for critical analysis that does not at every moment recapitulate the logic of instantiation.

In "The Order of Discourse," his most direct attempt to grapple with the persistence of this logic, Foucault refers to "the smallest units that were traditionally recognized and which are the hardest to contest: the instant and the subject" (69). The audacity and wager of Foucault's thought is to imagine that the instantiation relation as the basis of scholarly analysis might be dispensed with and that such a task must begin by disputing the unity of those supposedly most fundamental entities. For Foucault, "it is . . . not a matter of the *succession* of instants in time, nor of the *plurality* of different thinking subjects. It is a question of caesurae which *break up the instant* and *disperse the subject* into a plurality of possible positions and functions" (69). "Beneath" and "independently" of such notions, he writes further, "we must conceive relations . . . which are not of the order of succession (or simultaneity) within one (or several) consciousnesses; we must elaborate—outside of the philosophies of the subject and of time—a theory of discontinuous systematicities" (69). But what might this look like? A theory that attempted to remain true to the principle of discontinuous systematicities would no longer take for granted the validity of explanatory codes and concepts that—like all explanatory procedures—presuppose subjectivities, ideologies, authors and authorial projects, and sociological and demographic categories that originate outside discourse. A *theory* of "discontinuous systematicities" would seem, therefore, to be a contradiction in terms.

What is behind the need for such a theory, as articulated half a century ago? And what has happened to this project since Foucault's own writing and thinking came to an end? Was it abandoned with the demise of Foucault himself? That is to say, is it an idiosyncratic, merely "subjective"

project, or was Foucault responding to certain historical forces and challenges that had and continue to have their own trajectory? What, indeed,
is the relationship between the historicity of such challenges and the critical subjectivities that apprehend and make sense of them? Is anything to
be gained by conceiving of those projects in creative terms, as Foucault
seems to have done, rather than representational ones?[24] What, in fact, are
the current prospects for Foucault's vision of a theory of "discontinuous
systematicities"?

One of the premises of this book is that Foucault's imperative of a theory of discontinuous systematicities might be thought of not as a merely
theoretical or speculative provocation but as a historical development. The
most likely domain for the emergence of such a theory, however, is not the
work of theorists and scholars of literature but the mode of contemporary
novelistic production that I have been calling postfiction. Furthermore, the
nature of this emergence is not primarily formal or representational but
takes place at the limits of what the work's formal and discursive elements
are able to register. That is to say that it is difficult, if not impossible, to
improve upon contemporary novelistic practices in coming up with a way
of "systematizing" discontinuity. To the extent that the present work
remains within the theoretical register, it too falls short of grasping the
thought of which contemporary fiction is capable or of understanding the
full implications of the postfictional formation.

Postfiction is not, strictly speaking, a new literary form or genre. Postfiction is not simply a development in the novel (although it is that), nor is
it a proposition that predominantly impacts literary criticism—implying,
say, a "noninterpretive" method of reading—although there are implications for critical practice that are explored in this book. Postfiction
denotes, rather, the collapse of an ideological structure, one that has, until
recently, organized the production and reception of literature (and many
other activities besides). We see that structure operating in such normative
definitions of the novel as the following:

> Narratives are about human beings, the ideals and norms that guide their
> lives, the passions that drive them, and the action they take. Since charac-
> ters and their ideals form the true, living center of narrative genres, novels
> propose substantial hypotheses about human life and imagine fictional
> worlds governed by them. These hypotheses describe distinct human types,

their relation to ideals, their patterns of behavior, and their links to the community in which they live. The novel ponders the meaning of life and of human interactions, just as epic and tragedy did before it. . . . Novels portray individuals in different ways, as strong souls, sensitive hearts, or enigmatic psyches.[25]

What is being described here is nothing more or less than a fabric of connectivity. In the various connecting words and phrases in this passage (the word "about" in the phrase "Narratives are about human beings," the claim that novels propose substantial hypotheses and that those hypotheses describe distinct human types, or that the novel ponders the meaning of life)—in these formulations, the logic of instantiation as the governing logic of the novel is sustained but also normativized, obscured from view. Under the guise of saying almost nothing, Thomas Pavel here establishes the permanence of the most fundamental of all aesthetic ideologies: the instantiation relation.

I have earlier referred to this logic as a "degree zero" of connection. What is denoted in those nouns and the connecting verbs that accompany them (*are about* human beings, *propose* substantial hypotheses, *imagine* fictional worlds, *describe* human types, *ponders* the meaning of life, etc.) is in each case a very complicated relation. Its ideological quality consists in its relative invisibility, its "degree-zero" quality. Its force is to be found precisely in its "obviousness," for who could possibly object on ideological grounds to a logic of "connection"? Isn't this the basis of everything we do as critics and thinkers? Certainly, to develop a mode of critical analysis that did not participate in that logic would be challenging, to say the least.

But my aim is not merely to analyze the logic of instantiation—the ideological basis of all contemporary critical discourses—but to show how a strain of contemporary writing locates itself (its own thought) *in the interstices of* the relations that seem to be presupposed by those words and phrases. Such writing does not, in other words, accept the instantiation relation (the relation of "fiction") as a given but opens up gaps and spaces *within* the apparent unities denoted by such phrases as "human beings," "human types," "substantial hypotheses," "fictional worlds," or "the meaning of life." It's that new situatedness that we may provisionally call "postfiction."

Postfiction, then, is less a genre than a logic—one that is radically at odds with the logic of instantiation—and the forms of its manifestation are not limited to novels. The term applies to films, artworks, and critical and philosophical writing as much as to works of literature. Nevertheless, it is contemporary novelistic production that enables us to think most immediately the existence of this logic, a logic that, I will argue, is immanent to the form of the novel and as necessary to it as the logic of instantiation. Postfiction is a name for work—of whatever genre—that helps us to think (and thus think outside) the logic of instantiation.

After all, even "fiction" is a term from criticism; it has never been especially important to writers of literature. Postfiction is best conceived as a continuation of the historical trajectory of the novel, not a break with it. Postfiction is a means of preserving or recovering the notion of literature as a mode of thought that is not reducible to the language of ideology or the language of interests. Literature thinks, but that capacity to think has nothing to do with the representation of thoughts.

Postfiction, then, is as much an evolution in modes of *critical reading* as it is a development of the novel. It is a principle that detaches the thought of the work from that which is instantiated in the work, and it does so by reconfiguring what is meant by thought itself. That reconfiguration happens by close attention to the nature of *the thought that the work makes possible*. And what postfiction makes possible, I will argue, is a nonanchored, nonsubjective thought, a *thought without perspective*, which is also to say, without a communicative function. Postfictional thought is located not positively, in any element instantiated in the work, but in the work's interstices. Postfiction is a distinct mode of connection no longer predicated on representation or the "degree-zero" links of instantiation but on their dissolution.

IS DISCONNECTION ALSO A CHRONOTOPE?

A change, then, in the connective infrastructure of the novel has been taking place. However, the nature of that change is not best grasped as a matter of scale or as a historical or spatial extension of a logic that was already in place but, rather, as a break with all logics of typicality, comparison, motivation, and character. One effect of the break is that *its own historical status becomes indeterminate.* Thus, it is impossible to say that the break happened at a particular historical juncture—say, in the period since Benedict Anderson wrote *Imagined Communities*—or that the paradigm it introduces chronologically succeeds those of fiction, the novel, or the nation. Perhaps, rather, the break happened long ago. Perhaps, still more radically, it was already implicit in the change that Anderson's work describes so precisely.

The most significant innovation of *Imagined Communities* was not its analysis of the nation as an imagined form but its presentation of the modes of connection in works of fiction in terms of instantiation rather than representation. Like Bakhtin, Anderson understood that the modes of linkage in fictional works do not depend for their legitimacy on being thinkable or representable in the consciousness of the writing subject herself. For Anderson, the unstatable quality of novelistic connection is underwritten by the structure of simultaneity that functions as a degree-zero order of connection. Time ("a complex gloss upon the word 'meanwhile'"), allied with space ("a fixity that fuses the world inside the novel with the world outside") steps in to supply a sensorimotor continuity in the absence of a personal or ideational one (25, 30). Bakhtin's work brings this out still more clearly. For once we understand the fabric of novelistic connection as chronotopic—Bakhtin's great achievement in "Forms of Time and of the Chronotope"—it becomes possible to understand the limits of the chronotope, which is also to say, *the fact of the chronotope as a limit.* Modes of connection predicated precisely on that limit become, for the first time, conceivable.

The thinker who has most directly conceptualized the fact of a limit to chronotopic thinking and thus the possibility of an outside to the chronotope or the emergence of nonchronotopic forms of thought is Gilles Deleuze. For Deleuze, space-time is itself a limit, one that constitutes "all the disciplines that define themselves through creative activity," including "science," "philosophy," and "filmmaking."[26] Whether through the invention of "functions" (in the case of science), "concepts" (in the case of philosophy), or "blocks of duration/movement" (in the case of cinema), such disciplines communicate "at the level of something that never emerges for its own sake, but is engaged in every creative discipline: the formation of space-times."

Deleuze, however, is particularly interested in one exception to this pattern: the work of the French filmmaker Robert Bresson. In Bresson's films, writes Deleuze,

there are seldom complete spaces. They are spaces we could call disconnected. For example, there is a corner, the corner of a cell. Then we see
another corner or part of the wall. Everything takes place as if Bressonian space was made up of a series of little pieces with no predetermined
connection. . . . Bresson was one of the first to make space with little disconnected pieces, little pieces with no predetermined connection. . . . At
the limit of all of these attempts at creation are space-times. Only space-
times. Bresson's blocks of duration/movement will tend towards this type
of space among others.

(315)

For Deleuze, the question of a limit to space-times is not a question of the
disappearance of connections as such but of the emergence of new linkages
outside the "predetermined" connections of character, plot, and theme. In
films such as Bresson's *The Trial of Joan of Arc* and *Pickpocket*, the principle of connection is "the hand": a cinematographic image. "This is not theory or philosophy," says Deleuze.

It cannot be deduced like that. . . . Bresson's type of space gives cinematographic value to the hand in the image. The links between the little bits of
Bressonian space—due to the very fact that they are bits, disconnected pieces
of space—can only be done manually. . . . Only the hand can effectively make
connections between one part of space and another.

(315–16)

The logic of this claim could be illustrated by the many shots in *The Trial
of Joan of Arc* in which hands, isolated from the bodies they belong to, convey signals, deliver food and drink to Joan in her cell, rise together in
prayer, open and close doors, inscribe mysterious and inaccessible verdicts
on paper, or, finally, carry torches to ignite the fire beneath Joan's bound
body or twist in agony behind her back as she is engulfed by the flames. The
value of the hand in Bresson is "cinematographic"—not, then, philosophical, ethical, cognitive, financial, or in any other way fungible. By "cinematographic," Deleuze means precisely that the hand is *not* translatable. The
image of the hand is a mode of thought, but one predicated upon disconnection rather than connection, exteriority rather than interiority, the event
rather than interpretation. For Deleuze there is no thought *in general*. An

FIGURE 5.1. *Procès de Jeanne d'Arc*, dir. Robert Bresson, Agnes Delahaie Productions, 1962.

FIGURE 5.2. *Procès de Jeanne d'Arc*, dir. Robert Bresson, Agnes Delahaie Productions, 1962.

FIGURE 5.3. *Procès de Jeanne d'Arc*, dir. Robert Bresson, Agnes Delahaie Productions, 1962.

FIGURE 5.4. *Procès de Jeanne d'Arc*, dir. Robert Bresson, Agnes Delahaie Productions, 1962.

idea is always rooted in a particular practice: painting, the novel, philosophy, or cinema. Ideas are creative; they are not subjective entities, and so philosophy is not privileged over any other activity as a mode of thought. One does not need philosophy to think (313). Indeed, philosophy is not a discipline devoted to thinking; it's a discipline that is involved in a particular *practice*: the creation or invention of concepts. Philosophy is not a category devoted to understanding all the other practices; it's a practice with its own procedure and rationale.

If the hand, as an image of disconnection in Bresson's films, resists immediate recombination as a connection, it is because what is disconnected in Bresson's cinema is, precisely, connection itself. What Deleuze calls the sensorimotor "collapse" in modern cinema appears to signal nothing less than the dismantling of the chronotope.[27]

What Deleuze says about hands in Bresson recalls what Bakhtin says about "the new modes of linkage" signaled by Dostoevsky's works. Repeating an observation by the Russian critic Vasily Komarovich, Bakhtin notes that Dostoevsky's works are held together *not* by some principle of "unity" but by what Komarovich calls "chunks of reality" ripped out of "the normal and predictable chain of the real" and transferred to "Dostoevsky himself" or to his protagonists:

> The monologic unity of the world is [hence] destroyed in a Dostoevsky novel, but those ripped off pieces of reality are in no sense directly combined in the unity of the novel: each of these pieces gravitates toward the integral field of vision of a specific character; each makes sense only at the level of a specific consciousness. If these chunks of reality, deprived of any pragmatic links, were combined directly as things emotionally, lyrically, or symbolically harmonious in the unity of a single and monologic field of vision, then before us would be the world of the Romantic, the world of Hoffman, for example, but in no way could it be Dostoevsky's world.
> (*PROBLEMS*, 20–21)

The unity of Dostoevsky's works can never be found internalized in any such "chunk of reality"—in a particular idea put forward by a character, say—since in Dostoevsky no idea is ever present in the separate or disembodied form that would enable it to become a principle of authorial representation. No idea in Dostoevsky is ever endorsed by the work; no idea is "true or untrue" (93) because no idea in Dostoevsky is anything but an object of representation (23), an entity that is tied to a specific point of view within the novel. As a principle of connection, ideas in Dostoevsky are therefore exterior—as exterior as the hands in Bresson's *The Trial of Joan of Arc*. They signal coexistence in space rather than evolution toward an "ultimate whole" or "systemic unity" (*Problems*, 93). For Bakhtin, "not a single element of [Dostoevsky's works] is structured from the point of view of a nonparticipating 'third person.' In the novel itself, nonparticipating 'third persons' are not represented in any way. There is no place for them, compositionally or in the larger meaning of the work. And this is not a weakness of the author but his greatest strength" (18).

Two authors may briefly be examined here to illustrate how Deleuze's principle of "disconnected" spaces might be extended to contemporary writing: the Scottish novelist James Kelman and the French winner of the 2014 Nobel Prize for Literature, Patrick Modiano.

The Limits of the Chronotope: James Kelman

Kelman's writing is one of the most consistent contemporary realizations of the principle of "exteriority" that Bakhtin locates in Dostoevsky's work, in which the *coexistence* and *interaction* of elements and ideas are emphasized over, say, the evolution of an idea within a narrative of a character's psychological development (*Problems*, 28). Almost any work of Kelman's might be used to make this case.

Take, for example, the 1994 novel *How late it was, how late*. Sammy Samuels, an unemployed construction worker, is the novel's protagonist and its almost exclusive site of focalization. At the beginning of the novel, Sammy, who has been arrested and beaten by the police, wakes up newly blind in a police station cell. His blindness will persist for the course of the novel and will thus define all his thoughts and perceptions through its remaining 350 pages—which means that every "chunk of reality" is framed and formed by Sammy's blindness. Not a single visual entity appears in the third-person narrative other than as imagined or remembered by Sammy himself. Yet not even this most indisputable and central aspect of Sammy's reality is given any third-person confirmation. The very category of blindness belongs to Sammy; it is never used objectively or disembodiedly: "So that was him. Blind. He was blind. Okay. Blind. That was that. Ye know. Okay. There ye are. So be it. So fucking be it" (56). Even to call *How late it was, how late* a story about a "blind" man is to introduce a category of understanding to Kelman's text that is only present in the text as an "object of representation." As Ally, another character puts it, "Naybody can jump inside yer head and take a look and go: Alright, the guy's blind, that's it over and out, beyond dispute. . . . They cannay do that" (235). Such difficulties are among the many quandaries caused for criticism by Kelman's work.

Following the same logic, the possible *causes* of Sammy's blindness remain unconfirmed, indeed unaddressed, at the level of the text. When Sammy attends an interview to assess his eligibility for disability benefit, a cause is both asserted and resisted. Sammy has told a preliminary officer that the police "gave [him] a doing" (103), yet he won't press a compensation claim against the police. His entitlement to benefits is dependent upon "a cause that is available to verification"; however, Sammy reasons that, since the police did not "intend" to take his sight, any such cause is mere speculation. "I mean if they went at me with a blade and then dug out my eyes then I'd be straight in for compensation, know what I mean" (104, 105). The chunk of reality that is operating connectively here is not the question of causation or even the philosophical dilemma raised by the indeterminacy of the origins of Sammy's blindness. It is nothing other than the succession of statements: Sammy's application for benefits alongside his refusal to apply for compensation, Sammy's sense of a legitimate grievance alongside his refusal to acknowledge it or to pursue the legal channels open to him. There is no reconciliation of the two sets of statements in the text; there are no conclusions drawn, no "connection" made that would constitute their reconciliation. This is not to say that there is no connection to be made, only that none *is* made. The difference in Sammy's two statements is not an empirical difference between, for example, ideological perspectives or between militant personality traits and submissive ones. It is rather what Deleuze calls an "absolute and ultimate Difference"—a difference "at the heart of a subject," a difference *internal* to each sign or entity that prohibits any connection between them.[28] This failure of connection is also the interruption of a conventional chronotopic formation.

In "Kelman and World English," Michael Gardiner addresses the question of whether Kelman is legible as a writer of "world literature"—the question, that is, of whether his work is comprehensible according to the "literary-system" chronotope, the system delimited at one end by the "core" and at the other by the "periphery" or, as Moretti puts it, by a triumvirate of "foreign form," "local material," and "local form."[29] To read Kelman as such, contends Gardiner, is to "individuate and ethnicise" his writing (100) in ways that, we might say, the work resists by installing a pure or "absolute" difference in place of a merely empirical difference between preconstituted identities. "The impulse of core culture," says Gardiner, "will always be to make peripheral writing *visible* and therefore easier to place; it will want to see the world's literary Englishes as non-comparable, specific and ethnic, and even, as refusing English altogether" (101). Kelman's use of vernacular Glaswegian dialect makes him susceptible to such readings, yet those readings fail to acknowledge the central quality of his work: the absence of "perspective." Kelman's "unwillingness to 'perspectivise' narration," comments Gardiner, "makes difficult the packaging of ethnic difference for global literary markets, in which there is a constant, core-driven demand for vernacular" (102).[30]

Is such a development—replacing a chronotopic continuity over time with a discontinuity in space—truly a "break" with the chronotope, or is it, on the contrary, an experience of the *limits* of the chronotope, an experience that—like all our experiences as soon as they become narratable—is itself chronotopic? The same question might be asked of the figure of the bridge at the beginning of Coetzee's *Elizabeth Costello*. Does such an explicitly figurative image also function chronotopically, like the classic chronotope of the road, or does it, on the contrary, dismantle the chronotopic connections between space and time, for example, by extending the qualities of free indirect discourse potentially to all discourse?

The most compelling answer is provided in the final pages of Bakhtin's essay, where, in a discussion that is over almost before it is begun, Bakhtin makes reference to a "special semantic sphere" that "exceeds the bounds" of his study. This sphere is that of the figure already mentioned who exists at the limits of the chronotope: the author. Not the *image* of the author but the author-creator *himself*, the figure who, in his "unresolved and still evolving contemporaneity," remains chronotopically heterogeneous to the world represented in his work. It is at the threshold of this "special semantic sphere," perhaps, that we should situate the principle of coexistence in Dostoevsky's writings, as well as in these works by Kelman and Coetzee. In an enigmatic moment in his essay, Bakhtin refers to this special sphere as "purely chronotopic" (256). If we accept this designation, then disconnection—by which I mean, now, modes of linkage that take place outside the "predetermined" forms of "authorship," commentary, disciplines, etc.—would be not a break with, or a collapse of, chronotopic regimes of thought but the perfection of the chronotope. At the borders of the chronotope, then, we encounter not the birth of *non*chronotopic thought but the sphere of the "purely chronotopic," a new mode of connection in real space-time and a form of simultaneity that succeeds—in the sense of *coexisting with*—the "homogeneous, empty time" of modernity and of the realist novel.

The Pure Chronotope: Patrick Modiano

A final illustration will, I hope, bring out the nature of the pure chronotope even more clearly. Patrick Modiano's novel *Dora Bruder*, published in 1997, tells the story of a failed attempt to discover the fate of Dora Bruder, a fifteen-year-old girl who disappeared in Paris in 1942, from the point of view of a narrator who never registers any separation between himself and Modiano, the book's author.

Dora Bruder, a novel about a nonencounter that transpires not on a road but over a period of fifty years, might initially be thought to be a classic chronotopic work. Modiano's narrator, observes Michael Wood, reviewing the novel shortly after the publication of the English translation,

> registers lapses of time, situates himself at meticulously specified distances from a series of past moments: eighteen years ago, ten years after that, six years earlier than that. He is remembering whole patches of the past, but what he really can't forget is the barren present, the year on the current calendar. Time is not regained, it is segmented and catalogued, remembered as lost, the very precision of the memory a form of alienation.[31]

The narrator fastens onto certain hypotheses concerning Dora Bruder's fate that are not substantiated and that would not have explanatory value even if they were. Was the girl whom Modiano's father remembers as a fellow detainee in the police van on the night he was arrested in February 1942 Dora Bruder? The dates match, but the idea is present in the book only as a speculation.[32] What was the weather like on the day, December 14, 1941, that Dora escaped from the Saint-Coeur-de-Marie boarding school where she had been living since May 1940? How did the school's mother superior let her parents know that she was missing? By telephone, waiting until the Monday morning after her disappearance, or immediately, by sending a nun to her parents' residence? How did Dora survive the four months until, police records show, she "regained the maternal domicile" in April 1942? (73). Why did she run away a second time? (84). What were the circumstances in which she was arrested and sent to the Tourelles internment center before being transferred to the camp at Drancy on August 13 and, on September 18, put on a convoy for Auschwitz? Was her mother Cécile, a Hungarian Jew who was not arrested until January 1943, able to visit her daughter at Tourelles that summer? (118). Could the dealer in secondhand goods whom Modiano remembers meeting twenty-three years later (long before he knew of the existence of Dora Bruder), a man who would have been eighteen at the time of the occupation of Paris and who lived near the Porte de Clignancourt—the same neighborhood as Dora Bruder—could that man have met her, known her story? Such questions remain unanswered, unanswerable.

Within the body of his text Modiano makes explicit the chronotopic principle of the work, its rule of connection: "I feel as though I am alone in making the link between Paris then and Paris now, alone in remembering all these details. There are moments when the link is strained and in danger of snapping, and other evenings when the city of yesterday appears to me in floating gleams behind that of today" (41). There is nothing ordained in the connections Modiano is making, nothing but happenstance, the existence of "flukes, encounters, coincidences" (112). The "chunks of reality" that hold the work together are simply the succession of remembered, uncovered, or imagined events: the likelihood that Dora Bruder used the métro station at Simplon, *alongside* Modiano's own frequent use of the same station twenty years later (37); the significance of the adjacent Rue de Picpus and the Saint-Coeur-de-Marie boarding school to Dora Bruder's story, *alongside* the setting of an episode just a few streets away in Modiano's 1990 novel *Voyage de noces*, written while Modiano was preoccupied with Dora Bruder's story; the publication, with Gallimard, of a first novel by one Albert Schaky—a man who had once resided in the same apartment in which Modiano later lived with his father—in 1938 at the age of twenty-one, *alongside* the publication of Modiano's first novel with the same press, and at the same age, exactly thirty years later (81–82); the title of that first novel by Modiano, *La place de l'Étoile, alongside* the prior publication, in 1945, of an identically titled novel by Robert Desnos, who by then had died in the camp at Terezin (83)—a work unknown to Modiano until shortly after the publication of his own book.

Like the hand in Robert Bresson or the succession of Sammy's thoughts and statements in *How late it was, how late*, these chunks of reality exist in a relation of pure exteriority to one another. No concept or explanatory apparatus connects them other than the figure of Modiano himself (the site of connection) and the words "coincidence" and "clairvoyance" (*voyance*) that he introduces into the narrative (42), but such words explain nothing. Like the word "blind" in Kelman's novel, they never ascend from the status of "object of representation" to become a "principle of representation."[33]

What Bakhtin calls the "purely chronotopic" is defined by the absence of such unifying principles from the work, the possibility that a work might be composed precisely out of that absence, the appearance of such principles only as objects of representation. In *Dora Bruder*—indeed, in his entire body of work—Patrick Modiano has discovered that a work can take shape around broken connections and subjective, unverifiable speculations. By these means, and *pace* Michael Wood, time *is* regained in Modiano, in the strictly Proustian sense laid out in the last volume of the *Recherche*: not, Proust says, as an exercise of contemplating "a past made arid by the intellect" or "a future which the will constructs with fragments of the present and the past" (although such struggles and reflections certainly take place in Modiano) but as an experience outside all represented time, an experience of "extra-temporal[ity]."[34] According to Proust's narrator, time is regained not by forging connections with the past but in the absence of such connections:

> I noticed cursorily that the differences which existed between every one of our real impressions—differences which explain why a uniform depiction of life cannot bear much resemblance to the reality—derive probably from the following cause: the slightest word that we have said, the most insignificant action that we have performed at any one epoch of our life was surrounded by, and coloured by the reflexion of, things *which logically had no connexion with it* and which later have been separated from it by our intellect which could make nothing of them for its own rational purposes, things, however, in the midst of which . . . the simplest act or gesture remains

immured as within a thousand sealed vessels, each one of them filled with things of a colour, a scent, a temperature that are absolutely different one from another, vessels, moreover, which being disposed over the whole range of our years . . . are situated at the most various moral altitudes and give us the sensation of extraordinarily diverse atmospheres.

(220–21)

The very condition for such experiences is the unavailability or the disappearance of connections based on "logical reasoning" or "the life of the mind" (223):

If, owing to the work of oblivion, the returning memory can throw no bridge, form no connecting link between itself and the present minute, if it remains in the context of its own place and date, if it keeps its distance, its isolation in the hollow of a valley or upon the highest peak of a mountain summit, for this very reason it causes us suddenly to breathe a new air, an air which is new precisely because we have breathed it in the past.

(221–22)

The chronotopic principle described in these passages is not calendrical time, or what Bakhtin calls "represented time." It has nothing to do with the incantation of dates in *Dora Bruder*, as ventriloquized by Wood— "eighteen years ago, ten years after that, six years earlier than that" (Wood, 30)—and everything to do with the *pure* chronotopicity of "represent*ing* time," a time in which the author him- or herself "moves freely" (Bakhtin, 255). Such moments, says Proust's narrator, may be described as "a fragment of time in the pure state" (224), for time is no longer subordinated to movements in space; rather, we are "freed from the order of time" (224). It is at the borders of the chronotope, therefore, that time is "regained" in *Dora Bruder*: at the borders of narrative, character, plot, and representation; at the borders, that is to say, of fiction itself.

Bakhtin devotes only a few fascinating paragraphs at the end of his essay to the sphere of the "purely chronotopic." The fullest implications of this proposition will be developed only much later, in an exploration of a different aesthetic form by a thinker who makes few overt references to Bakhtin in his work and who never—at least in print—uses the term "chronotope." That thinker is Gilles Deleuze, and the exploration in question takes place in the two volumes on cinema that Deleuze published in 1983 and 1985 respectively.[35] The concept of the "time-image" outlined in those books suggests not merely an analogy with Bakhtin's notion of the "pure chronotope" but that cinema itself, in its most radical development, comes into being as a philosophical exposition of Bakhtin's hypothesis. To read Deleuze in this way is not, therefore, simply to extend his work on cinema to the form of the novel nor to suggest that recent tendencies in novelistic practice are an effect of the influence of cinema. It is, rather, to return Deleuze's work on cinema *to its origins in the novel* and to suggest that contemporary fiction reveals a truth about, or a potentiality to, the novel that is inherent in the form itself.

It is toward Deleuze, therefore, and specifically to his work on cinema, that the inquiry into the contemporary forms and possibilities of novelistic aesthetics must turn.

FICTIONAL DISCOURSE AS EVENT

On Jesse Ball

The unfortunate implication of the central argument of this book—that the thought of the novel escapes the instantiation relation—is that any textual example falls short of its realization to the very degree that it may be invoked in support of it. However, this is the predicament of all works of theory (Roland Barthes speaks thus of theory's "blackmail"),[1] and it will not have failed to be noticed how gingerly I have been treading around the question of exemplarity. Of course, we cannot do without examples, and this is undeniably a work of theory, even as it insists that its object of study is beyond its grasp—that the novel's thought is impervious to the theoretical register. There comes a time, in the interstices perhaps, when midday passes for midnight and one must simply say what one means.

A 2014 work by the American novelist Jesse Ball, *Silence Once Begun*, can be located between two figures, the speaking subject and the work's silence— what Jacques Rancière calls the "mute speech" of literature.[2] A plot summary might read as follows: in a bar in Sakai, Japan, in October 1977 a twenty-nine-year-old man named Oda Sotatsu signs a written confession for a crime he did not commit—the murder of eleven elderly citizens who have disappeared, presumed killed, from the villages around Sakai—after Sotatsu loses a wager to an acquaintance named Sato Kakuzo and Kakuzo's girlfriend Jito Joo. The girlfriend gives Sotatsu's confession to the police, and the next morning Sotatsu is arrested. He refuses to cooperate with the authorities; to explain, confirm, or deny the supposed confession; to provide any details about his supposed crimes; to speak to a lawyer; or respond to remonstrations from his own family to retract the confession. After weeks of silence he is tried for the multiple murders. At his trial, Sotatsu does not address "the facts of the indictment"; he says that "while aware" of the case against him, he "can neither admit nor deny it" but that he "holds to the confession that he has signed, as he signed it."[3] Sotatsu is convicted; he does not appeal the verdict and is sentenced to death by hanging. A week after his execution, a procession appears in the streets of Sakai consisting of the eleven missing elderly men and women. They are led by a young man, the aforementioned Kakuzo, who from the steps of the city courthouse denounces both Sotatsu's conviction and a society that would execute a man on the basis of such "imaginary documents" as a confession (215).

Such are the events that are revealed to have happened in the course of the novel. However, they are hardly the events *of* the novel, for *Silence Once Begun* takes place in the mathematically minimal opening that, as Rancière says, is less a space than a line: "the straight line of the story and the 'literary' silences said to interrupt it" (*Mute Speech*, 123). Ball's novel comprises an introductory narrative and a number of documentary materials arising out of the case and assembled, thirty years later, by a writer named Jesse Ball, who, according to a short "Prefatory" section (signed "Jesse Ball, Chicago, 2012"), became interested in Sotatsu's story for personal reasons and traveled to Sakai in search of information about the case. Jesse Ball lays out the story with a minimum of artifice, presenting his findings in the form of transcriptions of police interrogations of Sotatsu, texts of contemporary newspaper reports, records of the narrator's interviews with Sotatsu's family members and other principals in the case (including Kakuzo and Jito Joo), framing commentaries on the material, and a few narrative interruptions, mostly containing details of a "factual" nature. The various angles presented on the case, such as the accounts of Sotatsu's personality by different family members, are frequently conflicting, and no explanation for Sotatsu's behavior is arrived at until the last third of the book, when Jesse Ball tracks down Jito Joo and, finally, Sato Kakuzo, the pair who, as a couple, persuaded Sotatsu to sign the confession and subsequently maintain his silence.

Like the earlier sections of Ball's book, the last third consists solely of purported documentary material: records of personal meetings with, and writings supplied by, Joo and Kakuzo. Most significantly, the two accounts of the case by Joo and Kakuzo are contradictory and irreconcilable. Irreconcilable, that is, as long as we attempt to hold on to an ideology of the unity of thoughts, desires, and motivations, as long as we attempt to achieve a "grammatical concatenation" of perspectives. Joo's story is provided in a letter to Jesse Ball, which is transcribed in full (179–96). The letter, the one passage of identifiably literary writing in the book, tells of Joo's growing love for Sotatsu as she continued to visit him in jail, a love she compares to "a gigantic train" that "carries everything" to Sotatsu that he needs and that is "more real than the world that surrounds it"; more real than the time she spends with Kakuzo, with whom she continues to live and sleep (185); and more real, by implication, than the life of freedom Sotatsu might attain by responding to his police interrogators or telling his story in court. Joo relates a vivid literary image that she used to console Sotatsu and reconcile him to his situation, a line of trees on the horizon that "moves within itself, its own length" (186), which they are about to enter together and that has nothing to do with anyone else:

> We are a prisoner and his love. For I am sometimes one and sometimes the other. You are one and then the other. We are diving in the thin and wild air, as if the spring has just begun. We are diving but we are composing the water beneath us with our dreams, and what I see gives me hope. I will return to you, my dear, and I will return to you and return to you and return to you. You will be mine and no one else's, and I will be the same. I will turn my face away, and look at you when I am elsewhere. I will look only at you.
> (187)

The final section of *Silence Once Begun* comprises a brief interview with Kakuzo and a number of documents supplied to Jesse Ball by Kakuzo. These documents describe an elaborate plan by Kakuzo to "overload" and thus "destroy" the idea of confession by inventing a crime that will not take place but that will nevertheless be punished (219). We are provided with Kakuzo's "blueprint" for the scheme (called the "Narito Disappearances") (212), an account of Kakuzo's theory of the "innate duplicity" of confession that underlies it (215–17, 219), and the conditions for implementing the plan successfully, which include the involvement of either "an unbreakable person (dedicated to the cause and understanding it thoroughly)" or "a person who will prove unbreakable based upon arbitrary reasons, reasons of peculiarity, i.e., an eccentric" (212). Kakuzo, a man with "an immense force of personality" (200), persuades a selection of "old people with odd views" to collaborate in staging their disappearance by relocating to a farm outside Sakai, leaving behind their possessions and property. Jito Joo is persuaded to participate by means of a wager (which Kakuzo wins by cheating) in which the loser will have to obey the other for the duration of a "project." "And from then on," Kakuzo tells us, "I had Jito Joo's complete obedience in all matters related to the Narito Disappearances" (221–22). After Sotatsu's arrest, Joo "fell into the role" of seducing Sotatsu "like an actress"—so much so that Kakuzo "didn't even have to tell her to go" to visit him. "She would just go on her own. I would wake her up and she would be gone" (227).

The questions raised by the discrepancies between Kakuzo's and Joo's narratives all involve Joo's motivations. Is she acting out of love for Sotatsu or from a prodigious (personal or political) commitment to Kakuzo's project? Is she an "unbreakable" person because she is "dedicated to the cause and understand[s] it thoroughly" or for reasons of "peculiarity" and "eccentricity" (i.e., because she loves Sotatsu)? Does Joo herself know which is the correct explanation? Is the narrative of her letter in earnest or a testament to the power of self-delusion? A mark of "unbreakability" or a symptom of "eccentricity"?

For Kakuzo, such questions are inconsequential. After all, he believes and is setting out to prove that, as he puts it in his manifesto, "we as humans believe we see things we do not see," that "we will stake our lives and reputations on the above," that "we as humans believe we have done things we have not," and that "we will stake our lives and reputations on that, too" (215–16). In other words, that the concepts of *love, self-belief, nobility of intentions*, and—given the nature of the language in Joo's letter—*literature*, like all subjective categories, are "innate[ly]" deceptive. The difference between the authenticity of Joo's love for Sotatsu and her manipulation of him for political ends is a subjective distinction that will not survive the successful realization of Kakuzo's project.

In fact, we should say *does* not survive it. Kakuzo's project is the staging of a crime—hence, a fiction. But the fiction is Jesse Ball's as much as it is

Kakuzo's; the project is Jesse Ball's to precisely the same degree that it is Kakuzo's. The successful realization of the Narito Disappearances is therefore the successful realization of *Silence Once Begun*. What makes Jesse Ball's novel a work that thinks (and thinks outside) the logic of instantiation, that thus approaches the possibility of a thought that is resistant to critical explication and elaboration, is not only what it calls into question (certain categories of thought: *motivation, pretense, delusion, confession, literature* itself) but the means by which it does so: the production of fictional discourse as an event.

PART III
The Free Indirect

Chapter Six

HOW DOES IMMANENCE SHOW ITSELF?

THE SENSE OF SENSE

The coming into existence of an artistic work is invariably conceptualized in spatial terms—as the *manifestation, translation, projection, actualization,* or *externalization* of an idea but also, more poetically, as the *traversal* of a certain ideal space: between a point at which the utterance has not yet taken place and one at which the utterance has been made, an idea incarnated, a work created. Such figures of expression (manifestation, translation, incarnation, actualization, a "simple bridging problem," etc.) introduce conceptions about the nature of what is expressed that seem to derive from the world in which the utterance has already taken place: the world of denotation. Thus "manifestation" and "expression" suggest a subject who speaks (who preexists the communication, controls it, and whose autonomy survives it), an idea or an intention to be communicated, and a degree of success attributable to the transmission. Such terms ascribe a temporal unity to the event of discourse, bounded on each side by a *before* and an *after.* To conceive of this process as the traversal of a space suggests that the thing or entity expressed has "extension" or substance, that, as such, it is subject to processes and material constraints that are independent of it, including aesthetic considerations, formal conventions, personal or institutional interests, ideological influences, and historical factors of various kinds.

The reality, according to Gilles Deleuze in his 1968 book *The Logic of Sense*, is far more elusive and paradoxical:

> On one hand, [that which is expressed] does not exist outside the proposition which expresses it; what is expressed does not exist outside its expression. That is why we cannot say that sense exists, but rather that it inheres or subsists. On the other hand, it does not at all merge with the proposition, for it has an objectness [*objectité*] which is quite distinct. What is expressed has no resemblance whatsoever to the expression.[1]

"No resemblance whatsoever . . .": the thing expressed and the expression are inseparable, but they lack any *relation* (for example, of morphological similarity, ideological homology, psychic condensation or displacement) that would enable the first to be derived from the second. The expressed does not "merge" with the expression yet is tied inseparably to it.

The consequences of this paradox for literary criticism and aesthetic theory are calamitous, for sense, if conceived in such terms, is impossible to represent or paraphrase satisfactorily. On the other hand, to talk of "consequences" is already to fail to grasp the implication. For the paradox of sense is not some "condition" that preexists and determines the failure of criticism; the paradox, rather, is *nothing other than* this unparaphraseability that conditions—but is everywhere denied by—the practice of criticism. Sense, for Deleuze, is not figured spatially but is "exactly the boundary between propositions and things" (22). The protocols of criticism (which include concepts as fundamental as "fiction" or "point of view") tend to propose a "sense of sense" located on one side or the other. Since sense cannot easily be named, since to name it is to attribute substance to what is insubstantial, and since naming and conceptualization introduce closure, an endpoint, to something that, in essence, subsists without closure—any theory of the novel, any literary criticism, any philosophy of literature, is caught in the predicament that what it has to say about the work pertains only to the order of the *already completed utterance*—a "sphere," says Deleuze, "in which I am already established" at the point of speech (28). Sense, to stay with Deleuze's terminology, is always "presupposed" and never articulated directly. When I speak, he says in *The Logic of Sense*, I only speak; it is impossible for me to "state the sense of what I am saying." To attempt to do so is to necessitate a further such clarifying statement, and so on ad infinitum.

Deleuze locates a beautiful illustration of this problem in one of the absurd situations imagined by Lewis Carroll in *Through the Looking Glass*. During Alice's encounter with the White Knight in chapter 8, the Knight offers to sing her a song:

> "The name of the song is called '*Haddocks' Eyes.*'"
>
> "Oh, that's the name of the song, is it?" Alice said, trying to feel interested.
>
> "No, you don't understand," the Knight said, looking a little vexed. "That's what the name is *called*. The name really *is* '*The Aged Aged Man.*'"
>
> "Then I ought to have said 'That's what the *song* is called'?" Alice corrected herself.
>
> "No, you oughtn't: that's quite another thing! The *song* is called '*Ways And Means*': but that's only what it's *called*, you know!"
>
> "Well, what *is* the song, then?" said Alice, who was by this time completely bewildered.
>
> "I was coming to that," the Knight said. "The song really *is* '*A-sitting On A Gate*': and the tune's my own invention."[2]

Deleuze's discussion of this passage appears in the fifth chapter (or "series") of *The Logic of Sense*, devoted to "sense." The problem under discussion is that of the "sense of sense," and, as the *Alice* episode illustrates, it is a problem of "infinite regress" (28). Deleuze calls this "Frege's paradox," referring to the letter that Bertrand Russell wrote to the German mathematician and philosopher Gottlob Frege in June 1902, alerting Frege to a contradiction in his attempt to establish the ontological primacy of concepts (i.e., sets) by deriving numbers from the concept—a deduction of his researches in mathematical set theory. Frege tries to show that numbers are nothing but the "extension" of concepts; that logic, in that sense, presupposes numbers (and vice versa); that number has a logical foundation and is therefore "natural": as Alain Badiou puts it (summarizing Frege), "the index of truth" and "an instance of pure thought."[3] Badiou characterizes Frege's proposition as follows: "Given any concept whatsoever, an object 'falls' under this concept if it is a 'truth-case' of this concept, if the statement that attributes to this object the property comprised in the concept is a true statement. In other words, if the object satisfies the concept" (16). For Frege, numbers reiterate the primacy of concepts, which is to say, the primacy of thought itself, beyond all sensation or mere attributes. Frege's system begins with zero as the number proper to the concept {not identical to itself} (since, according to Leibniz, every object is identical to itself) (18). Zero is thus identified with "the extension of all concepts which fail to be exemplified."[4] Russell's letter to Frege, written in German, challenges Frege's system by proposing a concept that would be irreducible to mathematical logic: the set of "all sets that are not members of themselves"; such a set could be a member of itself only if it were not a member of itself, and vice versa.

It will immediately be noticed that Frege's paradox (or, as it is more usually known, "Russell's paradox") bears close relation to the paradox of the instantiation relation introduced in chapter 3 as "Bradley's regress," after the work of the British philosopher F. H. Bradley. Russell's letter amounts to an assault on the instantiation relation that is held in place by the principle of identity at the center of Frege's system. The "Haddocks' Eyes" episode of *Through the Looking Glass*—an arbitrary name for the episode, insofar as the White Knight's song has four possible titles specified and an infinite number of virtual others—is a fable of the paradox of instantiation, that is to say, of the fallacy of a secondary relation between universals and particulars, including the relation implied in the formulation "sense of sense." The point at which the sequence of names (and names of names) comes to an end is always arbitrary: every name is by definition penultimate.

The implications of this paradox go to the heart of the literary-critical enterprise and the relation it purports to have with its object. When, for example, Dorothy Hale celebrates the operation of instantiation in the work of Zadie Smith ("One can falsify a description of oneself or lie in a statement of belief, but one can't counterfeit the way one sees, the point of view from which one makes sense of the world"),[5] we should ask: why call a halt to the cycle of false representations and truthful instantiations so soon, on arriving at the "point of view" of the author? When Frank Kermode claims that poets "help us to make sense of our lives" and critics to "mak[e] sense of the ways we try to make sense of our lives,"[6] the question that suggests itself, irrepressibly, is: Who will help us make sense of the ways critics make sense of the ways poets make sense of our lives? Who will help us make sense of sense itself?

The philosopher David Armstrong, on whom I drew in my account of the instantiation relation in chapter 3, acknowledges the close similarity between Frege's "concepts" and Armstrong's own understanding of "universals" and thus between Frege's notion of "extension" and Armstrong's concept of instantiation.[7] Similarly, we might compare Armstrong's solution to the paradox of instantiation discussed in chapter 3—an "ontology of states of affairs" (in other words, the *primacy* of the instantiation relation)—to the retort that Badiou constructs to Frege's theory of the primacy of the concept. Number, writes Badiou, comes first; "it is that *point of being* upon which the exercise of the concept depends" (22–23). No concept can be thought in the absence of number, just as, for Armstrong, no attribute can be thought in the absence of the object that instantiates it (and vice versa). To separate concept (which is to say, language) from number is to limit the thought of number to mere "numericality," a "banalization" of number that exists "outside all thought" (Badiou, 213). In this way, Badiou reveals the logic according to which instantiation, the instantiation relation, takes the form of *an ideology of number*, in which value and truth are scaled numerically, as in opinion polls, election voting, and the entire apparatus of the money economy and stock market investment—a logic that extends toward school and university rankings, social media "likes," and a tendency (attributed by Michel Foucault to "neoliberalism") to reduce all forms of private motivation to "interest."[8] In such formations we see the identification of public discourse with economics, of humanity with Adam Smith's *homo economicus*, and of rationality with the logic of "interest."[9]

Numericality, which Badiou does not hesitate to call a "regime" (51), likewise "follows from the simple law of the situation, which is the law of Capital" (213). On the other hand, the conception of number that Badiou dignifies with the phrase "the mathematical thought of Number" supports "no value, and has no truth other than that which is given to it in mathematical thought." Badiou's philosophy is an attempt to convoke such a thinking of number outside the "arithmetical" logic of mathematicians such as Frege and Giuseppe Peano, a thinking that will comprise no element of calculation, utility, or instrumental deployment. For Badiou, every thought worthy of the name deploys itself, in the current situation, as a "retreat" from all attempts "to make a truth of Number" (213).

For all the differences between Badiou and Deleuze (which Badiou has documented in several texts),[10] Deleuze's solution to the problem of infinite regress bears some similarity to this enterprise of Badiou's insofar as Deleuze's work in *The Logic of Sense* may be said to construct a place for thought in the interstices of conventional notions of literary meaning, that is, to take as both subject and object that element of sense that cannot be "extracted" using the formulation "sense of sense."

The instantiation relation, as we saw in chapter 3, concerns the relation between universal qualities and particular objects or bodies that are said to instantiate them. Its classical formulation is found most systematically expressed in Aristotle's foundational distinction between *what a thing is* and its *predicates* or *attributes*, in book Zeta of the *Metaphysics*, but also in Plato's theory of the forms outlined in books 7 and 10 of the *Republic*.[11] Stoic philosophy, on which Deleuze draws in the opening sections of *The Logic of Sense*, enables a radically different conception of this relation, in terms of bodies, on one hand, and the events that they undergo, on the other. In the Stoic conception (to use again the terms that we explored in part 2) there is no "instantiation relation" between universals and particulars. As Deleuze puts it, "what is more intimate or essential to bodies than events such as growing, becoming smaller, or being cut? . . . Mixtures are in bodies, and in the depth of bodies: a body penetrates another and coexists with it in all of its parts, like a drop of wine in the ocean, or fire in iron" (5).

But—as already discussed in chapter 4—instantiation is also applicable to certain theories of language and meaning: for example, to the relation between the *system of linguistic differences* that constitutes a language (Saussure's *langue*) and the individual speech act (*parole*) that constitutes the utterance. This problem of language as a problem of instantiation is addressed in Aristotle's *Metaphysics* in a section dealing with the being of ideas. The relation between primary being and "other categories" of being (1031a, 138), when it comes to language, concerns the distinction between being (the question of *what it is*) and meaning (the question of *what it is to be*). Primary beings, says Aristotle, are those whose qualities are "essential" to them—in which *what it is* and *what it is to be* are identical—while other beings are those whose qualities are "accidental."

For Aristotle it is clear that ideas are primary beings insofar as there is no difference between "what it is *to be*" (for example) and being itself. "What it is to be" cannot be said to be an *attribute* of being or to "belong" to being:

they are the same thing; the former is nothing but being's "definition" (Aristotle, 139). To take another example, "What it is to be good" and the idea of the good are the same; the idea of the good does not "participate" in what it is to be good. The same is true for the idea of the animal or the idea of Socrates (but not for propositions of "accidental" being, say, a white man, or three pens on a table). A difference would imply that "what it is to be good" is not good; the proposition is nonsensical. Thus, in Aristotle's metaphysics, Bradley's regress never gets off the ground. It would be "absurd," says Aristotle, "if one were to assign a name to each successive instance of what it is to be: for there would then be another beyond that; for example, what it is to be a horse should then have its own meaning added to the meaning of 'horse'" (141). Were "one" and "what one is" different, he goes on, "there would be an infinite regress; for there would be 'what one is,' which would be something belonging to 'one,' and these would be one; and, consequently, the same distinction could be made concerning the being of 'what it is to be one.'"

When Deleuze concerns himself in *The Logic of Sense* with that element in language that does not exist—that eludes "the action of the Idea" (2)—he is rejecting the instantiation model of language in two of its crucial aspects: first, the primacy and unity of the idea, that is, the fundamental difference between *definition* and *attribute*; and, second, the implication of a remainder or excess that could be unaccounted for by language and in which the primacy of being would be preserved. As Foucault puts it in *The Archaeology of Knowledge*, "words, sentences, meanings, affirmations, series of propositions do not back directly on to a primeval night of silence."[12] In the space between language as it is manifest—"as one reads and hears it, and also as one speaks it"—and "the absence of a formulation" there is nothing but "the conditions according to which the enunciative function operates"; in other words, no "profusion of things half said," no "sentences left unfinished," no "thoughts half expressed," no "endless monologue of which only a few fragments emerge." Such notions merely reassert the primacy of being and thus help raise that "transcendental obstacle" that philosophical discourse (beginning with Aristotle) "opposes to all analyses of language" (Foucault, 113).

The Logic of Sense attempts to situate itself, its own thought, in a space that is discursively uninhabitable, even by literature (although literature, like every form, is constituted by it): more accurately, a nonspace, a space of absurdity in the interval between sense and sense, which is to say, between being and instance. Another way to say this is that *The Logic of Sense* is about a hypothetical order of noninstantiated, "pure" events. *Pure* does not mean mysterious, hidden, enigmatic, or transcendent; it refers simply to events that are untroubled by the logic of the instance: by the logic of the ideal, on one hand, and the material (or the taking-place), on the other:

> It is no longer a question of simulacra which elude the ground and insinu-
> ate themselves everywhere, but rather a question of effects which manifest
> themselves and act in their place. These are effects in the causal sense, but
> also "effects" of sound, optics, or language—and even less, or much more,
> since they are no longer corporeal entities and are rather the entire idea.
> What was eluding the Idea has risen to the surface, the incorporeal limit,
> and represents now all possible *ideality*, the latter being stripped of its causal
> and spiritual efficacy.
> (7, TRANSLATION MODIFIED)

In the two *Alice* books, Lewis Carroll invents a series of what Deleuze calls "ideal games," games without a beginning or an end point, without a winner or loser:

> Not only does Lewis Carroll invent games, or transform the rules of known
> games [*jeux connus*] (tennis, croquet), but he invokes a sort of ideal game
> whose meaning and function are at first glance difficult to assess: for example,
> the caucus race in *Alice*, in which one begins when one wishes and stops
> at will; and the croquet match in which the balls are hedgehogs, the mallets
> pink flamingos, and the loops soldiers who endlessly displace themselves
> from one end of the game to the other. These games have the following in
> common; they have a great deal of movement, they seem to have no precise
> rules, and they permit neither winner nor loser. We do not "know" [*Nous
> ne "connaissons" pas*] such games, which seem to contradict themselves.
> (58, TRANSLATION MODIFIED)

And yet, in the conception of a sense located in the interstices of what is producible or "extractable," in the substitution of "Something" (*aliquid*) as a higher term than "Being" (*ousia*) (7), and in the unmistakably cinematic reference to "optical" and "sound" effects, appended to certain unspecified "language" effects, as well as to effects that are even smaller and slighter than those, unverifiable and perhaps imperceptible, what Deleuze is imagining, perhaps—and without naming it as such—is literature, a literature that no longer closes upon a meaning, indeed, is no longer referable to a subject of enunciation.

A THEORY OF THE CONTEMPORARY NOVEL?

A central claim of the "postfictional hypothesis," as it has been outlined in part 2, is that a certain condition of discourse has emerged in which forms of connection, such as those "fundamental categories of ethical and legal inquiry and evaluation" mentioned by Mikhail Bakhtin in "Discourse in the Novel" (349), are not only rendered questionable but dissolved from within or (which amounts to the same thing) preserved in a state of hollowness, instability, or indeterminacy.

For Bakhtin, such connective principles fall into two main groups, "objective" and "psychological," depending on whether the field of application is primarily social or biographical,[13] in other words, whether they function in relation to a whole that is external or internal to the novel, whether the novel is considered for what Dorothy Hale called its "social representativeness" (*Social Formalism*, 5) or its psychological truth. Political and economic *structures* (capitalism, imperialism, totalitarianism, domesticity), social and cultural "discourses" (racism and sexism), or sociological concepts (terrorism, alienation, criminality) give definition to the former, while concepts of *motivation* (such as madness, greed, vengeance, conscience, responsibility) are categories of the latter.

This distinction appears in Bakhtin's book on Dostoevsky. For Bakhtin, the revolutionary quality of Dostoevsky's work is that such links are "insufficient" in his work. That is, they do not bind the work together. Insofar as they appear at all, it is only at the level of "individual consciousnesses" (9). "The ultimate claims that hold his novelistic world together are a different sort entirely; the fundamental event revealed through his novel does not lend itself to an ordinary pragmatic interpretation at the level of the plot" (7). In such moments, Bakhtin's book on Dostoevsky, notwithstanding its value as a reading of Dostoevsky, also identifies the structural and organizational features of the contemporary novel.

In *The Theory of the Novel*, Georg Lukács identifies such connecting terms with the "form-giving" procedures of the novel: ways in which the novel constructs "biographical" (i.e., ethical) or historical limits in order to avoid the "continuum-like infinity" of the epic (81). Their structural importance is part of the logic of instantiation that governs and frames Lukács's early work on the novel, as signaled by the centrality to his account of the notion of "totality." By giving form, says Lukács, the novel seeks "to uncover and construct the concealed totality of life" (60). The totality of the world of the novel is always concealed, says Lukács, and never "given," not even in the form-giving process of the novel itself, which is why the paradigmatic novelistic narrative is the search or quest: "a way of expressing the subject's recognition that neither objective life nor its relationship to the subject is spontaneously harmonious in itself" (60). Should the hero's goals, or the way to achieve them, be given "in a psychologically direct and solid manner" (i.e., should they be spoken directly), this indicates their mere existence as "a psychological fact to which nothing in the world of objects or norms need necessarily correspond" (61). It is impossible, in other words, for the "totality" to be spoken directly in the work and retain its status as the totality.

As Lukács presents it, this logic is profoundly melancholy, insofar as the structure it is caught up in is "tragic." The novel form always relates to the totality as to something unencompassable, and it compensates for that unencompassability by circumscribing its material with "imposed limits" (81)—the imposition of which renders the shortfall apparent. The creation of forms, we read in *The Theory of the Novel*, is "the most profound confirmation of the existence of a dissonance" (72). No successful bridging is possible, only "a maximum conciliation," in the form of "the profound and intensive irradiation of a man by his life's meaning"—this combined with the realization that "a mere glimpse of meaning is the highest that life has to offer" (80). But a question has to be asked—one that has not, perhaps, been posed often enough of Lukács's text: at what level of engagement with the novelistic work, or to whom, is the dissonance apparent? At what level, that is to say, is the "melancholy" of formal conciliation experienced in its melancholic dimensions rather than its "conciliatory" ones (for example, as narrative closure, fictional psychobiography, or the happy fulfillment of genre expectations)? In conceptualizing it as such, is Lukács conveying the perspective of the ordinary reader, that of the professional critic, his own unique insights, or that of someone (something) else? And does this morose "substratum" to the novel form apply to every novelistic work, even those whose conciliations may be experienced as, say, spiritual, satirical, epiphanic, informational, or comic? Every form, he writes, "restores the absurd to its proper place as the vehicle, the necessary condition of meaning" (62). Perhaps. But at what level of awareness and analysis does the experience of form qua form recede and the "fundamental dissonance" that the form "resolves" become apprehensible *as such*? What principle, if any, determines the transformation of absurdity from the "vehicle, the necessary condition of meaning" into the immediate object of theoretical attention? And what would it take for the "absurdity"—what Lukács paraphrases, a few lines later, as "the futility of genuine and profound human aspirations, or the possibility of the ultimate nothingness of man"—to attain the status of a critically actionable insight, rather than simply the mark of one man's (or one historical moment's) dour "mood" (11)?

What all these questions are asking can be summed up in the following: how can we guarantee the nonsubjectivism of Lukács's intuition? One thing seems certain in Lukács's account of the novel: the hypothesis of the melancholy of novelistic form does not rest on any direct appearance at the level of the text. In fact, the "fundamental dissonance of existence" has no formal presence in the work at all.

RESOLUTION AS "DEFLECTION": LUKÁCS WITH CORA DIAMOND

In a dense but luminous short essay on Lukács's *Theory of the Novel*, Paul de Man observes that the book is written "from the point of view of a mind that claims to have reached such an advanced degree of generality that it can speak, is it were, for the novelistic consciousness itself."[14] De Man claims to find this quality in Lukács's work "strange" and off-putting; nevertheless, the truth about *The Theory of the Novel* that he touches on is that the work's central claims and insights are not of the order of verification because they are not of the order of representation. Lukács's work is not a theory in the sense of "a singular explanatory or evaluative account"—a sense that, D. N. Rodowick claims, did not appear prominently in the arts and humanities until the mid-twentieth century.[15] Lukács's theory of the novel is, rather, a ventriloquy of the abstract form of the novel were the novel to articulate its own thought in theoretical terms—terms of which novels themselves, in all their concretion, are both blissfully unaware and have no need. Lukács's *Theory of the Novel* would then be an exploration of a theoretical role attributed *to the novel itself*, an account of the novel as itself a theoretical form—a *subject*, rather than an *object*, of thought. The novel is not subjected to theorization in *The Theory of the Novel* but subjectivized—given the active role. The theorist is not Lukács but the novel itself. The negative formulations with which Lukács characterizes its thinking—not only "futility," "absurdity," and "nothingness" but "mature virility" (85), "irony" (84), "negative mysticism," and the "demonic" (90)—imply that the novel is the form of a world bereft of unity, a world that we, too, are condemned not to grasp when we engage it theoretically or synoptically, that the novel, in short, is capable of *a mode of thinking that we ourselves are not.*

And it is this implication that makes Lukács's *Theory of the Novel* an indispensable work for the present moment. For the task of theorizing a world of discontinuity, a world in which the most pressing theoretical undertaking is not to try to wrest the fragments into a semblance of unity but, on the contrary, to think disconnection as such—to think, as Foucault put it, "the relations between chance and thought," to think the "absence" of theory[16]—such a task is no longer that of the theorist or critic but of the novel.

A second series of questions suggests itself: Can we imagine a literature that, unlike Lukács's novel, would not content itself with formal "conciliations"? A literature that would neither affirm nor regret the "fundamental dissonance of existence"?—that would live it, which is to say, think it directly: *be* it, rather than "resolve" it through "formal" means? Can we imagine a literature without the "pathos of ineffability"—another form of "resolution" that seems to describe precisely the melancholy disposition of Lukács's *Theory of the Novel*?[17] And then, if it were possible to imagine it into being, what interest could such a literature hold, for "us"?

In a highly influential essay that deals partly with Coetzee's *Elizabeth Costello*, the American philosopher Cora Diamond asks a version of this question: "Can there be such a thing as philosophy that is not deflected from such realities?"[18] The word "realities" alludes to the phrase that provides Diamond with the title of her essay, "the difficulty of reality," a phrase she attributes to John Updike, although she is unable to source it satisfactorily.

This is appropriate, for the "difficulty of reality," like Lukács's "absurd," has a referent that is irreducibly experiential; it resists substantiation (like the fruitless search through the archives of the *New Yorker* one can imagine Diamond undertaking in search of the Updike reference):

> We take something in reality to be resistant to our thinking it, or possibly to be painful in its inexplicability, difficult in that way, or perhaps awesome and astonishing in its inexplicability. *We take things so.* And the things we take so may simply not, to others, present the kind of difficulty, of being hard or impossible or agonizing to get one's mind around.
>
> (45–46)

Diamond does not speak of this experience in the first-person singular. Rather, in a succession of readings (of Coetzee's *Elizabeth Costello*, a poem by Ted Hughes, and an essay by Stanley Cavell) she discusses analogous representations of it: as when Hughes—describing a photograph of six "profoundly, fully alive" men, all now dead—writes of feeling "demented" by the "contradictory permanent horrors" introduced by their still-smiling faces in the photograph (Diamond, 44). The experience, says Hughes, "shoulder[s] out / One's own body from its instant and heat." A second example from Diamond is when Elizabeth Costello speaks in her lecture at Appleton College of a "repel[lent]" knowledge that comes to her at certain moments of reading, fleeting moments during which "we live the impossible: we live beyond our death, look back on it, yet look back as only a dead self can."[19] What I know when I read, Elizabeth continues, "is what a corpse cannot know: that it is extinct, that it knows nothing and will never know anything any more. For an instant, before my whole structure of knowledge collapses in panic, I am alive inside that contradiction, dead and alive at the same time." This knowledge is not one that *Elizabeth Costello* gives us access to; Elizabeth is reporting on something that remains beyond the reach of the text.

When readers (such as Peter Singer, Wendy Doniger, and Barbara Smuts, official respondents to Coetzee's two 1997 lectures at Princeton University, published separately as *The Lives of Animals*) take Coetzee to be "presenting . . . a position on the issue [of] how we should treat animals" (Diamond, 49), they select one reading of Coetzee's text at the expense of another, suggests Diamond.[20] Such readers do not know—or rather, they "pass by"—the difficulty of reality "as if it were not there" (58); they take the concepts at work *in* Coetzee's novel to be those *of* the novel and the ethical quandaries outlined by Elizabeth in the work to be the ethical quandaries of the work. Elizabeth herself, in other words, is taken to be nothing other than a device for Coetzee, who remains in all such readings the expressive subject of the work. The difficulty of reality, the subjective form of which is *represented* in Coetzee's novel in the consciousness of the protagonist, is thus resolved—"deflected," to use the word that Diamond takes from Stanley Cavell[21]—into "discussion of a moral issue" (Diamond, 59).

The term "deflection" is important to Diamond in a way that it is not to Cavell. For Diamond, deflection describes rationalizations of unthinkable experiences, rationalizations that are therefore premature or consolatory. The implication of her use of the term, which is singular to Diamond, is that all rationalizations necessarily succumb to this prematurity. Thus we should bear in mind, for example, that the difficulty of reality has already been deflected in the subjective contemplation of it in Coetzee's novel. The "psychological" manifestation of the dissonance, a feature of every novel, is a "conciliatory" form, says Lukács, "to which nothing in the world of objects or norms need necessarily correspond" (61). Elizabeth's very awareness "of the limits of thinking, the limits of understanding" (Diamond, 52)—an awareness evident in the self-consciously speculative (as opposed to scholarly) nature of her reflections about animal thinking[22]—is *also* limited, then, in its capacity to, as Lukács says, "penetrate reality" (80): limited precisely by its "biographical" (or characterological) form. This is especially so since Coetzee, with thirty years of novelistic craftsmanship under his belt, is diligent enough to include plenty of detractors within his narrative, such as Norma, Elizabeth's prickly daughter-in-law, for whom Elizabeth's lecture is "rambling" and her comparison between the mental lives of humans and animals "naive" (Coetzee 75, 91); and Thomas O'Hearne, a philosopher at Appleton, who raises concerns about the historicity and the Western origins of the "animal rights movement," the shaky scientific grounds for giving animals the same legal basis as humans, and the "abstraction" of the case for animal rights (105–10). Deflection, says Cavell, characterizes all such formal rationalizations, including any philosophical position (say, skepticism or antiskepticism) that one might take in response to doubts (say) about the commonality of experience. The "difficulty of reality," paraphrases Diamond, does not survive its transformation into a "philosophical or moral problem" (Diamond, 57).

Diamond's essay does not seek to resolve this aporia at the heart of her concept of the "difficulty of reality" except through another figure of comprehension (and thus deflection): the "bodily life" that, she suggests at the end of her essay, may represent the limit to any attempt to establish an objective basis to this sense of a "coming apart of thought and reality" that she designates with the phrase (53, 78). For Diamond, the difficulty of reality testifies to the fact of bodily life, a dimension of existence that is both common to all beings and, precisely, the limit to commonality: "What response we may have to the difficulties of [Elizabeth's] lectures, the difficulties of reality, is not something the lectures themselves are meant to settle. This itself expresses a mode of understanding of the kind of animal we are, and indeed of the moral life of this kind of animal" (56). Lukács, too, is unable to resolve the aporia; the analysis in *The Theory of the Novel*, as we have discussed earlier, is organized around it. Accordingly, in his 1962 preface to the reissued edition of the book he will publicly disavow the "utopianism" and "lack of theoretical principle" (i.e., subjectivism) of the entire work (*TN*, 20–21).

Perhaps the natural position to take on the question of deflection is simply to accept that all thought is determined, indeed enabled, by "deflections" of various kinds, that deflection is the condition of possibility of thought. Perhaps "thought" (which is to say sense, the *sense* of sense, or indeed the "difficulty of reality") is nothing other than deflection's imaginary brother (or vice versa), the alibi of every disciplinary procedure and scholarly undertaking. Is it not possible to say that all philosophical systems and, certainly, the dominant protocols of literary criticism take as their point of departure some variant of this "conciliatory" notion? Isn't deflection the hidden extension of Aristotle's category of "primary being" (*ousia*)—the formal envelope of the many ways of "derivative" being, as opposed to the "simplicity" of primary being (*Metaphysics*, 1028a)? Doesn't the instantiation relation itself—the "degree-zero" connection outlined in part 2 of this book—depend upon a notion of deflection as the material expression of the unrepresentable yet unfalsifiable "watermark of self" that persists alongside and inseparably from it?

Two recent works of literary criticism help crystallize the degree to which this set of propositions underlies the main currents of literary scholarship at the present time.

Modes of Deflection (1): The "Political Novel"

Addressing the question of the "political novel" in her 2016 book *Bleak Liberalism*, Amanda Anderson distinguishes between the "formal" and the "immanent" presence of democracy in E. M. Forster's *Howards End*— between the "character-character argument" that constitutes much of the discursive fabric of Forster's work and the notion of community that appears, "beyond argument," in the grounds of the eponymous estate in the novel's final chapter.[23] For Anderson, the relationship between what she calls the "political substance" of the work and its formal deflections is complex but not fundamentally problematic (90). In Anderson's reading, the ideological substance of *Howards End* is found not in Margaret's explicit arguments for "connection" or in the unspoken "communitarianism of the novel's ending" but in the "relation between them" (97), that is to say, in the "clear indication of the limits of argument" *combined with* the "intractable clash of worldviews"—which is also to say, a "nonreflective 'being with'" that has no need of being spoken by the text (97). For Anderson, much depends on the fact that Margaret and Henry do not separate after the conversation in which she tells him that he must "see the connection if it kills you."[24] Their reconciliation (although it is barely that) is marked in the text not discursively—say, by Henry's recognition of Margaret's position or by an accommodation between them—but simply by his "quiescen[ce]" (97). The relationship between the formal and the existential is thus a relationship of instantiation, a "degree-zero" relation insofar as there is no need for the nature of the relationship to be made explicit. ("If the author has to say what he's doing, that means he hasn't done it.")

Importantly, however, the weight of Anderson's argument is not on the existential side of the relation but on the formal. Anderson is taking issue primarily with modes of scholarship—represented initially by the critic Simon During—that subordinate "conversational" forms of democracy to the novel's capacity to present "immanent and originary experience"— modes of scholarship, that is, that neglect or underplay the significance of "argument" in favor of a "lived relation to political commitment or belief" (79). Anderson's work distinguishes between spoken and unspoken content in order to argue that everything that is politically important in the novel (here, *Howards End*) takes place in the relation between the two. Her insistence on this point is clear in the adjectives "necessary" and "productive" that she uses to describe the tension between the two orders of political content (95). Thus, the novel is critically positioned in relation to a thought that is encoded in the work (through a combination of these two principles) and extractable from it. In the course of her discussion, the spoken/unspoken distinction maps roughly onto a number of other oppositions: embodied presence and impersonal critique, first-person and third-person perspectives, writers' own "beliefs and convictions about the conditions of political life" and the "complexity and difficulty" of living or enacting political ideals (78, 82)—terms that, taken together, comprehend the novel's capacity for thought and for politics. Anderson's argument is confined to a genre formation, the "political novel" (the understanding of which is inherited from liberal critics of an earlier generation, primarily Lionel Trilling and Irving Howe), and circumscribed by a notion of "liberal thought" that determines the scope of the discussion. In other words, Anderson's examination of the political novel takes place firmly within the terms of the instantiation relation, terms that are established by the category of "liberal aesthetics" that is the declared topic of *Bleak Liberalism*. A project such as Jacques Rancière's, to shift the terms in which we think about the politics of literature away from what is uttered (and not uttered) and toward what is perceived or sensed (or not perceived and not sensed), is within the terms of Anderson's engagement only to the extent that it is exemplary of a "dominant" tendency (represented also by During) to think of the politics of aesthetics in "immanent" or nonrepresentational terms, a tendency that Anderson is setting out to correct.

The same should be said of Theodor Adorno, whom Anderson refers to as an advocate of modernist works whose power is of a "formal and experiential" kind capable of "convey[ing] the suffering and thinned-out experience of an administered life" (83). The diachronic nature of Rancière's distinction between the "representative" regime and the "aesthetic" regime—the historical basis of his project on the politics of aesthetics—does not register within the terms of Anderson's discussion. Nor does any suggestion of a thought that could put into question the capacity of the liberal critical tradition to grasp, either directly (through "mediated telling") or indirectly ("narration by other means"), the political substance of the work (93).

From the perspective of the present discussion, however, the difference between Anderson's and During's positions is negligible. Both are operating within the instantiation relation, which constitutes the horizon of their attention. During wants to locate the truer form of democracy in the "radical, mystical" site of "the impenetrable mysteries of democratic futurity." At the end of his chapter on *Howards End*, During talks of democracy's fullest promise as "that of a romantic Spinozan, creative spiritual awakening," a promise that is available to Forster's readers only if they read his dialogue "literally," that is to say, noninterpretatively—a task that is "impossible," he concedes, given "the weight of figuration upon it" (121). Thus, in During's work, the same distinction that Anderson is navigating between is present in the two terms "compulsory democracy" and "mystical democracy."

Howards End is also a crucially important text for my argument (as spelled out in chapter 4). In my thinking, however, *Howards End* is considered from the point of view of the novelistic revolution that Forster's novel was in the process of *inaugurating*, rather than from the point of view of the nineteenth-century tradition of which Forster's work may be considered to mark the logical endpoint and culmination.

If a new thought could be identified in a literary work or range of works—a thought that would be comprehended neither by the "conversational" form of democracy, as During calls it (although I prefer Rancière's term "representational") nor by the "immanent" form (which finds its fullest theoretical articulation in the instantiation relation of the aesthetic regime)—then we could plausibly claim that a further redistribution of the sensible had taken place subsequent to the historical emergence of the aesthetic, a redistribution that would amount, therefore, to a new politics of literature. Any such development would be unanticipated in Rancière's work (that is to say, in the *letter* of his work, a point I will return to in chapter 8) or by the liberal tradition of reflection on the politics of the novel in either its classical version or its recent revival in Anderson's work. Inklings of such a form would nevertheless be detectable in Simon During's intuition of a "tragic" dimension in Forster's novel, in During's awareness of the "smothering" of democracy that takes place in our various critical compulsions to interpret the text, and in his apparent longing for (and inability to imagine) a mode of reading that would not involve interpretation (121–22).

Modes of Deflection (2): "Forms"

Caroline Levine's theoretical work *Forms: Whole, Rhythm, Hierarchy, Network* locates its corrective in the opposite direction: not the rediscovery of character-character argument or a renewed attention to the "immanence" of the idea in the work but, rather, a radically expanded notion of form in which both argument and immanence and the relation between them are beside the point because the question of thought, even as a problematic of the work, is beyond consideration. Levine's revision of the category of form seems to want to comprehend all previous uses of the term: Platonic and Aristotelian, Hegelian and Marxian, new critical and new formalist, sociological and structuralist, etc. Her concept of form incorporates elements such as ideas, materials, social categories, critical methods, theoretical approaches, concepts, abstractions, as well as literary forms themselves (Levine mentions free indirect discourse, the sonnet, and the "triple-decker novel").[25] Form, she specifies in the opening pages of the book, "will mean all shapes and configurations, all ordering principles, all patterns of repetition and difference" (3). Levine approaches these dimensions of form positivistically, in terms of what they allow us to do or perceive, rather than, for example, what they signify or occlude and omit. In place of signification and representation—the concepts with which literary theory has traditionally designated the work of form—Levine substitutes a new concept, "affordances," taken, she tells us, from "design theory," where it denotes "the potential uses or actions latent in materials and designs" (6): "Glass affords transparency and brittleness. Steel affords strength, smoothness, hardness, and durability. . . . A fork affords stabbing and scooping . . . The sonnet, brief and condensed, best affords a single idea or experience . . . while the triple-decker novel affords elaborate processes of character development in multiplot social contexts" (6).

The implications of that substitution are radical and substantial, since the concept of affordance (unlike meaning, significance, representation, thought, and so on) dispenses with the uncertainty and work of reading. Levine's notion of form is not just a synthesis of previous accounts; it also relocates form securely in the world, i.e., outside the self. The positionality of the researcher with respect to his or her object, the question of the author's intentions, the issues of narrative point of view and the reader's own situatedness and experience—questions that (contrary to an aside in Levine's work) treat the work precisely *not* as a "synchronic unity" but in its actuality as an event (52)—are inconsequential to Levine's scene of reading because they fall outside her understanding of "forms." The notion of "affordances" presumes the consistency of each form, the unidirectionality of its effects, and its separation from its field of influence.

Among the affordances of the novel is its ability to "conceptualize," says Levine (28), but that conceptualization has nothing to do with any order of thought undertaken by the novel itself. For Levine, the thought of the novel is the thought of the artist who produces the novel and that of the reader who receives it. The work is the means by which that thought is made available to both. "Like [Bruno] Latour," she writes, "I treat fictional narratives as productive thought experiments that allow us to imagine the subtle unfolding activity of multiple social forms" (19). Individuals are "users" of forms who are constitutionally unaffected by the forms they use, which is why particular writers and artists—"imaginative" users of forms, Levine calls them (7)—are repeatedly spoken of in her work as "skillful," "persuasive," "brilliant," "shrewd," "canny," and so on. Affordances are multiple and sometimes contradictory. Forms have a capacity for "disorganization as well as for organization," and their outcomes can be unexpected and ideologically unsettling" (104). This, of course, is a necessary principle of Levine's thinking if forms are to be upheld in their capacity to be "emancipatory" and "transformative" (28).

If there is an order of experience that is not included in this apparently capacious category of form, it is that which escapes the knowledge or comprehension of the writer or reader. "There are many events and experiences that do not count as forms," writes Levine,

> and we could certainly play close attention to these: fissures and interstices, vagueness and indeterminacy, boundary-crossing and dissolution. But . . . these formless or antiformal experiences have actually drawn too much attention from literary and cultural critics in the past few decades. . . . Too strong an emphasis on forms' dissolution has prevented us from attending to the complex ways that power operates in a world dense with functioning forms. (9)

What is left out of this notion of form, therefore, is the "dissonance" that, according to Lukács, lies behind every form, indeed, that every form comes

into existence to "resolve." Levine writes: "By making use of a formal feature of the Victorian novel that has not often been theorized—sheer length—
[Charles] Dickens puts an especially loose and baggy narrative form to use
to theorize networks in canny and persuasive ways" (127). But the insight
into networks afforded by Dickens's *Bleak House*, in Levine's work, fails to
extract anything from the novel beyond the self-evident features of the narrative. Network form, as she calls it, involves characters "act[ing] as nodes
in more than one different distributed network at a time" (125). Levine enu-
merates these networks as "the law, disease, economics, class, gossip, the
family tree, city streets, rural roads, and even global print and philanthropic
networks." By making "networks" rather than the social world the object
of her reading, Levine turns a refusal to extrapolate from forms or to establish connections between forms into a method. "*Bleak House* offers multiple
sources of suspense," she writes. "At any given moment, we know that we
cannot grasp crucial pathways between nodes, and this points us to our
more generalized ignorance of networks. We cannot even apprehend the
totality of the networks that organize us" (129). But the limitations attributed to Levine's rhetorical "we" do not pertain outside the interpretive
method she invents in *Forms*. For in fact, we have long known how to read
Bleak House (which is to say, to identify the critical pathways between its
nodes) and to do so without being overwhelmed by "the totality of the networks that organize us" (129). Anderson puts this well when she describes
the heightened moments of embodied indignation that punctuate Dickens's
impersonal, omniscient third-person narration:

> In such moments we are made to understand the principles and forms of life
> that are thwarted or denied by the prevailing system: legal and social jus-
> tice, unperverted childhood, individual self-development, and moral open-
> ness. These moments of critical intervention are a comment on the system
> otherwise being described in totalizing terms—they light up the informing
> evaluative perspective of the broader systemic critique.
> (*BLEAK LIBERALISM*, 49)

Pace Anderson, such "heightened" narrative moments are not even necessary for the global significance of the novel to be legible. For the "totality
of life," as Lukács observed crucially, is never itself spoken by the work, only,
at most, "the artist's relationship with that totality, his approving or

condemnatory attitude towards it" (*TN*, 53). It may be that *Bleak House* comes close to violating this principle and speaking the totality directly. E. M. Forster, for example, is in no doubt that *Bleak House* "denounces a social injustice," and for Forster this certainty puts the very status of the work as a "novel" in question (if only momentarily).[26] But this makes it all the more surprising that Levine should take this work by Dickens as her chief instance of "network form."

Levine, to be clear, is no instantiation critic. The insights made possible in her reading of *Bleak House* do not rise to the level of the instantiation relation—although not because the instantiation relation has collapsed in the nineteenth-century works she is reading but because it is collapsing in the period in which she is *writing*. Levine appears to recoil from the work of imaginative transcendence that is part of the infrastructure of the classic realist novel and factored into the reception of such works in advance. This recoil amounts to a programmatic refusal of aesthetic logic itself: the logic that enables a work such as *Bleak House*, without saying so explicitly— and precisely by assembling a vast concatenation of representative characters, recognizable social strata, and identifiable decrepit and negligent social institutions—to lay bare a system of social exclusion and exploitation, cruelty and turpitude, moral weakness, legal corruption and inefficiency. The "whole" or "totality" of Dickens's novel is found not in the "conjoined" multiplicity of networks without "necessary connexion" to which Levine limits the affordances of narrative (19), but in *ideas*, such as those listed in the previous sentence. In fact, exploitation, cruelty, injustice, etc., are not "forms" in Dickens. They are hypotheses put forward in the interstices of the work. As Deleuze writes of all experiences of belief and causality, they are modes by which the subject "transcends the given," since they require that the subject go "beyond what the mind gives it."[27] But that makes them no less a part of the work.

The same refusal of instantiation is a feature of Levine's treatment of the other forms that concern her in this work: "bounded wholes," "rhythms," and "hierarchies." The analysis that Levine offers of each of these forms is limited to their figuration in the body of the work in question. Bounded wholes, for example, can be either physical (prison cells, medieval churches) or conceptual (narrative closure, socially gendered spaces, nation-states). Their recategorization as "forms" means that they will be engaged with, in Levine's method, not as objects of "critique" or as resolutions of the "fundamental dissonance" that, for Lukács, remains the basis of the novel form but instead for the "genuinely emancipatory and transformative political work" that they do (28). However, not all political work undertaken by the novel is "emancipatory" or "transformative." Novels are also capable of dismantling ideas and concepts, replacing them with empty shells. The work of critique that a novel such as Joseph Conrad's *The Secret Agent* undertakes with respect to thought-forms such as "criminality," "legality," "morality," or "terrorism"—a kind of systematic disassembling of the concept by exposing the "fissures" that lie behind it—is beyond the reach of Levine's method as she presents it in *Forms*.

Approached from the perspective of Cora Diamond's notion of "the difficulty of reality," then, Levine's method could be summed up in a single word: deflection. There are nothing but deflections in Levine's notion of forms. When it comes to Dickens, for example, all causality, all ideas of relation between networks, seem to be removed from consideration simply by the fact of their absence from the consciousness of his characters. Such instantiated elements are thus, in Levine's terms, "formless."

In Diamond's discussion of Coetzee's *The Lives of Animals* and of the responses to that text by Peter Singer, Wendy Doniger, and Barbara Smuts, "deflections" take the form of ideas of ethical relevance (for example, the issue of "how we should treat animals"), which count as failures of reading because the work in question is located at a different moment in the evolution of the instantiation relation from *Bleak House*. *Elizabeth Costello* is a work whose central thought and concern—in Diamond's reading—is incapable of making any formal or "positive" appearance in the work. Thus to mobilize the instantiation relation in a quest for the work's thought, as Singer, Doniger, and Smuts do, is to be deflected from that thought. With Dickens, by contrast, one is deflected from the thought of the work if one *ignores* the instantiation relation. In Levine, that mode of deflection provides nothing less than a new methodological basis for literary research.

For both of these critics—who in other respects, as I hope to have made clear, have very different commitments and approaches—the "difficulty of reality" is no difficulty at all. Anderson and Levine are representative of the view that Diamond attributes to those who are free of Ted Hughes's "wonder" at the coexistence of life and death in a photograph or the "astonishment" felt by the writer and Holocaust survivor Ruth Klüger (another of Diamond's examples) at the intervention of a young woman at Auschwitz who saved her life when she was a twelve-year-old internee. "The men were alive, and now are dead; what's the problem?" ventriloquizes Diamond of Hughes. "Okay, some persons are altruistic," ventriloquizes Klüger, evoking those who respond to her story without a sense of wonder. "The girl who helped you was one of those who liked to help" (62).[28]

We might perform the same kind of ventriloquy with respect to Anderson and Levine. The confrontation between Margaret and Henry in *Howards End*, combined with its resolution in the novel's coda, writes Anderson, "upends" Jacques Rancière's distinction between the representative regime (the "formal" or conversational presence of democracy) and the aesthetic regime (immanence) by demonstrating that the two go hand in hand. Margaret's argument for connection is "privileged" by the narrative both directly—through "focalization and free indirect discourse"—and indirectly, through non-narrated elements (such as Henry's final, mute acquiescence) (Anderson, 96–97). So what's the problem? Any continuing adherence to the "difficulty of reality"—to the idea of a residue in *Howards End* that is unaccounted for by the alternatives of deliberation and immanence—is nothing but a failure to read, to properly attend to the conceptual work taking place in the relation between character-character dialogue and its limits. One can equally imagine Anderson directing such a remark to Cora Diamond or to Caroline Levine: to both the idealism of ineffability and the pragmatism of affordances. However (one wants to ask Anderson), what if one were no longer to consider free indirect discourse and focalization, or the placement of an epigraph, as dependable guides to the work's ideological affiliations? What if, say, they began to be read as procedures for dismantling authority, rather than for conferring it?

With respect to Levine, the gist of the ventriloquy would be in a direction opposite to that of Anderson. If you want a literature without the "pathos of ineffability" (one can imagine Levine saying), then we have such a literature already: in every novel that has ever been written. Pay attention only to what is said, rather than to what is not said. Treat literature as you would any other "form"—a table, a concept, a speech in Parliament, or a household implement: not for what it cannot give you, but for what it can (its "affordances"). Put aside the "difficulty of reality," which is not a form, so it doesn't exist.

As a theory of form, it's incontestable. To contest it requires invoking categories of experience that are, by definition, immaterial or, in Levine's terms, "formless." The "fundamental dissonance of existence" and "the difficulty of reality" are only the most obvious of these. Levine's theory also dispenses with the inherent contentiousness of conventional literary and historical interpretation: allegorical reading of various kinds, the necessarily "transcendent" narratives of causality that are never spelled out by the work (because the work is composed in the expectation of such interpretative faculties being brought to bear upon it), and all ideology critique.

Levine's theory of form is oblivious to a basic fact about the novel that this work and this chapter hope to have made irrefutable: that the instantiation relation—the principle of connection between the novel's elements and its whole—is a formal quality of the novel. To fail to pay attention to it is to fail to understand the novel form. Not only is the instantiation relation a form; it is novelistic form itself. The instantiation relation would certainly be worthy of consideration alongside the *wholes, networks, hierarchies,* and *rhythms* that Levine pays attention to in *Forms*. But, more to the point, such attention is meaningless without an understanding of the instantiation relation that structures and organizes each of these "forms."

If the instantiation relation is a form, should the same be said of the "difficulty of reality"? The short answer is no, for the difficulty of reality is not a form but an experience of the limits of form. Like the "fundamental dissonance of existence," the difficulty of reality is not a form—until, that is, it becomes one, until it is "resolved" or deflected.

The question of whether we can imagine a literature without the "pathos of ineffability" is therefore a question of whether a literature is possible that could defer, for the duration of the work and beyond, the betrayal of the difficulty of reality into resolutions, deflections, and forms.

The two sets of positions summarized in this chapter and represented in the questions raised by Diamond, on one hand, and the absence of such questions in the work of Anderson or Levine, on the other, are irreconcilable. The irreconcilability is signaled by the experiential nature of

Diamond's central concept, "the difficulty of reality." Earlier I said that Diamond never speaks of this experience in the first person. Nevertheless, her exposition of the concept, and the occasion for it, is framed in consistently personal terms in "The Difficulty of Reality and the Reality of Philosophy": "*I am concerned* in this paper with a range of phenomena" (43). "*What interests me* [in Hughes's poem] is the experience of the mind's not being able to encompass something which it encounters" (44). "*I want* to describe Coetzee's lectures ... as presenting a kind of woundedness or hauntedness" (47). "*I say* that that is how I want to describe Coetzee's lectures" (47). Diamond never breaks with this subjective and anticipatory mode, which is to say that every interpretive or expository action in the essay is oriented subjectively. This is so even at the essay's conclusion: "*What I want to end with* ... is to note how much that coming apart of thought and reality belongs to flesh and blood. *I take that* ... to be itself a thought joining Hughes, Coetzee, and Cavell" (78). Diamond thus creates a concept—the difficulty of reality—and a set of procedural aspirations that never completely vacate the realm of hypothesis. In the final paragraph of the essay, the possibility is explicitly entertained that the "failure" of thought connoted by the totemic phrase of her title may be a "confused" notion, lacking "content." Perhaps, she says, "a language, a form of thought cannot ... get things right or wrong, fit or fail to fit reality; it can only be more or less useful." In other words, evaluative terms such as "failure" and "difficulty," which exist on a continuum with the autobiographical framing of her essay, are forms of deflection from the "thought joining Hughes, Coetzee, and Cavell": the fact of embodiment.

INSTANTIATION AND THE LITERARY REGIME

What about the term "instantiation"? As I have described it, instantiation is a logic that is inherent to the novel form, according to which an entity (a person, an object, a linguistic sign, an encounter, a fictional description, a character trait) is asserted as a *case* or *instance* of a larger category, property, or concept, to whose reality it attests. The term "instantiation," as I am seeking to show, is indispensable for understanding the preoccupations and procedures of literary criticism at the present time. To remain oblivious to the presence of the instantiation relation in, say, a realist novel is to fail to grasp the work's substance, for the literary regime, as Jacques Rancière has observed, is formed by a "miscount" between the individualities of the work, on one hand, and the whole that unites those individualities, on the other. The discrepancy is present either as a "subtraction" (as in Flaubert's *Madame Bovary*, in which unifying ideas such as the love between Emma and Léon are present only as narratable exterior sensations) or as an "addition" (as in Proust, whose book comments on its own operations but in so doing enacts a "performative contradiction" with respect to its essence). This interior discrepancy or (Rancière's term) "dissensus" can never be brought into harmony, for it is "the law of literature" and not simply a fact of unpredictability in the work's reception.[29] The instantiation relation installs itself, for example, inside the reeds, dragonflies, water beetles, and sunbeams perceivable in the environs of Yonville, such that the "tall, slender grasses" and "thin-legged insects" noticed by Emma and Léon allude to—but at the same time *invent*—a connection of legibility with the characters' stirring emotions (Rancière, 61).[30] Instantiation is what Rancière describes as the "mode of intelligibility in which literature asserted its novelty and which it then passed onto those sciences of interpretation which believed that, by applying them to it in turn, they were forcing literature to cough up its hidden truth" (23). The structure is invented by the novel itself, which thus lays down traces that the standard interpretive protocols of literary criticism merely emulate.

To introduce the term "instantiation" into critical discourse, then, is to do two things at once. First, it is to propose a distinct analytic with which to understand a historical, aesthetic formation in which the thought of the work is for the first time unspeakable (although by no means unreadable)—in which any normative claim by the work itself is, by that very fact, enlisted in the work's accumulation of details. (Rancière calls this the "aesthetic regime.") Second, it is to register, in the identifiability of that formation, a historical limit or threshold beyond which this analytic is no longer pertinent, that is, to introduce a nominally later formation *from* which the formal disjunction or dissonance implied in the aesthetic regime is newly *thinkable*—thinkable *as such*, thinkable precisely *in its unthinkability*—and *in* which the instantiation relation is no longer the principle of the work's thought. The terms "instance" and "instantiation" signify, therefore, both positively and negatively; they both designate a technology or procedure of artistic expression associated with the novel form and signal the appearance of a certain aperture within that technology or procedure, an aperture peculiar to a newer critical moment (however we might delimit and situate that moment historically).

Even this (broadly speaking) contemporary situation of the "thinkability" of instantiation should not be understood in positive terms. When Deleuze refers to this development, as he does in *The Logic of Sense*, it is as a *loss* of belief, an *incapacity* to believe, rather than an emergent intuition or insight. Imagining a constituency of readers immune to the force of the problematic as he is outlining it, Deleuze writes:

> It is difficult to respond to those who wish to be satisfied with words, things, images, and ideas. For we may not even say that sense exists, either in things or in the mind; it has neither physical nor mental existence. Shall we at least say that it is useful, and that it is necessary to admit it for its utility? Not even this, since it is endowed with an inefficacious, impassive, and sterile splendor.
>
> (20)

Deleuze, then, is registering the same subjective incommensurability that we noted earlier in the discussion of Cora Diamond's position alongside that of Amanda Anderson and Caroline Levine. The critical insight that activates Diamond's readings is of the same unverifiable quality that underpins Deleuze's concept of "sense": an entity, says Deleuze, that can only be "infer[red] . . . *indirectly.*" Sense appears "for itself, in its irreducibility" as a break in the relation between word and concept that is constituted in the proposition (20). For Deleuze, it seems, as for Lukács, sense has no formal, evidentiary status.

The critical language we have encountered for giving expression to this development has been predominantly negative up to this point: disconnection, the "difficulty of reality," "fundamental dissonance," the "ultimate nothingness of man." The question that titles this chapter, "How does immanence show itself?"—a question that derives from an essay by Rancière referred to briefly in chapter 1—continues to be thus evaded, or deflected.[31] Whenever it has been enunciated in this chapter, it too has inevitably asserted itself in a negative form; e.g.: *How may the critic, especially the critic in conversation with a work of literature, avoid "deflecting" from the thought of the work in the very moment of reading it? Is not any writer and any critic who is determined to think the "difficulty of reality" directly—without framing it in "conciliatory" forms—doomed to unreadability and incoherence?* In such formulations, the question answers itself. The negative question, which puts in place the concept of deflection, is already a deflection.

The next chapter is devoted to another of those negative formulations: the sensorimotor "break" or "collapse," derived from Henri Bergson's philosophy of perception, that provides Deleuze with the terms of a historical event that organizes his analysis of twentieth-century cinema.

In Bergson's *Matter and Memory* we encounter nothing less than a nondeflected, nonconciliatory notion of perception in the concept of "pure perception" already alluded to briefly in chapter 5. Pure perception is not a human faculty, or an ideal, or a practice (artistic or otherwise). It is for Bergson an entirely hypothetical category predicated on the virtual existence of a being who, without memory, without a body, without, therefore, any subjective interest, would thus be capable of an "immediate and instantaneous" perception, a perception from which nothing is subtracted and in which there is no temporal or spatial lag.[32] Human perception, by contrast, is "sensorimotor," which means that it is located in the human organism and determined by actions (whether immediate, imminent, pending, or merely potential) that the organism must undertake in order to maintain its existence. In Bergson's theory, a perception is nothing but a deferred action: this is the sensorimotor schema in a nutshell. As Deleuze summarizes it, "we do not perceive the thing or the image in its entirety, we always perceive less of it, we perceive only what we are interested in perceiving, or rather what it is in our interest to perceive, by virtue of our economic interests, ideological beliefs, and psychological demands."[33]

For Deleuze, this "sensorimotor" and "subtractive" form of perception, centered in a human being, provides the model for the classical era of filmmaking, driven by plots, characters, and stories and featuring objects and locations that are only perceived by the camera insofar as they are part of an economy of diegetic and thematic meaning. It is this form of perception that is "shattered" by transformations in European cinema in the years after the Second World War (*C2*, 40). In works by directors such as Roberto Rossellini, Michelangelo Antonioni, and Jean-Luc Godard, the cinematic image is liberated from plot considerations and from the organizing principle of characters and motivations, or, rather, such considerations become incidental and peripheral to the image rather than central and determining. Modern cinematic perception is no longer subtractive, no longer determined by *interests*. To bring out the full implications of this event for the present work, cinema, we could say, no longer obeys the protocols of the instantiation relation. The spaces between action and perception "are now neither co-ordinated nor filled" (*C2*, 40–41), which means that the principle of connection that both organizes the diegesis and determines the possibility of an interpretive approach to the work drops out.

The negative associations of Deleuze's diagnosis of a "break" or "collapse" in the sensorimotor schema, as a basis for thought, are therefore misleading, for the sensorimotor break is for Deleuze a moment of real thought, although not one that is attributable to any particular philosopher or critic (not even Deleuze) but to cinema itself. In this way, Deleuze's work on cinema asks us to relinquish our attachment to the notion of thought as a power or capacity. "What forces us to think," writes Deleuze, quoting Antonin Artaud, is " 'the inpower [*impouvoir*] of thought,' the figure of nothingness, the inexistence of a whole which could be thought" (*C2*, 168).[34] And in fact, this notion of an "inpower" or "inexistence" is one way out of the predicament of "deflection" described earlier. For if we were to reconceptualize the difficulty of reality not as the "difficulty" or the "failure" of thought but precisely *as* thought, that is, if we could give up the sense of thought as "power," "capacity," "affordance," etc., and come to terms, instead, with what another description of Artaud's project calls the "impossibility of thinking which is thought,"[35] we might thereby bring an end to the logic of instantiation, the logic in which every manifestation, actualization, or expression of a thought is in turn subject to the ontologizing charge of "deflection" or the aestheticizing charge of "pathos."

For Deleuze, then, cinema is a form in which such a thought, a thought outside the logic of instantiation, becomes possible, albeit at the cost of transposing the seat of thought outside the human subject. Cinema arrives in Deleuze's work to supply a material basis for a conception of thought, a noninstantiated thought that, until that moment, has had no formal complement. Certainly, for Deleuze, the same set of possibilities is evident in literature. The central motifs of his consideration of cinematic thought (the existence of an "unthinkable" in thought and the perpetual presence of "another thinker in the thinker"), he says, have already been diagnosed "everywhere in literature" by Maurice Blanchot (*C2*, 168). But the challenges for literature in displaying such a thought are illustrated when, at the end of *Howards End*, Margaret Schlegel gives voice to a sentiment that is as close to Deleuze's notion of absolute difference—or "sense"—as anything in English literature: "It is only that people are far more different than is pretended. . . . It is part of the battle against sameness. Differences—eternal differences, planted by God in a single family, so that there may always be colour; sorrow, perhaps, but colour in the daily gray" (Forster, 328). This passage, like the novel's epigraph, is an instance of the "performative contradiction" in which the idea is a casualty of the very directness and clarity with which it is expressed. The instantiation relation is present in this formula no less than in the countryside of Yonville. In literature, this is to say, directness of speech in the expression of ideas is yet another mode of deflection.

In cinema, however, even if absolute difference (or the difficulty of reality) were to be verbalized, the legibility or legitimacy of the idea would not hang on such verbalization, for the thought of cinema is never aligned with statements made or theories advanced by an object in the field of vision. In the sensorimotor break of cinema, this is to say, the thinking of the interstice is no longer hypothetical; the cinematic image is the real thought of the interstice: the moment when the thought of the interstice and the interstice itself, *sense* and the *sense of sense*, are one.

This claim is the basis of the argument to be unfolded over the next two chapters, which deal respectively with Gilles Deleuze's contention of a sensorimotor break in cinema and Jacques Rancière's account of the aesthetic or literary "regime," an account that includes an unprecedented challenge to Deleuze's project on cinema—unprecedented insofar as it also offers as lucid an account of that project as we have anywhere. These readings will make the case that Deleuze's cinema books give us a way to talk about the thought of the novel that avoids the positivism with which practices of literary criticism and contemporary novel theory have approached the novel form, a positivism that ensures that the work's most profound stratum of thought remains unnoticed.

The stakes of this encounter between literature and cinema will become clear if we compare the proposition of the cinematic image as "the real thought of the interstice" with what Lukács says about the novel's "form-giving" qualities in *The Theory of the Novel* (60). With Lukács, we have only his word for it that the novel's "form-giving intention" may be read for the "fissures and rents," or the "nothing in the world of objects or norms" that underlies that intention, rather than for the forms as such—say, the "psychology of the novel's heroes" or the "given" concepts of crime or madness. Lukács's claims for the fundamental dissonance of existence that every form "resolves" (62) and for the "absurdity" that underlies every lurch toward meaning remain abstract—hypothetical—in their very substance and dependent, therefore, on the sensitivities of a likeminded reader. There is nothing in the novel that can underwrite such claims or provide a formal complement to them. If there were, Lukács says, it would amount only to "a psychological fact." Lukács's claims about the novel thus subsist as ideal ones, predicated on a level of abstraction that he will later condemn in his own early work. It is only with cinema, and only with Deleuze's account of it, that we can see or immediately apprehend this thought. Only in cinema does "the possibility of the ultimate nothingness of man" leave the realm of the subjective. Only with cinema, in other words, does the thought of the difficulty of reality appear in itself, undeflected and entirely lacking in pathos.

Chapter Seven

WHAT IS A SENSORIMOTOR BREAK?

Deleuze on Cinema

THE POSSIBILITY OF THINKING

Deleuze's cinema books advance a kind of historical thesis that is unknown elsewhere in Deleuze's work. This thesis proposes a transition from an analytic of the "movement-image" in *Cinema 1* (1983) to that of the "time-image" in *Cinema 2* (1985) and a corresponding historical evolution from the classical cinema, in which movement determines and frames all temporal experience, to the modern cinema, in which time is liberated from that subordination to movement and becomes perceivable and meaningful "in itself." Films such as Rossellini's *Germany Year Zero*, Ozu's *Late Spring*, or Welles's *The Lady from Shanghai* are transitional works in Deleuze's terms. They mark the beginning of what Deleuze calls the upheaval or collapse (C2, 1, 128) of the "sensorimotor system," Bergson's term for the corporeal basis of human perception, which lends its name in Deleuze's cinema books to the schema of narrative cinema. For, in an audacious move that will redefine the philosophical approach to cinema itself, Deleuze takes narrative cinema to be a realization of Bergson's theory of perception as "sensorimotor"—predicated upon action. Modern cinema, which departs from that schema, thereby opens a new order of perception and thought in the "time-image," the philosophical implications of which are as revolutionary as its artistic ones. Deleuze's analysis of cinematic thought provides us with both an image and a concept (a philosophical image) for a decentered

and deauthorized thought that is irreducible to the criterion of "interest"—
not hypothetically or ideally but in actuality.

A sensorimotor break, therefore, is a *moment in the history of cinema* in
which what is broken and displaced is the very principle according to which
mind and body may be comprehended together: "the link between man and
the world," as Deleuze put it (*C2*, 171–72). We can formulate the repercussions of this event in a number of ways, but among them is the proposition
that, after the sensorimotor break, the cinematic image is no longer referred
to a center of perception. A shift takes place in the narrative economy of
the visual sign, such that an image (that is to say, a cinematic movement) is
emancipated from the consciousness that would give such a movement
meaning. The movement no longer bears any necessary relation to narrative, philosophical, biographical, or ideological ends. The sensorimotor
break is a rupture in the very relation between the image and action. And
just as narrative is no longer the determining factor in any movement or
image, "aberrant" (non-narrative) movement is no longer incidental, relative to the narrative action, but becomes valid "in itself."

Bergson, or How to Preserve the Possibility of Thought in the Face of Its Materialist Critique

In Bergson's "sensorimotor" model of perception, perception is always
determined by "interests," meaning that Bergson's account is a materialist
theory of perception. The sense of "materialism" I am intending to retain
here is precisely that of Marx and Engels when they refer to "the phantoms
formed in the human brain" as "sublimates of [men's] material life-process."
The passage from *The German Ideology* is well known:

> Morality, religion, metaphysics, all the rest of ideology and their correspond-
> ing forms of consciousness, thus no longer retain the semblance of inde-
> pendence. They have no history, no development; but men, developing their
> material production and their material intercourse, alter, along with this
> their real existence, their thinking and the products of their thinking. Life
> is not determined by consciousness, but consciousness by life.[1]

The effect of these lines is to dismantle any idea of thought as independent or autonomous; indeed, it is not clear that the notion of thought as such

survives this challenge (and others, including that of psychoanalysis) in the modern period. Although Bergson's inquiry is oriented not around belief and ideology but perception—although, in other words, his critique is undertaken not at the level of social institutions and ideological concepts but at the level of the brain—its materialist underpinning bears some comparison to Marx and Engels's account of ideology. Like them, Bergson begins not from consciousness—"from what men say, imagine, conceive" (*The German Ideology*, 47)—but from "the reality of matter."[2] But for Bergson, "the reality of matter" cannot be located anywhere else than in "the totality of perceived images" (64). Marx and Engels differentiate "men in the flesh"—"real, active men"—from "men as narrated, thought of, imagined, conceived" (47). For Bergson, the difference is immaterial; the totality of matter means the absoluteness of representation or, better, "the totality of perceived images" (64). The difference is less one of content than of starting point. If one were to try to establish philosophical terms for thinking Bergson's project alongside that of Marx and Engels, one need only consider their critique of idealism as having, with Bergson, moved into and occupied the very place of perception from which the critique is undertaken. Their reference to "men in the flesh" would be for Bergson an instance of that privileged image that we call "the body"—"privileged" insofar as we refer all other images to it (43). Just as, for Marx and Engels, every image is altered when regarded through the prism of class struggle, so for Bergson every image, including those of the body and brain themselves, is fundamentally altered once we view it from the perspective (which is not a perspective) of the "aggregate of images" (43).

Closely associated with this starting point of the "totality of matter" is a second premise: the hypothesis of an order of "pure perception," predicated upon the theoretical existence of a being "placed where I am, living as I live, but absorbed in the present and capable, by giving up every form of memory, of obtaining a vision of matter both immediate and instantaneous" (26). This "hypothesis" becomes, in the course of just a few pages of *Matter and Memory*, a supposition "with which no theory of perception can dispense" (32). The mistake is to imagine perception on the model of the photograph. The "obvious" truth, says Bergson, is that "the photograph, if photograph there be, is already taken, already developed in the very heart of things and at all the points of space" (31). This is a photograph "without loss" and which is "translucent," insofar as there is no need for any "black screen" on which the image could be shown. This hypothetical photograph is a figure for the "virtual perception of all things" going on around us (32) (a phrase that, for Bergson, is equivalent to the very possibility of a material world) and for the virtual action of every object upon every other object, irrespective of our perception and experience of such events.[3]

The notion of a conscious self that is capable of perceiving such an image and of drawing conclusions, developing hypotheses, etc. is construed, then, only as a departure from that pure, virtual perception, for my perception begins "in the aggregate of bodies" and then "gradually limits itself and adopts my body as a centre" (64). Human perception emerges not as something added to matter (the totality of images) but as a limitation of it. Following this logic, Bergson rejects the idea that our perception produces "knowledge" of the object perceived (17); it is more like the opposite. Perception is corporeal, which means that it is subtractive: it "results from the discarding of what has no interest for our needs, or more generally for our functions" (30). The subject is formed, then, not as a center of determinacy but of "indetermination" (28). Extrapolating from Bergson's "subtractive" theory of subjectivity, we might say that the subject is not a site of action but of inaction; the very "activity" of the subject is in fact a principle of resistance to the incessant action of every atom upon every other atom in the universe. Again, the starting point—the "aggregate of images" rather than, say, the field of perception as referred to a privileged center—is what distinguishes Bergson's philosophy from one (such as Descartes's) that begins with, and is destined never to resolve, the existential predicament: the subject-object dichotomy.

Bergson's description of the sensorimotor system in the first chapter of *Matter and Memory* is worth quoting for its economy and compactness:

> Perception, understood as we understand it, measures our possible action upon things, and thereby, inversely, the possible action of things upon us. The greater the body's power of action (symbolized by a higher degree of complexity in the nervous system), the wider is the field that perception embraces. The distance which separates our body from an object perceived really measures, therefore, the greater or less imminence of a danger, the nearer or more remote fulfilment of a promise. . . . Consequently, our perception of an object distinct from our body, separated from our body by an interval, never expresses anything but a *virtual* action. But the more the

distance decreases between this object and our body (the more, in other words, the danger becomes urgent or the promise immediate), the more does virtual action tend to pass into *real* action. Suppose the distance reduced to zero, that is to say that the object to be perceived coincides with our body, that is to say again, that our body is the object to be perceived. Then it is no longer virtual action, but real action, that this specialized perception will express: and this is exactly what affection is. . . . Our sensations are, then, to our perceptions that which the real action of our body is to its possible or virtual action. Its virtual action concerns other objects, and is manifested within those objects; its real action concerns itself, and is manifested within its own substance.

(57–58)

Perception, action, and affection are thus mutually constitutive events within the sensorimotor schema; they are different from one another only by "degree" and separable only insofar as we insert a temporal lag between them, a lag in which the consciousness of the subject is entirely located. Subjectivity, we might say, is nothing other than that temporal lag of inaction and imperception.

Action, says Suzanne Guerlac, is for Bergson "a law of life, and perception follows from this law."[4] Naturally, the same goes for narrative cinema—or, at least, for approaches to cinema that proceed under the assumption of the comprehensibility of every sign we encounter in the work. Narrative cinema is an objectivization of Bergson's theory of perception, a perception in which nothing registers that is not the object or subject of some real or possible action. It is this corporeal, human-centered, inherently meaningful notion of perception that is "shattered from the inside," according to Deleuze, by transformations in European cinema in the years after the Second World War (*C2*, 40), when the image is liberated from plot considerations and from the organizing principles of character and person. Shattered—but replaced by what? By a new relation to movement, liberated from a center of determination (which for Bergson was always a center of indetermination). Movement becomes "aberrant," which is to say that characters "find themselves condemned to wander about or go off on a trip [*à l'errance ou à la balade*]" (*C2*, 41). Their presence in the film no longer has to do with revelations that they undergo, experiences they transmit, social positionalities they embody and with which the viewer may identify, or plot developments that are in the process of unfolding. Such characters "do not even have the consolation of the sublime, which would connect them to matter or would gain control of the spirit for them" (*C2*, 41). They are simply "seers," which is to say, vessels of what Deleuze calls "pure optical and sound situations" (41)—when a pragmatic function is replaced by a pure "seeing function" (19). In such moments, "the character or the viewer, and the two together, become visionaries." (The words "seer" [*voyant*] and "visionary" [*visionnaire*] carry no mystical connotations in Deleuze's work. Seers see, and visionaries employ vision.) Thus Deleuze contrasts the formally indistinguishable treatment of two-character dialogue in the films of the Hollywood director Ernst Lubitsch with that of the Japanese director Yasujiro Ozu, spelling out how the "one shot, one line" technique (in which shots and reverse-shots are correlated precisely with speakers) functions as an index of action in the former, whereas in Ozu the banality of the dialogue ("any dialogue whatever") ensures that the element of action "disappears in favour of the purely visual image of what a character *is*, and the sound image of what he *says*" (*C2*, 13–14).

With this decisive formal shift, cinema opens directly onto the world, bringing about "the identity of the mental and the physical, the real and the imaginary, the subject and the object, the world and the I" (16). And, we might add: the material and the ideal. Such sequences bring into being "direct time-images," where time is no longer presented indirectly, as representation (for example, the cut signifying "the next day"), but attains a "crystalline" presence, existing identically both inside and outside the diegesis. Examples mentioned by Deleuze include the famous ten-second perception image (or point-of-view shot) of the vase at the end of Ozu's *Late Spring* (1949) as Noriko lies awake in a hotel room in Kyoto,[5] but also less ostentatious shots, such as the camera's obsessional interest in the glass of milk Johnnie delivers to his wife, Lina, in Alfred Hitchcock's *Suspicion* (1941), the many views through an adjacent apartment window from the perspective of the incapacitated protagonist L. B. Jefferies in Hitchcock's *Rear Window* (1954), and such noted moments in Italian neorealism as the girl's contemplation of her own pregnant stomach at the beginning of Vittorio De Sica's *Umberto D.* (1952). In all these images, of course, a sensorimotor connection is retained, since the perception is still focalized through a character (following the model of free indirect style in literature) and because the plot element is relatively important to the image (although

Deleuze distinguishes Ozu's images as having greater "autonomy" in both respects) (16). Action, in other words, is merely postponed rather than transcended completely. And yet such character-image relationships, and the narrative conceits that enable them,[6] begin the transformation that will be more fully realized in the works of, say, Godard, Antonioni, Werner Herzog, and, in a later period, Abbas Kiarostami, Béla Tarr, and Tsai Ming-liang.

THE HISTORICAL ARGUMENT

What effects the "break," as Deleuze refers to it throughout his writing on cinema? At the end of *Cinema 1*, Deleuze offers an apparently conventional, historical explanation, mobilizing causes that are both "external" to cinema (functioning, then, as "materialist" explanations) and others that seem to draw on an inherent or "developmental" logic—a "history," in Marx and Engels's sense of the word (*Geschichte*):

> The crisis which has shaken the action image has depended on many factors which only had their full effect after the war, some of which were social, economic, political, moral and others more internal to art, to literature and to the cinema in particular. We might mention, in no particular order, the war and its consequences, the unsteadiness of the "American Dream" in all its aspects, the new consciousness of minorities, the rise and inflation of images both in the external world and in people's minds, the influence on the cinema of the new modes of narrative with which literature had experimented, the crisis of Hollywood and its old genres. Certainly, people continue to make SAS and ASA [narrative-driven] films: the greatest commercial successes always take that route, but the soul of the cinema no longer does.
>
> (*C1*, 206)

The sensorimotor break takes place at slightly different moments, depending on national-historical conditions, especially in relation to the Second World War. Why did the break happen "in Italy first, before France and Germany" (*C1*, 211)? The film industry in Italy had largely escaped the influence of fascism during the war and was able to point to the endurance of a spirit of popular "resistance" underlying the repression of the fascist years; thus, little ideological adjustment was needed for the "renewal" (*renouvellement*) of the cinematographic image to take place. France, by contrast, "aspired to belong to the circle of victors," an aspiration that favored the continuing ideological investment in "a properly French 'dream'" underpinned by the framework of a "traditional action-image" (211). The break was thus "belated" in France and was even more so in Germany: the "new German cinema," as the work of directors such as Herzog, Rainer Werner Fassbinder, and Wim Wenders came to be known, did not appear until the end of the 1960s. Thus, the "renewal" of the image is in fact the discovery, by the cinema, of effects and modes of thought that are immanent to it—its coming to terms with the "profound Bergsonianism of the cinema in general" (*C1*, 206). The logic is similar to that of Bergson's understanding of subjective perception in relation to "pure perception." The sensorimotor break is not precipitated by a particular director's vision or aesthetic practice but the opposite. Such visions or practices have the effect, rather, of delaying or deferring the break. If the sensorimotor break takes place, it is because it had already taken place long ago, with the discovery of the cinematographic image itself.

Cinematic Thought

Thus, the sensorimotor break is not only—and not primarily—a historical event but a figure of thought: the thought of cinema itself. It is cinema's emergence into its full potentiality—its "soul" (*C1*, 206). The thought of cinema is not the thought of the director who translates his or her idea to the screen; it is not the thought of the spectator, moved to reflection by the images or the unfolding of a narrative. In fact, the sensorimotor break is an interruption of the very links implied in such notions of "translation" and "reflection." As a figure of thought, the sensorimotor break dismantles at least three conceptual relations on which narrative cinema depends: it liberates thought from "action," whether imminent or deferred; it uproots thought from its supposed seat in the brain (a center of [in]determination); and it frees cinema from the task of representing thought, from reference. Thus, thought is no longer implicated in any subject-object relation. The sensorimotor break announces the arrival of a thought that has no obligation of communicability or comprehensibility, for it is a thought that is wholly free of "interest."

The sensorimotor break thus represents an escape, on the part of cinema, from the protocols of narrative realism, protocols with which writers and producers, actors and directors, financiers and proprietors, attempt to regulate the image, i.e., render the thought of the work identifiable and transferable. These protocols are set forth in what is perhaps the most influential English work of novel theory, Ian Watt's *The Rise of the Novel*, where they are underpinned by a set of premises that its author takes to be intrinsic to "the novel form in general": that the work "is a full and authentic report of human experience"; that it is "therefore under an obligation to satisfy its reader with such details of the story as the individuality of the actors concerned, the particulars of the times and place of their actions"; and that such details are presented "through a more largely referential use of language than is common in other literary forms."[7] It is difficult to find a more direct or efficient statement of the aesthetic ideology that I have been calling the instantiation relation.

Such protocols, then, define and determine the sensorimotor schema in cinema, as they do the instantiation relation in literature. With their disappearance in "modern" cinema, the question arises of what Deleuze's "seer" actually sees? If we take "see" to mean *recognize, comprehend, understand*—concepts that imply the deferred or virtual action that for Bergson is intrinsic to subjective perception—then what Deleuze's seer sees is, in a sense, nothing. Nothing, that is, but seeing itself. "The sensory-motor break makes man a seer who finds himself struck by something intolerable in the world, and confronted by something unthinkable in thought" (169). Between the intolerable and the unthinkable, Deleuze writes,

> thought undergoes a strange fossilization, which is as it were its powerlessness to function, to be, its dispossession of itself and the world. For it is not in the name of a better or truer world that thought captures the intolerable in this world, but, on the contrary, it is because this world is intolerable that *it can no longer think a world or think itself*. The intolerable is no longer a serious injustice, but the permanent state of a daily banality.
>
> (*C2*, 169–70)

What is the "something intolerable in the world" or the "something unthinkable in thought"? We have already encountered several answers to this question in the work of Cora Diamond (and the authors who interest her, Coetzee and Ted Hughes) and that of Georg Lukács. For Diamond, it is an experience of intellectual defeat that resists being thought to the extent that its very self-narration (as, say, a position of philosophical "skepticism," "defeat," or the "failure" of thought) amounts to a "deflection" of it.[8] In Coetzee's *Elizabeth Costello* the "something unthinkable" takes at least two forms: one "repellent"—for example, the knowledge of "what it is like to be a corpse," a knowledge that is both momentary, arriving in "instants at a time" when we sense our mortality, and separated from itself by the feelings (of repulsion) that accompany it; the other joyful—for example, the feeling of what it must be like "to be a bat," which is to say, to be "alive," an "embodied soul," a feeling that is graspable in a sensory and imaginative form, i.e., a form incompatible with Descartes's notion of thinking as cognition, "a kind of ghostly reasoning machine thinking thoughts."[9] The subjective and temporal limitations of these knowledges are the source of their paradoxical quality: "What I know is what a corpse cannot know: that it is extinct, that it knows nothing and will never know anything anymore. For an instant, before my whole structure of knowledge collapses in panic, I am alive inside that contradiction, dead and alive at the same time" (77). Lukács offers several abstract formulations for the something unthinkable, including, of course, the "fundamental dissonance of existence" and the "possibility of the ultimate nothingness of man" (*TN*, 62). Lukács, too, appears to yearn for the possibility of an "unresolved" (or non-"absorbed") experience of the dissonance, but such a possibility is present in his theory of the novel only in the terms "futility," "absurdity," and "nothingness" that designate what is absolutely foreclosed from the novel, except as its "basic *a priori* constituent, the fundamental structural element of the characters and events within it" (62). For Lukács, an absence of a sense of futility in the novel heralds no deliverance from the futility but the opposite: a lack of thought, a lapse into convention, and a capitulation to the world of "recognised but senseless necessities" (62).

In every such case, then, the "intolerable" or "unthinkable" is a negative principle: the fact of a discrepancy between thought and the forms available to it. The claim that anchors the present book, the proposition around which its every reading and analysis revolves, is, first, that the most direct, least "deflected" theoretical formulation of this experience, which haunts the novel form, is *the absence of an instantiation relation*; and, second, that this absent and unthinkable fact is not, *pace* Lukács, the "basic *a priori* constituent" of the novel, or a residue of the lost "perfection" from which the novel seeks consolation (31), but its destination: the point at which the novel is perpetually arriving, a principle of absolute heterogeneity that gestures back at the novel, and every novel, from the perspective of its realization.

The proposition that there is no instantiation relation attempts to give a theoretical articulation to an experience whose subjective element neither Diamond nor Lukács is able definitively to erase. But this "theoretical" formulation is far from simple. We have encountered at least two possible versions of it in the course of this discussion:

(1) the absence of an instantiation relation on the grounds that, as David Armstrong has it, objects do not exist without properties, and vice versa (if no apple exists without the properties of either redness or greenness, then the concepts of *green* and *red*—or indeed *apple*—are not fundamental or universal but secondary; what is fundamental is the "state of affairs" of a green, or red, apple);

(2) the absence of an instantiation relation in the name of an "outside" of thought, or what Marie-Claire Ropars-Wuilleumier, following Deleuze, calls "the constitutive in-between of every image."[10]

These two absences seem to be radically different. When—making reference to Blanchot—Deleuze writes of a thought that "addresses itself to an outside that has no form," this is in tension with Armstrong's refusal of "disjunctive and negative universals."[11] But it is important to remember a principle alluded to earlier: that it is in the very nature of an absence to be nongeneralizable. Thus, there can be no absence of an instantiation relation *in general*. The unthinkable that gestures to us in the work of Lukács and Diamond, Deleuze and Armstrong, Coetzee and innumerable writers of literature—including, say, Paul Auster, who writes of a "knowledge that exists, that comes into being beyond any possibility of putting it into words"; James Baldwin, who talks of an "incoherence" singular to the American experience, an incoherence that the "fact of color" simultaneously obscures, corroborates, and allows to remain in place; Maggie Nelson, who is unperturbed sharing her love of the color blue with "half the adults in the Western world," since she understands blue not as a universal property or a particular substance but as an "abundance" whose proper mode of apprehension is an "unseeing," an "unknowing," and an "undoing"; or Valeria

Luiselli, for whom any documentation of an experience results only in an assemblage of "all the moments that didn't form part of the actual experience"[12]—the unthinkable in these works *has no referent in common*, even when the formulations are identical. The unthinkable therefore resists theoretical elaboration. This is the problematic of the present work—and of novelistic form itself—in a nutshell, for the formulation "there is no instantiation relation" captures nothing whatsoever. One must be careful, in other words, not to translate the absence of an instantiation relation into the presence of a noninstantiable relation or the presence of an instantiable nonrelation.

However, what is remarkable in Deleuze's work on cinema is not only that this negative principle acquires an image that is adequate to it but that the image in question is precisely "philosophical" and not "aesthetic"; i.e., it is not momentary or present only "imaginatively," in a form that is paradoxical and unsustainable. It is, rather, material, stable, even objective. Cinema, that is to say, substantiates what Cora Diamond (or any philosopher or thinker) is only able to imagine: a "philosophy that is not deflected from such realities" (74). "The direct time-image is the phantom which has always haunted the cinema, but it took modern cinema to give a body to this phantom" (*C2*, 41). Cinema, then, is capable of thinking "directly" something that was only "indirectly" thinkable before: an absence of linkages, a break in the sensorimotor schema—and it does so without pathos, without subjective consolation, and without transcendental philosophies of expression. Unlike every thought that precedes it, cinematic thought thinks not simply a new relation but relationality itself. In the novel, says Lukács, "really existent relations" are obscured from view by the psychologizing forms that the novel imposes on the text, in which the trajectory of the hero's own story—typically a search—is expressed as the work's organizing principle: "the simple fact of seeking implies that neither the goals nor the way leading to them can be directly given" (*TN*, 60–61). The search is thus a sensorimotor image (a chronotope) that contains and displaces the "fissures and rents" that for Lukács are "inherent in the historical situation" of the novel (60). It should be obvious that no embodied thought in any novel with a protagonist, even one as formally reflective as *Elizabeth Costello*, can escape the status of "a psychological fact to which nothing in the world of objects or norms need necessarily correspond" (*TN*, 61).

This is the context in which cinema replaces Lukács's sensorimotor "seeker" with a nonsensorimotor alternative: a "seer" from whose vision or perception nothing is subtracted, whose "goals," and "the way leading to them," pertain only to the seer's body. The relation of such goals and trajectories to the sonorous and optical images onscreen is thus purely incidental. The seer is not a protagonist but more like an *anagonist*, a nonplayer or, in Jean Louis Schefer's phrase, a "being without qualities."[13] Cinema, says Deleuze, "is the pure vision of a non-human eye, of an eye which would be in things" (*C1*, 81). The most challenging, even outrageous implication, one that remains both unequalled in the philosophical tradition and unfathomed by it, is that cinematic perception is no longer subtractive, no longer determined by interests. And that with this expulsion of interest from the image, thought finally becomes possible.

What does such a thought look like?

THE ANY-INSTANT-WHATEVER, THE OUT-OF-FIELD, THE INTERSTICE

Like the status of the historical break, the status of the example is by no means straightforward in Deleuze's work on cinema, for reasons that have to do with the conception of thought that is operating through his project. Exemplarity—like judgment, like criticism, like all forms of knowledge, like philosophy itself—is a sensorimotor structure that presupposes a prior organization of the world according to concepts (universals) and instances (particulars), a relation of expression between the two that is rational and legible, and a reader or viewer capable of exploiting that legibility—by, say, drawing lessons from it. When examples appear in Deleuze's discussion they are accompanied by an insistence that nothing is thereby "sum[med] up [*résumé*]"; examples take their place "among others" (*C2*, 136/178). As Deleuze explains elsewhere, "all images combine the same elements, the same signs, differently."[14] The proliferation of films and directors across his two volumes on cinema further dissolves the possibility of any one figure or movement emerging in a privileged or vanguard (exemplary) position. Since what connects the different practices is the fact of a disjunction internal to each, the link between them lacks any positive principle or logic. "Each image is plucked from the void and falls back into it" (*C2*, 179). The void itself does not tolerate any consideration as an object of theoretical reflection.[15] Thus, the very "readability of the visual image" in modern cinema is of a special kind; it "no longer relates to a specific element . . . nor to an overall effect of the speech-act in the seen image" (246). The sensorimotor break is not the expression of a universality but the opposite: an exit from all regimes of thought predicated upon a relation between the universal and the particular.

Nevertheless, it is clear that certain pioneering directors such as Carl Dreyer, Robert Bresson, and Michelangelo Antonioni; or the filmmakers of the French new wave such as Jean-Luc Godard, François Truffaut, and Eric Rohmer; or inheritors and later practitioners such as Chantal Akerman and the partnership of Jean-Marie Straub and Danièle Huillet supply especially rich occasions for Deleuze to explore the possibilities of a cinema not of the idea or the positive term but rather of the "interstice," a cinema that "does away with all the cinema of Being = is" (C2, 180), a cinema of the "unthought in thought," a cinema that is able to "restore our belief in the world" by producing an image of precisely that in thought which is inaccessible to conceptualization (181–82). In the work of Godard or Straub-Huillet, cinema is itself thought; cinema has liberated itself from the task of *representing* thought. In Godard, says Deleuze, there is no "privileged" image or discourse; even "good" discourses, such as those of "the militant, the revolutionary, the feminist, the philosopher, the film-maker," are treated with the same "categorical" inflection—that is to say, *generically* (C2, 172). Thought in Godard happens elsewhere than in these representational moments, which is to say that it happens in cinema itself—*as* cinema.

The concepts that are relevant to Deleuze's analysis of cinema are thus not philosophical concepts but concepts specific to cinema. Such concepts enable cinema to constitute a form of knowing that is inaccessible to us or, at least, ungraspable without cinema. One such cinematic concept is the *any-instant-whatever* (*l'instant quelconque*). In the first chapter of *Cinema 1* Deleuze identifies a tension within cinema between the "privileged instant"—moments at which the great directors attempt to extract meaning from the moving image—and the "any-instant-whatever," the technological basis of the image. This is really an opposition between two forms of perception: human perception and the perception of the technical apparatus, the cinema itself. Referring to Eadweard Muybridge's early experiments photographing the movements of animals, which are presented in multiple series of successive moments, Deleuze points out the following: if there are privileged instants in Muybridge's pictures (for example, when the horse has one hoof on the ground, or none), "it is as remarkable or singular points which belong to movement, and not as the moments of actualization of a transcendent form." Deleuze draws from this a principle that will underpin the entire analysis of cinema through the two volumes:

> The privileged instants of Eisenstein, or of any other director, are still any-instants-whatever: to put it simply, the any-instant-whatever can be regular or singular, ordinary or remarkable. If Eisenstein picks out remarkable instants, this does not prevent him deriving from them an immanent analysis of movement, and not a transcendental synthesis. The remarkable or singular instant remains any-instant-whatever among the others.
> (5-6)

The passage establishes a close relation between the technical specificity of cinema, the apparatus (the fact of a movement-image being constructed out of a succession of "any-instants-whatever," twenty-four frames a second), and its "soul." From the beginning, according to Deleuze, cinema is in conflict with itself, for the temptation is always to extract privileged instants from the succession of any-instants-whatever, whether in Eisenstein's "dialectical" cinema or the "spiritual style" of a director like Bresson,[16] but also, of course, in every commercial film that is ever made.

Deleuze's thesis on movement is organized around this opposition between the privileged instant and the any-instant-whatever. The essence of cinema is to know—despite what *we* "know," despite what its practitioners, despite what Eisenstein "knows"—that *there are no privileged instants*, or, rather, that there are privileged instants only in so far as we impose our own interests, our own cuts or disconnections, on the movement-image. It is almost impossible to resist making such impositions; the process of producing and receiving the work involves innumerable such "cuts" and subtractions, moments at which we substitute already existing images for thought. We normally perceive only clichés, says Deleuze.

> But, if our sensory-motor schemata jam or break, then a different type of image can appear: a pure optical-sound image, the whole image without metaphor, brings out the thing in itself, literally, in its excess of horror or

beauty, in its radical or unjustifiable character, because it no longer has to be "justified," for better or for worse.

(*C2*, 20)

Deleuze presents this attention to the any-instant-whatever as a nondialectical (and therefore, in a certain sense, nonhistorical) inflection. Cinema is the expression of a shift, itself historical, in which meaning and history cease to operate dialectically, or are awakened to their nondialectical essence. A "developmental" conception of history is thus replaced by a "natural" history, a history told from the point of view of the entire (albeit still incomplete) history of cinema ("On the Movement-Image," 46). It is no longer possible, or necessary, to locate a synthesis of the disparate elements or moments in order to give those elements order and closure, to derive meaning from them. The "instants" of cinema are "equidistant" from one another and from the whole; no single moment emerges to unify and explain the rest. Insofar as cinema locates or searches for such moments, it flees from or suppresses its "essence." Jacques Rancière will later refer to this thesis, which defines the separation of "modern" cinema from the "classical" cinema, as Deleuze's "rigorous ontology of the cinematographic image."[17]

Deleuze explains the crucial distinction between modern (Dreyer, Bresson, Rohmer, Godard) and classical (D. W. Griffith, Lubitsch, Sidney Lumet, Sergei Eisenstein) cinema using two phrases: "the whole is the outside" and "the whole is the open" (*C2*, 179). Both refer to the relation between the images onscreen and the thought (or "whole") to which they give access: the out-of-field (or out-of-shot). Each phrase, then, imagines a distinct relation to instantiation. By "the whole is the open," what is meant is an out-of-field that "refer[s] on one hand to an external world which was actualizable in other images, [and] on the other hand to a changing whole which was expressed in the set of associated images. "The whole is the open" thus posits an out-of-field that is in continuity with what is in the shot, that is absent only incidentally, instantiated by what is visible.

"The whole is the outside," by contrast, refers to something like an absolute out-of-field: an out-of-field that has no hope of ever entering the shot. And yet, as we will see, the very distinction between a relative and an absolute out-of-field is, in the course of Deleuze's exposition, consigned to the paradigm of the sensorimotor schema.[18] What counts in the cinema of the break is no longer "the association or attraction of images" but "the interstice between images, between two images." "In Godard's method," writes Deleuze,

> it is not a question of association. Given one image, another image has to be chosen which will induce an interstice *between* the two. . . . The fissure has become primary, and as such grows larger. It is not a matter of following a chain of images, even across voids, but of getting out of the chain or the association. Film ceases to be "images in a chain . . . an uninterrupted chain of images each one the slave of the next," and whose slave we are. . . . It is the method of BETWEEN, "between two images," which does away with all cinema of the One. It is the method of AND, "this and then that," which does away with all the cinema of Being = is. Between two actions, between two affections, between two perceptions, between two visual images, between two sound images, between the sound and the visual: make the indiscernible, that is the frontier, visible. . . .
>
> Just as the image is itself cut off from the outside world, the out-of-field in turn undergoes a transformation. When cinema became talkie . . . the sound itself becomes the object of a specific framing which *imposes an interstice* with the visual framing. The notion of voice-off [*voix off*] tends to disappear in favour of a difference between what is seen and what is heard, and this difference is constitutive of the image.[19] *There is no more out-of-field.* The outside of the image is replaced by the interstice between the two frames in the image. . . . Interstices thus proliferate everything, in the visual image, in the sound image, between the sound image and the visual image. . . . Thus, in Godard, the interaction of two images engenders or traces a frontier which belongs to neither one nor the other.
>
> (179–81)

A well-known scene in Godard's 1967 film *Two or Three Things I Know About Her* illustrates both the startling innovativeness of Godard's cinema—hence, its intense relevance to Deleuze's claims—and the limited value of taking any such body of work as exemplifying, or still less epitomizing, those claims. Twenty-five minutes into the film, Juliette Janson enters a café, orders a Coke, and sits down at a table where a man reading a newspaper smokes a cigarette and a young woman reads a magazine. The sounds of a pinball machine off-screen are heard. As the three sit, reading, smoking, one of them stirring a cup of black coffee, a whispered voiceover narrates the action as follows: "This is how Juliette, at 3.37 p.m., saw turn the pages of that object that, in journalistic language, is called a 'magazine.' And this is how, 150 frames later, another young woman, her fellow, her sister [*sa semblable, sa soeur*], saw the same object. Where, then, is the truth—in full face or in profile? And anyway, what is an object?"

Two perception images are shown of the magazine, the first ("in profile") from Juliette's point of view (figure 7.1), the second ("in full face") from the perspective of the woman reading (figure 7.2). Juliette and the smoking man exchange looks; a barman, alerted to a noise behind him, turns around, then pours someone a drink. During the monologue, which is delivered by Godard himself, the ambient sounds of the café are muted. In an extended

FIGURE 7.1. *Deux ou trois choses que je sais d'elle*, dir. Jean-Luc Godard, Argos Films, 1967.

FIGURE 7.2. *Deux ou trois choses que je sais d'elle*, dir. Jean-Luc Godard, Argos Films, 1967.

sequence that one hesitates even to mention—for so closely identified with Godard's film and with Godard's work in general has it become that it threatens to emerge as a "privileged" instant—the lens of the camera approaches the surface of the coffee in a kind of framing that Deleuze calls "rarefied" (as opposed to "saturated") (*C1*, 12).[20] The voiceover might almost be a ventriloquy of the thought of cinema itself as Deleuze presents it in the last few chapters of *Cinema 2*:

> Maybe an object is what permits us to connect [*relier*], to move [*passer*] from one subject to another, therefore to live in society, to be together. But then, since social relations are always ambiguous, since my thought divides as much as it unites, since my speech brings closer by what it expresses, and isolates by what it omits, since a large gulf separates my subjective certainty of myself from the objective truth that I am for others, since I do not cease to find myself guilty even though I feel innocent, since each event changes my daily life, since I always fail to communicate, I mean, to understand, to love and to be loved, and each failure causes me to experience my solitude, since . . . since I cannot tear myself from the objectivity that crushes me, nor the subjectivity that exiles me, since I can neither rise to a state of being, nor fall into nothingness, I must listen, more than ever I must look around me at the world, my fellow, my brother [*mon semblable, mon frère*].[21]

What permits us to connect is an object, says Godard. Not a sentiment, a belief, an ethical principle or code of behavior, not, then, a thought of any kind. Such thoughts, in fact, do the opposite—which is precisely why the ideas expressed in this monologue, which is set in the temporal lag of inaction and imperception that we call subjectivity, cannot be equated with the thought of the film. The principle of the absence of any privileged discourses in Godard, then, must extend even to those that could be taken to paraphrase or ventriloquize the absence in question.[22] For, like the pages of the magazine, Godard's voiceover is "just an image" (to quote a phrase of Godard's, the meaning of which, again, has almost been eclipsed by its fame)[23]—or an "any-instant-whatever." Notwithstanding its felicity and appropriateness, the thoughts contained in any such utterance can have no privileged status with respect to the "thought" of the film. This also implies that the sentiments expressed cannot be taken to refer outside cinema—to the possibilities of establishing connections in society—or even to cinema's potential to establish such connections.[24] Thought in cinema happens in the interstices between images, says Deleuze, not in the images themselves. If a remark made in the film resonates with the thought of the interstice, that is happenstance, for the thought of the interstice cannot be instantiated, *even if such an instantiation should take place.* Instantiation is a reversible principle; it designates both a documentable event and an impossibility, for, as we have been saying all along, *there is no instantiation relation.* This is why, no matter how far Godard goes toward speaking the truth of the images, his voiceover undertakes no "resolution" of (or "clarified meditation" upon) the interstice but only induces a further interstice. As with *Elizabeth Costello,* Godard's monologue breaks with the site of authorship in the very fact of enunciation.

The connections between Deleuze's idea of cinematic thought and the ideas expressed in Godard's voiceover, then, are fortuitous, or "adventitious," to use Badiou's term.[25] The voiced sentiments are no more significant than any other but also, crucially, no less so. The fact that they are voiced neither privileges them nor delegitimates them. The truth of Godard's commentary—its cinematic truth, its "essence"—consists precisely in its difference *from itself,* in the interstice in which two meanings, one immanent, one transcendent, coexist, each simultaneously removing from the other its point of reference.

HEAUTONOMY

Toward the end of *Cinema 2,* Deleuze introduces the Kantian concept of heautonomy to characterize the relationship between the sound image and the visual image in the cinema of Godard and other directors, notably Marguerite Duras and Jean-Marie Straub-Danièle Huillet. The term "heautonomy" first appears in the introduction to the *Critique of Judgment,* where Kant describes a series of propositions that it is necessary to take up a priori (as a matter of principle, rather than a posteriori—from experience) if any knowledge of nature is to be attained or any inquiry whatsoever is to be undertaken. Namely:

> that there is in nature a subordination graspable by us of species under genera; that genera in turn approach one another under some common principle, so as to make possible a transition from one to another and so to a

higher genus [that is, a genus of genera—TB]; that, while initially it seems to our understanding unavoidable to assume as many different kinds of causality as there are specific differences among natural effects, they may nevertheless fall under a small number of principles which it is our task to discover, etc.[26]

Such propositions, taken together, amount to "a cognizable order of nature" and "a harmony of nature with our cognitive power" (24). In other words, a coherent, interconnected world, characterized—"in nature"—by relations of instantiation between, at the first level, species and genera (in which a species instantiates a genus) and, at a second level, between genera and "higher" genera (sets of sets)—ad infinitum. For Kant, however, "purposiveness in nature" (a plausible paraphrase of the instantiation relation) is a hypothesis beyond any possibility of substantiation. Its rationale is not merely autonomous but "heautonomous," meaning that its principles are prescribed not only to its object, nature, but to itself, the "subject" of the reflection. Heautonomous principles are not "determinative" but "reflective." Thus, with the notion of heautonomy, Kant invents a mode of *self-understanding of principles themselves*, an awareness of the enormousness of the differences "in the empirical laws of nature" that may underlie and exceed our attempts to grasp them, an awareness that is present in those very attempts.[27] Heautonomy designates, therefore, *the possibility of an impossibility*: the possibility that nature's products *not* be divided "into genera and species" (even if they happen to be so divided); the possibility that the very "principles by which we explain and understand one project in order to explain and grasp another as well" (25) may, in actuality, enable nothing of the sort; the possibility that the "coherent experience" we thereby construct "out of material that to us is so full of confusion (though actually it is only infinitely diverse and beyond our ability to grasp it)" is the expression of a fundamental incoherence—the truth of which lies, rather, in that ungraspable complexity; the possibility that examples mask an irreducible multiplicity.

The extraordinary implication of these sentences in Kant's introduction is that the concept of heautonomy—as present in that distinction between "confusion" (how the world appears to us) and "infinit[e] divers[ity]" (how the world appears to itself)—is an anticipation of the principle that underlies Deleuze's cinema books: the collapse of the "privileged instant" into the "any-instant-whatever" (the very principle, we said earlier, that is "ungrasp-able" without cinema). To return to a theme of the previous chapter, it seems that, for Kant, deflection is indeed "the condition of possibility of thought." Without the procedures of instantiation and exemplarity that deflect us from the infinite diversity, we are caught in the "confusion" that is their alternative: a subjectively distressing (but no less deflected) mode of experience. Nevertheless, the principle of the possible abolition or over-coming of all instantiation, all exemplarity, the possibility of a "nonde-flected" philosophy, the critical potential of the "extremity of difference": these are also present in Kant's thought in this fleetingly entertained notion of heautonomy—a figure that registers an order of being, or thought, out-side the bounds of any conceivable or actual relation of instantiation.[28]

Thus, when Deleuze appends the term "heautonomy" to the relationship between sound and image in modern cinema—in Godard's work and else-where—he is crediting cinema with making substantial, and so unignor-able, a thought that, in Kant, is only momentary and speculative (i.e., ignor-able). The separation of sound and image in modern cinema, the technical possibility of such a separation, is "the invention of a point of view which disconnects the sides" (C2, 251), that is no longer interested in reconciling two or more views of an object in the service of "truth." For the new point of view "establishes a void between them, in such a way as to extract a pure space, an any-space-whatever, from the space given in objects."[29] Speech acts themselves become "pure," says Deleuze, meaning that they "are no lon-ger components or dimensions of the visual image," for the integrated vision and sound of the "first stage" of the talkie—when, after the "indi-rect" or reported speech of the silent era, cinema discovers the possibility of "direct" speech—gives way, in the "second stage," to "two heautonomous images, an auditory image and an optical image, continually separated, dis-sociated, or unhooked by irrational cuts between them" (252). The new relation between the auditory and the optical is "non-totalizable" (256). "The speech-act is no longer inserted in the linkage of actions and reactions, and does not reveal a web of interactions anymore" (243). As in the conversa-tional shots and reverse-shots in Ozu's earliest sound films, verbal interac-tions in the cinema of the sensorimotor break are "no longer explained through individuals, any more than they derive from a structure" (227). In fact, cinematic treatments reveal something inherently "mad" and "schizo-phrenic" about conversations themselves (230).

Again, Godard's works from the mid-1960s offer a number of illustrations, including two unanchored, apparently improvised conversations in a café, one hour into *Two or Three Things*, the first between Juliette's husband, Robert, and a young unidentified woman, the second between a schoolgirl and a "Nobel Prize–winning" writer named Ivanoff.[30] In such scenes, says Deleuze, the fictional and the real "mix together so that they seem to be speaking to each other" (*C2*, 154). Conversation in such scenes is a "time-image" (155) in which interaction, the dynamic of inbetweenness, becomes visible *as such*, not simply the elements "external to it": the places and functions of the communication, the interests and motives of the conversation partners, their actions and reactions (230). Such elements are points of origination and summation that we tend to extract from them. The amazing discovery of cinema—which neither theater nor the novel is able to match (with the exception, according to Deleuze, of one or two authors whose work is contemporary with the emergence of cinema)—is that of "conversation for itself" (231).

DISCONNECTING THE SIDES: FREE INDIRECT SUBJECTIVE

If silent cinema, with its use of intertitles, may be analogized to indirect (or reported) speech, and the talkie to direct discourse, the cinema of the sensorimotor collapse, says Deleuze, generates a "free indirect" quality (*C2*, 242). However, this usage of free indirect discourse, which recurs many times throughout Deleuze's cinema books, does not simply transpose a technical description of a mode of reported speech and thought from literary-critical discourse. Deleuze is drawing on Pier Paolo Pasolini's essay "The 'Cinema of Poetry,'" where Pasolini, playing on the Italian term for point-of-view shot (*soggettiva*), refers to the perspective of the camera in the works of certain contemporary filmmakers (Antonioni and Bernardo Bertolucci as well as Godard) as *soggettiva libera indiretta*, a "free indirect subjective." Pasolini is differentiating between the forms of literature and cinema, pointing out that cinema does not have the same possibilities of "interiorization and abstraction" as the word; indeed, cinema "lacks the entire abstract and theoretical dimension which is explicitly involved in the evocative and cognitive act of the character's monologue."[31] The free indirect point-of-view shot is a uniquely cinematic mode that does not correspond to "free indirect discourse." It is not a technique or projected point

of view that remains in the control of a director or actor but a subject position in itself.

Deleuze takes up this set of ideas, but, without saying so directly, he
rejects Pasolini's distinction between cinema and the novel. Rather, Deleuze
seems to consider the very absence of interiority or unity that Pasolini
regards as unique to cinema to be precisely what film has inherited from
the novel. With Godard, writes Deleuze, cinema becomes "novelesque,"
meaning that Godard's use of language is characterized by the same per-
sistent and constitutive "borrow[ing]" that, for Mikhail Bakhtin, is intrinsic to the novel (C2, 187)—and the same logic applies to Godard's use of
genres, characters, even colors. Not a single moment in Godard's body of
work is susceptible to "resolution"; every moment escapes attribution:
"Godard gives cinema the particular powers of the novel. He provides himself with the reflexive types as so many interceders through whom I is
always another [*JE est toujours un autre*]" (187/244).[32]

Deleuze's thinking here draws on a critique of linguistic approaches to
language that he and Félix Guattari had earlier undertaken in *A Thousand
Plateaus*. That critique is indebted in turn to Vološinov's *Marxism and the
Philosophy of Language*, a work in which free indirect discourse (or, in
Vološinov's preferred nomenclature, "quasi-direct discourse") extends
beyond its status as a stylistic device for the reporting of speech and thought.
For Vološinov, what we have in quasi-direct discourse is "a completely *new*,
positive tendency in active reception of another person's utterance, a *special direction* in which the dynamics of the interrelationship between reporting and reported speech moves" (142).[33] As the commentator Charles Lock
has put it, free indirect discourse shows us "the discursive possibilities of
an entirely novel way of thinking."[34]

The great error of linguistic approaches, says Vološinov, is to frame the
phenomenon of free indirect discourse in relation to already existing categories of analysis (author, subject, sense, signification, *langue, parole*)—in
the light of which free indirect discourse appears as a "problem." Free indirect discourse is conceptualized by such approaches as "masked" discourse
(a term Vološinov quotes from the linguist Theodor Kalepky), a form of
indirect discourse whose distinction is simply that the speaker's identity,
and its relation to the narrator, is unspecified (*MPL*, 143–44). The predicament that free indirect discourse presents us with is thus limited to questions of identification and decipherment. Such questions presuppose that

free indirect discourse is simply a "modification"—or, in Adolf Tobler's words, "a peculiar mixture"—of direct and indirect discourse (142); that direct discourse is the prior category in relation to which indirect and free indirect discourse are subsidiary forms; that once we are able to identify the speaker and recover or reconstruct the direct statement of which the free indirect utterance is the "veiled" form, the problem of free indirect discourse is resolved. For Vološinov, however, no such problem exists, for "it is clear from the very start that, in terms of the *sense* of what is said, it is the character speaking" (144). Such difficulties arise, says Vološinov, only for "grammarians," who, in isolating the utterance from its social context, assume an abstract notion of sense embedded in the words and phrases themselves. "Linguistic" approaches to discourse thus ensure that the sense-event remains ungraspable; the resolution they effect is always partial or premature. By confining itself to "constants" of expression (author, subject, word, sentence, signified, *langue*, *parole*, etc.) rather than "variables" (the same elements considered as immanent to language), linguistics, observe Deleuze and Guattari, "ties the statement to a signifier and enunciation to a subject and accordingly botches [*rate*] the assemblage."[35]

"Assemblage" (*agencement*) is Deleuze and Guattari's term for the smallest possible unit of analysis with respect to any given instance of discourse—the smallest unit being, precisely, a collectivity or an encounter.[36] The concept of assemblage is thus a rejection of the unitary quality of words, ideas, concepts, subjects, significations. On the basis of the "necessarily social character" of these elements (*ATP*, 79–80), Deleuze and Guattari claim that "there is no individual enunciation" or even a "subject of enunciation," that "all discourse is indirect" (77), and that "a rule of grammar is a power marker before it is a syntactical marker" (76). There is no communication that is not social in origin and no imparting of information that does not impose an order on its recipient, for there are no facts that are not, first, *statements* of fact—that do not presuppose a response, either of recognition or refusal (whether or not they are met with such a response). There is no "nonlinguistic point of departure" to language (76). To give an order is thus to engage in a "redundancy" (75), since statements of fact are already imperatives whose normative force consists in the erasure or denial of their status as such.

It is here, also, that we should locate the violence of the instantiation relation: in the assumption of a nonlinguistic origin in any notion of a primary, universal quality and its secondary or particular instantiation in an object. Deleuze and Guattari claim that "language does not operate between something seen (or felt) and something said, but always goes from saying to saying." In doing so, they refuse not only the idealism of the speaking subject posited by "linguistics" but, again, the primacy of "Being" over "Something" posited by ontological philosophies. At the origin of language is not a sight seen or a sentiment felt but a moment of reported speech. The origin is a transmission of something heard, "what someone else said to you" (*ATP*, 76). Just as Bergson speaks of an "aggregate of images," a photograph "in the very heart of things," so we may speak of the primacy of "hearsay" over direct discourse, of an aggregate of words, sentences, formulations that precede, and hence are constitutive of, experience.[37]

These principles are central to Vološinov's philosophy of language also. For Vološinov, the fundamental unit of analysis is not the word or sentence, or the utterance, or, of course, the speaking subject and his or her expressive intentions, for no such entity exists "outside [its] material objectification in language" (152). To interpret any statement by reference to "subjective psychic factors and intentions" is to explain "an ideologeme of greater clarity and precision with another ideologeme of a vaguer, more muddled character" (153). The most elementary unit of Vološinov's philosophy of language is "the interaction of at least two utterances—in a word, dialogue" (117). In the absence of this principle, "not a single one of the categories of linguistics is of any value for defining a whole linguistic entity" (110). Every such category (author, subject, *langue*, *parole*, etc.) is an assemblage: "*Word* is a two-sided act. It is determined equally by *whose* word it is and *for whom* it is meant. As word, it is precisely *the product of the reciprocal relationship between speaker and listener, addresser and addressee*" (86). Linguistic subjectivism substitutes for the principle of the assemblage a principle of unity and origin, for example, the notion of an inner or subjective "personality," of which a word is conceived as the "expression." For Vološinov, the relation between word and subjectivity is the inverse of this. Expression begins not with the individual but with sociality. The subject is explained by the assemblage of enunciation, not the other way around:

> The word is an expression of social intercourse, of the social interaction of material personalities, of producers. The conditions of that thoroughly material intercourse are what determine and condition the kind of thematic and

structural shape that the inner personality will receive at any given time and in any given environment; the ways in which it will come to self-awareness; the degree of richness and surety this self-awareness will achieve; and how it will motivate and evaluate its actions. . . . The inner personality is generated along with language, in the comprehensive and concrete sense of the word, as one of its most important and most profound themes.

(153)

Vološinov's theory of language is thus a linguistic version of the ontological principle we have seen earlier articulated in David Armstrong's philosophy: that the most basic fact is not a propertyless entity, a "thing," but a state of affairs (Armstrong, 139).

Toward the end of *Marxism and the Philosophy of Language* Vološinov discusses a passage of free indirect discourse in Dostoevsky's novel *The Idiot*. Prince Myshkin is contemplating his troubled relationship with his love-rival Rogozhin: "And why had he, the prince, not gone up to him now, but turned away from him as if noticing nothing, though their eyes had met? (Yes, their eyes had met! and they had looked at each other.) Hadn't he wanted to take him by the hand and go *there* with him? Hadn't he wanted to go to him tomorrow and tell him that he had called on her?"[38] Passages of this kind, says Vološinov, are capable of a "play of intonations" that cannot be reproduced in any medium other than a prose conceived to be read silently (136). "Only this 'silencing' of prose," he goes on, "could have made possible the multileveledness and voice-defying complexity of intonational structures that are so characteristic for modern literature" (156). The multileveledness and complexity, that is to say, cannot be transposed to another medium. The thought made possible in free indirect discourse is not extractable or generalizable. Vološinov describes this thought not in terms of subjective shifts "within the confines of an individual psyche" (say, a character's vacillation between empathy and distance)—but as a combination of the perspectives of character and the author. That is, the character's "evaluative purview" (empathy) coexists with that of the author (distance). The "specificum" of quasi-direct discourse is "a matter of both author and character speaking at the same time" (144).

Few modern readers of *The Idiot* would agree with Vološinov's interpretation here. Even Vološinov's colleague Bakhtin, writing contemporaneously, insists that "a polyphony of battling and *internally* divided voices" is the primary mode in which "dialogicality" (a term we will return to in due course) is manifest in Dostoevsky's works.[39] However, the difference between externally and internally differentiated voices is inconsequential once we accept the principle, which is important to both Bakhtin and Vološinov, of the derivative nature (and thus "imprecision") of all "subjective psychic factors." For Vološinov, internal voices are dialogical long before the dialogicality is experienced subjectively (as, say, ambivalence or indecision)—indeed, *irrespective* of whether it is experienced as such. The vicissitudes of the word are individual only insofar as they are social, "the vicissitudes of the society of word-users" (157). "Language lights up the inner personality and its consciousness; language creates them and endows them with intricacy and profundity—and it does not work the other way" (153).

The key point for Vološinov is that the "expressive intonations" of quasi-direct discourse are distinctive and singular to the medium—prose—such that they cannot be transposed to, or replicated in, another artistic form—for example, the stage. No transposition of quasi-direct discourse can take place without compromising that which, as a thought, distinguishes it in the first place: its nonsubjective quality. The thought of free indirect discourse, in short, cannot be transferred, or "acted out," because *it cannot be inhabited subjectively* (156–57).

The case is more easily made if we present the distinct intonation of free indirect discourse as a combination of external perspectives. "After all," says Vološinov, "into that self-enclosed, individual world there can . . . be [no] infusion or spillover of the author's intentions." At the same time, the principle of the *intrinsic* (rather than extrinsic) sociality of enunciation (a point central to Deleuze and Guattari's discussion in *A Thousand Plateaus*) is thereby weakened, as the respective subjectivities of the character and the author, the *representing* and the *represented* consciousnesses, are left intact. The authentically Vološinovan view of free indirect discourse is more completely expressed, therefore, in Bakhtin's notion of "dialogicality," a term with which Bakhtin avoids the pitfalls of focalization implied in that of "free indirect discourse." For dialogicality is not a formal feature of the novel but *a propensity that is immanent within the novel form*, a condition toward which everything in the novel gravitates. Free indirect or quasi-direct discourse is a feature in almost every passage Bakhtin discusses, yet the concept never appears in his *Problems in Dostoevsky's Poetics* or in the essays collected in *The Dialogic Imagination*. When Bakhtin says that Dostoevsky was capable of "representing someone else's idea, preserving its full capacity to signify as an idea, while at the same time preserving a distance, neither confirming the idea nor merging it with [the author's] own expressed ideology" (*Problems*, 85), the distance (between author and idea, between narrator and character) is *infinite* (which is the same as saying that it is negligible). The dialogical relation cannot be conceptualized spatially, which means that no "resolution" of the relative investments of author and character in the views being expressed is possible or appropriate. Far from signifying the character's legibility to the narrator—as, say, Dorrit Cohn implies of free indirect discourse with her notion of "transparent minds"[40]— dialogicality in Dostoevsky represents the emancipation of the character from the author's (or narrator's, or critic's) field of vision. Any resolution of perspectives is provisional and subjective, a deflection from the real thought of the interstice—which is the element in free indirect discourse that remains after all readings and resolutions have been completed and disseminated. This thought is not inhabitable, since it is not the thought of the character, or of the author, or of the reader. Nor—most challenging of all in the present context—is the thought of the interstice the thought of the critic or theorist. The interstice is located not "within the confines of an individual psyche," says Vološinov, but only within a particular "linguistic construction" (155). Just as, for Deleuze, the cinematic apparatus is necessary in order to realize the thought of the sensorimotor collapse, so, for Vološinov and Bakhtin, written prose is the indispensable technology without which the thought of free indirect discourse is inaccessible and inconceivable.

This does not mean, of course, that the thought of free indirect discourse is the same as the thought of the sensorimotor collapse. No principle in common underlies the sensorimotor collapse and the free indirect, for again, the absence of an instantiation relation is not itself instantiable.

Nevertheless, the "proliferation" of interstices in and between images, including the image of the author and of his or her discourse, can be seen to take place in the context of both literature and film as an operation of incessant de- (and re-) subjectivation. To illustrate, let us return briefly to Godard's film *Two or Three Things I Know About Her*, where this proliferation extends to almost every image that we encounter in the course of the film, including its most consistent human presence, Juliette Janson. From the opening scenes of the film it is impossible to conceive of Juliette

separately from the actress who plays her, Marina Vlady, for each is introduced in turn by Godard's whispered commentary as she stands on a bal-
cony of the public housing development where Juliette lives. (The image of
Juliette is followed immediately by a second image, of Marina Vlady, that
induces an "interstice" with the first.) Both Juliette and Marina, we hear,
"are of Russian origin"; both have light brown, or perhaps dark chestnut,
hair—"I'm not sure which, exactly"; and both wear a blue sweater with yel-
low stripes. Juliette turns her head to the right, Marina to the left—"but
that means nothing." *Elle*, in the film's title, refers to both figures (as well
as to the "région parisienne" specified in the film's opening credits).

The subject of the free indirect, as actualized in *Two or Three Things*, is
not, therefore, Godard the filmmaker, or Juliette the protagonist, or Marina
the actor. It is not the unnamed young man in the café, whose hand (perhaps) holds the spoon we see stirring the coffee during the voiceover, for
the thoughts expressed in the voiceover are not the young man's (as if
Godard were ventriloquizing him, as James Joyce ventriloquizes the
thoughts of Leopold Bloom in the "Lestrygonians" episode of *Ulysses*).[41] The
subject is not—to name other possible contenders—capital, the commodity, or the proletariat (unless, following Lukács, we conceive the consciousness of the proletariat as an immaterial entity made up of the conjoined
"thought" and "existence" of the figure "whose mission it is to create the
future"—a figure who thus resides in that "unbridgeable 'pernicious chasm'"
of the present, as Ernst Bloch put it).[42] Rather, the subject of the free indirect is the conjoined-dissociated pair *Juliette-Marina* (the interstice constituted by their relation), the conjoined-dissociated pair *actor-character*. The
subject of the free indirect is the conjoined-dissociated trio of primary colors, red-yellow-blue, the interval between the color and its instantiation in
an object—for in Godard color itself has a heautonomous quality, its dimension as a subjective category or genre entirely displacing its supposed
objective dimension as a universal property. The subject of the free indirect is the conjoined-dissociated pair *audio-vision*, the thought-space
opened up in cinema by the technical possibility of their dissociation. It is
the conjoined-dissociated pair *grammar-sense* or that of *words-voice*; the
conjoined-dissociated pairs *intimacy-impersonality*, *being-attribute*, or
discourse-subject. Neither term in each pair is detachable from its fellow,
for the subject is the interaction itself: the event or encounter and its irre-
solvability. The posited identification of one term with the other is in each

case "impossible" and "paradoxical," as D. A. Miller says of the relation between narrator and character in Austen's works, both "presupposed" and "severed."[43] This is another formulation of what Kant means by "heautonomy."

And we may speak similarly, in the context of contemporary fiction, of the fiction-reality relation or the narrator-character relation as a "free indirect" that precedes and transcends, or survives, any subjectivation of thought in the work. We may speak, then, of an accumulation of coincidences in Patrick Modiano's novel *Dora Bruder* (discussed in chapter 5), coincidences that connect two habitual uses of the same métro station (by Dora and the narrator) twenty years apart; or two first novels with the title *La place de l'Étoile*, both published by Gallimard; or the mere existence of a man "the same age" as Dora Bruder, who "lived in the same neighborhood" as she did and so might have known her.[44] No common principle connects these terms, only the "imaginative leaps" that betray the writer's vocation, "the need to fix your mind on points of detail—to the point of obsession" (42–43).

We may speak of two novels both called *Period*: one by Dennis Cooper (an author), the other by Walker Crane (a fictional character); and of a complex structure of obsessive intradiegetical reading, according to which the characters in one of these works named *Period* behave and model themselves after the characters in the other.[45] We may speak of the two works being so intricately connected and interpenetrated in Cooper's text that it is difficult to establish which chapters and characters are part of which novel, which work—that of the author Dennis Cooper or that of the character Walker Crane—is subsidiary to which, or in which work or set of characters we should locate the expression and in which the imitation.

We might speak of a conjoined-dissociated pair of writers, both named Ben Lerner, in the novel *10:04* and of two identical texts titled "The Golden Vanity" attributed respectively to these two writers—one published separately in the *New Yorker*, the other embedded in the novel as a chapter and distinct from the first not by any textual variations (for there aren't any) or by the name of the author to whom they are attributed (the names are identical) but only in the assemblage responsible for it: as Vološinov would say, the "concrete, historical situation that engendered the utterance" (*MPL*, 99).[46] We may speak of two identical sets of opinions held by two different characters in Lerner's work, Ben and his student Calvin, opinions that are indistinguishable in their formulations, their nuances of meaning, and even their quotients of plausibility (that the FBI "fucks with citizens' phones"; that the works of the poet Geoffrey G. O'Brien can be said to "spider out on the page"; that "our society [cannot], in its present form, go on"). These identical opinions are in each case separated by an immaterial assemblage of attribution and identification, an unbridgeable gap that one character, Ben, names as illness ("I felt that something was seriously wrong with Calvin as soon as I saw him"), the other, Calvin, as the "institution" ("Wow. You want to pathologize me, too. I guess that's your job") (214–20).

We might speak of Sybil, the "bourgeois little bitch" imagined in Muriel Spark's *The Bachelors*, the fiancée of a character named Walter, whose fictionality is doubled and inverted by the fact that she "had never existed";[47] of Maryanne, the imaginary sister of a character in a story by Tao Lin, who isn't "restrained by time or space," who is "just *there*" and "not even a sister, really";[48] of a dog in another work by Cusk, a brown spaniel named either Taffy or Tiffy, who appears only as the subject of a reported quarrel over its name and whether it ever existed in the first place (*Transit*, 246–47).

We might speak of a fart emitted onstage by an actor rehearsing the role of W. H. Auden in a fictional play within a play by Alan Bennett—a fart the actor immediately attributes to his character;[49] or an "Interval" located between acts 1 and 2 of the same work, the limits and duration of which coincide precisely with the break taken by the fictional actors in rehearsal (51). (These differences, of course, illustrate not some contra-Vološinovan possibility of "act[ing] out" the thought of the free indirect but moments when drama, too, encounters the free indirect at its own limits and the capacity of theater—no less than cinema and the novel—to create crystalline formations that escape the instantiation relation.)

We might speak of two stories that coexist in J. M. Coetzee's novel *Slow Man*: the story of an author (Elizabeth Costello) and the story of her character (Paul Rayment), the two brought into a relation of reversibility that is inconceivable outside the circuits of virtuality and actuality that are made possible in fiction—just as the "expressive intonations" of Prince Myshkin, for Vološinov, are unspeakable and unreproducible outside the "silent register" of Dostoevsky's free indirect discourse (*MPL*, 156).[50]

What we are encountering in such moments of contemporary fiction has been articulated no more clearly than in the words of Charles Lock, commenting on Bakhtin's notion of dialogicality: "an event in the history of human culture: the eruption of the unspeakable into discourse, the separation of words from voices, of discourse from subjects."[51] In these images and episodes, past and present, virtual and actual, art and madness, expression and imitation, are simultaneously present—not as oppositions to be resolved but in their perfect reversibility and indiscernibility. Time is no longer an object of representation (as in the epic, "a poem about the past")[52] or a product of instantiation (as in the novelistic structure of the "imagined community," where time is the "homogeneous, empty" backdrop to a sensorimotor perspective shared by narrators, characters, and readers).[53] In these episodes, rather, time emerges as nothing less than a representing *subject*. The time-image in the contemporary novel is a crystalline formation, "a fragment of time in the pure state," in which it is no longer possible to distinguish the narrated event from the event of narration, for the distance between them is not closed, or resolved (in either direction), or transposed or deflected into something inhabitable or knowable, but preserved in its actuality and indeterminacy. It is here, in the interstice, or the "special semantic sphere" of the "purely chronotopic," as Bakhtin calls it, that the subjectivity of the work is located, and its thinking takes place, although the place in question does not exist in any spatial or conceptual sense at all.

PROFILING

The antithesis of the principle of noninstantiability (the idea of the absence of an instantiation relation) is, of course, nothing other than the logic of instantiation (a thought that is content to connect a system of preexisting qualities or properties with the persons and objects that embody them). One of the principal forms for the dissemination of the logic of instantiation is the activity and concept of "profiling," a term that currently operates, in the United States and elsewhere, in two main disciplinary and discursive contexts: "psychology" and "race." Both contexts involve the exploitation of intuitive or traceable connections. Associations are made on the basis of certain "raw" data (phenomenological impressions, perceived racial or demographic patterns, identifiable social trends, individuals' self-reported preferences and desires), certain conclusions are drawn, and certain social consequences ensue. Profiling, which we may define as the extraction of "constants" from such data, is a direct enactment of the logic of instantiation in the public sphere. Psychological profiling attracted particular attention in 2018 after 230 million profiles of American citizens were created by the British company Cambridge Analytica from data harvested over the previous four years from personal Facebook accounts.

The ideological force of profiling depends on the impression that it is nothing but a "degree-zero" connection, a technology that merely exposes relations that are already operating, whether we are aware of them or not. Of course, anyone, including an algorithm (a person with a computer), may extrapolate from a person's "intimate family connections" or social media "likes" and other "crumbs of personal data"[1] in order to construct a "profile" that is by definition legible, transposable, and monetizable, just as a police officer may draw certain conclusions about (say) a person's propensity to criminality from his or her racial appearance, accent, or make and condition of vehicle and subject such a person to search, harassment, restraint, or arrest (or worse). The relation between these two forms of profiling—"psychological" and "racial"—should be insisted upon, despite the fact that one may be based on statistical precedent and the other on subjective prejudice. The distinction between statistics and prejudice is itself ideological (indeed, the ideological opacity of the first is revealed by the ideological transparency of the second). To name "instantiation" as the ideology underlying such connections is to expand our understanding of the term "ideology" from the subjective domain to the ontological. Such expansion is possible—and imperative—once the "degree-zero" connections denoted by the term "instantiation" become newly thinkable, as, I contend, they are (increasingly) in the trajectory of the novel.

The principle of the absence of an instantiation relation—or better, of the *fundamental* nature of instantiation—holds to the notion that, despite the regularity with which instantiation relations are mobilized in the contemporary public sphere, and in the face of any evidence (statistical, anecdotal, psychological, psephological, commercial) that appears to support them, such relations are subjective phenomena inextricable from the positionalities that enable them to appear natural. Personality traits (such as the five "types" that, in 2007, formed the basis of a "myPersonality" Facebook application originated by the precursor to Cambridge Analytica, the Psychometrics Centre at Cambridge University—"Openness, Conscientiousness, Extroversion, Agreeableness, and Neuroticism") (Cadwalladr) no more exist as objectless properties than greenness and redness exist without the apples or other objects that "instantiate" them and no more than "criminality" exists without the social forces and relations that produce it and that the very term "criminality" obscures from view. This would be so even if such relations were borne out by empirical evidence, i.e., by "data." A statistical preference for red over green apples in the general population does not establish the existence of redness as an abstraction, and neither do subsequent changes in agricultural practice that might hope to address that general preference—even if they succeed in doing so. The link between race and criminality *is no truer when supported by statistical evidence than when it is not.* To think the absence of an instantiation relation is to think the impossibility of "profiling"—that is, to think the interstice that exists at the site of the connections that profiling (whether "racial" or "psychological") asserts as the substance of thought. The interstice persists whether or not a consumer demand can be identified and fulfilled using the technology of "profiling," whether or not a presidential election or political referendum can be won on the basis of voting tendencies that are revealed by its means, and whether or not a criminal conviction may be secured following a detainment or arrest based on subjective racial prejudice.

And that absence of an instantiation relation—that is to say, the thought of the interstice between an individual's likely political affiliations, as suggested by personal or demographic indicators, and his or her real affiliations, *even if the two should happen to coincide,* or between the likelihood of the presence of an illegal firearm in a vehicle's glove compartment, as reflected in the prejudices of the officer who accosts the driver, and the real contents of the glove box, *even if those contents should happen to gratify the officer's prejudicial assessment*—that absence is not thinkable in journalistic, consumer-marketing, data-analytical, or criminal-investigative discourses or even in the academic (literary-theoretical, political-philosophical) register of books such as this one. Just as the logic of instantiation has a natural subject position—the point of sensorimotor unity at which the connections endemic to profiling appear natural and intuitive or, alternatively, "original, groundbreaking" (Cadwalladr)—so the principle of the absence of an instantiation relation, or the "fundamental" quality of instantiation, has a natural standpoint from which the interstice is thinkable: the point of sensorimotor collapse (or principle of novelistic subjectivity) that I am calling the free indirect.

Chapter Eight

RANCIÈRE

Toward Nonregime Thinking

THE AESTHETIC REGIME

The title of this chapter takes the word "regime" from the work of Jacques Rancière, who in *Le partage du sensible* (2000) coins the term "artistic regimes" to conceptualize three historical stages in the evolution of the politics of aesthetics in the Western tradition.[1] In Rancière's writing, the term is intended as a rejection of the positivist inflection of concepts such as "modernity" and "postmodernity," which have typically been made to cohere by reference to subjective statements such as artists' manifestos and accompanying "exemplary works."[2] For Rancière, works of art and literature are determined as much by the conventions they define themselves in opposition to as by the artistic conceptions and practices that inform their production. The historical shifts indicated by the differences between one regime and another take place over decades, or centuries, and have none of the subjective explanations that the discourses of modernity and postmodernity often attribute to them—even if we consider, say, Virginia Woolf's reference to December 1910 as the moment when "human character changed" or Samuel Beckett's 1949 claim about the Dutch painter Bram van Velde as the first artist to escape the expressive "predicament" to be intentionally hyperbolic.[3] Rancière's regimes name not practices or interventions but complex social and historical formations that include works that meet specific formal criteria as well as others that violate them.

The notion of the artistic regime is central to all of Rancière's work on aesthetics. Indeed, it seems that for Rancière there is no artistic activity that is not implicated in one of three historically determined regimes of art. Rancière thus differentiates the "ethical" regime, the "representative" (or mimetic) regime, and the "aesthetic" regime. The first is a preartistic regime, predicated on the consensual values of the community. In the ethical regime, the distinction between the "true" (ideal) arts and their simulacra is established with epistemological certainty, such that the question of politics does not arise, for art, as a distinct mode of knowledge or experience, does not exist (*Politics of Aesthetics*, 21). The question at issue in the ethical regime is that of the work's effects on the "mode of being of individuals and communities," the ethos. The Mosaic prohibition on graven images, articulated in the Second Commandment, is part of this regime,[4] as is Plato's figure of the cave, according to which art is an unambiguously secondary and derivative activity. Having thus defined and identified the "ethical" regime, Rancière pays little further attention to it, for there are no "politics of aesthetics" in the ethical regime.

The second, "representative" regime is also a preaesthetic formation. Its world is that of fine arts and letters, of edifying dramatic productions and pleasing chamber performances, and by implication it includes the norms and taboos that place certain themes and works outside the bounds of representability. Only in the second regime, then, is there a kind of material deemed "unrepresentable." Pierre Corneille's *Oedipe*, his seventeenth-century adaptation of *Oedipus Rex* for the French stage, which omits the violent excesses of Sophocles's original work, is for Rancière a characteristic work of the representative regime. Corneille's adaptation dispenses with the tragic paradoxes of Sophocles's play (the dénouement of which turns on a knowledge that is simultaneously known and not known) by introducing characters into the plot who will resolve the pathos of the protagonist in a dramatic rather than interior form. Corneille's rewriting of the play thus reinstitutes "a certain order of relations between what can be said and what can be seen."[5] (Such reordering or redistribution of the perceptible is, for Rancière, an example of the politics of aesthetics. Corneille's intervention is a specifically reactionary one because it reintroduces a hierarchy of representability into the sensible, consigning certain objects and subjects to the invisible.) If Plato is the authorizing thinker of the ethical regime, it is Aristotle who, by first identifying mimesis as a distinctive quality of art, supplies "criteria of discrimination" with which to evaluate the productions of the representative regime.[6] This Aristotle, of course, in his interpretation of *Oedipus Rex*, casually elides the very elements that Corneille deemed unrepresentable in the play.[7] Aristotle, says Rancière, substitutes for the pathos of Sophocles's hero a "theory of dramatic action that makes knowing a result of the ingenious machinery of reversal [*peripateia*] and recognition [*anagnorisis*]."[8] Aristotle, in other words, is the great classical thinker of the sensorimotor imbrication of perception and action.[9]

The "aesthetic" regime, the third in Rancière's schema, is the most important for Rancière's project, as well as for the present study, since it is the regime that pertains to the modern period and to our own era. In the aesthetic regime "there are no longer appropriate subjects for art" and thus no inappropriate subjects either ("Are Some Things Unrepresentable?," 118). Rancière draws on Gustave Flaubert's many reflections about art in his correspondence, where we find the first theoretical formulations of what Rancière will call the aesthetic regime in the French tradition: "Yvetot is as good as Constantinople" says Flaubert, in a famous letter to Louise Colet written during the composition of *Madame Bovary*. What Flaubert means, says Rancière, is that "the adulteries of a farmer's daughter are as good as those of Theseus, Oedipus or Clytemnestra. There are no longer rules of appropriateness between a particular subject and a particular form, but a general availability of all subjects for any artistic form whatsoever" (118). If political activity, as Rancière puts it, "reconfigures the distribution of the perceptible" by "introduc[ing] new objects and subjects onto the common stage," the aesthetic regime—irrespective of what individual works may do—is the historical formation in which any subject position can speak and any object can make an appearance. The aesthetic regime "makes visible what was invisible, it makes audible as speaking beings those who were previously heard only as noisy animals."[10] Under the protocols of the aesthetic regime, the sensible itself is, for Rancière, a basis for the existence of "something in common," that is to say, a community.

One of the most dramatic implications of Rancière's account of the aesthetic regime for critical discussions of contemporary literature is in challenging approaches that explain modern art and literature by reference to some unprecedented or traumatic event that exceeds available forms of representation. Theodor Adorno's supposed dictum about the impossibility of poetry "after Auschwitz" and Jean-François Lyotard's definition of "modern" and "postmodern" art as formal responses to a world in which the capacity to "conceive" has surpassed the capacity to "present" both, for Rancière, fail to note the irrefutable fact that there is nothing unrepresentable in modern art and literature.[11] Antirepresentative art, says Rancière—whether in the form of nonfigurative abstraction or parodic irony—"is constitutively an art without unrepresentable things." A black square on a canvas or a carton of household cleaning pads is no less appropriate a subject for art than a row of poplars in Giverny or an allegorical depiction of a saint's temptation in the wilderness. In the aesthetic regime "there is no longer a language or form which is appropriate to a subject, whatever it might be" (137). That liberation of subject matter from a particular language or form is, for Rancière, precisely the "democracy" of the aesthetic regime. Lyotard and—by implication—Adorno transpose Immanuel Kant's concept of the sublime from nature to art when they introduce a notion of the unrepresentable into modern aesthetics. For Rancière, Kant's idea of the sublime "draws us outside the domain of art" (132). The sublime has to do with "nature's inability to attain to an exhibition of ideas," as Kant puts it. An intuition of the sublime is an experience of the "futility" with which reason, faced with the totality of nature, will "step in" to attempt to grasp that totality conceptually.[12] The sublime, in other words, is more properly an experience of the ethical regime, since it is manifested not in a kind of art but in the restraint from any kind of artistic effort on the grounds of its inadequacy.

When Rancière forecloses the question of representation from aesthetics, he is revealing an unspoken affiliation with the aesthetic regime, one that is apparent, also, in the very terms in which he defines the politics of aesthetics. The politics of literature, he says in the opening sentences of *The Politics of Literature*, "does not concern the personal engagements of writers in the social or political struggles of their times" (3). Politics is not a question of giving voice to an unrepresented identity formation or of bringing into visibility a particular cause or struggle, for such notions presuppose a representative dimension to the work. Politics is best thought of, rather, using a formulation that has become indelibly associated with Rancière's work, the "distribution of the sensible": "Politics is the construction of a specific sphere of experience in which certain objects are posited as shared and certain subjects regarded as capable of designating these objects and of arguing about them" (3).

Thus, when Rancière excludes all moral or subjective dimensions from the question of representability, he is doing so by reference to the protocols of the aesthetic regime *as he defines them*. Naturally, individual critics and artists regularly protest the inappropriateness (in terms of repugnancy, and even immorality) of particular works or artistic treatments.[13] But such evaluations, which contain an implicit commandment prohibiting or censoring the image (and the same is true of positive evaluations that celebrate the "restraint," "tact," or "delicacy" of other works) have no relevance to aesthetics, strictly speaking, for there is no problem of appropriateness in the aesthetic regime. Whatever the subject matter, "the language exists and the syntax exists" (126). Rancière illustrates this point by comparing a passage from the Buchenwald survivor Robert Antelme's memoir *The Human Race* dealing with toilet rituals in the camp to a passage in *Madame Bovary* that describes Emma sewing silently in the kitchen while Charles contemplates the movement of dust over the stone floor and the distant sound of a laying hen. Both passages, observes Rancière, have a "paratactic" quality, treating "small perceptions . . . side by side" and foreclosing any possibility of reference to some larger idea, even while the "nocturnal silence" that prevails in both passages solicits a readerly interpretation predicated on its existence. The ideational affirmation in both passages, this is to say (for example, the suggestion of Antelme's "fundamental membership in the human race" despite the inhumanity of the circumstances he depicts, and the implication of an incipient mutual attraction between Charles and Emma), takes place only in conditions of the idea's literal absence. The effect of the appearance of any such idea would be only to establish its secondary, derivative status; the interpretive imagination would immediately be directed elsewhere. Rancière comments on Antelme's text as follows: "The experience of a programmed de-humanization quite naturally finds itself expressed in the same way as the Flaubertian identity between the human and the inhuman, between the emergence of an emotion uniting two beings and a little dust stirred up by a draught in a farm kitchen"—that is to say, paratactically ("Are Some Things Unrepresentable?," 126). Thus, the mode of Antelme's work, Rancière says, "is not born out of the camp experience" but shares its style with Albert Camus's *L'étranger* and "the American behaviourist novel" (125).[14] Parataxis is a distinct kind of relation in which the "whole" (or idea) of the text is present *only and exclusively* in its "parts." Far from emerging from the singular trauma of the Holocaust, parataxis is the mode of the aesthetic regime itself, as established (or authorized) by Flaubert. Flaubert's own word for this mode is "style," reconceived not as a tool of expression, the mastery of which would signal a full understanding of the modes of available discourse appropriate to a particular communicative task and a given social situation; style is rather "an absolute manner of seeing things."[15] Style (as Theodor Adorno, a great philosophical practitioner of parataxis, might put it) is a "cessation, a suspended moment of the process," as much as it is a revelation.[16]

Parataxis, then—the formal organization of the work around a "mute middle point through which every word seeks to be refracted and that it must express"—is a degree-zero principle of connection.[17] The nature of the connection is unspeakable except in the most abstract terms (e.g., "refraction"). The only speakable element of the paratactical connection is the fact of it. And so, another way of articulating the historical shift in Rancière's system—from the representative regime to the aesthetic regime—is to talk about a transition from representation (a mode in which the connection is visible, speakable) to instantiation (an invisible, unspeakable connection that is inadvertent, that "can't help" but be revealed, and whose nature and limits are most persuasively registered by its presentation as a perspective: "the point of view from which one makes sense of the world").[18]

Rancière's own relation to these two regimes, and to the artistic regime system as a whole, is ambiguous, not least in the fact that the choice of the term "regime" would seem to be freighted with implications of ideological significance that Rancière never endorses. Rancière does not explicitly favor one regime over the others, nor does the term "regime" itself appear to carry negative connotations in Rancière's writing. The relation between aesthetics and politics is not for Rancière a problematic but a given. There does not seem to be, for Rancière, a specific project implied in the politics of aesthetics. The aesthetic regime does not have any moral or political obligations; there is no art or literature that is not "political," that does not posit a partition of the sensible. Rancière's regimes of art, writes Gabriel Rockhill, "act as immanent conditions that only exist in actual historical configurations"[19]—meaning that there is no existence to each regime apart from the works that comprise it: "Since [Rancière's] particular case studies are not individual instantiations of general rules, they do not serve as examples of transcendental historical principles."

That last formulation is especially interesting in the context of a consideration of the role of instantiation in the history and theory of the novel. Rockhill's implication is that Rancière's regimes are not "transcendental" (or universal)—that there is nothing determining about them. At the same time, as Rockhill puts it, the relevance of the regimes is not limited in terms of either material practice (they comprehend drawing, painting, literature, music, films, art of all kinds) or history (the artistic regimes "span the totality of theoretical and cultural production at any given moment in history") (158–59). The nonuniversal, nondetermining quality of the artistic regime system is a necessary postulate of Rancière's project if he is not to be liable to the charge of issuing normative edicts about what is proper or improper to art. However, its universal, historical dimension is also necessary if the aesthetic regime is to retain any diagnostic value—if it is to be more than a rationalization, after the fact, of an aggregate of expressive decisions made by individual writers and artists. This is the great tension and predicament of Rancière's project on aesthetics. Like the principle of the equality of intelligence in Rancière's earlier work *The Ignorant Schoolmaster*, the necessity of the regime system seems to be a condition of Rancière's critical practice; one might almost call it a "heautonomous" principle, the tenets of which apply primarily to the subject of the reflection rather than its object. Rockhill characterizes the universalism of Rancière's project as a "polemical universal," one that exists solely in "concrete acts of struggle" rather than as some "a priori" abstract foundation (161). In this light, the fact that certain real utterances—such as the claims of "repugnancy" and "loathsomeness" adduced earlier—must appear anomalous with respect to the larger historical patterns identified by the regime system seems to betray a normative element in Rancière's work.[20] Nevertheless, Rancière's project presents the main argument of this book with its most formidable theoretical challenge, insofar as the sensorimotor collapse is for Rancière nothing more than a development within the protocols of the aesthetic regime.

To ask whether a nonregime mode of thought is possible is to introduce the question of a limit to Rancière's system of artistic regimes when it comes to the contemporary period. It is to ask whether there is a power of art or a capacity for thought that is captured in, say, Deleuze's analytic of the sensorimotor collapse or in Lukács's veiled references to an "unsurmounted" element in the novel (*TN*, 70–71, 84) but unaccounted for by Rancière's notion of the aesthetic regime. The contentiousness of the question arises from the fact that there is no indication in Rancière's own work that a "non-regime" mode of thought is possible. On the contrary; the aesthetic regime is a regime in a sense that seems not only to remove any possibility of an exit from it but to suggest that, with the appearance of the aesthetic regime, everything oppressive or normative about the system of the "regime of the arts" disappears. The aesthetic regime, says Rancière in *The Politics of Aesthetics,*

> is the regime that strictly identifies art in the singular and frees it from any specific rule, from any hierarchy of the arts, subject matter, and genres. . . . The aesthetic regime asserts the absolute singularity of art and, at the same time, destroys any pragmatic criterion for isolating this singularity. . . . It . . . establishes the autonomy of art and the identity of its forms with the forms that life uses to shape itself. . . . The aesthetic state is a pure instance of suspension, a moment when form is experienced for itself.
> (23–24)

In other words, the regime of aesthetics is precisely *the regime of the non-regime.* The paradox is the same as that of Rancière's definition of literature as mute speech, or his definition of the novel as the "nongeneric genre," or his identification of a relation in nineteenth-century literature between "the sorrow of characters" and "the happiness of books."[21] There *is* an "unsurmounted" element in the artwork, a discrepancy between action and perception, expression and content, or between "ways of speaking, ways of doing and ways of being" (*PL,* 11)—but that discrepancy is not an effect of the crisis of realism or the loss of "belief" that Deleuze nominally locates in the postwar period; it is what makes the work a work of art in the first place.

Again, Rancière stops short of endorsing or expressing any kind of affiliation with the aesthetic regime.[22] However, a positive framing is offered by the commentator Robert St. Clair, for whom the aesthetic regime is the most convincing realization of democracy in Rancière's thought: "In its indifference to subject matter, the aesthetic regime of art is . . . an egalitarian one, exemplifying the logic of dissensus, the contingency of discourses and practices of donation, and the capacity of any body to do or potentially be otherwise."[23]

The stakes of Rancière's rejection of any case for a radical shift in the modern constitution of art and literature since the appearance of the aesthetic regime (including those advanced by Sartre, Barthes, and Jean-François Lyotard) become most explicit when Rancière directly engages Deleuze's work on cinema. For Rancière, Deleuze's hypothesis of a "sensorimotor collapse" in twentieth-century cinema—a break in "the linkages of situation-action, action-reaction, excitation-response" that had organized the action-image of narrative cinema (*C1*, 206)—simply rediscovers and reformulates the protocols of the aesthetic regime that have been in place for two hundred years. Far from being the site of a decentered and deauthorized thought, a thought that is irreducible to criteria such as "interest" or "history"—far from achieving, then, the redemption of thought from its materialist critique or the inauguration of a new, unprecedented thought—the sensorimotor collapse is a belated restaging of the break in European thought that constitutes the appearance of the aesthetic itself. By an aesthetic idea, says Kant in the *Critique of Judgment*, "I mean a presentation of the imagination . . . to which no determinate thought whatsoever, i.e., no *concept*, can be adequate, so that no language can express it completely and allow us to grasp it."[24] Rancière wants to insist that the lack of "justification" that Deleuze finds in cinematic images of the sensorimotor break is nothing other than this lack of "determination" of the aesthetic idea. In the "empty spaces" of Ozu's work, or the "disconnected spaces" of Bresson's, says Deleuze, the parts "are not connected and are beyond all narrative or more generally pragmatic justification" (*C1*, 15). To insist that such images participate in the "regime" of aesthetics is to claim that there is a logic even in the sensorimotor break that makes those images referable to the "expressive ends" of the filmmaker.[25] "Logic," "distribution," "regime," "form," "schema": all these terms presuppose a sensorimotor connection that has its explanation in the interests of the bodily organisms in which the perception is centered. It is, in other words, to refuse the historical hypothesis of the sensorimotor collapse.

Rancière is interested in art and literature not for the singularity of vision of particular works but as a historical formation in which the logic of paradoxicality is paramount (a thought materialized in the absence of thought, a form of knowledge that is "intuitive" because inimical to conceptualization, a perception that is hindered rather than facilitated by the faculty of vision). For Rancière, the politics of literature is a matter not of the direct representation of social or political struggles or the writer's personal implication in those struggles but of the indirect presence (or instantiation) of relations and distributions of perception that have a political valence, particularly when they change. As Rancière puts it, the phrase "politics of literature" assumes that there is "an essential connection between politics as a specific form of collective practice and literature as a well-defined practice of the art of writing" (*PL*, 3). "Essential" means having no need of being specified, because, with sufficient readerly and interpretive attentiveness, the connection is legible. Literature—the literary regime—can be understood as the appearance of an order of legibility, which is a "mechanism" (*dispositif*) with three elements: the "indifference" of writing with respect to meaning or content, a practice of "symptomatic reading" that approaches indifference as itself something to be interpreted, and the ambiguity or plurality of such interpretations (*PL*, 9).

It is in accordance with this principle of legibility that Rancière detects a suppressed "allegorical" dependency in Deleuze's account of the sensorimotor break, a quality that is especially apparent in the work of two directors who are prominent in the story of the transition from the movement-image to the time-image, namely, Alfred Hitchcock and Tod Browning. The allegorical element in their films—the motor "paralysis" of Hitchcock's heroes such as Jeff (*Rear Window*) and Scottie (*Vertigo*), the self-mutilation of Tod Browning's circus performer Alonzo (*The Unknown*)—is a remnant of subjective expression that, Rancière implies, is present in all of Deleuze's readings that insist upon its absence (*FF*, 115–19). In other words, in Deleuze's work, the crisis of meaning cannot be the basis of a reading unless it is also present as an allegory. For Rancière, the theoretical deficit of Deleuze's claim for a sensorimotor collapse is the fact that it is simply illegible without such thematic treatments: "it is very difficult to specify, in the shots themselves or in their sequential arrangement, the traits by which we would recognize the rupture of the sensory-motor link, the infinitization of the interval, and the crystallization of the virtual and the actual" (*FF*, 118). By implication, no such unambiguous images of the collapse are possible. There is, in fact, no "sensorimotor collapse," no achieved "void" or "interstice" between sound and image or between action and perception—only allegorical images or diegetical depictions of characters (or authors) experiencing the collapse existentially. "The movement-image is 'in crisis,'" says Rancière, "because the thinker [Deleuze] needs it to be" (116).

Rancière's reading of Deleuze raises a number of questions: Is the aesthetic regime really the last word on the relation between aesthetics and politics, as Rancière seems to insist? And if so, what implications of the term "regime" remain in formulations such as "regimes of the arts" and "aesthetic regime"? Does not the use of the word "regime" risk consolidating the literary institution as a *particular* distribution of the sensible—a codification and thus restriction of the sphere of the sensible, rather than, say, the opening to emancipation and equality that Rancière seems to intend in his theorization of it?[26] In other words, doesn't Rancière's very project of *theorizing* the aesthetic regime undermine (or deflect) its emancipatory possibilities? To state the question in its most paradoxical form: Can the theory of the aesthetic regime *survive itself*?

And one last question: Is the difference between Rancière's decision to conceptualize aesthetics as a "regime"—to approach the aesthetic as a complex historical formation in which even the act of naming and conceptualizing it is implicated—and Deleuze's refusal of the name "aesthetics," his attempt to conceptualize the sensorimotor collapse as an exit of thought from all "regimes" and orders of thinking—is this difference anything other than a different orientation to language, a different relation to the ontology of naming itself?

My approach to these questions will be to try to establish a differentiation within Rancière's notion of the aesthetic regime: a differentiation that follows, or redraws, the line between what is speakable and unspeakable in theoretical discourse. This differentiation will undermine certain manifest elements of Rancière's project, especially his rejection of any case for a fundamental shift in the relation between aesthetics and politics in the last two hundred years, but it will also make the case that Rancière's real contribution to contemporary aesthetics is found in an affiliation with the aesthetic regime that runs deeper than the lip service we occasionally catch him paying to it.

HITCHCOCK: CINEMA OF COMPLETION

The instantiation relation—a "degree-zero" order of connection, in which every detail of the work speaks, but in a language of relations and connections rather than of words or actions—has its cinematic analogue in the formal elegance and thematic legibility of the works of Alfred

Hitchcock. What is legible in Hitchcock's works are not perceptions, thoughts, experiences, and ideas present to the characters themselves but rather relations (between characters or within characters) that exist outside perception. Hitchcock's body of work thus effects a new and distinctive relationship between cinema and thought. "Each image in its frame, by its frame, must exhibit a mental relation," says Deleuze:

> The characters can act, perceive, experience, but they cannot testify to the relations which determine them. These are merely the movements of the camera, and their movements toward the camera. Hence the opposition between Hitchcock and the Actors Studio, his requirement that the actor acts in the most simple, even neutral, way, the camera attending to what remains. This remainder is the essential or the mental relation. It is the camera, and not a dialogue, which *explains* why the hero of *Rear Window* has a broken leg (photos of the racing car, in his room, broken camera). . . . Hitchcock . . . no longer conceives of the constitution of a film as a function of two terms—the director and the film to be made—but as a function of three: the director, the film and the public which must come into the film, or whose reactions must form an integrating part of the film (this is the explicit sense of suspense, since the spectator is the first to "know" the relations).[27]
> (*C1*, 201–2)

Thus, Hitchcock's films sustain a logic of "perpetual tripling" (201) in which the actor and the acted upon, the assassin and the victim, are accompanied by a relation between the two: a third "fundamental" entity. If a crime is committed in a film by Hitchcock, it is not by one man for his own reasons (hatred, revenge, a desire for freedom) but by two men, each of whom will commit a murder for the other. If a wife suspects her husband of wanting to kill her, the important element is not the suspense—whether her suspicion is well founded, or why she drinks a glass of milk she knows to be poisoned—but "how the gimlet of suspicion perforates the unity of a couple."[28] Exchange, note Eric Rohmer and Claude Chabrol, as in the exchange of murders in *Strangers on a Train* (1951), has its "psychological equivalent" in the suspicion of *Suspicion* (1941) (67). The theory of relations, says Deleuze,

> is the key element of logic and can be both the deepest and the most amusing element. . . . Hitchcock's characters are certainly not intellectuals, but

have feelings that can be called intellectual feelings . . . in that they are mod-
eled on a varied play of experienced conjunctions[:] *because . . . although . . .
since . . . if . . . even if. . . .* In all these cases the relation introduces an essential instability between the characters, the roles, the actions, the set. The
model of this instability will be that of the guilty and the innocent. But, also,
the autonomous life of the relation will make it tend towards a kind of equilibrium, even though it may be devastated, desperate or even monstrous. The
innocent-guilty equilibrium, the restitution to each of his role, the retribu-
tion upon each for his action, will be achieved, but *at the price of a limit which
risks corroding and even effacing the whole.*
(*C1*, 202–3, MY EMPHASIS)

By focusing on relations rather than signifying structures, Hitchcock brings
cinema to its "completion" (204). Completion, however, is also a limit. Hitchcock's works surmount the unsurmounted element (the distance between
two characters) in a "terrible equilibrium" or mental image, but the cost is
the materialization of "a limit which risks corroding and even effacing the
whole" (203).

What lies beyond the limit? What stays unsurmounted in the formal sur-
mounting constituted by the "terrible equilibrium" of the Hitchcockian
remainder? What is beyond "legibility," and what kind of critical, philosophical, political, or historical value should be attributed to the "corrosion" of the
whole? These are all versions of the question we have been asking about the
aesthetic regime (in this chapter) and the instantiation relation (in this book).
Hitchcock's work is a formal exemplar of both. What is the virtue of introducing into the realm of concepts a formlessness that must escape even the
form that is "formlessness" itself—a nondeflected philosophy from which
even the concept of deflection is a deflection?[29] Are interstices of thought
really worthy of sustained theoretical consideration, or receptive to it? Is
there, as the young Lukács might have put it, something in the subjective
intuition of "the ultimate nothingness of man" that retains philosophical or
political substance, outside its "absorption into literary form"?

THE INTERSTICE: REALIST FORM OR CRYSTALS OF TIME?

Rancière's answers to these questions give us the clearest point of tension
and difference between Deleuze's project and his own. For Deleuze, cinema

actualizes an image of the interstice in the form of the "crystal image," in which "fundamental dissonance" is no longer a merely hypothetical or subjective experience but attains a sensuous, material reality. The discrepancy between actual and virtual is not resolved formally. Rather, their relation is inverted, the inseparability and reversibility of the two terms produced as a temporal continuity. For this reason, says Deleuze, "the organization of the crystal is bipolar, or rather two-sided" (C2, 90). This is precisely Deleuze's case for the revolutionary nature of cinema. The crystal image brings into visibility such organizers of experience as the distinction between original and imitation, present and past, future and present, soul and form, seats of inspiration and the world of convention. The crystal image is a thought that has no need of theory, a thought beyond conceptualization. In crystalline formations—such as every mention of money in cinema, where the cinema "confronts its own most internal presupposition" (C2, 78); or the diegetic appearance of an actor as a character (as in the films of Tod Browning), when the figure onscreen turns an irreducibly "double face" toward the camera and the work achieves a "poetry of the unassignable" (C2, 72); or the discovery of "conversation for itself" in Godard—time appears not indirectly, as an object of representation, but directly, as a "perpetual self-distinguishing" (C2, 82). A moment as fleeting as the statement by Orson Welles's Michael O'Hara in *The Lady from Shanghai*, delivered over images of canoes laden with provisions, troubadours playing guitars and violins, a seemingly endless retinue of servants and attendants hoisting aloft lanterns and platters stacked with food—"Mr. Bannister's picnic party was most typical of him. A lot of trouble and a great deal of money went into it, but it was no more a picnic than Bannister was a man"—cannot fail to bring to mind the "internalized relation with money" of cinema itself (C2, 77).[30] In Werner Herzog's films a transformed perceptual economy, as in Herzog's almost indefinite extension of pure optical and sound situations, establishes the conditions for an exit from the action-image, that is to say, from the logic of grammatical concatenation (Vološinov). Herzog's is a hubristic cinema in which it is impossible to say who is really the deranged visionary: Herzog or his crazed protagonists.[31]

In Rancière's reading of Deleuze's cinema books, whenever such crystal images appear Rancière suppresses their autonomy by reasserting their narrative, "sensorimotor" function. For Rancière, crystal images are nothing but instances of the double or paradoxical order of referentiality in which a particular figure (say, the omnipresent film camera in Dziga Vertov's *Man with a Movie Camera* or the passive protagonist in Hitchcock's *Vertigo*) invites two mutually incompatible and undecidable readings. On one hand, a reading for the nonsubjective intensities, the decentered gaze that obtains in the image; on the other, a reading for the gaze's "centrality." On one hand, the possibility, with Vertov's "machine-eye," of putting "perception into matter"; on the other, the imperialism of that gesture, undertaken by an "omnipresent cameraman" and an editor without whom no life can be breathed into "images inert in themselves" (*FF*, 110). On one hand, the technological "communism" of "the universal exchange of movements"; on the other, a "technological voluntarism" that, in the same gesture, "subjects all reality" to the vision of a "panoptic eye": "Cinema thus emerges as the art privileged to unite opposites: the extreme of voluntary alignment of all movements under the control of a centralizing eye, and the extreme of abdicating all intent to the profit of free development of living energies."[32]

Béla Tarr and Joseph Conrad

Accordingly, Rancière's account of the work of the Hungarian director Béla Tarr begins with a refusal of the hypothesis of a shift from realism into "metaphysic[s] and formalis[m]" in Tarr's later films.[33] What we find halfway through Béla Tarr's body of work, when the shots become progressively longer and the movements of the camera are increasingly autonomous with respect to the characters, is not a sensorimotor break but a redistribution of perception—the very redistribution characteristic of the aesthetic regime. The liberation of the camera from the action-image and the long sequence shots are extensions of Tarr's realism. They are how Tarr, with each film, "delves a little deeper" into "the reality that people live" (4, 5). Likewise, Tarr's use of nonprofessional actors is not, primarily, a challenge to the categories of actual and virtual, as it might have been for Deleuze (fictionality apparently plays no part in Rancière's understanding of Béla Tarr); it represents rather an extension of cinematic attention to "people to whom this story might have happened." The experience in question is that of "any socialist individuals whatever" (*individus socialistes quelconques*) (8/14).

With this ironized use of the Deleuzian construction, Rancière is honing the polemical element in his reading. For the social identity of Tarr's characters matters deeply in Rancière's account,[34] and the same goes for

Tarr's settings, especially the rural landscapes of later films such as *Sátán-tangó* (1994) and *The Turin Horse* (2011). These landscapes are not "any-spaces-whatever"—spaces without "coordinates," as Deleuze defines them, whose signifying powers are "independent of the states of things or milieux which actualize them" (*C1*, 120). On the contrary: Tarr's settings are for Rancière "primary character[s]" in his films (*Béla Tarr*, 70), places where people are "enclosed in their solitude" (4) and where psychic narratives, such as the cycles between pessimism and optimism—"expectation of the identical" and "hope for change"—are set in motion (73). The interstices that, for Deleuze, identify a distinctly cinematic thought are for Rancière simply the gaps (*écarts*) intrinsic to realism as a form—the gaps of the instantiation relation: "Stories demand that we retain, from each situation, the elements capable of being inserted into a schema of causes and effects" (9). The time in which Béla Tarr's later, more melancholic films take place "is not the morose, uniform time of those who no longer believe in anything" (9). Again, the unnamed interlocutor seems to be Deleuze, for whom "the modern fact is that we no longer believe in this world" (*C2*, 171). This broken "link between man and the world" is, for Deleuze, the occasion for cinema to generate a new object of belief: the interstice, which is to say, the infinite deferral that appears at the heart of—and comes to displace—the action-image (the "schema of causes and effects"). Deleuze's strongest statement of this new foundation of belief appears in the eighth chapter of *Cinema 2*:

> We no longer believe in a whole as interiority of thought—even an open one; we believe in a force from the outside which hollows itself out, grabs us and attracts the inside. We no longer believe in an association of images—even crossing voids; we believe in breaks which take on an absolute value and subordinate all association.
>
> (212)

For Rancière, by contrast, the time of the late work of Béla Tarr is "the time of pure, material events, against which belief will be measured for as long as life will sustain it" (9). The emphasis is on a continuing measurement and relationality, rather than an exit from such structures.

Literature, of course, is able to grasp explicitly any idea that may be put into words, including, then, the belief in a "force from the outside" that could enter into and "hollow out" any such idea. Near the beginning of *Heart of Darkness*, Conrad's nameless outer narrator contrasts the tales of its internal narrator Marlow with the "direct simplicity" of ordinary seamen's yarns, the meaning of which "lies within the shell of a cracked nut." To Marlow, on the contrary, "the meaning of an episode was not inside like a kernel but outside, enveloping the tale which brought it out only as a glow brings out a haze, in the likeness of one of these misty halos that sometimes are made visible by the spectral illumination of moonshine."[35] In *Heart of Darkness* we are at the outset of just such a tale. For Rancière, writing in *The Lost Thread*, this passage confirms the degree to which Deleuze's thematic of the sensorimotor collapse is anticipated by the protocols of literature, the art form that cannot brush against any such "force from the outside" without thereby bringing it into the warmth.[36]

Conrad, says Rancière, was the first writer to give "theoretical" expression to the "new fictional fabric" discovered by Flaubert, in which a texture of meaning is located in the pure relationality of the milieu. In Conrad, therefore, the "equality of phrases," literature's capacity for a nondiscriminating "solidarity with all lives" (34) that was discovered by Flaubert fifty years earlier, is threatened by a process of subjectivation that enfolds Conrad himself as soon as that equality is "transformed" into a "philosophy of life" (31). Once the novelist comes to *believe* in the vanity of any notion of free, independent thought, a belief plausibly expressed in the Flaubertian conception of a "milieu of meaning [that] is itself devoid of meaning" (30), the vanity reasserts itself, both in the claim to that belief and, especially, in the development of an artistic practice informed by it. (We are back in the grip of "Bradley's regress.") Thus, Conrad's work is ensnared in a perpetual oscillation between the "milieu" and the "story" (36), between experience, in all its unthinkability, and "deflection." This oscillation is the internal constitution of writing itself. Conrad's works, says Rancière, far from heralding a new "perspectivist relativism" (a code for the "sensorimotor break" in this book that never once mentions Deleuze), rather ensure "the absolute truth of a present by renewing the mode of its presence" (41). "Renewing the mode" of presence means multiplying the moments that combine to make up an event and relegating in significance privileged moments, such as those of action and determination. This is why, for Rancière, Jim's jump from the *Patna* in chapter 9 of *Lord Jim*, a jump that is never narrated in its taking place but only in its telling—in the sensations, perceptions, memories, feelings, dreams that anticipate and follow it—is exemplary.[37] Jim's leap is "the cut of the inconceivable that separates it defin-itively from the possible linkages of narrative action" (40). Jim's leap, in other words, stands for the sensorimotor break but demonstrates its per-fect imbrication with the sensorimotor schema in works of literature.

For Rancière, there are two "great arts of the word." One—literature—is the art of what we cannot see; the other—rhetoric—is the art of arousing action. The first has constitutive gaps; the second does not. One has irony baked into it—knowing what it means without saying it; the other says what it means and means what it says. In practice, the two are inseparable: "each makes use of the other in its own way" (*Béla Tarr*, 6). Thus, the two poles of modern cinema—the sensorimotor collapse that, for Deleuze, distin-guishes the thought of cinema and the action-oriented, character-focused principles that organize the movement-image—both belong "indiscernibly," according to Rancière, to the aesthetic regime (*FF*, 122; *Intervals*, 6). The pos-sibility of a wisdom concealed "behind the forms," as Lukács puts it, a formless thinking that is not "surmount[ed]" as novelistic irony (*TN*, 84)—a thought that, by contrast with what came before it, thinks not the link but its interruption, its "heautonomous" quality—such a possibility, apparently, is as much an abstraction for Rancière as it later came to seem to Lukács himself.

PENULTIMACY

It has been a contention of this book, or an article of faith, that—like cin-ema for Deleuze—the concept of instantiation enables us to access a rela-tion of nonequivalence or discontinuity at the center of all "degree-zero" connections, such as those that operate in all "profiling." If there is a kind of thought that is content to make connections between qualities or properties, on one hand, and the persons and objects that embody them, on the other, and to draw inferences based on those connections, there is also a thought that is *not* content to do so or that finds satisfaction, rather, in contemplating the failure or loss of such connections—which is also to say, in pondering the discrepancy as an inherently worthwhile object or occasion of thought. When the Assistant Commissioner in Conrad's *The Secret Agent* visits an Italian restaurant and, with a "pleasant" sensation, feels his own identity dissolving;[38] when he reflects on the disappearance of all "national and private characteristics" in the "immoral atmosphere" of the restaurant and on how its patrons seem only to exist inside that establishment, liberated of all "professional, social or racial" identity—a liberation mirrored in the "unstamped respectability" of the restaurant's "fraudulent" cuisine—is his pleasurable delirium really explicable as Conrad's deepening realism, a delving into "the reality of a situation" (*Béla Tarr*, 8)? Are the Assistant Commissioner's thoughts really sensorimotor in nature, i.e., reducible to his bodily interests and confined to his characterological envelope? Are the sensations depicted those of "lived time" only? And is the episode best read as a "renewal" of—rather than an escape from or a dismantling of—the present? "There is only the real," writes Rancière in *The Lost Thread*,

> that is to say a set of conditions—natural as much as social—whose ultimate connection escapes all mastery, as well as humans that turn this real into both the place of their daily bread and the theatre of their illusions—illusions that are themselves perfectly "real" since they alone furnish humans with the reasons to live and act in this real.
>
> (35)

But is Rancière speaking in his own voice here? Is he truly content with such explanations—or is there in Rancière, too, a hidden commitment to a dimension of experience or thought that passes all understanding? What if the secret object of this sentence in Rancière were the very order of "ultimate connection" about which Rancière says nothing (except that it escapes "mastery") as he transitions to the "perfectly 'real'" illusions of human consciousness? What if Rancière's own writing were read not for the story he seems always to be telling us, about the mutual imbrication of the intelligible and the sensible (what Virginia Woolf called the "series of gig lamps symmetrically arranged," on one hand, and the "luminous halo" on the other)?[39] What if we read him for what, in the formal and discursive context of his writing, *he is not able to reflect on*: the hypothesis of an "ultimate connection" in Conrad that forces Rancière to contort the conceptualization of the aesthetic regime in order to accommodate it; or the lack of a "perceptive center" in Béla Tarr's work (the very quality, according to Deleuze, that distinguishes cinematic thought), which may be brought into Rancière's conception of the aesthetic regime only on condition that it be presented as part of the palette of textural effects available to the filmmaker (*Béla Tarr*, 66)?

What if we read these sequences in Rancière's late work, then, for the exit from the instantiation relation that the story of the aesthetic regime makes thinkable, even as it insists upon its impossibility? What if the Flaubertian "compromise"—the formula in which the "sensible states" are always being sacrificed to the "artifice of causal fiction" (*Lost Thread*, 40)—were replaced, in our reading of Rancière himself, by the Deleuzian alibi or "pretext," the inverse procedure (exemplified most clearly in Deleuze and Guattari's book on Kafka) in which the critical attention shifts to the "line of escape" that traverses every formal solution, every attempt at closure or resolution?[40] What if the deaths of Emma Bovary, Septimus Smith, and Albertine—characters who, in Rancière's account, are killed by their authors for the sake of the aesthetic regime (*Lost Thread*, 62–63) (i.e., to prevent the "infinitization" of the interval)—what if these fictional deaths were understood not as means of resolving the conflict between the "shower of atoms" or the "splash of color on a beach," on one hand, and the plot, on the other, but as "blockages"—momentary interruptions of becoming, testaments to the fact that, as Deleuze puts it in relation to cinema, "we are not yet ready for a true 'reading' of the visual image" (*C2*, 179)? And what if Rancière's own seemingly categorical utterances were regarded not as final but penultimate—a penultimacy extending even to the word "total" or the word "regime"?[41]

Perhaps this is simply to read Rancière himself and the absolute distinction between the representative and the aesthetic regimes that is central to his work on aesthetics according to the standards of the aesthetic regime, a discourse born, Rancière says elsewhere, "as the refusal of its name."[42] Rancière wants to insist on the perfect "appropriateness" of the name "art," indeed of all names, but that appropriateness is possible only on the basis of Rancière's own paradoxical formulation of the aesthetic regime—as "the place of the adequation between a sensible different from itself and a thought different from itself, a thought identical to non-thought" ("What Aesthetics Can Mean," 19). Perhaps the aesthetic regime itself is nothing less than a Deleuzian "assemblage," a machine for the production of an "equality of phrases" and for dismantling all questions of appropriateness and inappropriateness. Just as the real political sympathies of *The Secret Agent* are revealed by Conrad's consistent disparagement of their every bodily representative—the anarchists are fat, lazy, vicious, sociopathic, mentally confused, and morally reprehensible—so, perhaps, the extent of Rancière's true affiliation with the aesthetic regime is unspoken or dissembled, operating at a level that critical discourse is able to register only negatively.

In which case, the real significance of Rancière's project would consist in an even more radical refusal of the logic of instantiation than Deleuze's: not a refusal of language but a refusal *in* and *by way of* language. Naming, in Rancière's own writing (the names "regime," "aesthetics," as well as "unity," "out-of-field," and "appropriate"), would be understood to take place always under the auspices of a secret decommissioning of the name. The plausibility of such a reading, which radically shifts the stakes of Rancière's work on the relation between aesthetics and politics, would depend, of course, on the lack of any reference to it in Rancière's writing. If there is an exit from the aesthetic regime, an exit even from the "nonregime" of aesthetics, it could not emerge as a theorizable object or identifiable historical shift in a theoretical project such as Rancière's. Rancière is the most novelistic of aesthetic theorists, perhaps, because of his intuition that the thought of the novel has no use whatsoever for theory.

THE PRIMACY OF RELATION: SAMUEL BECKETT

Samuel Beckett's third "dialogue" with the French art critic and historian Georges Duthuit, on the painter Bram van Velde—a text alluded to earlier in this chapter—gives us further terms by which we might understand the space of tension or irreconcilability between Deleuze's project to cast cinema as the location of a thought that takes place outside the logic of instantiation and Rancière's refusal of any such gesture. In this dialogue, which was composed by Beckett after an exchange of letters with Duthuit, Beckett declares van Velde to be the first artist to, on one hand, "accept a certain situation," that of being helpless to paint, and on the other, to "consent to a certain act," that of painting despite there being "nothing to paint and nothing to paint with."[43] Van Velde's work takes place, therefore, in a zone of disconnection between painting and its motivation, where the question of "perfectly 'real'" illusions does not apply, for van Velde's work no longer needs "reasons to live and act in this real." Van Velde is the first artist, according to Beckett, who is not concerned with expression—either his own or that of "humanity." His art is "inexpressive," meaning that it is "bereft . . . of occasion in every shape and form" (121). By "occasion," what Beckett means is "relation"—the relation between "the artist and his occasion" (124).[44] Because van Velde's work is bereft of occasion, there is no relationality to be found in his work. Van Velde, according to Beckett, is the first artist whose work breaks the "degree-zero" connection between the work and the "watermark of self"—the space that is bridged by "the point of view from which one makes sense of the world."

To speak of van Velde's work interpretatively—using conjunctions such as *because, although, since, if,* or *even if*—is to reconstruct such a relation by referring the work to its subject. Thus Duthuit asks Beckett whether it could be said of van Velde's art that this absence of relation is precisely his "predicament," that this predicament is what van Velde's work may be said to "express." Beckett retorts by distinguishing between being "short" of something and being "without" it: "the one is a predicament, the other is not" (122), the implication being that what is distinct about van Velde is that he has freed himself from any such relationality and thus any such predicament. Van Velde is free of the expressive predicament because his work "submits wholly to the incoercible absence of relation," meaning that he paints not out of a *sense* of its absence but out of its absence. He does not paint the pathos of the lost relation, for the loss is in no way the object of his work. Not only is there no relation; there are no terms in which the relation might be spoken about as present or absent (125). Van Velde, then, is the first artist to escape the predicament of modern painting itself—the predicament that both Lukács and Cora Diamond have attempted to give philosophical expression to, as explored in chapter 6 of this work—and to do so without simply constituting it as "a new term of relation." Van Velde paints the difficulty of reality (or the fundamental dissonance of existence) without the difficulty being deflected into an "occasion." The object of van Velde's painting is not the thing itself but, in Beckett's words, "the thing that hides the thing," or as van Velde put it, "what hinders us from seeing."[45] No better paraphrase could be found, perhaps, for what Diamond calls the "difficulty of reality."

What Beckett is convinced is present in van Velde—an achieved disconnection, a nondeflected artistic practice—is, of course, unverifiable.[46] Looking at van Velde's works with Rancière, one might say that it is difficult to specify, either in the blocks of color themselves or in their spatial arrangement, the "traits" by which we would recognize such an absence (*FF*, 118).[47] To identify the "forms" of an absent relationality, of course, would be the surest way of "deflecting" it. As Beckett says, referring to Duthuit's question about van Velde, "No more ingenious method could be devised for restoring him, safe and sound, to the bosom of Saint Luke" (121–22). The authentically Rancièrian approach to the works of van Velde would be, perhaps, only a further twist on Beckett's own: not to read the work in search of the expressive "predicament," or to read in search of its absence, but to assume its absence from the outset as the presupposition and condition of one's reading. Such a procedure might offer the only possible route out of the aesthetic regime, an exit that would be neither acknowledgeable nor theorizable as one.

Rancière concludes his essay on Deleuze's cinema books ("From One Image to Another?") by noting the "near-total indiscernibility between the logic of the movement-image and the logic of the time-image" (*FF*, 122). This insight should be reframed not as the fatal blow to Deleuze's cinema project but as its crucial lesson. Not even for Deleuze is the time-image outside the movement-image. That the time-image is not itself thinkable, perceivable, or verifiable, that it cannot be instantiated outside the movement that materializes it, is not the great weakness of Deleuze's work on cinema. Its weakness is the degree to which it *is* those things.

A "nonregime" mode of thinking, the capacity of art for a kind of thought that exceeds sensorimotor explanations (in terms of possible action, bodily interests), can never be named or conceptualized. Thus none of the despondent words with which Lukács characterizes the world before the creation of forms—"nothingness," "absurdity," "futility," or the merely "existent"—rises to the level of the concept (*TN*, 62). When Lukács conceives of a positive sphere of experience beyond the reaches of form, he speaks in abstract terms of "the innermost recesses of the soul" (62). To insist, as does Rancière, that there is no unrepresentable or unspeakable element in the aesthetic regime may be the only consistent way to reserve a place of thought at the limits of form itself. How better to do justice to the unrepresentable than by refusing to acknowledge it? How else to register the unspeakable than by not speaking it? What if the most substantive difference between Rancière's work on literature and Deleuze's work on cinema were that Deleuze insists on retaining as an object of his inquiry precisely what Rancière, out of an even more rigorous adherence to its essence, dispenses with altogether? What if it were Rancière who came closest to the freedom from the expressive predicament that Beckett attributes to Bram van Velde—precisely by not expressing it?

CONCLUSION

The Indeterminate Thought of the Free Indirect

Despite the consistency with which this book has tried to argue against the adequacy of instantiation as a logic of literary interpretation, no such negative principle can provide the basis of a general theory of the novel, since, in so doing, the principle becomes substantial; that is, it enters into the kind of form-content relation that is its antithesis. For Georg Lukács, the form-content relation is the source of the novel's "hazardous" quality (*TN*, 73), where the novel's status as "a true-born form in the historico-philosophical sense," its capacity to attain "the true condition of the contemporary spirit" (i.e., the novel's thought) is most at risk of being forsaken in favor of some object of theoretical knowledge or reflection at the level of content.

The form-content relation is also, of course, the defining principle and predicament of critical discourse. It is in order to avoid simply inscribing itself inside this relation or this predicament that this book has not sought to correct or update earlier theories of the novel in order to (for example) account for contemporary novelistic developments. Such earlier theories falter not in the quality of their insights about the novel or in their failure to anticipate such developments but in their attempts to theorize the novel in the first place. Once we reconceive the novel not as a form but as a logic, once we understand the work of the novel not in terms of representation but as a thought that is always emerging—a thought of which the novel is the *subject* rather than a *vehicle* and that is present not in any work or body of work or in some projected stage or historical phase of the novel but in its collective orientation—it becomes apparent that the critical-theoretical register perpetually comes up against its own limits in the novel. That is why this book has insisted on the principle of the novel's untheorizability and has pressed the viability of a thought that *it is itself unable to formulate theoretically*, a singular thought whose positive presentation, without instantiation, occurs only in novelistic discourse.

The novel coheres as a *form*, says Lukács, when it "establishes a fluctuating yet firm balance between becoming and being"—that is, when the novel, "by transforming itself into a normative being of becoming, surmounts itself" (*TN*, 73). The meaning of the passage bears comparison with one of the central claims of this book: that the logic of "instantiation" and the logic of the "interstice" are both immanent to the form of the novel. The moment of formal coherence is the moment the work becomes critically legible, accessible to theoretical analysis. But this moment is fraught with danger for the novel—that of becoming a "caricature," what Lukács calls an "entertainment novel": a work that is "bound to nothing and based on nothing" (73). As Lukács points out, the critical legibility of the novel is also the condition in which the problems and dissonances of the work are resolved "as a matter of content," a resolution that he describes as "a marked convergence between ethic as an interior factor of life and its substratum of action in the social structures" (74).

These pages in *The Theory of the Novel*, on which we have expended much interpretive energy in the course of this book, are closely argued, but the implication seems to be that this resolution at the level of content—a sensorimotor resolution insofar as the congruity is established as a "substratum of action"—is no less subjective (and hence, in Lukács's terms, abstracted from the "totality") "if it remains unexpressed" (74). Thus the instantiation relation—a "degree-zero" connection, which does not require that the nature of the relation be stated explicitly—is established as a constitutive element of the novel, alongside an awareness of its limits, in the form of

a subjectivity which sees through the abstract and, therefore, limited nature of the mutually alien worlds of subject and object, understands these worlds by seeing their limitations as necessary conditions of their existence and, by thus seeing through them, allows the duality of the world to subsist. (74–75)

The element in the novel that has concerned the present work is this potentially *unsurmounted* element that Lukács was the first to notice and formulate as a dissonance that escapes, or precedes, "the creation of forms" (34). This dissonance, I have been arguing, is opened up for attention by recent developments in the novel, most immediately, the "postfictional" experiments that were the concern of part 2. But the same significance can be attributed to the feature or logic of the "free indirect," the focus of discussion in part 3, especially the last section of chapter 7. For Deleuze and Guattari, as well as for Vološinov, free indirect discourse is both a mode of representing speech and thought—a stylistic device implicitly framed by a set of absent linguistic "constants" that enables the subject of the utterance to be identified and the sense determined—*and* an element that precedes, and survives, the constitution of subjectivized discourse. It is thus a theory, or a thought, that can operate in the absence of personal attribution. Free indirect is not only, and not primarily, a particular *use* of language; it is also an experimental hypothesis, advanced by literature itself, about the capacity of language to function in an interstitial or nonsubjective space. In this context, according to Deleuze and Guattari, free indirect *discourse* has an "exemplary" status born of its capacity to present (directly, syntactically) the determining influence of the assemblage. In free indirect discourse, write Deleuze and Guattari,

> there are no clear, distinctive contours; what comes first is not an insertion of variously individuated statements, or an interlocking of different subjects of enunciation, but a collective assemblage resulting in the determination of relative subjectification proceedings, or assignations of individuality and their shifting distributions within discourse. Indirect discourse is not explained by the distinction between subjects; rather, it is the assemblage, *as it freely appears in this discourse*, that explains all the voices present within a single voice . . . the languages in a language, the order-words in a word. (*ATP*, 80, MY EMPHASIS)

This distinction—between free indirect discourse as a "stylistic device" and as a theory of language—might be rephrased as a question: Is free indirect discourse a specifically novelistic *form* (a mode of *representing* speech and thought) or a novelistic technology for effecting an *escape* from form (a mode of *thought*)?

In an essay published in 2000, the critic Frances Ferguson calls free indirect discourse "the novel's one and only formal contribution to literature."[1] Ferguson is expressing something that is a point of conviction for this book also: that few if any formal features can be said to define the novel and that free indirect discourse is a mode of thinking that is singular to it. But Ferguson's conception of free indirect discourse as a "form" means that, like other contemporary critics (notably Franco Moretti and D. A. Miller),[2] she cannot conceive of any approach to free indirect discourse that does not involve resolving the "problem" of free indirect discourse in subjective or ideological terms. Ferguson rejects older readings of Jane Austen (by such critics as Wayne Booth and A. Walton Litz) that identify in the work a "clearly available narrative position from which to judge Emma," a position that, in the case of Booth and Litz, would be implicitly critical of Austen's protagonist (171). Ferguson's approach, rather, addresses the paradox according to which "Emma Woodhouse is the heroine even when she produces a series of misjudgments and statements that are rude or at least insensitive"—in which we "recognize Emma as good even when she is not" (164). This paradox is that of the instantiation relation, which in Austen's works, according to Ferguson, takes the form of a negative correlation between the meaning of the work in the "aggregate" and the level of the individual signifier. The very values apparently upheld by the text as a whole are flouted and betrayed by the novel's heroine, who is no less revered by the text on that account. Ferguson's term for the ideological element that resolves this paradox is the "communal," a feature that is present in the novel only implicitly or by derivation, as a consequence of attentive critical reading. The sophistication of Ferguson's reading is the sophistication of the instantiation relation itself, in direct contrast to the kind of readings represented by Booth's criticism. Thus: "The brilliance of [Austen's] deployment of free indirect style is that it recognizes what we might want to think of as a communal contribution to individuals" (164). "Austen uses a community to foreshadow an individual's actions—to say of Emma, from the very outset, that she will have come out right by the end." Moretti characterizes the same element as the "intermediate, almost neutral third voice" of the "achieved social contract" (396, 399).

Such a formulation seems in accordance with Vološinov's refusal to credit "subjective psychic factors and intentions" with explanatory power in instances of free indirect discourse. However, Lukács's discussion of the "inner form of the novel" leaves us in no doubt that subjective explanations are rarely, if ever, matters of representation but rather of instantiation. Such values as "community" or "sociality," if endorsed by the work as "content" (whether overtly or implicitly), are "even more subjective than the overt manifestation of a clearly conscious subjectivity" (*TN*, 74). Ferguson therefore overstates the radicalism of the transition from representation (Booth, Litz) to instantiation (Moretti, Ferguson herself) in critical discourse. In both stages, a sensorimotor schema is in operation, the only difference being that in the former, what is visible (or audible, or legible) is present without remainder, whereas in the latter, as Jacques Rancière has stated, what is visible takes the paradoxical form of "the visible which does not make visible."[3]

What Booth, Moretti, and Ferguson are unable to render critically significant is the interstice (between fiction and reality, actual and virtual, narrator and character, character and character, or within a single character) that, I have been claiming, is the basis of every use of free indirect discourse. The interstice survives every critical reading, for such readings cannot help but privilege one or another opposing term, or some relation (dialectical, affective, philosophical, moral, etc.) that is held to bridge them. The greatest contrast with the work of Moretti and Ferguson may be drawn, perhaps, using Ann Banfield's notion of "unspeakable sentences," with which Banfield recognizes a fundamental division between the subject position of spoken language (*representing* speech and thought) and that of written discourse (*represented* speech and thought). Banfield's pioneering work culminates in the claim that "the writer of fiction nowhere 'speaks' in the novel," that, consequently, the knowledge produced by the text "can be considered as a knowledge in some sense unknown, its properties not self-evident, not available to the introspection of the conscious speaking subject who possesses it."[4] Despite the fact that both Ferguson and Moretti approvingly cite Banfield, there is no bridge between these two understandings of the primary significance of free indirect discourse: one focused on rationalization and resolution (Ferguson, Moretti, et al.), the other on interstices (Banfield).

In certain works by modern and contemporary authors—Muriel Spark's *The Driver's Seat* (1970), James Kelman's *A Chancer* (1985), Rachel Cusk's trilogy of works beginning with *Outline* (2015)—it is possible to identify such an indeterminate space of thought, for the narrative position of these works is subjectively uninhabitable, although for reasons other than those adduced by Vološinov or Banfield—namely, that they relate their stories in a voice bereft of affective resonance.[5] Thus, Moretti's formula characterizing the Toblerian view of free indirect discourse—"emotions, plus distance"—also fails to capture the effect of free indirect discourse in these works.[6] Nor can we readily speak of some "third voice" that, like Ferguson, Moretti conceives of as the "social" or "communal," for there is no such resolution. The effect, rather, is like the dysfunctional dramatic production imagined in the last few pages of Vološinov's *Marxism and the Philosophy of Language*, an illustration of what would happen were a literary seat of perception to be established for acting out the pure thought of the free indirect: "The reported speech will begin to sound as if it were in a play where there is no embracing context and where the character's lines confront other lines by other characters without any grammatical concatenation" (*MPL*, 157). Like Vološinov's hypothetical drama, these texts by Spark, Kelman, and Cusk lack any "grammatical concatenation" (or point of sensorimotor unity) that would make the perspective of the work subjectively inhabitable—even when, as happens at certain moments in these works, feelings are represented from outside, as "content." One of Cusk's characters, a playwright named Anne, describes herself rejecting every idea for a work as soon as a concept or theme presses itself upon her as the work's aggregate meaning: "*tension*, for instance, or *mother-in-law*" (*Outline*, 232). Presently, the feeling of discomfort extends beyond the domain of Anne's own writing to works by other writers and even to her experience of her acquaintances: "She was having a drink with a friend the other night and she looked across the table and thought, *friend*, with the result that she strongly suspected their friendship was over" (232–33). Were there a sensorimotor "convergence" (as Lukács styles it) in Cusk's narrative, in which Anne's poetic (or neurotic) interiority were met with a corresponding sympathy (or irony) in the narrator, and thus framed with a complicitous (or satirical) inflection, Cusk's narrative would fall into the camp of "paradox," a mode of resolution through deferral of the work's values (or, conversely, that of critical condemnation à la Booth and Litz, another mode of resolution). But there is no such convergence in Cusk and thus no resolution—nor, we could say, "deflection" in Cora Diamond's sense. In such moments, literature discovers a way to imagine itself as no longer a subjective form at all.

NOTES

INTRODUCTION. UNTHINKING CONNECTIONS

1. "Violating the Form: Rachel Cusk and Alexandra Schwartz in Conversation," *FSG Work in Progress*, September 7, 2018, https://fsgworkinprogress.com/2018/09/07/violating-the-form/.

2. Rachel Cusk, *Outline* (New York: Farrar, Straus and Giroux, 2014), 70.

3. W. G. Sebald, in James Wood, "An Interview with W. G. Sebald," *Brick: A Literary Journal* 59 (Spring 1998): 25–26, 27.

4. W. G. Sebald, *The Rings of Saturn* (New York: New Directions, 1998), 187–88.

5. Guido Mazzoni, *Theory of the Novel*, trans. Zakiya Hanafi (Cambridge, MA: Harvard University Press, 2017), 51.

6. Teju Cole, *Open City* (New York: Random House, 2012), 161.

7. Renee Gladman, "The Sentence as a Space for Living: Prose Architecture," *TRIPWIRE: a journal of poetics* 15 (2019): 98, https://tripwirejournal.files.wordpress.com/2020/03/tripwire15.pdf.

8. Renee Gladman, *Calamities* (Seattle, WA: Wave, 2016), 48, 104–5. The quotation about drawing is from the artist Monika Grzymala.

9. Jacques Rancière, *Mute Speech*, trans. James Swenson (New York: Columbia University Press, 2011), 83.

10. Jean-Philippe Deranty, "Regimes of the Arts," in *Jacques Rancière: Key Concepts*, ed. Jean-Philippe Deranty (Durham, UK: Acumen, 2010), 117.

11. Louis Althusser, "A Letter on Art in Reply to André Daspre," in *Lenin and Philosophy and Other Essays* (New York: Monthly Review, 2001), 152.

12. Aristotle, *Poetics*, trans. Anthony Kenny (Oxford: Oxford University Press, 2013), 9.1451a–b.

13. I. A. Richards, *Principles of Literary Criticism* (London: Routledge & Kegan Paul, 1960), 272.

14. Ian Watt, *The Rise of the Novel: Studies in Defoe, Richardson, and Fielding* (London: Hogarth, 1987), 62.

15. Northrop Frye, *Anatomy of Criticism: Four Essays* (Harmondsworth: Penguin, 1990), 52.

16. Wayne C. Booth, *The Rhetoric of Fiction*, 2nd ed. (Chicago: University of Chicago Press, 1983), xiii.

17. Fredric Jameson, "The Case for Georg Lukács," in *Marxism and Form: Twentieth-Century Dialectical Theories of Literature* (Princeton, NJ: Princeton University Press, 1971), 161.

18. Dorothy J. Hale, *The Novel and the New Ethics* (Stanford, CA: Stanford University Press, 2020), ix, 127.

19. Mikhail Bakhtin, "Forms of Time and of the Chronotope in the Novel," in *The Dialogic Imagination*, trans. Caryl Emerson and Michael Holquist (Austin: University of Texas Press, 1981), 243.

1. THE PROBLEM OF FORM

1. Immanuel Kant, *Critique of Judgment*, trans. Werner S. Pluhar (Indianapolis, IN: Hackett, 1987), 176–77.

2. Jacques Rancière, *Mute Speech*, trans. James Swenson (New York: Columbia University Press, 2011), 124.

3. Charles Dickens, *Bleak House*, ed. Nicola Bradbury (Harmondsworth: Penguin, 1996), 734.

4. Mark Twain, *The Adventures of Huckleberry Finn*, ed. John Seelye (Harmondsworth: Penguin, 1985), 235.

5. Leslie A. Fiedler, *Love and Death in the American Novel* (Harmondsworth: Penguin, 1984), 30.

6. Ben Lerner, *10:04* (New York: Faber and Faber, 2014), 237.

7. On the question of the shortcoming of formal or generic definitions of the novel, the insights of the Russian philosopher and critic Mikhail Bakhtin are unsurpassed. Every formal definition of the novel proposed by literary theorists, Bakhtin points out, can be advanced only with a reservation that "immediately disqualifies it altogether as a generic characteristic." He continues: "Some examples of such 'characteristics with reservations' would be: the novel is a multi-layered genre (although there also exist magnificent single-layered novels); the novel is a precisely plotted and dynamic genre (although there also exist novels that push to its literary limits the art of pure description); the novel is a complicated genre (although novels are mass produced as pure and frivolous entertainment like no other genre); the novel is a love story (although the greatest examples of the European novel are utterly devoid of the love element); the novel is a prose genre (although there exist excellent novels in verse)." Mikhail Bakhtin, "Epic and Novel," in *The Dialogic Imagination: Four Essays*, trans. Caryl Emerson and Michael Holquist (Austin: University of Texas Press, 1981), 8–9. The meaning of Bakhtin's observation has not been explored, nor really even considered, in the field of novel studies. However, it is centrally important to a primary contention of the present work: that the novel is less a *form* than a *logic*, the implications of which extend well beyond the practice

of literature and into our critical procedures and modes of intellectual and political engagement.

8. Martin Heidegger, *What Is Called Thinking?*, trans. Fred D. Wieck and J. Glenn Gray (New York: Harper & Row, 1968), 8.

9. V. N. Vološinov, "Discourse in Life and Discourse in Art (Concerning Sociological Poetics) (Appendix I)," in *Freudianism: A Marxist Critique*, trans. I. R. Titunik (London: Verso, 2012), 179 (emphasis added).

10. Percy Lubbock, *The Craft of Fiction* (1921; London: Jonathan Cape, 1965), 59, 92.

11. Georg Lukács, "Realism in the Balance," trans. Rodney Livingstone, in Theodor Adorno et al., *Aesthetics and Politics* (London: Verso, 1980), 48.

12. E. M. Forster, *Howards End* (1910; Harmondsworth: Penguin, 1985), 3; Fredric Jameson, *The Political Unconscious: Narrative as a Socially Symbolic Act* (Ithaca, NY: Cornell University Press, 1981), 9.

13. Mikhail Bakhtin, *Problems of Dostoevsky's Poetics*, trans. Caryl Emerson (Minneapolis: University of Minnesota Press, 1984), 25. "Social indexicality" is associated with the emergent field of linguistic anthropology and is partly inspired by the work of Pierre Bourdieu; see Tom McEnaney and Michael Lucey, "Introduction: Language-in-Use and Literary Fieldwork," *Representations* 137 (Winter 2017): 1–22. "Social formalism" is a coinage of the critic Dorothy J. Hale with which she characterizes the tendencies of novel theorists to approach the work primarily for its quality of "social representativeness." Social formalists, says Hale, "imagine in particular that the form of the novel can accurately instantiate both the identity of its author and the identity of the subject the author seeks to represent." Dorothy J. Hale, *Social Formalism: The Novel in Theory from Henry James to the Present* (Stanford, CA: Stanford University Press, 1998), 5.

14. Pierre Bourdieu, *The Rules of Art: Genesis and Structure of the Literary Field*, trans. Susan Emanuel (Stanford, CA: Stanford University Press, 1995), 3. For *Verneinung*, see Sigmund Freud, "Negation," trans. James Strachey, in *On Metapsychology: The Theory of Psychoanalysis* (Harmondsworth: Penguin, 1991), 436–42.

15. Jacques Rancière, "Literary Misunderstanding," in *The Politics of Literature*, trans. Julie Rose (Cambridge: Polity, 2011), 42.

16. Georg Lukács, *Studies in European Realism*, trans. Edith Bone (New York: Howard Fertig, 2002), 145; henceforth *SER*.

17. Barbara Foley, *Marxist Literary Criticism Today* (London: Pluto, 2019), 96.

18. Thomas Pavel, *The Lives of the Novel* (Princeton, NJ: Princeton University Press, 2013), 18.

19. Georg Lukács, *The Theory of the Novel: A Historico-Philosophical Essay on the Forms of Great Epic Literature*, trans. Anna Bostock (Cambridge, MA: MIT Press, 1971), 74. Throughout this book, page references to Lukács's *The Theory of the Novel* will be signaled using the abbreviation *TN* (unless the source is obvious from the context).

20. Besides realism, ethics, and irony, we might mention a fourth term that has lately come to play the same role of comprehending the constitutive gaps in the novel, giving rise to a new field of literary theory and criticism: "affect." As such, certain pitfalls of "affect theory" have been recently highlighted by Fredric Jameson in the context of a discussion of *Madame Bovary*: "We have to be sure that we do not ourselves too readily identify [Emma Bovary's] dissatisfaction after the fact, and add

in diagnoses which, old or new, tend in advance to reify something it was the very intent and burden of Flaubert's art to leave unidentified—better still, to identify as being unidentifiable and unavailable in the first place." Fredric Jameson, "Realism and the Dissolution of Genre," in *The Antinomies of Realism* (London: Verso, 2013), 142.

21. In *History and Class Consciousness* (1922), Lukács will discover a new name (and an explanation) for the world's "fragility" and "fundamental dissonance" in the concept of class struggle and thus a rationale for what will be a decades-long, increasingly complex critical commitment on Lukács's part to realism. However, class struggle and class consciousness are also not "forms" for Lukács, as his insistence on the "imputed" (*zugerechnet*) quality of class consciousness makes clear. Class consciousness is a consciousness that would be "neither the sum nor the average of what is thought or felt by the single individuals who make up the class." Georg Lukács, *History and Class Consciousness: Studies in Marxist Dialectics*, trans. Rodney Livingstone (London: Merlin, 1971), 64–65, 51.

22. Aristotle, *Metaphysics*, 1026b, 1030b.

23. Catherine Gallagher, "The Rise of Fictionality," in *The Novel*, vol. 1: *History, Geography, and Culture*, ed. Franco Moretti (Princeton, NJ: Princeton University Press, 2006), 340.

24. For Anton Chekhov's distinction between "answering the questions" and "formulating them correctly" see his letter to Alexei Suvorin, October 27, 1888, in *Anton Chekhov's Life and Thought: Selected Letters and Commentary*, trans. Michael Henry Heim, in collaboration with Simon Karlinsky (Berkeley: University of California Press, 1975), 117.

25. Jacques Rancière, "Are Some Things Unrepresentable?" in *The Future of the Image*, trans. Gregory Elliott (London: Verso, 2007), 124; Gustave Flaubert, *Madame Bovary*, trans. Lydia Davis (New York: Viking, 2010), 20.

26. Kant, *Critique of Judgment*, 183.

27. Theodor W. Adorno, *Aesthetic Theory*, trans. Robert Hullot-Kentor (Minneapolis: University of Minnesota Press, 1997), 311.

28. Maurizio Lazzarato, *Experimental Politics: Work, Welfare, and Creativity in the Neoliberal Age*, trans. Jeremy Gilbert et al. (Cambridge, MA: MIT Press, 2017), 149–50.

29. M. M. Bakhtin, *The Dialogic Imagination: Four Essays*, trans. Caryl Emerson and Michael Holquist (Austin: University of Texas Press, 1981), 333.

30. Toni Morrison, *Playing in the Dark: Whiteness and the Literary Imagination* (New York: Random House, 1992), 4–5.

31. Amitav Ghosh, *The Great Derangement: Climate Change and the Unthinkable* (Chicago: University of Chicago Press, 2016), 121, 125.

32. Robert Walser, *The Tanners*, trans. Susan Bernofsky (New York: New Directions, 2009), 64.

33. Letter to Georges Duthuit, March 9, 1949, in *The Letters of Samuel Beckett*, vol. 2: *1941–1956*, ed. George Craig, Martha Dow Fehsenfeld, Dan Gunn, and Lois More Overbeck (Cambridge: Cambridge University Press, 2011), 140, 139.

34. Gilles Deleuze, *Cinema 2: The Time-Image*, trans. Hugh Tomlinson and Robert Galeta (London: Athlone, 1989), 163.

35. Olena Hankivsky, "Rethinking Care Ethics: On the Promise and Potential of an Intersectional Analysis," *American Political Science Review* 108, no. 2 (May 2014): 256. Intersectionality is not a methodology, a field of research, or a political program but a metaphor for a certain situation of discrimination or oppression that is experienced in a plurality of forms. As such, it is distinguished by the absence of positive terms. In Kimberlé Crenshaw's initial articulation of the metaphor in relation to the experience of women of color, those terms are sex (meaning sex discrimination) and race (meaning race discrimination). Kimberlé Crenshaw, "Demarginalizing the Intersection of Race and Sex: A Black Feminist Critique of Antidiscrimination Doctrine, Feminist Theory, and Antiracist Politics," *University of Chicago Legal Forum* 1989, no. 1, article 8 (1989): 49. Neither sex nor race has the status of an identity claim by those caught in the intersection; on the contrary, identity is a status foisted upon them by the discrimination itself. Barbara Foley has recently observed that intersectionality falls short of providing an "explanatory framework" for the multiple oppressions it describes. Barbara Foley, "Intersectionality: A Marxist Critique," *New Labor Forum* 28, no. 3 (2019): 10. For Foley, this fact speaks to the "inadequacy" of intersectional social theory, which offers "no account of why this 'matrix' exists in the first place." Thus to claim that the novel is intersectional in its essence is to place the novel's essence not only on the boundaries of form as such but in a differential relation to all forms and explanatory frameworks, including those put forward in the body of the work itself. It also speaks to the simple fact that there can only be a racist novel, a capitalist novel, and even a "protest novel" in tension with and as a foreclosure of the qualities that make the work a novel. In the protest novel, said James Baldwin memorably, "it is categorization alone which is real." James Baldwin, "Everybody's Protest Novel," in *Collected Essays*, ed. Toni Morrison (New York: Library of America, 1998), 18.
36. Toni Morrison, "Academic Whispers" (a talk given at Johns Hopkins University in March 2004), in *The Source of Self-Regard: Selected Essays, Speeches, and Meditations* (New York: Vintage International, 2020), 198–99.
37. Kingsley Amis, *Lucky Jim* (1954; New York: Penguin, 2002), 242.
38. Ian McEwan, *Saturday* (New York: Random House, 2005), 281–82.
39. In an insightful reading of McEwan's novel, Frances Ferguson summarizes this quality of the novel as follows: "Henry really doesn't understand the world of minds that the literature [his poet daughter] Daisy is always urging on him depicts, and Daisy doesn't have much interest in the world of brains with which Henry constantly grapples. In addition, Henry's wife, Rosalind, doesn't understand him." For Ferguson, the term that underpins the supposed discrepancy is "professionalism," a form in which each character's distinctive expertise is recognized (by Henry and by the novel) without the need for a discursive plane of understanding between them. Frances Ferguson, "The Way We Love Now: Ian McEwan, *Saturday*, and Personal Affection in the Information Age," *Representations* 100 (November 2007): 50.
40. A notion of virtuosity also, bizarrely, seems to frame *Saturday*'s treatment of ethnicity. Just as every Perowne family member is a prodigy of his or her chosen pursuit, so no ethnically or culturally coded character is endowed with personal features that are anything other than typologically consummate and exemplary. The novel's most important black character, a Nigerian teenager named Andrea, is

introduced as follows: "[Henry] admired her spirit, and the fierce dark eyes, the perfect teeth, and the clean pink tongue lashing itself round the words it formed." This sentence is immediately followed by the first mention of the novel's only American character: "It took Jay Strauss, an American with the warmth and directness that no one else in this English hospital could muster, to bring her into line" (9).

41. Adolf Tobler in 1887 is widely credited with first identifying the phenomenon. See V. N. Vološinov, *Marxism and the Philosophy of Language*, trans. Ladislav Matejka and I. R. Titunik (Cambridge, MA: Harvard University Press, 1986), 142; henceforth *MPL*; Franco Moretti, *Graphs, Maps, Trees: Abstract Models for Literary History* (London: Verso, 2007), 81–82. Ann Banfield provides an overview of the evolution of the critical terminology in *Unspeakable Sentences: Narration and Representation in the Language of Fiction* (Boston: Routledge and Kegan Paul, 1982), 277–78n14.

42. James Joyce, *Dubliners* (Harmondsworth: Penguin, 1992), 175; Vološinov, *MPL*, 151.

43. See, respectively, Monika Fludernik, *The Fictions of Language and the Languages of Fiction: The Linguistic Representation of Speech and Consciousness* (London: Routledge, 1993), 5; Moretti, *Graphs, Maps, Trees*, 82; James Wood, *How Fiction Works*, 10th anniversary ed. (New York: Picador, 2018), 9.

44. Franco Moretti, "Serious Century," in *The Novel*, vol. 1: *History, Geography, and Culture* (Princeton, NJ: Princeton University Press, 2006), 399; D. A. Miller, *The Novel and the Police* (Berkeley: University of California Press, 1988), 25.

45. Peter Boxall, *The Prosthetic Imagination: A History of the Novel as Artificial Life* (Cambridge: Cambridge University Press, 2020), 157–58.

46. Henry Green, *Surviving: The Uncollected Writings of Henry Green*, ed. Matthew Yorke (New York: Viking Penguin, 1992), 139.

47. Hans Robert Jauss, *Toward an Aesthetic of Reception*, trans. Timothy Bahti (Minneapolis: University of Minnesota Press, 1982), 43–44; cited by Moretti, "Serious Century," 398.

48. Anne-Lise François, *Open Secrets: The Literature of Uncounted Experience* (Stanford, CA: Stanford University Press, 2008), 14.

49. The term "focalization" was coined by Gérard Genette to denote the point of view of any passage of narrative prose. After Genette, the concept comes into its own in discussions of free indirect discourse. Gérard Genette, *Narrative Discourse: An Essay in Method*, trans. Jane Lewin (Ithaca, NY: Cornell University Press, 1980), 189–94.

50. Mikhail Bakhtin, "Epic and Novel," in *The Dialogic Imagination: Four Essays*, trans. Caryl Emerson and Michael Holquist (Austin: University of Texas Press, 1981), 8–9. See also note 7.

2. AGAINST EXEMPLARITY: W. G. SEBALD

1. Alain Badiou, *Logics of Worlds: Being and Event 2*, trans. Alberto Toscano (London: Continuum, 2009), 18.

2. Agustín Zarzosa, "The Case and Its Modes," *Angelaki: Journal of the Theoretical Humanities* 17, no. 1 (March 2012): 41, 50–51.

3. See Immanuel Kant, *Practical Philosophy*, trans. Mary J. Gregor (Cambridge: Cambridge University Press, 1996), 593n.

4. Lauren Berlant, "On the Case," *Critical Inquiry* 33, no. 4 (special issue: *On the Case*, ed. Lauren Berlant) (Summer 2007): 666.

5. Jacques Rancière, *The Politics of Literature*, trans. Julie Rose (Cambridge: Polity, 2011), 9.

6. Toril Moi, *Revolution of the Ordinary: Literary Studies After Wittgenstein, Austin, and Cavell* (Chicago: University of Chicago Press, 2017), 88, 90.

7. Ludwig Wittgenstein, *Philosophical Investigations*, trans. G. E. M. Anscombe, P. M. S. Hacker, and Joachim Schulte (Oxford: Wiley Blackwell, 2009), 38, 36 (§§71, 67).

8. Immanuel Kant, *Critique of Pure Reason*, trans. J. M. D. Meiklejohn (London: J. M. Dent and Sons, 1934), 114–15.

9. Onora O'Neill, "The Power of Example," *Philosophy* 61 (January 1986): 11–12. "All we can do," writes Winch (in the passage quoted by O'Neill), "is to look at particular examples and see what we *do* want to say about them; there are no general rules which can determine in advance what we *must* say about them." Peter Winch, *Ethics and Action* (London: Routledge and Kegan Paul, 1972), 182.

10. W. G. Sebald, *Vertigo*, trans. Michael Hulse (London: Harvill, 1999), 106–7. Quotations from W. G. Sebald's works are from published English translations, all of which (with the exception of the posthumous collections *Campo Santo* [2005] and *A Place in the Country* [2013]) were produced in collaboration with Sebald.

11. In a review of Lynne Sharon Schwartz's edited volume *The Emergence of Memory: Conversations with W. G. Sebald*, Evelyn Toynton notes the "strained" connections of Sebald's work as one of a number of possible detractions from the case for his "greatness." Evelyn Toynton, "The Other Side of Silence: W. G. Sebald's Melancholy Art," *Harper's Magazine*, April 2008, 100.

12. Mark R. McCulloh, *Understanding W. G. Sebald* (Columbia: University of South Carolina Press, 2003), 63.

13. Sebald has commented insightfully on this theme of interconnectedness in several interviews. See, for example, Joseph Cuomo, "A Conversation with W. G. Sebald," in *The Emergence of Memory: Conversations with W. G. Sebald*, ed. Lynne Sharon Schwartz (New York: Seven Stories, 2007), 96–97.

14. Charles Dickens, *Bleak House* (Harmondsworth: Penguin, 1996), 256.

15. Georg Lukács, "Realism in the Balance," trans. Rodney Livingstone, in Ernst Bloch et al., *Aesthetics and Politics* (London: NLB, 1977), esp. 36–37. See also *The Meaning of Contemporary Realism*, where Lukács extends this characterization to (among others) William Faulkner, Robert Musil, Samuel Beckett, and Franz Kafka. Georg Lukács, *The Meaning of Contemporary Realism*, trans. John and Necke Mander (London: Merlin, 1963), 17–46.

16. The link between exemplarity and subjectivity is most fascinatingly spelled out by Theodor W. Adorno, whose philosophical project consists in the systematization of a method whose end would be not identity but nonidentity. In *Negative Dialectics* he describes identity as a thinking in terms of class or set and nonidentity as a thinking of singularity: "Cognition of nonidentity . . . seeks to say what something is, while identitarian thinking says what something comes under, what it exemplifies or represents, and what, accordingly, it is not itself." Theodor W. Adorno, *Negative Dialectics*, trans. E. B. Ashton (London: Routledge, 1990), 149.

17. Giorgio Agamben, *The Coming Community*, trans. Michael Hardt (Minneapolis: University of Minnesota Press, 1993), 9.

18. Brian Massumi reads Agamben's aphorism on the example in *The Coming Community* as if Agamben were celebrating its ambiguities rather than using them as his point of departure. For Massumi, the ambiguity of the example seems to speak not of its normative qualities but of its "experimental" ones. Brian Massumi, *Parables for the Virtual: Movement, Affect, Sensation* (Durham: Duke University Press, 2002), 17–19. Agamben aligns exemplary logic with noncreative, metaphysical, even fascistic thinking. Massumi's imagination goes in the opposite direction: exemplarity enables us to avoid the fallacy of "applying" concepts, as long as we approach the use of the example "experimentally" (17–18). Every example, he says, "harbors terrible powers of deviation and digression" (18). It is those powers of digression that will foster experimentalism, if one allows the examples and the details (which threaten the coherence of the example) to multiply—if, that is, we suspend the logic of exemplarity from every example. Jessica Dubow—in the only other work I have seen that pays attention to Sebald's writing as a navigation of a relation to exemplarity—likewise proposes that the "historical case form," a symptom of the "urge to unity," might, "once reconfigured be the very medium for properly opposing" that urge. Jessica Dubow, "Case Interrupted: Benjamin, Sebald, and the Dialectical Image," *Critical Inquiry* 33 (Summer 2007): 828. The sense of Sebald's challenge to the logic of exemplarity is therefore strong in Dubow, even as her analysis, like Massumi's, rests on the "ambiguity" of the example. Dubow is thus the latest in a line of contemporary thinkers of the example (including Moi and Massumi) for whom the usefulness of exemplarity might be retained with a mental act of will by which we can avoid universalizing its concepts or conceiving their boundaries as "exclusionary." I prefer to emphasize the sense of a trajectory in Sebald's work, as tracing a line of flight toward a nonexemplary, wholly non-normative world, irrespective of its realizability.

19. Saidiya Hartman, "Venus in Two Acts," *Small Axe: A Journal of Criticism* 26 (June 2008): 2.

20. Saidiya Hartman, *Wayward Lives, Beautiful Experiments: Intimate Histories of Social Upheaval* (New York: Norton, 2019), 18.

21. J. M. Coetzee, *The Master of Petersburg* (New York: Penguin, 1995), 235.

22. I. A. Richards, *The Philosophy of Rhetoric* (Oxford: Oxford University Press, 1936), 97.

23. In an analysis of what he calls the "example effect," which he specifies as nothing less than the "possibility of philosophy," Eric Hayot addresses the inverse implication, claiming that "no ethical argument about an experience that arrives to us as a text can be made in a manner that separates it from its examples." Thus (he continues), "any evidentiary argument belongs at least partially to the examples on which it draws." Eric Hayot, *The Hypothetical Mandarin: Sympathy, Modernity, and Chinese Pain* (Oxford: Oxford University Press, 2009), 26, 29. Hayot's response to this implication is to present his examples in such a way as to "suspend" the normalizing transition from the particular to the general "at precisely the moment at which the individual anecdote, citation, sentence, or episode threatens to cross over into general principle, there to be replaced by a rule or state of things that effectively erases the anecdote's or citation's importance *qua* itself—that is, its existence as something other than an example of some idea." Hayot is thus one of the contemporary thinkers of the example (see note 18) who

attempt to navigate its inherently normative implications with procedures of interior qualification.

24. Agamben's concept of *whatever being* is derived from Gilles Deleuze's formulation "un espace quelconque" ("any space whatever"), which recurs throughout *Cinema 1* and *Cinema 2* to designate the sense of a "pure space" detached from any stratified order or relation to a whole. See Gilles Deleuze, *Cinema 2: The Time-Image*, trans. Hugh Tomlinson and Robert Galeta (London: Athlone, 1989), 251.

25. Catherine Gallagher, "The Rise of Fictionality," in *The Novel*, vol. 1: *History, Geography, and Culture*, ed. Franco Moretti (Princeton, NJ: Princeton University Press, 2006), 342.

26. Thomas Keenan, *Fables of Responsibility: Aberrations and Predicaments in Ethics and Politics* (Stanford, CA: Stanford University Press, 1997), 46.

27. Keenan's observation about the double register of exemplarity is another mobilization of Kant's distinction, already alluded to, between two apparently synonymous words, "instance" (*Beispiel*) and "example" (*Exempel*). The first names a cognitive discourse ("a presentation of a concept merely for theory"), the second an instructional ("practical") one. Kant, *Practical Philosophy*, 593n.

28. J. M. Coetzee, *Elizabeth Costello* (New York: Viking, 2003), 7–8.

29. Coetzee's entire literary output has been characterized by restiveness over the category of identity. Characters such as Friday in *Foe* (Harmondsworth: Penguin, 1987), Michael in *The Life and Times of Michael K* (London: Vintage, 1998), and Vercueil in *Age of Iron* (New York: Penguin, 1998) are all "great escapees," in the words of the unnamed medical officer in the second part of *Michael K*, who thus retain their enigmatic (nonexemplary) status within and beyond the confines of the text. "Your stay in the camp," the medical officer says of Michael, "was merely an allegory . . . of how scandalously, how outrageously a meaning can take up residence in a system without becoming a term in it" (*Life and Times*, 166)—without, that is, becoming exhausted by structures of exemplarity.

30. V. S. Naipaul, *An Area of Darkness* (New Delhi: Penguin, 1968), 44–45.

31. Thus we meet Ramnath, a stenographer, who, because it is not his job to type—because typing a letter that he has taken down in shorthand will violate his identity, his being as a "steno"—will not type (48–49). We meet Malhotra, his supervisor, recently returned to India from Europe, caught between the social aspirations of his European education and the badges of food, caste, dress, and income with which Indian marriage proposals are considered and by which his are refused (51–52). We meet Jivan, a Bombay street boy, who, even as he rises through a succession of jobs, selling advertising for a magazine, working as a clerk, and finally owning his own taxi, continues to sleep on the pavements of Bombay (53–45). We meet Vasant, a stockbroker of humble origins who, even when he becomes rich, continues to work from a tiny cubby-hole and to go without lunch (54). We meet Bunty, a business executive in a British firm and an example of the "new [native] aristocracy" that has replaced one set of (Indian) caste practices with a new set, originating in the obsolete British colonial system (58–59).

32. Edward W. Said, "Bitter Dispatches from the Third World," in *Reflections on Exile and Other Essays* (Cambridge, MA: Harvard University Press, 2000), 103.

33. Carol Jacobs's *Sebald's Vision* (New York: Columbia University Press, 2015) is predicated on the idea that Sebald's writings offer a "continuously changing meditation"

on the mutual "entanglements" of stories of violence and natural devastation with scenes of vision and documentation "and a dizzying practice of thinking and representing" such entanglements. However, she adds, it is impossible to dispel the suspicion that "we may not be able to learn anything at all" from them (xii).

34. Roland Barthes, *Camera Lucida: Reflections on Photography*, trans. Richard Howard (New York: Hill and Wang, 1981), 4.

35. James Wood, "An Interview with W. G. Sebald," *Brick: A Literary Journal* 59 (Spring 1998): 24. For Jacques Rancière, however, all novelistic prose has "a degree of mutedness" about it. Indeed, for Rancière, muteness is precisely the form of eloquence specific to the literary regime. Rancière, *The Politics of Literature*, 14. The questions that are opened up by this observation impact upon both Sebald's project and Rancière's, as well as on claims about a "new mode of seeing" (Jacobs, *Sebald's Vision*, xiv) in Sebald's work: is the muteness that Sebald aspires to produce in his writing anything more than the "muteness of the letter" that Rancière ascribes to the novel form as such? What does it mean for a late-twentieth-century writer to strain toward that which, for the philosopher of aesthetics, is effortlessly produced in the fiction of the nineteenth century—and in every work of fiction since then—simply as a condition of the form? In other words, is there an ethical necessity, or even an aesthetic distinctiveness, to Sebald's project beyond that of the novel as such? (In chapter 8 I return to these quandaries in the context of the encounter between the work of Jacques Rancière and that of Gilles Deleuze.)

36. W. G. Sebald, "Kafka Goes to the Movies," in *Campo Santo*, trans. Anthea Bell (New York: Random House, 2005), 153–54.

37. Franz Kafka, *The Diaries of Franz Kafka, 1910–23* (Harmondsworth: Penguin, 1964), 109.

38. The phrase "Faint white of the low neck of a blouse" appears in a diary entry dated October 12, 1911, from a description of a young woman referred to only by the initial "R." Kafka, *Diaries*, 73–74.

39. Didi-Huberman attributes the phrase to Gérard Wajcman. See Georges Didi-Huberman, *Images in Spite of All: Four Photographs from Auschwitz*, trans. Shane B. Lillis (Chicago: University of Chicago Press, 2008), 27.

40. I refer to the American English–language edition, trans. Anthea Bell (New York: Random House, 2001), which has 298 pages. The British edition, at 415 pages long (London: Hamish Hamilton, 2001), approximately retains the spacing of the 417-page German edition (München: Carl Hanser Verlag, 2001).

41. In a 2006 essay in *MLN*, John Zilcosky notes the threat posed to Sebald's project by these tensions. In *Austerlitz*, he comments, "Sebald comes perilously close . . . to the melodramatic 'impulse toward dramatization' and 'desire to express all' that he had scrupulously avoided in the earlier fictions and, what is more, had criticized in other Holocaust representations such as *Schindler's List*." John Zilcosky, "Lost and Found: Disorientation, Nostalgia, and Holocaust Melodrama in Sebald's *Austerlitz*," *MLN* 121, no. 3 (April 2006): 694–95.

42. Maya Jaggi, "Recovered Memories," *Guardian*, September 22, 2001.

43. W. G. Sebald, *The Rings of Saturn*, trans. Michael Hulse (London: Harvill, 1998), 38–40, 193–95.

44. See Dan Jacobson, *Heshel's Kingdom* (Evanston, IL: Northwestern University Press, 1998), ix–xi.

45. Gilles Deleuze, *Cinema 1: The Movement-Image*, trans. Hugh Tomlinson and Barbara Habberjam (London: Athlone, 1986), 206–7. In Deleuze's typology of cinematic images, synsigns are signs that refer to the organic unity of the situation.
46. Deleuze, *Cinema 2*, 180.
47. Jacques Rancière, "The Shores of the Real," in *The Edges of Fiction*, trans. Steven Corcoran (Cambridge: Polity, 2020), 116.

3. THE INSTANTIATION RELATION

1. Gilles Deleuze, *Foucault*, trans. Seán Hand (Minneapolis: University of Minnesota Press, 1988), 48.
2. I therefore disagree with Michael Holquist when he counts Lukács's *The Theory of the Novel* among a list of theoretical works that "seek to elevate one kind of novel into a definition of the novel as such." Michael Holquist, introduction to Mikhail Bakhtin, *The Dialogic Imagination*, trans. Caryl Emerson and Michael Holquist (Austin: University of Texas Press, 1981), xxvi–xxvii. However, Holquist is right to note that Bakhtin's theory of the novel explicitly rejects this formal understanding of the novel.
3. This is what Franco Moretti means when he says (correctly) that "the great theories of the novel have been theories of modernity" and (again correctly) that the "insistence on the market" in his own work is "a particularly brutal version thereof." Franco Moretti, *Distant Reading* (London: Verso, 2013), 176. A theorized novel is one whose place in the ideological and consumer economy has been rendered transparent. Moretti thus opposes consumption and modernity to "aesthetics." I will discuss Moretti's work more fully in what follows.
4. J. M. Coetzee, *Elizabeth Costello* (New York: Viking, 2003), 1.
5. This suggestion might seem naïve in the light of an observation about Coetzee's work made by Stephen Mulhall: "If we are already within the fictional world at the beginning of the first paragraph, then the bridge to it must already have been built and crossed." Stephen Mulhall, *The Wounded Animal: J. M. Coetzee and the Difficulty of Reality in Literature and Philosophy* (Princeton, NJ: Princeton University Press, 2009), 177. For Mulhall, that is to say, the conceit of Coetzee's opening paragraph is a sleight of hand. Everything in *Elizabeth Costello*, including the opening paragraph, is a fiction that we have already acceded to by opening the book. "In short, a work of fiction cannot contain or embody the problem of the opening as a problem, even in its opening sentence; for it must already have opened in order to do so, and so must already have relied upon our willingness to pass over the bridge and its building. It can only, therefore, gesture towards a mystery of its own constitution as something essentially mysterious—at once mundane and miraculous, and always already beyond its grasp" (177). We are thus "where we want to be" from the first syllable. But Mulhall's observation is based on a purely technical, formal definition of the novel—as a genre born of "the desire to make reality apparent to the reader" (142)—a desire that is implicitly ascribed to every author, who is treated as the originator of the complex speech act that is a novel and of the ideas it contains. According to Mulhall's history of the novel, "novelists repeatedly subject their inheritance of realistic conventions to critical questioning in order to re-create the

impression of reality in their readers" (145). Thus, the problematic stated *in* the work—the problem of "realism," the problem of "ideas"—is assumed by Mulhall to be the problematic *of* the work. Coetzee's text is held to be ultimately comprehensible, therefore, within the realist conventions of the novel. As Mulhall puts it, "the darkness can be read, and what appear to be gaps are nothing of the kind" (151). My point of departure is quite different. Contemporary realism aspires not to "make reality apparent to the reader" but, on the contrary, to separate reality from itself, i.e., to make apparent the nonequivalence, or interstice, that exists at the site of the real. Coetzee's novel is part of an emerging postfictional universe in which figures of literary analysis such as author, reader, narrator, protagonist, character, idea, medium, metaphor, genre, representation, fiction, and reality are nothing more than formal categories that novelists have long resigned themselves to inhabiting. As modes of communication or thought, they collapsed long ago; they survive only in readings limited to the repetition of already existing thoughts. In the emerging postfictional universe, that is to say, they cease to function.

6. "Represented speech and thought" is Banfield's term for what is more usually called, in English, "free indirect discourse" or "free indirect style," after the Swiss linguist Charles Bally's 1912 coinage *style indirect libre*. Ann Banfield, *Unspeakable Sentences: Narration and Representation in the Language of Fiction* (Boston: Routledge and Kegan Paul, 1982), 12. For Banfield, the opposition between pure narration and represented speech and thought defines the formal limits of possible focalization in narrative fiction (185).

7. D. A. Miller, *Jane Austen, or, The Secret of Style* (Princeton, NJ: Princeton University Press, 2003), 64.

8. The term "infinitization" is used by Jacques Rancière, with a mostly pejorative inflection, in relation to Gilles Deleuze's work on cinema. Jacques Rancière, *Film Fables*, trans. Emiliano Battista (Oxford: Berg, 2006), 118. I will return to this use of the term in chapter 8.

9. The phrase "grammatical evidence" is also taken from Banfield's *Unspeakable Sentences* (189).

10. Mikhail Bakhtin, *Problems of Dostoevsky's Poetics*, trans. Caryl Emerson (Minneapolis: University of Minnesota Press, 1984), 24. In an insightful discussion of several moments in Coetzee's work when fictional characters express views that are close to Coetzee's own, Carrol Clarkson compares the first sentences of Coetzee's novel *Diary of a Bad Year* to the famous opening of Jane Austen's *Pride and Prejudice* ("It is a truth universally acknowledged, that a single man in possession of a good fortune, must be in want of a wife"). *Diary of a Bad Year* begins: "Every account of the origins of the state starts from the premise that 'we'—not we the readers but some generic we so wide as to exclude no one—participate in its coming into being." Carrol Clarkson, *J. M. Coetzee: Countervoices* (Houndmills, Basingstoke: Palgrave Macmillan, 2009), 79, 85–86. Clarkson's observation about the presence of "a syntax which deflects personal agency" (86) in Austen's and Coetzee's texts is beautifully relevant to the reflection on realism in *Elizabeth Costello* ("Realism has never been comfortable with ideas")—except, that is, for her technical explanation of the apparatus of deflection as a "syntax." For no such syntax of deflection is discernible in the *Elizabeth Costello* passage (or, perhaps, in *Pride and Prejudice* or *Diary of a Bad Year*). The deflection of personal agency takes place by structural rather than

rhetorical means. Each passage is in free indirect discourse, a form of discursive deflection *that is not marked syntactically*. Impersonality in Coetzee (and, I would venture, in Austen also)—"the impersonal 'one' or 'we,'" as Clarkson describes it (86)—is not a syntax of deflection but a syntax *from which* deflection must take place. Personal deflection in Coetzee is not an operation that is accessible to a "linguistic" analysis of the text; free indirect discourse is discernible only by paying attention to the "whole utterance" (to use a term from V. N. Vološinov), rather than to isolatable fragments of text (Vološinov, *MPL*, 101). Furthermore, the views expressed by Coetzee's characters are not simply *close to* Coetzee's own (Clarkson uses the double negative "not unrelated to") but *indistinguishable* from them. Thus, what Clarkson calls the "difficulty" of establishing the "source of the point of view or opinion expressed" in Coetzee's recent work (86) amounts to not merely an ambiguity but the *dissolution* of point of view as a signifying problematic. There is, in short, *no point of view to establish* in Coetzee's recent writing.

11. James Joyce, *Ulysses* (1922; London: Bodley Head, 1960), 11; E. M. Forster, *Howards End* (1910; Harmondsworth: Penguin, 1985), 44.

12. Wayne C. Booth, *The Rhetoric of Fiction*, 2nd ed. (Chicago: University of Chicago Press, 1983), xiii–xiv.

13. In assessing the afterlife of Booth's *The Rhetoric of Fiction* it is worth noting that the predicament into which Booth places a hypothetical "intelligent," "non-professional" reader when reading the "sordid adventures" narrated in Céline's novels—that Céline is neither "undeniably there" in his first-person narrators nor "undeniably dissociated" from them (379–80, 383–84), and on the basis of which Booth condemns Céline's work as finally "immoral" and "meaningless"—is one that certain professional readers of Coetzee have also attached to *Elizabeth Costello*. When the philosopher of ethics Peter Singer objects to Coetzee's eponymous protagonist as a "marvellous device" that enables Coetzee to advance arguments without taking personal responsibility for them, he is making the same assumptions about the "morality" of literary technique as Booth. "Costello can blithely criticize the use of reason, or the need to have any clear principles or proscriptions, without Coetzee really committing himself to these claims." Peter Singer, in J. M. Coetzee, *The Lives of Animals* (Princeton, NJ: Princeton University Press, 1999), 91. Incidentally, Booth later revised his views in the light of the publication of Mikhail Bakhtin's work in English—most notably in an introduction to the 1984 English translation of Bakhtin's *Problems in Dostoevsky's Poetics*. "If I had not been ignorant, like almost everyone else, of the work of Bakhtin and his circle," he writes, "I might have grappled with [Bakhtin's] much more sophisticated attack on the 'author's voice' in fiction, one that would have forced me to reformulate, if not fundamentally to modify, my claim that 'the author's judgment is always present, always evident to anyone who knows how to look for it.'" Wayne Booth, introduction to Bakhtin, *Problems*, xix.

14. Relevant works include Louis Althusser, "Ideology and Ideological State Apparatuses (Notes Towards an Investigation)," trans. Ben Brewster, in *Lenin and Philosophy and Other Essays* (New York: Monthly Review Press, 2001); Max Horkheimer and Theodor W. Adorno, "The Culture Industry: Enlightenment as Mass Deception," in *Dialectic of Enlightenment*, trans. Edmund Jephcott (Stanford, CA: Stanford University Press, 2002); Theodor W. Adorno, "Art, Society, Aesthetics," in

Aesthetic Theory, trans. Robert Hullot-Kentor (Minneapolis: University of Minnesota Press, 1997), 1–15; Pierre Bourdieu, *Distinction: A Social Critique of the Judgement of Taste*, trans. Richard Nice (London: Routledge and Kegan Paul, 1984).

15. Mark McGurl, *The Program Era: Postwar Fiction and the Rise of Creative Writing*, Cambridge, MA: Harvard University Press, 2009, 233.

16. Franco Moretti, *Distant Reading* (London: Verso, 2011); see especially the essays "Conjectures on World Literature" (43–62), "The Slaughterhouse of Literature" (63–89), "More Conjectures" (107–19), and "The Novel: History and Theory" (159–78).

17. Moretti's reference to Fergus's work is to her analysis of library borrowing trends in *Provincial Readers in Eighteenth-Century England* (Oxford: Oxford University Press, 2006), 108–16. Moretti also cites Walter Benjamin's discussion of distraction (*Zerstreuung*) at the end of "The Work of Art in the Age of its Technological Reproducibility," the key text for understanding the relationship between the rise of industrial capitalism and the destruction of the aura. See the third version of Benjamin's essay, trans. Harry Zohn, in *Selected Writings*, vol. 4: *1938–1940* (Cambridge, MA: Harvard University Press, 2003), esp. 267–69.

18. In "More Conjectures," Moretti responds to objections from Jale Parla and Jonathan Arac that the differentiation of the logics of core and periphery, and his thesis of a "compromise" between "local" material and "foreign" forms, adopts the point of view of the "unavowed[ly]" Anglophone core (Arac, 44) at the expense of the periphery. In his response, Moretti concedes that compromise is not limited to the periphery, that "literary form is *always* a compromise between opposite forces," and that such a thesis was a leitmotif of his "intellectual formation" (116). This "corrective," of course, changes nothing about the systematizing, economic nature of Moretti's model. The thesis of "formal compromise" sidelines entirely the hypothesis of expression, which is to say, thought. See Jonathan Arac, "Anglo-Globalism?" *New Left Review* 2, no. 16 (July–August 2002): esp. 38–40, 43; Jale Parla, "The Object of Comparison," *Comparative Literature Studies* 41, no. 1 (2004): 116–25.

19. Walter Benjamin, "On the Concept of History," trans. Harry Zohn, *Selected Writings*, vol. 4: *1938–1940* (Cambridge, MA: Harvard University Press, 2003), 391–92.

20. G. W. F. Hegel, *Aesthetics: Lectures on Fine Art*, trans. T. M. Knox (Oxford: Clarendon, 1975), 1:89.

21. Fyodor Dostoyevsky, *Notes from Underground / The Double*, trans. Jessie Coulson (Harmondsworth: Penguin, 1972), 112–18; see Bakhtin, *Problems*, 253.

22. F. H. Bradley, *Appearance and Reality: A Metaphysical Essay*, 9th impression, authorized and corrected (1893; Oxford: Clarendon, 1930), 16.

23. Stephen Mumford, *David Armstrong* (Stocksfield: Acumen, 2007), 28.

24. D. M. Armstrong, *A World of States of Affairs* (Cambridge: Cambridge University Press, 1997), 114.

25. Armstrong, *A World of States of Affairs*, 113–38; Bradley, *Appearance and Reality*, 61–63.

26. Dorothy J. Hale, "*On Beauty* as Beautiful? The Problem of Novelistic Aesthetics by Way of Zadie Smith," *Contemporary Literature* 53, no. 4 (Winter 2012): 821–22.

27. Samuel Delany, *Trouble on Triton* (Hanover, NH: University Press of New England, 1996), 6.

28. Dorothy J. Hale, *Social Formalism: The Novel in Theory from Henry James to the Present* (Stanford, CA: Stanford University Press, 1998), 5.

29. Fredric Jameson, "Postmodernism and Consumer Society," in *The Anti-Aesthetic*, ed. Hal Foster (Port Townsend, WA: Bay, 1985), 115–16. As Jacques Rancière's work on literature and aesthetics has made clear, it is a mistake to conceive of realism as the "representational" mode with which twentieth-century literature had to break; on the contrary, realism is "the emancipation of resemblance from representation." Thus, the entire emergence of the aesthetic regime in modernity, in Rancière's terms, is a shift from the logic of representation to the logic of instantiation. "The new novel—the novel called realist—is criticized for a primacy of description over action. The primacy of description is in fact that of a form of the visible which does not make visible, which deprives action of its powers of intelligibility—that is, of its powers of ordered distribution of knowledge-effects and pathos-effects." "The aesthetic revolution establishes this identity of knowledge and ignorance, acting and suffering, as the very definition of art. In it the artistic phenomenon is identified as the identity, in a physical form, of thought and non-thought, of the activity of a will that wishes to realize its idea and of a non-intentionality, a radical passivity of material being-there.... This regime of thinking ... identifies artistic phenomena as intellectual phenomena in as much as they are modes of a thought that is immanent in its other and inhabited by its other in turn." Jacques Rancière, *The Future of the Image*, trans. Gregory Elliott (London: Verso, 2009), 122, 119.

30. Fredric Jameson, *Postmodernism, or the Cultural Logic of Late Capitalism* (Durham, NC: Duke University Press, 1990), 5.

31. The result of this project is Dorothy J. Hale, *The Novel and the New Ethics* (Stanford, CA: Stanford University Press, 2020).

32. Zadie Smith, "Love, Actually," *Guardian*, November 1, 2003; "Fail Better," *Guardian*, January 13, 2007; "Read Better," *Guardian*, January 20, 2007. Henceforth, parenthetical page references to Hale's 2012 essay will include a second reference for the essay's republication (in extended form) in Hale's 2020 book *The Novel and the New Ethics*.

33. Only the first and third of these passages are among the examples mentioned by Hale.

34. Mikhail Bakhtin, "Discourse in the Novel," in *The Dialogic Imagination: Four Essays*, trans. Caryl Emerson and Michael Holquist (Austin: University of Texas Press, 1981), 308.

35. Zadie Smith, *White Teeth* (New York: Vintage, 2001), 25.

36. Frank Kermode, *The Sense of an Ending: Studies in the Theory of Fiction* (New York: Oxford University Press, 1967), 3.

4. THE POSTFICTIONAL HYPOTHESIS

1. I take the term "characterological" from the work of Amanda Anderson, who, in *The Way We Argue Now*, observes that the discourse of metatheoretical commentary has been inseparable from a discourse of "characterology." For Anderson, the work of pragmatist philosophers such as William James, Richard Rorty, Barbara Herrnstein Smith, and Stanley Fish is marked by a (deliberate or inadvertent) "incorporation of the dimension of character into the discussion of intellectual practice." Amanda Anderson, *The Way We Argue Now: A Study in the Cultures of*

276

4. THE POSTFICTIONAL HYPOTHESIS

Theory (Princeton, NJ: Princeton University Press, 2006), 121. Anderson's argument directly concerns instantiation insofar as the body of scholarship she is concerned with implicitly distinguishes between the "beliefs" of certain thinkers, which are held to be foundational, and "style," which "gives expression to those beliefs, but could easily do so in any number of ways" (127): "We have become accustomed to hearing pragmatists called smug, or rationalists depicted as defensive and uptight. The hermeneut of suspicion is paranoid; the p.c. [politically correct] brigade oppressively pious" (134). In contrast to the tendency to separate such "ascriptions" from "formal argument," Anderson's move toward "characterological" analysis, she says, "reorients us toward the question of whether and how certain ideas can be expressed as a way of life or, less encompassingly, as forms of practice vitally significant to any larger conception of the good" (121). In other words, Anderson's perspective on liberalism and ideology is founded on the ineradicability of character from our theoretical and ideological discourses.

2. J. M. Coetzee, *Elizabeth Costello* (New York: Viking, 2003), 8.

3. Carrol Clarkson, *J. M. Coetzee: Countervoices* (Houndmills, Basingstoke: Palgrave Macmillan, 2009), 86. See chapter 3, note 10.

4. In his indispensable commentary on Lukács's *The Theory of the Novel*, J. M. Bernstein calls the shift of emphasis in this paragraph "confused if not contradictory." J. M. Bernstein, *The Philosophy of the Novel: Lukács, Marxism, and the Dialectics of Form* (Minneapolis: University of Minnesota Press, 1984), 189. For Bernstein, the passage founders because of Lukács's unacknowledged "appropriation" of a Schlegelian conception of Romantic irony, one that "runs contrary to the main lines of argument in his text" (191), inflecting his thinking in a "cosmic" and "metaphysical" direction. Irony in Lukács registers not the Schlegelian opposition between finite and infinite but the division between "discrete experience" and "conceptual form" (191). The struggle that drives Lukács's relation to the novel down a melancholy, despondent path, implies Bernstein, is one tormented by the unavoidable inscription of the form of the novel as a "dialectic of interpretation and representation." In Lukács's novel, continues Bernstein, "the epical desire for objectivity is always defeated by the interpretative, form-giving moment" (194). I share Bernstein's desire to liberate Lukács's thought from the very "theses alien to it" that Lukács apparently ends up affirming (202). However, the distinction that remains unconceptualized in Bernstein's analysis and that leads him to see the cosmic and metaphysical as the alternative to the "conceptual" and the "experiential" is between representation and instantiation. Lukács does not conceptualize this distinction either. Nevertheless, the case I am making here is that in some part of his thinking— indicated in that allusion to a space "behind the forms"—Lukács wants to liberate the thought of the novel not merely from conceptualization but from the relation of instantiation also.

5. E. M. Forster, *Howards End*, ed. Oliver Stallybrass (Harmondsworth: Penguin, 1985), 44.

6. D. M. Armstrong, *A World of States of Affairs* (Cambridge: Cambridge University Press, 1997), 114.

7. Jacques Rancière, "Literary Misunderstanding," in *The Politics of Literature*, trans. Julie Rose (Cambridge: Polity, 2011), 43. See also Rancière, "Are Some Things Unrepresentable?" in *The Future of the Image*, trans. Gregory Elliott (London: Verso,

2007); Gavin Arnall, Laura Gandolfi, and Enea Zaramella, "Aesthetics and Politics Revisited: An Interview with Jacques Rancière," *Critical Inquiry* 38, no. 2 (Winter 2012): 289–90.

8. Gustave Flaubert, *Madame Bovary*, trans. Lydia Davis (New York: Viking, 2010), 82.

9. Jacques Rancière, "The Thread of the Novel," *Novel: A Forum on Fiction* 47, no. 2 (Summer 2014): 206.

10. See chapter 3, note 10.

11. E. M. Forster, *Aspects of the Novel* (London: Penguin, 2005), 130. Apart from Melville and Lawrence, Forster puts forward two further examples of the "prophetic" writer in *Aspects of the Novel*: Emily Brontë and Fyodor Dostoevsky. Forster defines prophecy not as "foretelling the future" but as an "accent" in the work of a novelist whose theme is "the universe, or something universal"—even though the prophet "is not necessarily going to 'say' anything about the universe" (116). To read the work of prophetic writers, the critic needs not the temperament of "classification" but "an ear for song" (118). With the figure of the "prophet," then, even Forster—who seems, in *Howards End*, the modern writer slowest to grasp the terms of the new literary regime—identifies a seam of "purely sensuous form-giving" that transcends the limitations of point of view.

12. Frank Kermode describes the intrusive moments in Forster's interpolations as "deliberately [tearing] the web of the tale [in order to] make such announcements": Frank Kermode, "Here She Is" (a review of *On Beauty* by Zadie Smith), *London Review of Books* 27, no. 19 (October 6, 2005): 13–14.

13. Ann Banfield, *Unspeakable Sentences: Narration and Representation in the Language of Fiction* (Boston: Routledge and Kegan Paul, 1982), 141.

14. Banfield is referring to Roy Pascal's *The Dual Voice: Free Indirect Speech and Its Functions in the Nineteenth-Century European Novel* (Manchester: Manchester University Press, 1977). However, the figure most frequently associated with the view that free indirect style "merges" the voices of narrator and character is Gérard Genette, *Narrative Discourse: An Essay in Method*, trans. Jane E. Lewin (Ithaca, NY: Cornell University Press, 1980), 174–75. V. N. Vološinov, discussed further in what follows, takes issue with the work of the Swiss critic and linguist Adolf Tobler on similar grounds; see *MPL*, 142.

15. Walter Benjamin, "Little History of Photography," trans. Edmund Jephcott and Kingsley Shorter, in *Selected Writings*, vol. 2: *1927–1934* (Cambridge, MA: Harvard University Press, 1999), 510.

16. Mikhail Bakhtin, *Problems of Dostoevsky's Poetics*, trans. Caryl Emerson (Minneapolis: University of Minnesota Press, 1984), 233.

17. Gilles Deleuze and Claire Parnet, *Dialogues II*, trans. Hugh Tomlinson and Barbara Habberjam (London: Continuum, 2002), 51–52; Gregory Flaxman, *Gilles Deleuze and the Fabulation of Philosophy* (Minneapolis: University of Minnesota Press, 2012), 216.

18. Ian Watt, *The Rise of the Novel: Studies in Defoe, Richardson, and Fielding* (London: Hogarth, 1987), 62.

19. D. M. Armstrong, *Universalism and Scientific Reason*, vol. 1: *Nominalism and Realism* (Cambridge: Cambridge University Press, 1978), 113.

20. To further illustrate how this important principle could inform an engagement with works of literature, we might return to Mark McGurl's *The Program Era: Postwar*

Fiction and the Rise of Creative Writing (Cambridge, MA: Harvard University Press, 2009), specifically to his account of the relation between Flannery O'Connor's work and the institution of the creative writing program in the United States. According to McGurl, what is instantiated in O'Connor's work is instantiation itself—instantiation being, in McGurl's acute analysis, the aesthetic ideology of the American creative writing program. "The idea of 'self-expression,'" writes McGurl, "is not obliterated in the postwar formation but is rotated to the minor position in relation to the more widely touted cluster of values that includes impersonality, technique, and self-discipline. In other words, the dictum 'write what you know' (from personal experience) is not negated by the dictum 'show don't tell,' but is folded into a larger entity that includes both positive and prohibitive imperatives (something like 'show, don't tell, what you know')" (147). Thus McGurl identifies and dissects the aesthetic-ideological formation known as the Iowa doctrine; he even describes it—using Louis Althusser's phrase—as an "ideological state apparatus" (175; see Louis Althusser, *Lenin and Philosophy and Other Essays* [New York: Monthly Review Press, 2001], 96). In O'Connor's work, this doctrine is detectable in the singular combination of impersonalization and focalization that McGurl, using the discourse of creative writing handbooks, calls "third person limited" narration, a paradoxical formulation that suggests the same shift from representation to instantiation that Hale calls "the novelistic aesthetics of alterity": "It was Flannery O'Connor's achievement . . . to maximize the ironic distance between her central focalizing characters and her disembodied narrators, and to attest thereby to the cognitive limits of any embodied human life, including certainly the author's fragilely embodied own" (143). McGurl continues: "This way of reading rather flagrantly puts her person back into her 'impersonal' narration. Not only must we rely on our knowledge of the author's biography in doing so, but we more or less dismiss the relevance of a potential distinction between O'Connor as author and her impersonal narrators, merely insisting that we see that narrator as only a partial manifestation of a larger autopoetic process that also involves the construction of her characters" (145–46). Despite the self-distancing rhetoric ("This way of reading," "flagrantly"), the biographical approach described here is precisely the one McGurl himself advocates in *The Program Era*. A reading of these relations according to David Armstrong's model would suggest *not* a logic of instantiation operating between O'Connor's writing (or the "theology" underlying it), on one hand, and the "show don't tell" regime of the creative writing program, on the other, but a relation of "synonymity" among all three formations (the work, the theology, and the "Iowa doctrine"). Each expresses a "content" that is tied to the instance in question, but that content is not the instantiation relation but the nonexistence or collapse of that relation. Nothing links these instances "horizontally," even though the content in each case—or in Armstrong's terms, the "proposition"—happens to be identical. There is, to repeat, no absence of an instantiation relation *in general.*

21. Ferdinand de Saussure, *Course in General Linguistics*, trans. Roy Harris (Chicago: Open Court, 1983), 118–20.
22. Jacques Derrida analyzes the centrality of this binary to Saussure's work in *Of Grammatology*, trans. Gayatri Chakravorty Spivak, corrected ed. (Baltimore, MD: Johns Hopkins University Press, 1997), 30–65.

23. Gilles Deleuze and Félix Guattari, "November 20, 1923—Postulates of Linguistics," in *A Thousand Plateaus*, trans. Brian Massumi (Minneapolis: University of Minnesota Press, 1987), 79–80.

5. THE LOGIC OF DISCONNECTION

1. Michel Foucault, "The Order of Discourse," trans. Ian McLeod, in *Untying the Text*, ed. Robert Young (Boston: Routledge & Kegan Paul, 1981), 51.
2. Mikhail Bakhtin, "Forms of Time and of the Chronotope in the Novel," in *The Dialogic Imagination*, trans. Caryl Emerson and Michael Holquist (Austin: University of Texas Press, 1981), 84.
3. Henri Bergson, *Time and Free Will: An Essay on the Immediate Data of Consciousness*, trans. F. L. Pogson (Mineola, NY: Dover, 2001), 92.
4. Gary Morson and Caryl Emerson, *Mikhail Bakhtin: Creation of a Prosaics* (Stanford, CA: Stanford University Press, 1990), 368, 371.
5. J. M. Coetzee, *Elizabeth Costello* (New York: Viking, 2003), 16.
6. Immanuel Kant, *Critique of Pure Reason*, trans. J. M. D. Meiklejohn (London: J. M. Dent and Sons, 1934), 45, 49.
7. A chronotope, observe Morson and Emerson, is always an answer to a problem posed in the work; indeed, the chronotope is the condition of both the problem and the resolution. And the problem is by definition a problem of connection. Thus, the chronotope is the site of everything "theoretical" in the work. "What is the relation of human action to its context? Is the context mere background, or does it actively shape events? Are actions dependent to a significant degree on where or when they occur? . . . Are the same kinds of actions plausible or possible in different historical and social contexts . . . ? What kind of initiative do people have: are they beings to whom events simply happen, or do they exercise choice and control, and if so, how much and of what kind? Is time open, with multiple possibilities, or is it scripted in advance? Depending on the degree and kind of initiative people have, what kind of ethical responsibility obliges them? What kind of creativity is possible? . . . Is there a concept of the 'personal' or private as opposed to the public? Are people understood as entirely 'exterior' or is there real interiority, and if so what kind? If that interiority is socially and historically shaped, does that shaping happen differently from the shaping of public selves and roles? . . . How does the past impinge on the present, and what is the relation of the present to possible futures? Is the greatest value placed on the past, the present, the immediate future, or the distant future?" (369–70). These questions are versions of the same central problematic: what is the nature of the connection between a work and the world? In other words, what does it mean to speak in and with a literary work in general and a specific work in particular?
8. Jorge Luis Borges, "Pierre Menard, Author of the *Quixote*," in *Collected Fictions*, trans. Andrew Hurley (New York: Penguin, 1998), 88–95.
9. "I seem to speak, it is not I, about me, it is not about me," says the narrator of Beckett's *The Unnamable* near the beginning of the text. "What am I to do, what shall I do, what should I do, in my situation, how to proceed? . . . The best would be not to

begin. But I have to begin. That is to say I have to go on." Samuel Beckett, *Molloy, Malone Dies, The Unnamable* (New York: Knopf, 1997), 331, 332.

10. Karl Marx, *Early Writings*, trans. Rodney Livingstone and Gregor Benton (Harmondsworth: Penguin, 1992), 352.

11. Foucault's few direct analyses of literary writers do not make any use of the category of "literature." In *Death and the Labyrinth*, on the work of Raymond Roussel, or *The Thought from Outside*, on Maurice Blanchot, what Foucault is interested in is a specific procedure or set of procedures: "Roussel belongs to a series of writers who exist in English, exist in German, exist in all languages. They are writers who have literally been obsessed with the problem of language, for whom literary construction and the 'interplay of language' are directly related. I couldn't say that was a tradition because, in fact, it's a tradition that disappears with each writer as if it were so individual to each writer that it could not be transmitted but is rediscovered every time." Michel Foucault, *Death and the Labyrinth: The World of Raymond Roussel*, trans. Charles Ruas (London: Athlone, 1987), 175–76. See also Michel Foucault, "Maurice Blanchot: The Thought from Outside," trans. Brian Massumi, in *Foucault/Blanchot* (New York: Zone, 1987), 12.

12. Mikhail Bakhtin, *Problems of Dostoevsky's Poetics*, trans. Caryl Emerson (Minneapolis: University of Minnesota Press, 1984), 49.

13. Writing about the style of Foucault's texts, Claire Colebrook has observed similarly that "the question 'Who speaks?' is increasingly difficult to answer in relation to Foucault's texts." Insofar as they speak, they do so "from within a style already given"; thus his texts "never fully own their style." Claire Colebrook, "A Grammar of Becoming: Strategy, Subjectivism, and Style," in *Becomings: Explorations in Time, Memory, and Futures*, ed. Elizabeth A. Grosz (Ithaca, NY: Cornell University Press, 1999), 137–38.

14. Michel Foucault, *Power/Knowledge: Selected Interviews and Other Writings 1972–1977*, trans. Colin Gordon et al. (New York: Vintage, 1980), 192–93.

15. Gilles Deleuze, *Foucault*, trans. Seán Hand (Minneapolis: University of Minnesota Press, 1988), 13–14.

16. Henri Bergson, *Matter and Memory*, trans. Nancy Margaret Paul and W. Scott Palmer (London: George Allen and Unwin, 1911), 26.

17. Richard Handler, *Nationalism and the Politics of Culture in Quebec* (Madison: University of Wisconsin Press, 1988); Benedict Anderson, *Imagined Communities: Reflections on the Origin and Spread of Nationalism*, rev. ed. (London: Verso, 1991).

18. Rebecca Walkowitz, *Born Translated: The Contemporary Novel in an Age of World Literature* (New York: Columbia University Press, 2015), 26.

19. There are several writers who do not fit Walkowitz's thesis or who complicate it. The most obvious is the difficult and troubling figure of James Kelman. Kelman's most formally challenging novel, *Translated Accounts*, does not get a mention in *Born Translated*—because, I think, it emerges from a different artistic and political ethos than those of the writers Walkowitz is concerned with. Kelman uses the conceit of incompetent translation precisely to produce a "nonstandard version" of English—so nonstandard as to test the limits of comprehensibility. *Translated Accounts* is a "born-translated" novel, then, in a different sense than in the works that Walkowitz writes about: one that, precisely, resists translation. *Translated Accounts* is an "accented" work, to use Walkowitz's term (37)—but not in a way that "register[s] . . .

the voices of . . . immigrant characters" but, rather, that seems to foreclose them. Kelman's work exerts the pull of the local as the absolutely singular, and it confounds global portability not by holding to an older model of modernist "untranslatability" but precisely by way of translation.

Something similar might be said of a writer whom Walkowitz does discuss directly, Kazuo Ishiguro. Walkowitz's discussion of Ishiguro turns on the phrase "unimaginable largeness," used by Stevens, the butler-narrator in *The Remains of the Day*, to explain and justify his assiduous attention to the household silver. Walkowitz rightly wants to complicate readings that have tended simply to ironize Stevens's sentiments. For Walkowitz, Ishiguro's own work *does* support an idea of "enlarged thinking." *The Remains of the Day*, she writes, asks us to see "analogy and contiguity between the act of polishing silver and the act of negotiating peace treaties" (114)—even if Stevens's own version of that call is not always to be "taken seriously or to be admired" (115). Stevens's problem, says Walkowitz, is that he fails to translate enough. Walkowitz is here attempting to resolve a problem in Ishiguro's works that has troubled every critic writing on him. Yet it could be that the problem of Ishiguro has to be grappled with more directly, in a way that Kelman's very different treatment of translation can help us to understand. What if the "ethical" quality of Ishiguro's work, which almost every critic has struggled to articulate—a task that is also a premise of Walkowitz's reading—were simply *not available to critical discourse*? The problem of Ishiguro that Walkowitz struggles with, therefore, may not be resolvable within the terms of a conventional critical approach to his work.

20. The "geography" of the world republic of letters, writes Casanova, "is based on the opposition between a capital, on the one hand, and peripheral dependencies whose relationship to this center is defined by their aesthetic difference from it. It is equipped . . . with its own consecrating authorities, charged with responsibility for legislating on literary matters, which function as the sole legitimate arbiters with regard to questions of recognition. Over time, owing to the work of a number of pioneering figures remarkable for their freedom from nationalist prejudice, an international literary law came to be created, a specific form of recognition that owes nothing to political fiat, interest, or prejudice." Pascale Casanova, *The World Republic of Letters*, trans. M. B. DeBevoise (Cambridge, MA: Harvard University Press, 2014), 12.

21. Michael Gardiner, "Kelman and World English," in *The Edinburgh Companion to James Kelman*, ed. Scott Hames (Edinburgh: Edinburgh University Press, 2010), 99.

22. Erich Auerbach, *Mimesis: The Representation of Reality in Western Literature*, trans. Willard R. Trask (Princeton, NJ: Princeton University Press, 2013), 74.

23. See also Mariano Siskind, "The Globalization of the Novel and the Novelization of the Global: A Critique of World Literature," *Comparative Literature* 62, no. 4 (2010): 352.

24. Foucault concludes his interview (with Lucette Finas) with the following remark: "It seems to me that the possibility exists . . . for bringing it about that a true discourse engenders or 'manufactures' something that does not as yet exist, that is, 'fictions' it" (193).

25. Thomas Pavel, *The Lives of the Novel* (Princeton: NJ: Princeton University Press, 2013), 17–18.

26. Gilles Deleuze, "What Is the Creative Act?" in *Two Regimes of Madness*, trans. Ames Hodges and Mike Taormina (New York: Semiotext(e), 1986), 315.

27. Gilles Deleuze, *Cinema 2: The Time Image*, trans. Hugh Tomlinson and Robert Galeta (London: Athlone, 1989), 128.

28. Gilles Deleuze, *Proust and Signs*, trans. Richard Howard (London: Athlone, 2000), 41.

29. Franco Moretti, *Distant Reading* (London: Verso, 2013), 57.

30. A discussion of Kelman's 1984 novel *The Busconductor Hines* by the Warwick Research Collective (WReC) presents a compelling alternative reading of Kelman's oeuvre, one that attempts to preserve the chronotopic principle of "commentary" and indeed that of the "world literary system" itself. Implicitly rejecting a merely biographical reading of Kelman's hero Rab Hines, the significance of which would be limited to the protagonist's mental decline, WReC writes: "The breakdown of [Hines's] linguistic ability is better read as a psychosomatic registration, on one disintegrating body, of the effect of generalized top-down social violence. As time and space are compressed in the novel, setting, narrative expression and organization are altered to draw attention to the ways in which shifts in the regional economy are affecting local conditions of production and development, shattering the stability of social relations and challenging cemented class solidarities. The reader is deliberately confronted with the limitations of Hines's cognitive competence, his inability to put his own abruptly transformed and diminished life into larger objective perspective or relief." Warwick Research Collective, *Combined and Uneven Development: Towards a New Theory of World Literature* (Liverpool: Liverpool University Press, 2015), 140. This coexistence of biographical and social instability in Kelman's work is well observed, yet WReC's move from the level of character to that of the social is undertaken too quickly. What is unobserved and left unanalyzed in *Combined and Uneven Development* is that Hines's failure of "perspective" is repeated at the level of the narration and that that *narrative* failure of perspective is not "progressive," as WReC takes Hines's to be, but a consistent principle of the narration from the outset. As in *How late it was, how late*—indeed as in every work of fiction Kelman has published—Kelman's narrator does not present any perspective, critical or otherwise, on the protagonist or his opinions or life trajectory. WReC acclaims Kelman's "modernism" for its ability to "perform" the instability of "social relations and . . . cemented class solidarities," a task for which modernist techniques are "superbly suited" (140). But much is taken for granted in that word "perform"— including, of course, a certain "connectivity." The nature of that connectivity, here and in the following passages, seems to be more allegorical than realist, yet WReC neither names nor theorizes the relation in such terms (I have italicized the key phrases): "*The Busconductor Hines*'s narrative style *is hinged to* the traumatic, disorderly experience of (environ)mental collapse: his perspective is progressively fractured *as* the wrecking ball approaches the tenements" (140); "the overall effect is a growing textual disorder as the novel progresses, and this *is symptomatic of* the approaching material disintegration and social and economic capitulation" (141); "the threat of the loss of physical shelter and of long-term social security generates a form of representative instability that *indexes* Hines's own struggles to comprehend a reordered world"; "the tonal shift between regular sentence structure and a more scattered, unhinged commentary *hints at* the way in which the functionality

of modernist idealism and 'communal' spatial organization has given way to a social world unsupported by public infrastructural ecologies" (142); "a physical and social disaggregation and disorganization that Kelman's literary modernism must somehow seek to *register*" (142). Like the verbal forms used by Pavel to denote the modes in which "novels" connect to the world (*are about, propose, imagine, describe, ponder*, etc.), the italicized terms in these sentences gloss over the problem of relationality that the present book—and, I am arguing, literary works themselves—make central to the discussion of contemporary literature.

31. Michael Wood, "J. xx Drancy. 13/8/42," *London Review of Books* 22, no. 23 (November 30, 2000): 30–31.

32. Patrick Modiano, *Dora Bruder*, trans. Joanna Kilmartin (Berkeley: University of California Press, 1999), 51. Later, Modiano learns that Dora Bruder could not have been the girl in the police van—but that only raises a further unresolved question: who could the girl have been? (52–53).

33. Clairvoyance is no special "gift" of the novelist, says Modiano's narrator; it merely signals "the need to fix your mind on points of detail . . . so as not to lose the thread and give in to natural laziness" (43).

34. Marcel Proust, *In Search of Lost Time*, vol. 6: *Time Regained*, trans. Andreas Mayor and Terence Kilmartin, rev. by D. J. Enright (London: Vintage, 1996), 224, 222.

35. The importance of Bakhtin's notion of the chronotope to Deleuze's work on cinema is revealed explicitly in the recordings and transcripts of Deleuze's seminars on cinema, given over four years at the University of Paris VIII (Vincennes) between 1981 and 1985 and published online at "La voix de Gilles Deleuze," http://www2.univ-paris8.fr/deleuze/. On October 30, 1984, near the beginning of the opening session of the fourth seminar, "Cinema and Thought," Deleuze identifies two methodological aspects common to the work of all philosophers: a "temporal" and a "spatial" aspect. The first (temporal) refers to the order, progress, and organization of thoughts, the second (spatial) to the determination of the "goals, means and obstacles of thought"—the *why* and the *how*. Deleuze characterizes this dual aspect using Bakhtin's notion of the chronotope, which Deleuze translates as "space-time": "[Bakhtin] tells us, for example, that the question 'What is the novel?' implies the extraction [*dégagement*] of the chronotope specific to the novel. That is to say, of a type of space-time presupposed by the novel. Similarly I would say that there is a chronotope of thought, and that every method, from [this] double point of view— the temporal order of thoughts, on one hand, the distribution of goals, means and obstacles, on the other—refers to a chronotope of thought, a chronotope that can undergo variations and mutations, and that is never given. What is given, at best [*au besoin*], is a method, but what is presupposed is not given. It takes a special effort to bring it out [*le dégager*]. . . . It is in [the chronotope] that philosophical discourse develops, but it itself is not the object of philosophical discourse. . . . It can only be marked out [*jalonné*]. . . . The chronotope is essentially marked out and signaled by cries."

Deleuze goes on to draw an analogy with the distinction between the cries and songs of birds: "In philosophy there are discourses, but these are not the same thing as cries. Discourses are the song of philosophers. It is their way of singing; and then there are philosophical cries. One risks missing this and thereby forming an idea of philosophy as a dead thing. One equates it with the discourses it elaborates, and a philosophical cry can always be translated in terms of discourse. But then something resists, and so not. If one has the slightest feel [*goût*] for philosophy, one knows very well that these are cries, and that there philosophy finds its points of birth, its points of life."

It is apparent from this passage that two distinct conceptions of the chronotope are of interest to Deleuze: the "spatio-temporal continuum," on one hand, and the "pure chronotope," on the other. These conceptions approximate, respectively, the "sensorimotor schema" and the "sensorimotor break" in *Cinema 1* and *Cinema 2*, or—to draw an analogy with a moment in Deleuze's earlier work *The Logic of Sense* (discussed in the next chapter)—a sense that is expressed without remainder in the proposition and a sense that must be extracted from it, a sense that subsists independently of the proposition and is unexhausted by it. Gilles Deleuze, *The Logic of Sense*, trans. Mark Lester with Charles Stivale (New York: Columbia University Press, 1990), 31–32.

INTERLUDE. FICTIONAL DISCOURSE AS EVENT: ON JESSE BALL

1. Roland Barthes, *Roland Barthes*, trans. Richard Howard (Berkeley: University of California Press, 1994), 54.
2. Jacques Rancière, *Mute Speech*, trans. James Swenson (New York: Columbia University Press, 2011).
3. Jesse Ball, *Silence Once Begun* (New York: Vintage, 2014), 75.

6. HOW DOES IMMANENCE SHOW ITSELF?

1. Gilles Deleuze, *The Logic of Sense*, trans. Mark Lester with Charles Stivale (New York: Columbia University Press, 1990), 21 (translation modified). I have followed Hazel E. Barnes's translation of *objectité* in Sartre's *Being and Nothingness: An Essay on Phenomenological Ontology* (London: Routledge, 1969), 633. Hugh Tomlinson and Graham Burchell offer "objectality" as an alternative in their translation of Gilles Deleuze and Félix Guattari's *What Is Philosophy?* (New York: Columbia University Press, 1995), 3n.
2. Lewis Carroll, *The Annotated Alice: Alice's Adventures in Wonderland* and *Through the Looking-Glass*, ed. Martin Gardner (Harmondsworth: Penguin, 1970), 306.
3. Alain Badiou, *Number and Numbers*, trans. Robin Mackay (Cambridge: Polity, 2008), 18. See also Gottlob Frege, "Frege on Russell's Paradox," in *Translations from the Philosophical Writings of Gottlob Frege*, ed. Peter Geach and Max Black (Oxford: Basil Blackwell, 1960), 234.
4. Edward N. Zalta, "Gottlob Frege," in *The Stanford Encyclopedia of Philosophy*, ed. Edward N. Zalta, Winter 2016 ed., https://plato.stanford.edu/archives/win2016/entries/frege/.
5. Dorothy J. Hale, *The Novel and the New Ethics* (Stanford, CA: Stanford University Press, 2020), 108.

6. Frank Kermode, *The Sense of an Ending: Studies in the Theory of Fiction* (New York: Oxford University Press, 1967), 3.

7. D. M. Armstrong, *A World of States of Affairs* (Cambridge: Cambridge University Press, 1997), 29.

8. Michel Foucault, *The Birth of Biopolitics*, trans. Graham Burchell (Houndmills, Basingstoke: Palgrave Macmillan, 2008), 267–69. J. M. Coetzee's novel *The Schooldays of Jesus* (London: Harvill Secker, 2016) features several spokespersons for this ideology of "numericality," including the minor character of señor Robles, David's first mathematics teacher. After arranging three pens and three pills on a table, he asks David: "What do these [indicating the pens] and these [indicating the pills] have in common?" " 'Three,' says the boy. . . . 'So what have we learned?' And, before the boy can answer, he informs him: 'We have learned that three does not depend on what is in the set, be it apples or oranges or pens or pills. Three is the name of the property that these sets have in common. . . . We have learned that each number is the name of a property shared by certain sets of objects in the world' " (27–28). David, whose thinking of number is outside the logic of instantiation, protests vehemently (but is ignored): "It's not the same three because the pens are different" (27).

9. In December 2016, Robert Reich, professor of public policy at UC Berkeley and former secretary of labor from 1993 to 1997, responded insightfully to a question from the broadcaster and journalist Amy Goodman about insinuations on Twitter by President-elect Donald Trump that the *Washington Post* had ulterior motives for criticizing him during his presidential campaign: "When Donald Trump goes after Jeffrey Bezos, publisher of the *Washington Post*, because of some notion that Amazon and Bezos are worried about a possible anti-trust action that Trump might inspire, that is designed to undermine the credibility in the public's mind of anything that the *Washington Post* might publish. . . . By creating this kind of conspiracy theory, this paranoid notion about the press, and planting it in the public's mind, the public, or at least a portion of the public, is led to think that [nothing] that the *Washington Post* . . . says is justified, or true." *Democracy Now!* December 20, 2016, https://www.democracynow.org/2016/12/20/protest_boycott_everything_robert_reich_on. Conspiracy theories, the doctrine of "fake news," and the regime of "numericality" are all implicated in a neoliberal ideology that removes from consideration everything outside the logic of calculability and "interest" or, rather, that constitutes as the basis of its theory of reality a subject defined by the principle of "an irreducible, non-transferable atomistic individual choice which is unconditionally referred to the subject himself" (Foucault, *Birth of Biopolitics*, 272). To state this more provocatively: a line connects Zadie Smith's conception of the writer's duty as "to express accurately their way of being in the world" and her hypothesis of "the watermark of self that runs through everything you do" to Adam Smith's model of *homo economicus*, which (according to Foucault) functions as "an individual subject of interest within a totality which eludes him and which nevertheless founds the rationality of his egoistic choices" (278).

10. Alain Badiou, *Deleuze: The Clamor of Being*, trans. Louise Burchill (Minneapolis: University of Minnesota Press, 2000); Alain Badiou, "The Event According to Deleuze," in *Logics of Worlds (Being and Event 2)*, trans. Alberto Toscano (London: Continuum, 2009), 381–87.

11. Aristotle, *Metaphysics*, 1028a (Zeta), trans. Richard Hope (Ann Arbor: University of Michigan Press, 1960), 130; Plato, *The Republic*, trans. Desmond Lee (Harmondsworth: Penguin, 1974), 255–64, 359–77.

12. Michel Foucault, *The Archaeology of Knowledge*, trans. A. M. Sheridan Smith (New York: Pantheon, 1972), 112.

13. Mikhail Bakhtin, *Problems of Dostoevsky's Poetics*, trans. Caryl Emerson (Minneapolis: University of Minnesota Press, 1984), 7.

14. Paul de Man, "Georg Lukács's *Theory of the Novel*," in *Blindness and Insight: Essays in the Rhetoric of Contemporary Criticism*, 2nd rev. ed. (Minneapolis: University of Minnesota Press, 1983), 52–53.

15. D. N. Rodowick, *Elegy for Theory* (Cambridge, MA: Harvard University Press, 2014), 57.

16. Michel Foucault, "The Order of Discourse," trans. Ian McLeod, in *Untying the Text*, ed. Robert Young (Boston: Routledge & Kegan Paul, 1981), 69.

17. "Pathos of ineffability" is a phrase from Martin Jay's 1996 essay "For Theory," where it refers to a certain antitheoretical tendency to consider "all concepts and a fortiori all theories . . . as violations of their objects." Thus "theory" is identified with the police, and its object is conceived as "an innocent victim falsely labeled as something it is not." Martin Jay, "For Theory," *Theory and Society* 25, no. 2 (April 1996): 173.

18. Cora Diamond, "The Difficulty of Reality and the Difficulty of Philosophy," in Stanley Cavell et al., *Philosophy and Animal Life* (New York: Columbia University Press, 2008), 74.

19. J. M. Coetzee, *Elizabeth Costello* (New York: Viking, 2003), 77.

20. The responses to Coetzee's 1997 lectures (by Marjorie Garber as well as Peter Singer, Wendy Doniger, and Barbara Smuts) are included in J. M. Coetzee, *The Lives of Animals* (Princeton, NJ: Princeton University Press, 1999), 73–120.

21. Stanley Cavell, *Must We Mean What We Say? A Book of Essays* (New York: Charles Scribner's Sons, 1969), 247, 260.

22. See, for example, the story Elizabeth tells about Sultan, a chimpanzee whom the German psychologist Wolfgang Köhler used as the subject of an experiment in Tenerife in the 1910s and who (Elizabeth imagines) is "at every turn . . . driven to think the less interesting thought" by the procedures of Köhler's experiment (72–74).

23. Amanda Anderson, *Bleak Liberalism* (Chicago: University of Chicago Press, 2016), 97.

24. E. M. Forster, *Howards End*, ed. Oliver Stallybrass (Harmondsworth: Penguin, 1985), 300.

25. "Triple-decker" is the informal term that academic specialists of Victorian literature use to designate the serially published British novel that first appeared in book form in three volumes.

26. E. M. Forster, *Aspects of the Novel* (London: Penguin, 2005), 184.

27. Gilles Deleuze, *Empiricism and Subjectivity: An Essay on Hume's Theory of Human Nature*, trans. Constantin V. Boundas (New York: Columbia University Press, 1991), 24.

28. This story is told in Klüger's memoir *Still Alive: A Holocaust Girlhood Remembered* (New York: Feminist Press at CUNY, 2003), 103–9.

29. Jacques Rancière, *The Politics of Literature*, trans. Julie Rose (Cambridge: Polity, 2011), 43.

30. See Gustave Flaubert, *Madame Bovary*, trans. Lydia Davis (New York: Penguin, 2010), 82.

31. Jacques Rancière, "Literary Misunderstanding," in *The Politics of Literature*, trans. Julie Rose (Cambridge: Polity, 2011), 42.

32. Henri Bergson, *Matter and Memory*, trans. Nancy Margaret Paul and W. Scott Palmer (London: George Allen and Unwin, 1911), 26. This being is "virtual," just as the existence of pure perception is "hypothetical"—but they are both no less real for that.

33. Gilles Deleuze, *Cinema 2: The Time-Image*, trans. Hugh Tomlinson and Robert Galeta (London: Athlone, 1989), 20. Henceforth and in successive chapters page references to Deleuze's *Cinema 1: The Movement-Image*, trans. Hugh Tomlinson and Barbara Habberjam (London: Athlone, 1986); and *Cinema 2: The Time-Image* will be preceded by the abbreviations C1 and C2 respectively, except where the source is obvious from the context. A second page number following an oblique stroke (/) refers to the French editions: *Cinéma 1. L'image-mouvement* (Paris: Éditions de Minuit, 1983); *Cinéma 2. L'image-temps* (Paris: Éditions de Minuit, 1985). Occasionally, small changes have been made when quoting the published English translations.

34. With the notion of *impouvoir*—the "powerlessness to think" as an element intrinsic to thought—Deleuze is partly drawing on an essay on Artaud by Maurice Blanchot, in *The Book to Come*, trans. Charlotte Mandel (Stanford, CA: Stanford University Press, 2002), 36. Versions of this notion appear elsewhere in Deleuze's philosophical writing, such as in the question of the "essence" of the work of art and its manifestation that arises in his early book *Proust and Signs* (1964). Deleuze's formulation of that question anticipates the previously mentioned question from Rancière: "Precisely how is essence incarnated in the work of art? Or, what comes down to the same thing, how does an artist-subject manage to 'communicate' the essence that individualizes him and makes him eternal?" Gilles Deleuze, *Proust and Signs*, trans. Richard Howard (London: Athlone, 2000), 46. But the more troubling question is posed a few pages earlier: "What is an essence as revealed in the work of art?" Deleuze's answer—"It is a difference, the absolute and ultimate Difference" (41)—will lead him to embark on the work he will later refer to as "the first book in which I tried to 'do philosophy'": *Difference and Repetition*, trans. Paul Patton (New York: Columbia University Press, 1994), xv. But even the clarification he offers in *Proust and Signs* luminously anticipates the notion of *impouvoir*. Absolute difference in Proust, he says, is not an "empirical" or "extrinsic" difference between two things or objects, but "an internal difference"—a proposition he explains with a quotation from Proust himself: "a difference that, if there were no such thing as art, would remain the eternal secret of each man" (41). In a 2017 article, Raymond Bellour identifies a shift in the relation between thought and the image in Deleuze's oeuvre, a shift that for Bellour reflects Deleuze's encounter with Félix Guattari. From the moment of their first collaboration, Bellour observes, Deleuze appears to abandon the quest for a "thought without image," as the images begin to "stream in from everywhere as thoughts, a profusion of insistent visions." Raymond Bellour, "'Art Resists, Even If It Is Not the Only Thing That Resists,'" trans. Allyn Hardyck, *Critical Inquiry* 44, no. 1 (Autumn 2017): 42. Before that encounter, in Bellour's account,

Deleuze's thought had seemed to come up against a limit represented by the impossibility of thinking difference directly, "in itself"; this is the note on which *Difference and Repetition* ends: "Difference is not and cannot be thought in itself, so long as it is subject to the requirements of representation" (262). However, we can equally emphasize another element in Deleuze's trajectory, apart from the meeting with Guattari: the encounter with cinema. Until that point, Deleuze's work has been preoccupied with negative formulations for a (noninstantiated) thought for which there is, and could be, no corresponding image. With the appearance of cinema in Deleuze's philosophical work, the thought of *impouvoir* finds for the first time an image that is adequate to it: the direct time-image. It is in this respect that *Cinema 1* and *Cinema 2* may be said to constitute, as D. N. Rodowick half-jokingly suggests, "a 700-page-long footnote to *Difference and Repetition*." D. N. Rodowick, *Philosophy's Artful Conversation* (Cambridge, MA: Harvard University Press, 2015), 108.

35. Maurice Blanchot, *The Book to Come*, trans. Charlotte Mandell (Stanford, CA: Stanford University Press, 2003), 36–37.

7. WHAT IS A SENSORIMOTOR BREAK?
DELEUZE ON CINEMA

1. Karl Marx and Frederick Engels, *The German Ideology: Part One, with Selections from Parts Two and Three*, ed. C. J. Arthur, 2nd ed. (London: Lawrence and Wishart, 1974), 47.

2. Henri Bergson, *Matter and Memory*, trans. Nancy Margaret Paul and W. Scott Palmer (London: George Allen and Unwin, 1911), 30.

3. It is from Bergson's notion of pure perception, no doubt, that Marcel Proust derived his idea of the "immeasurable keyboard," the virtual basis of all music, according to which "here and there only . . . some few among the millions of keys of tenderness, of passion, of courage, of serenity, each one different from all the rest . . . have been discovered by a few great artists who do us the service . . . of showing us what richness, what variety lies hidden . . . in that vast unfathomed and forbidding night of our soul which we take to be an impenetrable void." Proust's narrator speculates further: "Perhaps it is not-being [*le néant*] that is the true state and all our dream of life is inexistent [*inexistant*]; but, if so, we feel that these phrases of music, these conceptions which exist in relation to our dream, must be nothing either." Marcel Proust, *In Search of Lost Time*, vol. 1: *Swann's Way*, trans. C. K. Scott Moncrieff and Terence Kilmartin (London: Vintage, 1996), 420–21, 422.

4. Suzanne Guerlac, *Thinking in Time: An Introduction to Henri Bergson* (Ithaca, NY: Cornell University Press, 2006), 111.

5. In fact, the film presents two perception-images of the vase, of six and ten seconds respectively, separated by a shot of Noriko's face lapsing into melancholy.

6. Consider, for example, the broken leg of L. B. Jefferies ("Jeff") in *Rear Window*, which ensures the perpetual deferral of his action and, thus, a buildup of tension of deferred action, which is shared by the viewer. Such conceits are dispensed with relatively early in Ozu's body of work. Indeed, according to Deleuze, Ozu never has need of them.

7. Ian Watt, *The Rise of the Novel: Studies in Defoe, Richardson, and Fielding* (London: Hogarth, 1987), 32.

8. Cora Diamond, "The Difficulty of Reality and the Difficulty of Philosophy," in Stanley Cavell et al., *Philosophy and Animal Life* (New York: Columbia University Press, 2008), 78.

9. J. M. Coetzee, *Elizabeth Costello* (New York: Viking, 2003), 77–78.

10. Marie-Claire Ropars-Wuilleumier, "Image or Time? The Thought of the Outside in *The Time-Image* (Deleuze and Blanchot)," trans. Matthew Lazen with D. N. Rodowick, in *Afterimages of Gilles Deleuze's Film Philosophy*, ed. D. N. Rodowick (Minneapolis: University of Minnesota Press, 2010), 17.

11. Gilles Deleuze, *Foucault*, trans. Seán Hand (Minneapolis: University of Minnesota Press, 1988), 87; D. M. Armstrong, *A World of States of Affairs* (Cambridge: Cambridge University Press, 1997), 46.

12. Paul Auster, "White Spaces," in *Collected Poems* (Woodstock, NY: Overlook, 2004), 156; James Baldwin, "Notes for a Hypothetical Novel," in *Collected Essays*, ed. Toni Morrison (New York: Library of America, 1998), 223, 227; Maggie Nelson, *Bluets* (Seattle: Wave, 2009), 61–63; Valeria Luiselli, *Lost Children Archive* (New York: Knopf, 2019), 102.

13. Jean Louis Schefer, *The Ordinary Man of Cinema*, trans. Max Cavitch, Paul Grant, and Noura Wedell (South Pasadena, CA: Semiotext(e), 2016), 9. For more on the anagonist, see my "The Anagonist," *Novel: A Forum on Fiction* 53, no. 3 (November 2020): 307–16.

14. Gilles Deleuze, "On the Movement-Image," in *Negotiations: 1972–1990*, trans. Martin Joughin (New York: Columbia University Press, 1995), 49.

15. This point evidently differentiates the procedures of Deleuze's thought from the reading that Alain Badiou subjects him to in his 1998 book *The Clamor of Being*. The difference is registered in the title of Badiou's book, a quotation from the final sentence of Deleuze's *Difference and Repetition*: "A single and same voice for the whole thousand-voiced multiple, a single and same Ocean for all the drops, a single clamour of Being for all beings." Gilles Deleuze, *Difference and Repetition*, trans. Paul Patton (New York: Columbia University Press, 1993), 304. The tenor of Badiou's reading of Deleuze is to positivize and ontologize the void in Deleuze, which is to say, to displace the principle of multiplicity or heterogeneity by that of the "univocity of being." According to Badiou, it is not the "void" but the "case" that never becomes an object for thought in Deleuze's work. Alain Badiou, *The Clamor of Being*, trans. Louise Burchill (Minneapolis: University of Minnesota Press, 2000), 14–15. Badiou's misstep is to posit a relation between the concept and particular "cases" of it as the point of departure of Deleuze's philosophy and thus to retain the concept as the exemplar of thought. For Badiou, accordingly, each of Deleuze's studies comprises "an almost infinite repetition of a limited repertoire of concepts, as well as a virtuosic variation of names, under which what is thought remains essentially identical" (15). We can keep open, for the time being, the question of whether (or by how far) the difference between Deleuze and Badiou is more than rhetorical. "Clamor," after all, is not a term of ontology but of voice, expression. However, the fact that Badiou makes no reference to the qualification that precedes that final sentence in *Difference and Repetition*—that the single cry of Being can be heard "only at the point at which the extremity of difference is reached"—seems to betray a

tendentiousness in his reading. On the other hand, Badiou's insistence that "what is submitted to trial by the adventitious multiple of cases *never stops experiencing itself* as self-identical" (my emphasis) may be read as a formal acknowledgment of the central condition of Deleuze's reconstitution of a materialist basis for thought: the radical separation of thought from a human subject, from experience. Perhaps the division between Deleuze and Badiou, or between multiplicity and "univocity of being," is simply the division between a philosophy that has dispensed with the need for a final grounding in experience and one that has not (or that refuses that possibility in the name of "philosophy" and the "concept"). Again, for Deleuze, thought has nothing to do with the concept. For a considered exposition of the relations between Deleuze and Badiou, see Clayton Crockett, *Deleuze Beyond Badiou: Ontology, Multiplicity, and Event* (New York: Columbia University Press, 2013).

16. "Spiritual style" is a phrase coined by Susan Sontag to denote the centrality of Bresson's formal procedures to the emotional quality of his films. Susan Sontag, "Spiritual Style in the Films of Robert Bresson," in *Robert Bresson*, ed. James Quandt (Toronto: Toronto International Film Festival Group, 1998), 57–71.

17. Jacques Rancière, *Film Fables*, trans. Emiliano Battista (Oxford: Berg, 2006), 107.

18. In so doing, Deleuze takes a step beyond what was thinkable in *Cinema 1*, for in the opening pages of the first volume he insists that "there is always out-of-field, even in the most closed image." *C1*, 18.

19. The French Anglicism "voix-off" designates what in English is conventionally known as "voiceover." The spatial implications of "-off" are crucial to Deleuze's purposes in this passage. The English translators of Deleuze's text are thus right to reject the usual English term.

20. Such rarefied images are exemplified for Deleuze in Carl Dreyer's cinema, especially *Gertrud* (1964): "the more the image is spatially closed, even reduced to two dimensions, the greater is its capacity to open itself onto a fourth dimension, which is time, and onto a fifth, which is Spirit [*l'Esprit*], the spiritual decision of Jeanne [d'Arc] or Gertrud." *C1*, 17–18.

21. Translation mine. A transcript appears in Alfred Guzzetti, *Two or Three Things I Know About Her: Analysis of a Film by Godard* (Cambridge, MA: Harvard University Press, 1981), 132–38.

22. To consider the film as an "essayistic" work in which Godard puts his own ideas into the mouths of the characters shows the same kind of limited understanding that we saw in the previous chapter in various responses to Coetzee's novel *Elizabeth Costello*. An audio commentary on *Two or Three Things* by the film historian Adrian Martin, included on the 2009 Criterion DVD release, is illustrative. The film, says Martin, is "sometimes dismissed as being the first of Godard's films where the characters don't really work as anything but mouthpieces for Godard's own ideas and theories and slogans and quotations." Martin doesn't quite endorse this view, but his qualification of it is subjective rather than formal ("the more I've watched it I really think there's a strange tenderness in this movie"). In an essay written shortly after the film's release, Marie-Claire Ropars-Wuilleumier makes the same criticism in a more formal register, characterizing *Two or Three Things* as "the film of a film, in which . . . fragments close to those of *Vivre sa vie* or *Une Femme mariée* are

presented in their raw state, while Godard asks questions on their meaning while quoting Merleau-Ponty." The "destruction" of thought, a virtue of Godard's earlier films, she says, is replaced in *Two or Three Things* by the "manifestation" of this thought in "the heaviness of clarified meditation." Marie-Claire Ropars-Wuilleumier, "Form and Structure, or the Avatars of Narrative," trans. Royal S. Brown, in *Focus on Godard*, ed. Royal S. Brown (Englewood Cliffs, NJ: Prentice-Hall, 1972), 104. Martin, citing this essay, agrees, calling *Two or Three Things* "a somewhat uneven film," thus repeating another disconcerting tendency of critics, when it comes to *Two or Three Things*, to indulge in subjective evaluation of a film that so comprehensively neutralizes it, a tendency epitomized in Alfred Guzzetti's detailed reading of the film, where Guzzetti differentiates in qualitative terms—and, again, in an impressionistic rather than formal register—its various episodes. Alfred Guzzetti, *Two or Three Things I Know About Her: Analysis of a Film by Godard* (Cambridge, MA: Harvard University Press, 1981), 5–6, 271–75; Adrian Martin, audio commentary, *Two or Three Things I Know About Her*, DVD, dir. Jean-Luc Godard (New York: Criterion, 2009), 25:00–45:00. Such approaches miss the point of Godard's film not empirically or in the details—many incidental observations in these readings are invaluable, even indispensable—but globally and thus completely.

23. The phrase "Ce n'est pas une image juste, c'est juste une image" was used as an intertitle in Godard's and Jean-Pierre Gorin's film *Le vent d'est* (*Wind from the East*), dir. Groupe Dziga Vertov (Italy, France, West Germany, 1970).

24. According to Guzzetti, the crucial question of this scene is what Godard—or the narrator—might mean when he associates "the possibility of being together" with "the mediation of objects" (133). Guzzetti proposes an ingenious reading: "Restoring the link between, or passing from, one subject to another . . . is an act that can be performed only with respect to the image track and only at the level of its syntax. Godard's very portrayal of this act as possible . . . depends on the perfect suitability of his verbs *relier* and *passer* as descriptions of the physical task of editing, where, in order to pass from one shot to the next, one first cuts apart strips of film and then restores a link between them, that is, splices them together. Apart from film . . . passing from one subject to another is a contradiction in terms, for . . . subjectivity is inescapable. . . . Being together, as defined in [Godard's] commentary, is a possibility that belongs specifically and exclusively to the rhetoric of the film image" (133–35). Ingenious, but finally unbalanced and compromised by that "specifically and exclusively."

25. Alain Badiou, *Deleuze: The Clamor of Being*, trans. Louise Burchill (Minneapolis: University of Minnesota Press, 2000), 17.

26. Immanuel Kant, *Critique of Judgment*, trans. Werner S. Pluhar (Indianapolis, IN: Hackett, 1987), 24. For an etymological explanation of Kant's coinage, see Juliet Floyd, "Heautonomy: Kant on Reflective Judgment and Systematicity," in *Kants Ästhetik/Kant's Aesthetics/L'esthétique de Kant*, ed. Herman Parret (Berlin: Walter de Gruyter, 1998), 205.

27. Paul Guyer comments pertinently as follows: " 'Heautonomy' must characterize the *epistemic status* of these principles: it must mean precisely that these principles are ones that it is useful for us to adopt for our theoretical (or practical) purposes, and which are not precluded by the necessary conditions of the possibility of experience, but which cannot be numbered among the latter either." Paul Guyer, "Kant's

Principles of Reflecting Judgment," in *Kant's Critique of the Power of Judgment: Critical Essays*, ed. Paul Guyer (Lanham, MD: Rowman and Littlefield, 2003), 14.

28. Again, the contrast between Deleuze and Badiou is instructive. Rejecting the thesis of Deleuze's "postmetaphysical modernity" and the image of Deleuze as the "joyous thinker of the world's confusion" (9, 10)—a phrase he glosses to mean the non-explicability of the world either by "the One" or by "the Multiple"—Badiou insists that Deleuze's is an "abstract" philosophy, meaning that there is a unity to the heterogeneity (or, in the terms I have been exploring, a *general* absence of an instantiation relation). Badiou names the unity with a phrase that attempts to bring the quotient of positivity in the conception as close to zero as possible: "the quasi-organic consistency of conceptual connections" (17). However, in the light of Kant's notion of heautonomy, it is possible to suggest that Badiou's insistence on unity and univocity, his unwillingness to entertain any principle of multiplicity without denominating it, his premature use of the word "confusion" (in place of, say, infinite diversity), and even the mildly facetious claim—citing Plato—that "principles do exist" (17) are nothing but presuppositions undertaken for the sake of "an order that our understanding can cognize" (Kant, 25). In other words, that they are heautonomous. This would be to posit the difference between Deleuze and Badiou as primarily chronological. By insisting upon the principle of unity—or, for that matter, that the "adventitious multiple of cases never stops experiencing itself as self-identical," a proposition that Kant's notion of heautonomy directly refutes—Badiou succumbs to the temptation toward subtraction too soon—indeed, at the first opportunity, given how foundational is the principle of univocity to his project. In actual fact, it is Kant, of all thinkers, who with that nonsubjective formulation "infinit[e] divers[ity]" holds out the possibility of deferring the resolution for a while longer.

29. In a moment that anticipates the elaboration of my argument in the present chapter, Fredric Jameson locates the same freedom from "side-taking" in Henry James's use of free indirect discourse. Fredric Jameson, "The Swollen Third Person, or, Realism After Realism," in *The Antinomies of Realism* (London: Verso, 2013), 183. For Jameson, the critical questions that open up in the face of a work such as James's *The Wings of the Dove* (Does the text really condemn Merton Densher as a "gigolo" and Kate Croy as "a designing woman"? Are such judgments "extraliterary" or part of the work?) represent "the last traces of the traditional narrative category of destiny or the irrevocable"—categories, he says, that will be swept away by the modern inundation of points of view, which will render all moral judgments and evaluations "relative, in the sense of irrelevant" (184). In the face of such multiplicity, the serious writer, asserts Jameson, will tend to "keep faith" with the one point of resistance to "the weakening of all the joints and joists, the bulkheads and loadbearing supports, of narrative as such" in modern literature, namely, "affect," by which Jameson means a kind of bodily experience that "eludes language and its naming of things (and feelings)." Thus, with the decline of narrative in modernity, affect, says Jameson, is the sole point of "singularity in the everyday" (29, 184). In holding to this principle, however (while declining to elaborate on its constitution, for its proper form, he says, is modernism, not realism, putting it outside the declared topic of *The Antinomies of Realism*), Jameson stops short of registering the sensorimotor collapse that, according to Deleuze, is the remarkable achievement and substance of cinematic thought.

30. Guzzetti is oblivious to this "schizophrenic" quality when he casually identifies both Robert and Ivanoff as "surrogate[s]" of Godard (277, 283). The same goes for Alistair Whyte, who claims that the scene with Ivanoff tells us beyond any doubt that Godard "does not consider Soviet communism to be an answer": Alistair Whyte, introduction to Jean-Luc Godard, *Three Films: A Woman Is a Woman, A Married Woman, Two or Three Things I Know About Her* (New York: Harper and Row, 1975), 15.

31. Pier Paolo Pasolini, "The 'Cinema of Poetry,'" in *Heretical Empiricism*, trans. Ben Lawton and Louise K. Barnett (Washington, DC: New Academia, 2005), 176–77.

32. Deleuze here refers explicitly to Bakhtin's concept of heteroglossia, which, as put forward in "Discourse in the Novel," seems to provide him with a standard for what cinema may be capable of, that is to say: "the obliteration of a whole or of a totalization of images, in favour of an outside which is inserted between them; the erasure of the internal monologue as whole of the film [*comme tout du film*], in favor of a free indirect discourse and vision; the erasure of the unity of man and the world, in favour of a break which now leaves us with only a belief in this world." *C2*, 187–88.

33. *Quasi-direct discourse* is a translation of the German "*Die uneigentliche direkte Rede*," the title of a 1922 paper by the linguist Gertraud Lerch; the term means, literally, "improper" (unowned, unappropriated) direct discourse. Lerch was retheorizing and renaming what was at that time known predominantly as *Das erlebte Rede*—"lived discourse."

34. Charles Lock, "Double Voicing, Sharing Words: Bakhtin's Dialogism and the History of the Theory of Free Indirect Discourse," in *The Novelness of Bakhtin: Perspectives and Possibilities*, ed. Jørgen Bruhn and Jan Lundquist (Copenhagen: Museum Tusculanum Press, 2001), 87.

35. Gilles Deleuze and Félix Guattari, "November 20, 1923—Postulates of Linguistics," in *A Thousand Plateaus*, trans. Brian Massumi (Minneapolis: University of Minnesota Press, 1987), 82; henceforth *ATP*.

36. Gilles Deleuze and Claire Parnet, *Dialogues II*, trans. Hugh Tomlinson and Barbara Habberjam (London: Continuum, 2002), 51.

37. There is an interesting analogy to this insistence on the primacy of indirect over direct speech in the formal approach to archival material recently developed by the literary historian Saidiya Hartman and spelled out in her essay "Venus in Two Acts," *Small Axe: A Journal of Criticism* 26 (June 2008): 1–14. When Hartman describes the archive of African American slavery as constituted in its entirety by "rumors, scandals, lies, invented evidence, fabricated confessions, volatile facts, impossible metaphors, chance events, and fantasies"; when she describes the predicament of the scholar in the archive, faced with the impossibility of teasing out the lives of the people that suffered from the "terrible utterances that condemned them to death, the account books that identified them as units of value, the invoices that claimed them as property, and the banal chronicles that stripped them of human features" (3); when she despairs over the "formidable obstacle[s] or constitutive impossibilit[ies]" represented by the materials of her discipline (12), the violence she is describing is the ordering violence of an imperialist gaze *that passes off its own indirect discourse as mere procedure*: enumeration, characterization, accounting, and typifying. When she posits the opportunities open to a scholarship faced with the silence of the archive as limited to that of "displacing the received or authorized account" by imagining "what might have happened or might have been said or might have been

done" (11), her hope is to "engulf authorized speech in the clash of voices" and thus "topple the hierarchy of discourse" (12). Indirect discourse is thus, for Hartman, not a further obstacle to historical truth but a resource to bring to bear against the regime of direct discourse. It is on such grounds that Hartman refuses to "give voice" to the slave, for "dead girls are unable to speak." The challenge, rather, is to find a mode with which to approach the paradox of historical lives that "[become] visible only in the moment of their disappearance" (12). Hartman finds no potential for the evolution of this "impossible writing" in critical discourse, for scholarly writing, precisely by remaining within the limits of the "sayable," is destined to reproduce the omissions of the archive. The fullest development of Hartman's project to date is her 2019 book *Wayward Lives, Beautiful Experiments: Intimate Histories of Social Upheaval* (New York: Norton, 2019), a work already discussed briefly in chapter 2.

38. Fyodor Dostoevsky, *The Idiot*, trans. Richard Pevear and Larissa Volokhonsky (London: Knopf, 2002), 232; quoted in Vološinov, *MPL*, 156.

39. Mikhail Bakhtin, *Problems of Dostoevsky's Poetics*, trans. Caryl Emerson (Minneapolis: University of Minnesota Press, 1984), 250; my emphasis.

40. Dorrit Cohn, *Transparent Minds: Narrative Modes for Presenting Consciousness in Fiction* (Princeton, NJ: Princeton University Press, 1978), 111–12; quoted in Frances Ferguson, "Jane Austen, *Emma*, and the Impact of Form," *Modern Language Quarterly* 61, no. 1 (March 2000): 170.

41. James Joyce, *Ulysses* (London: Bodley Head, 1960), 190–234. The better analogue to Godard's free indirect voiceover in *Two or Three Things* is the passages of interspersed third-person narration that parody different styles of discourse in the "Cyclops" episode of *Ulysses* (376–449). Take, for example, the passage that introduces the series of submissions from the deceased Paddy Dignam to certain spiritual denizens of the "heavenworld" and to those left behind: "In the darkness spirit hands were felt to flutter and when prayer by tantras had been directed to the proper quarter a faint but increasing luminosity of ruby light became gradually visible, the apparition of the etheric double being particularly lifelike owing to the discharge of jivic rays from the crown of the head and face" (389). Such passages—as may easily be established by practical demonstration—respond especially well to whispered recitation.

42. Georg Lukács, *History and Class Consciousness*, trans. Rodney Livingstone (London: Merlin, 1971), 204.

43. D. A. Miller, *Jane Austen, or, The Secret of Style* (Princeton, NJ: Princeton University Press, 2003), 60.

44. Patrick Modiano, *Dora Bruder*, trans. Joanna Kilmartin (Berkeley: University of California Press, 1999), 112.

45. Dennis Cooper, *Period* (New York: Grove, 2000).

46. Ben Lerner, "The Golden Vanity," *New Yorker*, June 18, 2012, 66–73; Ben Lerner, "The Golden Vanity," in *10:04* (New York: Faber and Faber, 2014), 61–81.

47. Muriel Spark, *The Bachelors* (Harmondsworth: Penguin, 1963), 70.

48. Tao Lin, "Love Is the Indifferent God of the Religion in Which Universe Is Church," in *Bed* (New York: Melville House, 2007), 139.

49. "That's Auden farting, not me." Alan Bennett, *The Habit of Art* (London: Faber and Faber, 2009), 28.

50. J. M. Coetzee, *Slow Man* (London: Secker and Warburg, 2005).

51. Charles Lock, "Double Voicing, Sharing Words: Bakhtin's Dialogism and the History of the Theory of Free Indirect Discourse," in *The Novelness of Bakhtin: Perspectives and Possibilities*, ed. Jørgen Bruhn and Jan Lundquist (Copenhagen: Museum Tusculanum Press, 2001), 85.

52. M. M. Bakhtin, "Epic and Novel," in *The Dialogic Imagination*, trans. Caryl Emerson and Michael Holquist (Austin: University of Texas Press, 1981), 13.

53. Benedict Anderson, *Imagined Communities: Reflections on the Origin and Spread of Nationalism*, rev. ed. (London: Verso, 1991), 24–25.

INTERLUDE. PROFILING

1. Carole Cadwalladr, "'I Made Steve Bannon's Psychological Warfare Tool': Meet the Data War Whistleblower," *Guardian*, March 18, 2018.

8. RANCIÈRE: TOWARD NONREGIME THINKING

1. Jacques Rancière, *The Politics of Aesthetics: The Distribution of the Sensible*, trans. Gabriel Rockhill (London: Continuum, 2004), 20.

2. "Understanding Modernism, Reconfiguring Disciplinarity: Interview with Jacques Rancière on May 11, 2015," trans. Patrick M. Bray, in *Understanding Rancière, Understanding Modernism*, ed. Patrick M. Bray (London: Bloomsbury Academic, 2017), 264.

3. Virginia Woolf, "Mr. Bennett and Mrs. Brown," in *Theory of the Novel: A Historical Approach*, ed. Michael McKeon (Baltimore, MD: Johns Hopkins University Press, 2000), 746; Samuel Beckett, *Proust* and *Three Dialogues* (with Georges Duthuit) (1949; London: John Calder, 1965), 121–22. I will return to Beckett's reading of Bram van Velde at the end of this chapter.

4. Exodus 20:4.

5. Jacques Rancière, *The Aesthetic Unconscious*, trans. Debra Keates and James Swenson (Cambridge: Polity, 2009), 11–14, 17. Rancière also pays attention to Voltaire's 1719 adaptation (*Oedipe*), which similarly "correct[s]" the implausibility of Sophocles's story by finding another candidate (Philoctetes) for the murder of Laius (15).

6. Jacques Rancière, *Aesthetics and Its Discontents*, trans. Steven Corcoran (Cambridge: Polity, 2009), 65.

7. Aristotle, *Poetics*, 1452a–1452b.

8. Jacques Rancière, *The Aesthetic Unconscious*, trans. Debra Keates and James Swenson (Cambridge: Polity, 2009), 19.

9. Carl Power makes, in passing, almost exactly this point in "Bergson's Critique of Practical Reason," in *Bergson, Politics, and Religion*, ed. Alexander Lefebvre and Melanie White (Durham, NC: Duke University Press, 2012), 177. Aristotle, says Power, shares with Bergson (as well as other modern thinkers such as Heidegger, Wittgenstein, and Bourdieu) "a propensity to see the human agent, not as a locus of representations, but as a being who is immediately engaged in the world and whose understanding of self and other is first and foremost expressed in practice."

10. Jacques Rancière, *The Politics of Literature*, trans. Julie Rose (Cambridge: Polity, 2011), 4. Future references will appear in parentheses with the abbreviation *PL*.

11. Theodor W. Adorno, *Prisms*, trans. Samuel Weber and Shierry Weber (Cambridge, MA: MIT Press, 1981), 34; Jean-François Lyotard, "Answering the Question: What Is Postmodernism?" trans. Régis Durand, in *The Postmodern Condition: A Report on Knowledge* (Minneapolis: University of Minnesota Press, 1984), 78.

12. Immanuel Kant, *Critique of Judgment*, trans. Werner S. Pluhar (Indianapolis, IN: Hackett, 1987), 127–28 (§29). A few pages later Kant calls the Commandment against graven images "the most sublime passage in the Jewish Law" (135).

13. For example, a review in the *Guardian* newspaper refers to a documentary film about suicides at the Golden Gate Bridge in California (*The Bridge*, dir. Eric Steel [USA, 2006]) as perhaps "the most morally loathsome film ever made." Andrew Pulver, "The Bridge," *Guardian*, February 16, 2007. The French filmmaker Claude Lanzmann, a central figure in these debates, refers to the exhibition *Mémoire des camps*, curated at the Paris Hôtel de Sully by Georges Didi-Huberman, which concluded with four photographs taken by members of the Sonderkommando at Auschwitz, as "an immoral attempt at deconstruction with pedagogic pretensions." Claude Lanzmann, *The Patagonian Hare: A Memoir*, trans. Frank Wynne (New York: Farrar, Straus and Giroux, 2012), 467.

14. The phrase "behaviorist novel" (*roman behaviouriste*) is not an established term in English criticism. However, a possible connection with what has been called the "radical behaviorist" philosophy of William James suggests that Rancière may have in mind William's brother Henry James (and other writers of the period). The critic Matthew Guillen draws a direct link between Henry's writing and William's philosophy, surmising that the formal features of Henry James's work betray a working assumption that "the ultimate object of artistic and linguistic expression, consciousness, is elusive precisely because it is, to a fair degree, illusory." Guillen goes on to quote the view of art put forward in an 1893 letter from William James to Theodore Flournoy, where James opines that the quality of a work consists in its ability to tell "all sorts of things to different spectators, of none of which things the artist ever knew a word." See Matthew Guillen, "On Being and Becoming Isabel Archer: The Architectonic of Jamesian Method," *Revue française d'études américaines* 92 (May 2002): esp. 114; and Ralph Barton Perry, *The Thought and Character of William James*, vol. 2: *Philosophy and Psychology* (Boston: Little, Brown, 1935), 256.

15. The phrase "an absolute manner of seeing things" is from Flaubert's letter to Colet of January 16, 1852; quoted in Jacques Rancière, *Mute Speech*, trans. James Swenson (New York: Columbia University Press, 2011), 115.

16. Theodor W. Adorno, *Aesthetic Theory*, trans. Robert Hullot-Kentor (Minneapolis: University of Minnesota Press, 1997), 6.

17. Robert Hullot-Kentor, "Translator's Introduction," in Adorno, *Aesthetic Theory*, xiv.

18. Zadie Smith, "Love, Actually," *Guardian*, November 1, 2003; Dorothy J. Hale, *The Novel and the New Ethics* (Stanford, CA: Stanford University Press, 2020), 108.

19. Gabriel Rockhill, *Radical History and the Politics of Art* (New York: Columbia University Press, 2014), 160.

20. Similarly, in an essay written for the Brazilian daily newspaper *Folha de São Paulo* in November 2003—part of an extraordinary series collected under the title "Chronicles of Consensual Times"—Rancière offers a reading of three films (Clint

Eastwood's *Mystic River* [USA, 2002], Gus Van Sant's *Elephant* [USA, 2003], and Lars von Trier's *Dogville* [Denmark, UK, Sweden, France, Germany, Netherlands, 2003]) that do not rise to the level of the aesthetic regime, for these are films of "consensus." Rancière thus seems to flout the principles of his own approach to aesthetics when he concludes that, in the wake of the 9/11 attacks, American cinema has entered a "nihilistic" phase (the term is Rockhill's). The most natural political analogue of that nihilism is George Bush's doctrine of "infinite justice" in Iraq. *Elephant, Dogville* and *Mystic River* present us with a world in which "sin, the law and authority are radically absent"; that is, in which "there is no reason for crime, other than the very absence of reasons." The message of such films, according to Rancière, is that "we must not demand that justice be too just." The most remarkable revelation of this essay is, first, the evident normative affiliation with the aesthetic regime underlying this analysis and, second, the powerlessness of the concept of aesthetic regime when it comes to works that successfully foreclose the emergence of some "grammatical concatenation" at their center. See Rockhill's essay "The Politics of Aesthetics: Political History and the Hermeneutics of Art," in *Jacques Rancière: History, Politics, Aesthetics*, ed. Gabriel Rockhill and Philip Watts (Durham, NC: Duke University Press, 2009), 195–215.

21. Rancière, *Mute Speech*, 51; Rancière, *Aisthesis: Scenes from the Aesthetic Regime of Art*, trans. Zakir Paul (London: Verso, 2014), 48.

22. Because of this tendency, Rancière's work is unusually dependent on the work of commentators who put into words what Rancière himself is reluctant to state forthrightly, for reasons that are evident in his book *The Ignorant Schoolmaster*. Paraphrasing the French philosopher and educator Joseph Jacotot, the subject of his study, Rancière writes: "To explain something to someone is first of all to show him he cannot understand it by himself. Before being the act of the pedagogue, explication is the myth of pedagogy, the parable of a world divided into knowing minds and ignorant ones, ripe minds and immature ones, the capable and the incapable, the intelligent and the stupid." Jacques Rancière, *The Ignorant Schoolmaster: Five Lessons in Intellectual Emancipation*, trans. Kristin Ross (Stanford, CA: Stanford University Press, 1991), 6. The great challenge in reading and interpreting Rancière's project stems from the fact that Rancière evacuates the position of the teacher at every moment in his own writing. "Whoever emancipates doesn't have to worry about what the emancipated person learns. He will learn what he wants, nothing maybe" (18). The notion of understanding is profoundly alien to Rancière's conception of the role of the intellectual and of the capacity of philosophy not only to describe but to participate in the redistribution of the sensible.

23. Robert St. Clair, "Regimes of Art," in *Understanding Rancière, Understanding Modernism*, ed. Patrick M. Bray (London: Bloomsbury Academic, 2017), 257.

24. Kant, *Critique of Judgment*, 182 (§49).

25. Jacques Rancière, *Film Fables*, trans. Emiliano Battista (Oxford: Berg, 2006), 116. Future references will appear in parentheses with the abbreviation *FF*. See also Jacques Rancière, *Béla Tarr, the Time After*, trans. Erik Beranek (Minneapolis, MN: Univocal, 2013), 66.

26. How does Rancière's insistence on the democratic nature of "absolutized style" fare, for example, when faced with the observation by the American writer Toni Morrison that canonical American literature has been founded on a four-hundred-year

obliviousness to the real presence of Africans and African Americans in the United States? Toni Morrison, *Playing in the Dark: Whiteness and the Literary Imagination* (New York: Vintage, 1993), 4–5. Is not Morrison alluding to the fact that literature's universally emancipating potential will always be considered pending from the perspective of the people who inhabit the subject positions of that potential emancipation? Isn't this perpetually deferred quality obscured by the exercise of theorizing the literary regime as such—rather than theorizing, say, the historical and political circumstances in which a *particular* distribution of visibility becomes dominant?

27. With his reference to Hitchcock's conflict with the Actors Studio, Deleuze is no doubt evoking episodes such as the story Hitchcock related to François Truffaut, during their famous week-long conversation in 1962, about working with Montgomery Clift on the film *I Confess*. "I had a conflict with Clift. I said, 'Monty, I want you to look up at the hotel.' So he said to me, 'I don't know whether I would look up to the hotel.' I said, 'Why not?' He said, 'I may be occupied by the people below.' I said, 'I want you to look up to the hotel windows. And please do so.' . . . Now I was telling the audience: across the street is the hotel. So an actor is going to try and interfere with me, organizing my geography. That's why all actors are cattle." *Hitchcock/Truffaut*, dir. Kent Jones (France and USA, 2015).

28. Eric Rohmer and Claude Chabrol, *Hitchcock: The First Forty-Four Films*, trans. Stanley Hochman (New York: Frederick Ungar, 1970), 66.

29. "Even formlessness has form," says the writer Ali Smith in *Artful* (New York: Penguin, 2014), a work composed of four texts delivered at St. Anne's College, Oxford, in February 2012 for the Weidenfeld Visiting Professorship in European Comparative Literature (76). The text in which this sentence appears is the second, "On Form," which, like the others, comprises a draft of a lecture found on an unnamed writer's desk after her death by the writer's partner, the primary narrator of the work. Her narration intersperses the texts of the lectures with memories of her life with the writer and accounts of the writer's ghostly reappearances. So *Artful* has the structure of a novel. Thus, the claim about formlessness also being—or having—a form loses its reliability the moment it is articulated. The effect of the formal conceit of Smith's work is to erode or displace every site of "grammatical concatenation" in the book, especially that which is identified with the authorship of the lectures. Is this work insisting, like the unnamed lecturer, that form is ubiquitous and "environmental"? (74) That the effects of a form are exhausted by its affordances?—that, just as "a people's songs will tell you about the heart and aspirations of that people, like their language and their use of it will tell you what their concerns are, material and metaphysical, their artforms will tell you everything about where they live and the shape they're in"? That there is nothing that doesn't have form, and no effect of a work that is not a "meeting of opposites," of "different things"? (72) Such assertions appear in *Artful* only alongside the narrator's reading of them, a reading that frequently deflates or disidentifies with the lectures' content. As in Deleuze's account of the sensorimotor break, we might say that the speech-act in Smith's *Artful* "turn[s] in on itself and hollow[s] itself out," losing any relation to the world of reference and imposing, instead, of the "rational cut" of the sensorimotor schema, the "irrational cut" of the interstice (*C2*, 243, 248). In this regard, the effect of Smith's work is perhaps better captured by a quotation jotted down by the lecturer on one of the drafts and reproduced by the narrator: "Think what it would be to have a work

conceived from outside the *self*, a work that would let us escape the limited perspective of the individual ego, not only to enter into selves like our own but to give speech to that which has no language" (89). This passage, which is from Italo Calvino's *Six Memos for the Next Millennium*, trans. Patrick Creagh (London: Vintage, 1996)—another work made up of lectures that were never delivered because of the author's sudden death—is speculative and makes no claims to normativity or even plausibility ("Think what it would be . . .") (124). But in a work defined not by aesthetic protocols but by a new regime of art, or a movement beyond all regimes, only an utterance placed in such a way as to strip it of authority would have any hope of touching the idea of the work. To attempt to paraphrase that idea is to give it an authority that would not withstand its appearance in the work itself. Thus, such a paraphrase fails to capture its essence. Nevertheless, I attempt one here: There *is*, precisely, a formlessness without form, which is to say, a limit to form; connections may be broken, and the break remain graspable, without it thereby constituting a new connection; and such a limit or break opens onto a subject of thought that is without any identifiable center or attribution.

30. *The Lady from Shanghai*, dir. Orson Welles (USA, 1948).

31. *Fitzcarraldo*, dir. Werner Herzog (Germany, 1982), tells the story of an opera impresario obsessed with the idea of building a theater in the Peruvian jungle. Having secured financial backing with great effort—again, this financial and imaginative expenditure applies as much to Herzog's enterprise as to Fitzcarraldo's—and having progressed by steamboat many miles up the Pachitea River, it becomes necessary to transport the steamer physically over a mountain ridge in order to reach the adjacent but otherwise inaccessible Ucayali River. At this stage in the production, Herzog hires several hundred Peruvian Indian laborers/extras, with whom he constructs a series of winches set into the mountainside and hoists the boat physically over the ridge. Again, such moments in cinema exemplify its propensity to create crystalline images in which the distinction between actual and virtual—in the form of the generic distinction between documentary and fiction, say—is annulled not as a theoretical or artistic exercise but in actuality.

32. Jacques Rancière, *The Intervals of Cinema*, trans. John Howe (London: Verso, 2014), 35. This, of course, is the same tension that runs through every debate and discussion on the merits of free indirect discourse. Is free indirect discourse an intrusion of the author or narrator into the character's point of view or, on the contrary, a liberation and devolution of perspective from the author or narrator to the character? Does free indirect discourse imperialize or democratize? And we could identify this same tension at the heart of every political and philosophical critique of the Enlightenment tradition. When we advance a critique of the universalizing apparatus of colonial discourse, for example, are we doing so in the name of a *more* universal—because less provincialized, less centralized—point of view or in renunciation of the possibility of any unsituated, disembodied knowledge? Is the problem of colonial discourse its universalism or its provincialism? Is the remedy to that problem universal embodiment or disembodied universality? These tensions are partly about time. Are we looking for a solution that pays attention to the necessarily degraded realities of the here-and-now or one that inhabits a transformed relation to time as becoming? The essence of politics is "dissensus," says Rancière, in "Ten Theses on Politics," in *Dissensus: On Politics and Aesthetics*, trans. Steven

Corcoran (London: Continuum, 2010), 38. But does not any such claim about the "essence of politics" amount to the imposition of a consensus?

33. Rancière, *Béla Tarr, the Time After*, 4. Occasionally I will refer to the French text, *Béla Tarr, le temps d'après* (Paris: Capricci, 2011), in which case the page reference to the French edition will follow in the same parenthesis, separated by an oblique stroke.

34. Paraphrasing this claim about Béla Tarr, we might say that what Werner Herzog achieves by the on- and off-screen use of "extras" in *Fitzcarraldo*, in Rancière's schema, is not a crystal image but a redistribution of the sensible, a redistribution signaled by the appearance of *any indigenous individuals whatever* (thus bringing into visibility the specific lifeworld of indigenous communities).

35. Joseph Conrad, *Heart of Darkness*, ed. Paul O'Prey (Harmondsworth: Penguin, 1985), 30.

36. Jacques Rancière, *The Lost Thread: The Democracy of Modern Fiction*, trans. Steven Corcoran (London: Bloomsbury Academic, 2017), 29–30.

37. Joseph Conrad, *Lord Jim*, ed. Cedric Watts and Robert Hampson (Harmondsworth: Penguin, 2000), 124–25.

38. Joseph Conrad, *The Secret Agent*, ed. Tanya Agathocleous (Peterborough, Ont.: Broadview, 2009), 141.

39. Virginia Woolf, "Modern Fiction," in *The Common Reader: First Series* (1925; Orlando, FL: Harcourt, 1984), 150.

40. Gilles Deleuze and Félix Guattari, *Kafka: Toward a Minor Literature*, trans. Dana Polan (Minneapolis: University of Minnesota Press, 1986), 21. The word "pretext" is used by Dana Polan in his "Translator's Introduction," xxiii.

41. In a 2015 interview, responding to a question about his relation to the concepts of "modernism" and "modernity," Rancière states: "I always write within defined conjunctures." Thus, even such a central principle of his work as "the total critique of the concepts of modernism and modernity . . . needs to be placed in its context." Rancière, "Understanding Modernism, Reconfiguring Disciplinarity," 263. This seemingly straightforward claim opens up an ambiguity in Rancière's critical discourse. On one hand, the implication seems close to Deleuze's claim in "What Is the Creative Act?" that having an idea "is not something general," that "an idea . . . is already dedicated to a particular field." Gilles Deleuze, *Two Regimes of Madness: Texts and Interviews, 1975–1995*, trans. Ames Hodges and Mike Taormina (New York: Semiotext(e), 1998), 312. On the other hand, the insistence on a particular "conjuncture" for the event of one's writing suggests that the conjuncture is also a limit, that thought, or at least the type of thought that is communicable in writing, has a field of applicability and another field (or an out-of-field) in which that applicability is forgone.

42. Jacques Rancière, "What Aesthetics Can Mean," trans. B. Holmes, in *From an Aesthetic Point of View: Philosophy, Art, and the Senses*, ed. Peter Osborne (London: Serpent's Tail, 2000), 18.

43. Samuel Beckett, *Proust* and *Three Dialogues*, 119–20.

44. In a letter to Georges Duthuit written during the composition of the dialogue, Beckett makes clear this primacy of relation in his thinking about van Velde's work: "[Bram's painting] is new because it is the first to repudiate relation in all these

forms. It is not the relation with this or that order of opposite that it refuses, but the state of being in relation as such, the state of being in front of. We have waited a long time for an artist who is brave enough, is at ease enough with the great torna-does of intuition, to grasp that the break with the outside world entails the break with the inside world, that there are no replacement relations for naive relations, that what are called outside and inside are one and the same. I am not saying that he makes no attempt to reconnect. What matters is that he does not succeed. His painting is, if you will, the impossibility of reconnecting." Letter to Georges Duthuit, March 9, 1949, in *The Letters of Samuel Beckett*, vol. 2: *1941–1956*, ed. George Craig et al. (Cambridge: Cambridge University Press, 2011), 140.

45. Samuel Beckett, "Peintres de l'empêchement," in *Disjecta: Miscellaneous Writings and a Dramatic Fragment*, ed. Ruby Cohn (London: John Calder, 1983), 135; my translation. Bram van Velde's remark (as reported by Cäsar Menz) is cited, in the context of Beckett's phrase, by David Lloyd, "Beckett's Thing: Bram van Velde and the Gaze," in *Beckett's Thing: Painting and Theatre* (Edinburgh: Edinburgh University Press, 2016), 121.

46. By "present" I mean, of course, *not* present. Trying to be funny, or else out of simple exhaustion and desperation (or both), Beckett adds that we might equally describe this quality of van Velde's work as "the presence of unavailable terms" of relation (125). But the apparent symmetry of the two formulations is belied by the principle insisted on in the present work, that the critique or critical overcoming of the instan-tiation relation takes two distinct but incompatible forms: on one hand, the assertion of the *fundamental* nature of instantiation (as in D. M. Armstrong's "ontology of states of affairs"); on the other, the suggestion of an outside to (or escape from) the instantiation relation. There is no meeting ground between these propositions.

47. Nina Power reports once asking Jacques Rancière, in English, what he thought about Samuel Beckett: "He paused for a moment before replying: 'I 'ave no affinity for 'im.' " Jacques Rancière and Nina Power, "Interview with Jacques Rancière," *ephem-era* 10, no. 1 (2010): 78.

CONCLUSION. THE INDETERMINATE THOUGHT
OF THE FREE INDIRECT

1. Frances Ferguson, "Jane Austen, *Emma*, and the Impact of Form," *Modern Language Quarterly* 61, no. 1 (March 2000): 159.

2. Franco Moretti, "Serious Century," in *The Novel*, vol. 1: *History, Geography, and Cul-ture*, ed. Franco Moretti (Princeton, NJ: Princeton University Press, 2006), 364–400; D. A. Miller, *Jane Austen, or, The Secret of Style* (Princeton, NJ: Princeton Uni-versity Press, 2003).

3. Jacques Rancière, "Are Some Things Unrepresentable?" in *The Future of the Image*, trans. Gregory Elliott (London: Verso, 2009), 121.

4. Ann Banfield, *Unspeakable Sentences: Narration and Representation in the Language of Fiction* (Boston: Routledge and Kegan Paul, 1982), 272, 273.

5. Muriel Spark, *The Driver's Seat* (1970; New York: New Directions, 1994); James Kel-man, *A Chancer* (Edinburgh: Polygon, 1985); Rachel Cusk, *Outline* (New York:

Farrar, Straus and Giroux, 2015); Rachel Cusk, *Transit* (New York: Farrar, Straus and Giroux, 2016); Rachel Cusk, *Kudos* (New York: Farrar, Straus and Giroux, 2018).

6. Franco Moretti, *Graphs, Maps, Trees: Abstract Models for a Literary History* (London: Verso, 2005), 82.

INDEX

absolute difference (Deleuze), 149, 193, 287n34

absurdity, of the world (Lukács), 25, 173–75, 194, 204, 253

actions, and reactions, 216–17, 239

addressivity, principle of, 93–94, 103

Adorno, Theodor W., 27–28, 81, 179, 233–34, 236, 267n16

aesthetic regime, 13, 26, 40, 103, 131–32, 179–80, 186, 193, 231–41, 248, 249–51, 296–97n20; exit from, 208, 238, 241, 251, 253

affect, 263–64n20, 292n29

affordances (Levine), 181–82, 184, 186–87, 298n29

Agamben, Giorgio, 46–47, 49–50, 67, 268n18

Akerman, Chantal, 208

Althusser, Louis, 5, 278n20

"Always historicize!" (Jameson), 21

Amis, Kingsley, 32, 34

anagonist, 207, 289n13

Anderson, Amanda, 178–80, 186–87, 190, 275–76n1

Anderson, Benedict, 10–11, 134–37, 142

Antelme, Robert, 235

Antonioni, Michelangelo, 191, 201, 208, 217

any-instant-whatever (Deleuze), 208–10, 213, 215–16. *See also* privileged instant

any-space-whatever (Deleuze), 216, 245–46

Appel, Alfred, 108

Arac, Jonathan, 83, 274n18

Area of Darkness, An (Naipaul), 53–55, 62–63

Aristotle, 6, 7, 25, 168–69, 177, 181, 232–33, 295n9

Armstrong, D. M., 9, 85–86, 100–101, 124–25, 133, 167, 205, 221; on language, 114–15

Artaud, Antonin, 192, 287n34

artistic regimes (Rancière), 4–5, 26–27, 103, 231–41

assemblage (Deleuze and Guattari), 110, 219–20, 226, 250, 257

Auden, W. H., 226

Auerbach, Erich, 137

aura, 81–82, 83, 274n17

Auschwitz, 60, 63, 151, 186, 233, 296n13

Austen, Jane, 2, 35, 66, 76, 104, 105, 110, 225, 258, 272–73n10

Auster, Paul, 205
autonomy: of art, 80, 97, 110, 238; of thought, 7–8, 196–97

Badiou, Alain, 39, 165–68, 214, 289–90n15, 292n28
Bakhtin, Mikhail, 22, 28, 37, 78, 87, 218; chronotope, 10–11, 124–27, 137, 142, 149–50; on dialogicality, 110, 221–23, 226–27; on discourse as an object of representation, 28, 78; on the English comic novel, 92; on free indirect discourse, 12–13; on heteroglossia, 93; on the impossibility of a formal definition of the novel, 38, 262–63n7, 271n2
Bakhtin, Mikhail, works: "Discourse in the Novel," 123–24, 129–30, 293n32; "Forms of Time and of the Chronotope in the Novel," 124–27, 137, 142, 149–50; *Problems of Dostoevsky's Poetics*, 130, 146–47, 171, 222–23, 273n13
Baldwin, James, 205, 265n35
Ball, Jesse, 6, 155–59
Bally, Charles, 272n6
Balzac, Honoré de, 22–23, 125
Banfield, Ann, 10, 76, 77, 105–7, 109, 112, 259–60, 266n41, 272n6
Barthes, Roland, 87, 239; on photography, 56, 59
Beckett, Samuel, 267n15, 300–301n44, 301n45; Rancière on, 301n47; *Three Dialogues*, 29–30, 231, 251–54, 301n46; *The Unnamable*, 30, 128, 279–80n9
Beethoven, Ludwig van, 78, 100–101, 104, 109
being, 85, 211; as opposed to something, 170, 220; being-attribute relation, 168–69, 224–25; and exemplarity, 55; being-meaning relation, 168–69; primary vs. accidental, 168–69, 177
being without qualities (Schefer), 207
belief in the world (Deleuze), 246, 293n32
Bellour, Raymond, 287–88n34
Benjamin, Walter, 83, 106–7
Bennett, Alan, 226

Bergson, Henri, 124–25, 132–34, 195–99, 202, 203, 220; *Matter and Memory*, 133, 191, 197–99, 288n3
Berlant, Lauren, 40
Bernstein, J. M., 276n4
Bertolucci, Bernardo, 217
Bezos, Jeff, 285n9
Bhagavad Gita, 54
biographical form, 2, 60–62, 112–13, 172, 176
Blanchot, Maurice, 192–93, 205, 287n34, *Bleak House* (Dickens), 18, 44, 75, 183
Bloch, Ernst, 224
Booth, Wayne C., 7, 78–79, 80, 83, 88, 96–97, 101, 258–59, 273n13
Borges, Jorge Luis, 128
Bourdieu, Pierre, 22, 27, 80, 295n9
Boxall, Peter, 35
Bradley, F. H., 85–86, 166
Bradley's regress, 85–86, 114, 166, 169, 247. *See also* Russell's paradox
Bresson, Robert, 143–47, 208, 209, 210, 239
Brontë, Emily, 277n11
Browning, Tod, 240, 244
Bush, George W., 297n20

Calvino, Italo, 298–99n29
Cambridge Analytica, 228, 229
Camus, Albert, 235
capital, 167, 224
capitalism, 28, 171
Carroll, Lewis, *Through the Looking Glass*, 165–66, 170
Casanova, Pascale, 137, 281n20
case, 40, 188, 289–90n15
Cavell, Stanley, 175, 176, 188
Céline, Louis-Ferdinand, 273n13
certainty, loss of, 1–2, 29, 66, 74
chance, 63, 122–23, 125, 127, 131, 132, 134, 174, 293n37
characters, 1, 18, 26, 28–29, 141, 218, 222–24; actor-character relation, 224; character types, 23, 139–40; narrator-character relation, 225; as objects, 130; question of motivations, 11, 30–31, 129, 130, 157, 158, 159, 191–92

Chekhov, Anton, 26, 264n24
chronotope (Bakhtin), 10–11, 124–27,
206, 283–84n35; defined, 124, 279n7;
Deleuze on, 142, 146, 283–84n35; as
ideology, 11; image of authorship as,
126; limits of, 11, 142, 147–50; pure,
149–54, 227, 284n35; world literary
system as, 137, 282n30
cinema, 12, 170–71, 216; cinematic
apparatus, 12, 30–31, 209, 223;
classical, 191, 195, 210; modern, 195,
210; narrative, 199, 202; relation to the
novel, 154, 217–18; silent, 216; talkie,
211, 216, 217; and thought, 12, 192, 194,
202, 208, 213–14, 216, 251
Cinema 1 and Cinema 2 (Deleuze), 193,
199, 201–19, 241–46, 269n24, 284n35,
287–88n34
Clarkson, Carrol, 98, 104, 272–73n10
class consciousness, 264n21
clichés, 209
close reading, 82–83
Coetzee, J. M.: as inventor of assemblages,
110; chronotopes in, 126; Diamond on,
188, 203–5; free indirect discourse in,
76; Hale on, 88; relation to identity,
269n29; use of present tense, 76
Coetzee, J. M., works: Diary of a Bad
Year, 104, 272–73n10; Elizabeth
Costello, 5–6, 52–53, 74–79, 81, 84, 92,
97–99, 100, 104–5, 115, 122–23, 126,
149, 174–77, 185, 204, 206, 214, 271n3;
The Lives of Animals, 175–76, 185,
273n13; The Master of Petersburg,
48–49; Schooldays of Jesus, 285n8;
Slow Man, 226
Cohn, Dorrit, 223
Cole, Teju, 2, 6
Colebrook, Claire, 280n13
colors, as attributes, 25, 218, 224; as
thought, 29
comic novel, 92
concepts, 165–67, 207
confession, 156; innate duplicity of,
157–58, 159
connections: aleatory, 63; in Bleak
House (Dickens), 44; bridge as image
of, 102; between chance and thought,
132; as capacity of the novel, 18;
chronotope as form of, 124, 279n7;
critical interpretation as, 6, 32, 131,
140; as definition of the realist novel,
21–23; degree-zero principle of, 87,
102–3, 109, 132, 135, 140–41, 142, 177,
178, 228–29, 236, 241; disconnection
and, 10, 32, 34, 65; in Dostoevsky,
130; ethics as form of, 21, 23–24, 34;
in Howards End (Forster), 101–5,
178; in How late it was, how late
(Kelman), 148; irony as form of, 21,
24–25; between literature and life,
102; objective vs. psychological, 171;
between past and present, 152–53;
Rancière on, 103; realism as form of,
21–23; in Sebald, 42–44; ultimate,
249; between the work and the
world, 4, 21, 74–75, 86, 279n7,
282–83n30
Conrad, Joseph, 88
Conrad, Joseph, works: Heart of
Darkness, 247; Lord Jim, 247–48; The
Secret Agent, 185, 248–51
conversations, in cinema, 216–17, 244
Cooper, Dennis, 6, 225
Corneille, Pierre, 232
Crenshaw, Kimberlé, 265n35. See also
intersectionality
criminality, as form, 33, 34, 171, 185,
229–30
critical discourse, 6, 17, 35, 71, 83, 111, 114,
140, 166, 251, 255
critical practice, 17–19, 71–72, 164
crystal images, 63, 200, 227, 243–45,
300n34
crystalline formations. See crystal
images
Cusk, Rachel, 1, 6, 226

death of the author (Barthes), 108, 109
deflection (Clarkson usage), 98, 105,
272–73n10
deflection (Diamond usage), 174, 176–78,
185, 187–88, 190–94, 204, 206, 216,
223, 243, 247, 252–53, 260

degree-zero connection, 10, 87, 102–3, 109, 132, 135, 140–41, 241, 252; instantiation as, 177–78, 256; parataxis as, 236; profiling as, 228–29, 248

Deleuze, Gilles, 11–12, 65, 71, 110, 184; on cinema, 30–31, 40, 153–54, 214, 237–39, 283–84n35; on difference, 148–49, 193; positive conception of literature, 171, 192–93; theory of multiplicity, 132, 289–90n15, 292n28

Deleuze, Gilles, works: *Cinema 1* and *Cinema 2*, 193, 199, 201–19, 241–46, 269n24, 284n35, 287–88n34; *Difference and Repetition*, 287–88n34, 289n15; *Kafka: Toward a Minor Literature*, 250; *The Logic of Sense*, 12, 164–66, 168–71, 190, 284n35; *Proust and Signs*, 287n34; *A Thousand Plateaus* (with Guattari), 119, 218–22, 257

de Man, Paul, 173

democracy: and distant reading, 82–83; immanent vs. conversational, 178–80, 186; Rancière on, 234, 238

Derrida, Jacques, 80, 278n22

Descartes, René, 198, 204

De Sica, Vittorio, 200

dialogicality, 13, 93, 221–23, 226–27; absolute, 14, 94

dialogue, 220

Diamond, Cora, 174–77, 185–87, 203–6, 252

Dickens, Charles, 46, 50, 54, 63, 65, 66; *Bleak House*, 18, 44, 75, 183–85

Didi-Huberman, Georges, 60, 270n39, 296n13

difficulty of reality (Diamond), 174–77, 185, 186–88, 190–94, 252

direct discourse, 4–5, 90, 129, 193, 293–94n37; analogy with cinema (talkie), 216–19

disconnection, 6, 10, 44, 72, 83–84, 100, 174, 190, 251; in Bresson, 142–43; defined, 149–50

discontinuity, 31, 127, 174; as methodology, 132

discontinuous systematicities, theory of (Foucault), 11, 138–39

discourse, 121–24, 132; as event, 131, 159, 163; Foucault on, 132; legal, 129–30; noninstantiating, 126; political, 18; sociological, 129–30, 138; theoretical, 155

distance, 35, 54, 122–24, 221, 223. *See also* perspective

distant reading (Moretti), 81–83

Doniger, Wendy, 175

Dora Bruder (Modiano), 150–53, 225, 283n32

Dostoevsky, Fyodor, 84, 110, 125–26, 146, 171, 221, 130, 277n11; as character in *The Master of Petersburg* (Coetzee), 48–49; Vološinov on, 221–22, 226

Dostoevsky, Fyodor, works: *The Idiot*, 221–22, 226; *Notes from Underground*, 84

drawing, as practice, 3

Dreyer, Carl, 208, 210, 290n20

Dubow, Jessica, 268n18

Duchamp, Marcel, 28

Duras, Marguerite, 214

duration (Bergson), 125, 133

During, Simon, 177–80

Duthuit, Georges, 29–30, 251–52, 300–301n44

Eagleton, Terry, 87

Eisenstein, Sergei, 209, 210

Elizabeth Costello (Coetzee), 5–6; effect on critical discourse of, 111–13; as event in the history of the novel, 76, 104–5; exemplarity in, 52–53; Mulhall on, 78, 271–72n3; problem of enunciation in, 185, 214; "the problem of the opening," 74–77, 97–98, 99, 100; problem of realism in, 77–79

Emerson, Caryl, 125, 127, 279n7

empathy, 35, 221

Engels, Friedrich, 196

enigmaticalness, 42

entertainment novel (Lukács), 51, 52, 73–74, 256

environmental crisis, 29

epic, 51, 99, 112, 140, 172

ethics, 29, 73–74, 87, 98, 129, 185; as connecting term of the novel, 23; and

perception, 54–55; of reading, 79; as a regime of art, 232, 234; in Sebald, 66
event: Deleuze on, 168–70; dialogicality as, 226–27; of discourse, 131, 159, 163; *Elizabeth Costello* (Coetzee) as, 76, 104–5; narrated and narrating, 227; pure, 170, 246; sensorimotor break as, 196, 202; of the work, 34, 156
example, theorized, 49, 50
exception, 40, 82–83
exemplarity, 8–9, 82–83, 112, 155, 216; defined, 39; and the Holocaust, 60; as logic of being, 54; and perception, 53–54; refusal of, 42, 46, 50, 65; rhetorical, 50–51; semantic, 50–51; as a sensorimotor structure, 207; tenor and vehicle of, 49, 54, 59–60, 62
expression: 4, 11, 17, 26, 29–30, 31, 36, 60, 81, 83, 90, 106, 116, 124–25, 127, 206, 220, 222, 227, 239, 254; Beckett on, 251–53; Deleuze on, 164; and the expressed, 164; figures of, 163; ideological quality of, 5; Vološinov on, 116–17
expressivity, 137–38

Fassbinder, Rainer Werner, 202
Faulkner, William, 88–89, 267n15
Ferguson, Frances: on free indirect discourse, 258–60; on McEwan's *Saturday*, 265n35
fiction: as critical term, 141, 164; Foucault on, 131, 281n24; Gallagher on, 25–26, 50; ideology of, 5; and reality, 2, 225; relation to postfiction, 10; relation to truth and falsehood, 10, 112; truth-telling capacity of, 23, 50; twenty-first-century, 18
Fiedler, Leslie, 18–19
Fielding, Henry, 50, 92–93
Fish, Stanley, 275–76n1
Flaubert, Gustave, 233, 235–36, 247, 250, 263–64n20, 296n15; *Madame Bovary*, 20–21, 26–27, 36, 103, 189, 233
Flaxman, Gregory, 110
focalization, 76, 77–78, 91, 101, 106, 109, 126, 186, 200, 222, 266n49, 272n6

Foley, Barbara, 23, 265n35
form: and content, 20, 41, 73, 98, 255; of formlessness, 298–99n29; as ideology, 5, 34; Levine's revision of, 181–82; as the limit of thought, 34, 84; and material, 20; novelistic, 20; and relationality, 31; Smith on, 298–99n29
forms: novelistic, 31, 38, 172; space and time as, 126–27
Forms (Levine), 181–87
Forster, E. M., 21, 110; on *Bleak House* (Dickens), 184
Forster, E. M., works: *Aspects of the Novel*, 104, 277n11; *Howards End*, 89–91, 100–105, 178–80, 192–93, 277n11
Foucault, Michel, 130–32, 280n11, 280n13, 281n24
Foucault, Michel, works: *The Archaeology of Knowledge*, 129, 169; *The Birth of Biopolitics*, 167, 285n9; "Maurice Blanchot: The Thought from Outside," 131, 280n11; "The Order of Discourse," 11, 121–24, 127–32, 134, 138–39, 174
fragility: of the world (Lukács), 24, 25, 31, 42, 264n21
François, Anne-Lise, 36

framing: rarefied vs. saturated, 213
Frankfurt School, 80
free indirect, 5, 11–12, 37–38, 224, 225, 226, 257; logic, 257; subject of, 224
free indirect discourse: analogy with sensorimotor collapse, 216–19; Bakhtin on, 129–30; in Coetzee, 76, 126; Cohn on, 223; competing theories of, 35–38, 218–19, 299–300n32; in critical discourse, 109, 129; Deleuze and Guattari on, 257; defined, 77; and dialogicality, 222; Ferguson on, 258–60; as a form, 181, 257–58; in Forster's *Howards End*, 101, 186; in Foucault, 130–31; as merging of character and narrator, 106; Miller on, 35, 76, 258; Moretti on, 35, 258–60; as narratorless (Banfield), 106, 109; as

free indirect discourse (*continued*)
noninstantiating discourse, 77; in
Zadie Smith, 90; thought and, 5,
221–23, 257; universalization of, 77,
79, 105, 111, 126, 149, 299n32. *See also*
quasi-direct discourse
free indirect style, 5, 200, 258, 272n6
free indirect subjective (*soggettiva libera
indiretta*) (Pasolini), 12–13, 217–18
Frege, Gottlob, 165–67
Freud, Sigmund, 22
Frye, Northrop, 7

Gallagher, Catherine, on fictionality, 25,
28–29, 50
Gandhi, Mohandas, 55
Gardiner, Michael, 137, 148–49
Gates, Henry Louis, 87
gaze, 54–55, 59, 92–93; holy, 61
Genette, Gérard, 87, 266n49, 277n14
genius, 17, 31
genres, 208, 218, 224, 238; limitation of
regarding the novel, 10
Ghosh, Amitav, 29
Gladman, Renee, 2–3, 6
Godard, Jean-Luc, 191, 201, 208, 210–11,
217, 218; *Two or Three Things I Know
About Her*, 211–14, 223–24
Gordimer, Nadine, 75
Gorky, Maxim, 22–23
grammatical concatenation (Vološinov),
157, 244, 260, 297n20, 298n29
grammatical evidence (Banfield), 78, 101,
105–6, 272n9
grammatical regime, 111
Green, Henry, 35
Griffith, D. W., 210
Grzymala, Monika, 3
Guattari, Félix, 218, 250, 257, 287–88n34
Guerlac, Suzanne, 199
Guyer, Paul, 291–92n27
Guzzetti, Alfred, 291n22, 291n24, 293n30

Habit of Art (Bennett), 226
Hale, Dorothy J., 9, 86–88, 90, 96, 98,
103–4, 166, 171
Handler, Richard, 134

hands, 3; in Bresson, 143–47, 152
Hankivsky, Olena, 253n35
Hartman, Saidiya, 47–49, 293–94n37
Hayot, Eric, 268–69n23
heautonomy, 214–17, 224, 225, 237, 248,
291–92n27, 292n28
Hegel, G. W. F., 84, 181
Heidegger, Martin, 19, 295n9
Herzog, Werner, 201, 202, 244;
Fitzcarraldo, 299n31, 300n34
heteroglossia (Bakhtin), 93, 293n32
historical materialism, 7–8, 81
historico-philosophical approach
(Lukács), 44–46, 84, 255
Hitchcock, Alfred, 200, 240, 241–43,
298n27; *Rear Window*, 240, 242,
288n6; *Vertigo*, 240, 245
Holquist, Michael, 271n2
homo economicus, 167, 285n9
Horkheimer, Max, 81
Howards End (Forster), 78, 89–91,
100–105, 109, 178–80, 192–93
Howe, Irving, 179
Hughes, Ted, 175, 185–86, 188, 203–4
Huillet, Danièle, 208, 214

ideas: of artistic works, 4, 163; being of,
168–69; in *Bleak House* (Dickens),
184; in Dostoevsky, 146–47; in
Elizabeth Costello (Coetzee), 76–78,
97, 271–72n5; in *Howards End*
(Forster), 102, 178–80; instantiated,
25–28; Levine on, 181–85, 186–87;
Lukács on, 98–99; in *Madame Bovary*
(Flaubert), 189; noninstantiated,
71–72. *See also* meaning; sense;
thought
identity principle, 166; Coetzee on,
269n29
ideologeme, 28, 220
ideology, 13–14, 186; aesthetic, 14, 80,
131–32, 140, 203; of expression, 5; of
fiction, 5; of form, 5, 13–14; and
literary criticism, 101, 140; Marx and
Engels on, 196–97; novelistic, 24, 29,
139–40; novel's escape from, 38; of
number, 167; ontological, 229

imagined community (Anderson), 10–11, 134–35, 142, 227
immanence, 22, 43, 178–79
impersonality, 107
India, and exemplarity, 53–55
indirect discourse, 4–5, 90, 129, 219, 257, 293–94n37; analogy with silent cinema, 216–19
instances, 40, 188, 207; in fiction, 25, 50
instantiation: as aesthetic representation, 27; in cinema, 210; in critical discourse, 103–4, 114; defined, 25, 188, 216; distinct from expression and representation, 116, 118–19; historical shift from representation to, 87–88, 89, 91–92, 94, 100–105, 108–9, 142, 189–90, 236, 259, 275n29; as intrinsic to novel form, 25, 74, 100, 103, 140–41, 172, 187, 188, 256; logic of, 28, 38, 39, 41, 72, 88, 108–9, 124, 138, 141, 159, 192, 228, 251, 255; in nature, 214–15; primacy of, 119, 124–25, 167; of qualities or attributes, 25, 85, 100–101, 168, 205, 248; as theory of language, 114–20, 168–69, 219–20; of time and space, 125
instantiation relation: absence of, 95, 104–5, 114–15, 127, 128, 132, 168, 204–6, 214, 223, 229; Armstrong on, 85–86, 101, 114–15, 167, 205, 278n20; and Bradley's regress, 86, 166; chronotopes as, 11, 128; collapse of, 105, 113–14, 184; defined, 26, 85, 241; as degree-zero relation, 177; and fictionality, 25–26, 140; as a formal quality of the novel, 27, 187, 256; in Howards End (Forster), 102, 104–5; implications of Foucault's work for, 128; ideological nature of, 27, 140, 203; instantiability of, 114–15, 118; in language, 219–20; and literary criticism, 85–89, 179; in nature, 215; novel's exit from, 11–13, 38, 104, 155, 226, 250; paradoxicality of, 17, 20–21, 25, 166, 258–60, 278n20; as presupposition of the rhetoric of fiction, 97; in Zadie Smith, 166

interests, 141, 167, 192, 195–96, 202, 207, 209, 239, 249
intersectionality, 31–33, 253n35
interstice: in Bleak House (Dickens), 184; in cinema, 12, 96–97, 155, 193, 208, 210–11, 214, 246; in contemporary fiction, 272n5; Deleuze on, 12, 168, 170–71, 208, 210–11, 246, 298n29; in Elizabeth Costello (Coetzee), 113; and free indirect discourse, 223–24, 230, 259; in Godard, 211, 223–24; as immanent to the novel, 256; Levine's rejection of, 182; as literature, 170–71; in McGurl, 110; as noninstantiable, 214; and pure chronotope, 227; Rancière's rejection of, 240, 243–48; between sound and image, 211; as thought, 140–41, 168, 193, 214; as the unthought in thought, 208
irony: as connecting term of the novel, 24–25, 248; as form, 24, 33, 35, 174; as objectivity of the novel, 24–25
Irving, John, 108
Ishiguro, Kazuo, 281n19

Jacobs, Carol, 269–70n33, 270n35
Jacobson, Dan, 64
Jacotot, Joseph, 297n22
James, Henry, 87, 292n29, 296n14
James, William, 296n14
Jameson, Fredric, 7–8, 21, 27, 88, 96, 292n29; on affect, 263–64n20
Jauss, Hans Robert, 36
Jay, Martin, 174, 286n17
Joyce, James, 35, 75, 224; "The Dead," 35; Ulysses, 52, 78, 224, 294n41

Kafka, Franz, 58–59, 63, 111, 250, 267n15
Kalepky, Theodor, 218
Kant, Immanuel, 17, 27, 41, 124, 214, 225, 234; concept of the sublime, 234; Critique of Judgment, 214–15, 239; Critique of Pure Reason, 41, 126–27; distinction between instance and example, 40, 269n27; on heautonomy, 214–16, 225, 292n28
Keenan, Thomas, 50–51, 269n27

Kelman, James, 6, 11, 147–50; WReC on, 282n30
Kelman, James, works: *The Busconductor Hines*, 282n30; *A Chancer*, 259–60; *How late it was, how late*, 147–48, 282n30; *Translated Accounts*, 280–81n19
Kermode, Frank, 94, 96, 166–67, 277n12
Kiarostami, Abbas, 201
knowledge, 1, 32, 82, 198; Auster on, 205; Banfield on, 107–8, 259; that of cinema, 208–9; collapse of, 27; criticism as a form of (Morrison), 32; of degree, 54–55; as theme of Coetzee's *Elizabeth Costello*, 204; writing's capacity for, 107
Komarovich, Vasily, 146
Klüger, Ruth, 186

language: adequacy and inadequacy of, 72; bridge image, 119; as chronotopic, 126; Deleuze and Guattari on, 219, 222; instantiation model of, 114–20, 168–69, 251; in the novel, 203. *See also* concepts
Lanzmann, Claude, 296n13
Latour, Bruno, 182
Lawrence, D. H., 104
Lazzarato, Maurizio, 28
legibility, 4, 8, 26–27, 28, 38, 76, 189, 207–8, 229, 240, 243, 256
Leibniz, Gottfried Wilhelm, 166
Lerch, Gertraud, 37, 293n33
Lerner, Ben, 6, 19, 225–26
Levine, Caroline, 181–87
Lin, Tao, 6, 17, 226
linguistics, 29, 218–20; Saussurean, 115–18, 168
literature: capacity to grasp any idea, 246–47; concept of, in Jesse Ball, 158–59; Deleuze on, 171, 192–93; Foucault on, 128; Rancière's definition of, 249
literary regime (Rancière), 65–66, 188–89, 193
Litz, A. Walton, 258–59
Lloyd, David, 301n45

Lock, Charles, 218, 226–27
Logic of Sense (Deleuze), 12, 164–66, 168–71, 190, 284n35
Lubbock, Percy, 20, 26
Lubitsch, Ernst, 200, 210
Luiselli, Valeria, 6, 205–6
Lukács, Georg, 7, 12, 27, 32, 44, 48, 72, 190, 203–5, 224; fundamental dissonance of existence, 76–77, 83, 173–74, 182–83, 184–85, 187, 190, 194, 204, 244, 252, 264n21; on realism, 22–23, 26
Lukács, Georg, works: *History and Class Consciousness*, 224; *The Meaning of Contemporary Realism*, 44, 267n15; "Realism in the Balance," 21, 22–23; *Studies in European Realism*, 26, 32; *The Theory of the Novel*, 23, 24–25, 44, 46, 49, 51, 60–61, 72–74, 97–100, 112–13, 172–74, 176–77, 193–94, 204, 206, 237–38, 243, 248, 253, 255–57, 258–59
Lumet, Sidney, 210
Lyotard, Jean-François, 233–34, 239

Marx, Karl, 128, 181, 196
Marxism, 21; and thought, 7–8; Marxist literary criticism, 23; Lukács's, 24; structural, 80
Marxism and the Philosophy of Language (Vološinov), 37, 116–19, 125, 218, 225, 260
Massumi, Brian, 49, 268n18
materialism, 196–97, 201
Mazzoni, Guido, 2
McCulloh, Mark R., 43
McEwan, Ian, 32–34, 265n39, 265–66n40
McGurl, Mark, 80–84, 105, 108–10, 113, 277–78n20; as a writer of postfiction, 109
meaning, of a work, 20, 21, 81, 102, 119–20. *See also* ideas; sense; thought
meaning of life, as theme of the novel, 139–40, 172
Melville, Herman, 104
mereology, 115, 116. *See also* part-whole relation

Miller, D. A., 225; on free indirect discourse, 35, 76, 258
Mitchell, Margaret, 23
Modiano, Patrick, 6, 11, 147, 150–53, 225, 283n32
Moi, Toril, 40–41, 49
Moretti, Franco, 81–84, 271n3; distant reading, 81–83; on free indirect discourse, 35, 258–60; on world literature, 81–82, 137, 148–49
Morrison, Toni, 29, 31–32, 297–98n26
Morson, Gary, 125, 127, 279n7
motion, Bergson on, 133
movement-image, 195, 209, 253
Mulhall, Stephen, 78, 271–72n5
multiplicity, 132–34, 289–90n15, 292nn28–29; distinction between spatialized and pure, 132, 215
Mumford, Stephen, 85, 114–15
musicality, as instantiable quality, 25
Musil, Robert, 267n15
mute speech (Rancière), 17–18, 103, 155, 238, 270n35
Muybridge, Eadweard, 208–9

Nabokov, Vladimir, 108
Naipaul, V. S., 53–55, 60, 62–63, 269n31
names, 166, 241, 250–51, 253
narration: Banfield on, 105–8, 272n6; ellipsis in, 65; first-person, 1, 57, 179, 273n13; omniscient, 1–2, 35, 112, 183; perspectiveless, 282n30; present-tense, 76; pure, 105, 272n6; in Sebald, 1–2, 56–58, 61, 63; third-person, 112, 179, 183, 294n41; third-person-limited (McGurl), 278n20
Nelson, Maggie, 205
neoliberalism, 28, 38, 167, 285n9
networks, 19, 183–84
New Yorker magazine, 175
novel: as communication, 78, 84, 90, 101, 105, 108, 110, 141, 272n5; connective element, 21–22; disunity of, 73; as exceeding its formal qualities, 19; as form, 19, 187; historical evolution of, 19, 23, 34, 72, 81–82, 96, 141; ideology of, 24; as a logic, 255, 262–63n7; as a

mode of thought, 19, 34, 100, 141, 173–74, 255–56, 257; origins of, 72; subjectivity, 24, 25, 34, 227, 230; theory of, 5, 72–74, 124, 193, 255; thinking in, 13, 19, 24, 251; "unsurmounted element" in, 237–38, 243, 257; untheorizability of, 32, 256
novelistic aesthetics of alterity (Hale), 88, 94
numericality, 132, 165–67, 285n8, 285n9

O'Brien, Geoffrey G., 226
O'Connor, Flannery, 277–78n20
omniscient narration, 1–2, 35, 112, 183. See also narration
On Beauty (Smith), 89–92, 94, 97
O'Neill, Onora, 42, 267n9
"only connect . . ." (Forster), 21, 101–2
optical unconscious (Benjamin), 106–7
"Order of Discourse" (Foucault), 11
order-words (Deleuze and Guattari), 219, 257
Outline trilogy (Cusk), 1, 259–60
out-of-field, 210–11, 251, 290n18, 300n41
Ozu, Yasujiro, 195, 200, 216, 239, 288n5, 288n6

parataxis, 27, 235–36
Parla, Jale, 274n18
part-whole relation, 22, 51, 61, 82, 86, 115, 137, 188–89, 235–36. See also mereology
Pascal, Roy, 277n14
Pasolini, Pier Paolo, 12–13, 217–18
pathos of ineffability (Jay), 174, 186–87, 286n17
Pavel, Thomas, 23, 140, 282–83n30
Peano, Giuseppe, 167
penultimacy, 166, 250–51
perception: exemplary modes of, 54–56; pure (Bergson), 133, 191, 197–98, 202, 288n3; sensorimotor theory of, 191, 195, 196, 233; as subtractive, 191–92, 198, 207
Period (Cooper), 225
perspective, 1–2, 38, 86, 89, 92, 100, 105–6, 123–24; absence of, in

perspective (*continued*)
  Dostoevsky, 130; absence of, in
  Kelman, 149, 282n30; annulling
  of, 59–60, 126, 141; in Foucault,
  123–24, 131; multiplicity of, 71–72;
  perspectiveless thought, 141. *See also*
  point of view
photography: Benjamin on, 106–8; in
  Bergson, 197, 220; in Sebald, 56, 58–59
Picasso, Pablo, 39
Pisanello, 59–60
plagiarism, 31, 45
Plato, 168, 181, 232, 292n28
pluralism, 33–34
point of view, 9–10, 36–38, 41–42, 78–79,
  83, 86, 164, 181, 266n49, 273n10,
  277n11, 299n32; in Zadie Smith,
  89–92, 166, 236, 252. *See also*
  perspective
point-of-view shot, 217
politeness, 17, 31. *See also* sarcasm
political novel, 178–80
Politics of Literature (Rancière), 65–66,
  103, 234
possessive collectivism (Walkowitz),
  134–35
postfiction, 9–10, 43, 91, 94, 109, 111, 112,
  139; defined, 10, 85, 139–41, 272n5; as
  immanent to the form of the novel,
  141; as a logic, 141; as a practice, 257
postfictional hypothesis, 96–97, 171;
  Foucault and, 130
postfictional universe. *See* postfictional
  world
postfictional world, 43, 76, 85, 129, 272n5
postmodernity, 88
poststructuralism, 80
Power, Carl, 295n9
Power, Nina, 301n47
privileged instant (Deleuze), 208–9
Problems of Dostoevsky's Poetics
  (Bakhtin), 130, 146–47, 171, 222, 273n13
profiling, 228–30; defined, 228; as a
  degree-zero connection, 228–29, 248
Program Era (McGurl), 80–84, 105, 110,
  277–78n20
proletariat, 224

Proust, Marcel, 75, 152–53, 189, 288n3
psychology, 194; psychological profiling,
  228

quasi-direct discourse, 37, 218, 221–22,
  293n33. *See also* free indirect
  discourse

Rabelais, François, 93
race: discrimination, 265n35; as form, 31;
  racial profiling, 228–30
Rancière, Jacques, 22, 179, 186, 190,
  231–54; on cinema, 13, 210, 244–45,
  248, 296–97n20; on connections,
  65–66, 103; on the literary (aesthetic)
  regime, 26–27, 40, 65–66, 188–89;
  mute speech, 17, 155, 238, 270n35; on
  Sebald, 66
Rancière, Jacques, works: "Are Some
  Things Unrepresentable?" 233,
  275n29; *Béla Tarr, the Time After*,
  245–48; *The Ignorant Schoolmaster*,
  237, 297n22; *The Lost Thread*, 247–50;
  Mute Speech, 155–56; *The Politics of
  Aesthetics*, 231–32, 238; *The Politics of
  Literature*, 65–66, 103, 234
realism, 18, 21, 26, 77–78, 91, 104, 112, 203,
  272n5; as connecting term of the
  novel, 22–23; Lukács on, 22–23, 26;
  Rancière on, 275n29
referentiality, as quality of the novel,
  25–26, 76
regimes of art (Rancière), 4–5, 26–27,
  103, 231–41, 251, 298–99n29
Reich, Robert, 285n9
relationality, 27, 40, 206, 247; absence of
  in van Velde, 251–53; absolute, 29–34
relations: in Hitchcock's cinema, 241–43;
  as mode of thought of the novel, 29
representation, 26, 34, 208, 227; as ethical
  rather than technical problem of the
  novel, 74; historical shift from to
  instantiation, 87–88, 89, 91–92, 94,
  100–105, 108–9, 142, 189–90, 236, 259,
  275n29; logic of, 28; object vs.
  principle, 152; as regime of art, 103,
  179, 186, 232–33; representing and

represented consciousnesses, 153, 222, 227; of thoughts, 8, 112, 141

representative regime (Rancière), 179, 186, 232–33

represented speech and thought (Banfield), 5, 76, 77, 95, 105, 109, 111, 129–30, 257, 259–60, 272n6, 277n14

resolution, as formal quality of the novel, 12, 25, 42–43, 45, 173, 184–85, 187, 204–5, 219, 223, 256, 259–60; absence in Godard, 214, 218; chronotope as, 279n7

Rhetoric of Fiction (Booth), 78–79, 80, 83, 85, 97, 101, 273n13

Richards, I. A., 6, 49

Rise of the Novel (Watt), 6–7, 34, 113–14, 203

Rockhill, Gabriel, 236–37, 296–97n20

Rodowick, D. N., 173, 288n34

Rohmer, Eric, 208, 210

Ropars-Wuilleumier, Marie-Claire, 205, 290–91n22

Rorty, Richard, 275–76n1

Rossellini, Roberto, 191, 195

Roth, Philip, 88

Roussel, Raymond, 280n11

Russell, Bertrand, 165

Russell's paradox, 166. *See also* Bradley's regress

Said, Edward W., 55, 60

sarcasm, 17, 31, 110. *See also* politeness

Sartre, Jean-Paul, 239

Saturday (McEwan), 32–34

Saussure, Ferdinand de, 115–16, 118, 168

Scarry, Elaine, 90

Schefer, Jean Louis, 207

sculpture, 20, 29

Sebald, W. G., 1–2, 6, 8–9, 42–46, 50, 52, 55; use of photography, 56, 58–59

Sebald, W. G., works: *Austerlitz*, 60–67; *The Emigrants*, 56–58, 61, 65; "Paul Bereyter," 56–58, 61, 65; *The Rings of Saturn*, 63, 64–65, 99–100, 115; *Vertigo*, 42–43, 56, 59

sense, 164, 177, 190, 193. *See also* ideas; meaning; thought

sensorimotor break (Deleuze), 12–13, 191–93, 195–96, 208, 216; and Bakhtin's thought, 283–4n35; defined, 196, 199; as figure of thought, 192–93, 202–4, 206; as historical event, 196, 201–2; and Jameson, 292n29; Rancière's rejection of, 237, 239–41, 247–48; relation to free indirect, 223, 230; in Ali Smith, 298n29

sensorimotor collapse. *See* sensorimotor break

sensorimotor schema (Bergson), 142, 210, 259; analogy with Bakhtin, 284n35; Bergson's theory of, 198–99; and Conrad, 248–49; defined, 191; and the instantiation relation, 203, 230; realized in narrative cinema, 191, 195

sensorimotor system (Bergson). *See* sensorimotor schema

sentences, 2–3, 220; unspeakable (Banfield), 109

set theory, 61, 165–66

showing and telling, 26, 278n20

Silence Once Begun (Ball), 154–59

simultaneity, 133, 138, 142, 150

Singer, Peter, 175, 273n13

Siskind, Mariano, 137

Slow Man (Coetzee), 226

Smith, Adam, 167, 285n9

Smith, Ali, 6, 298–99n29

Smith, Barbara Herrnstein, 275–76n1

Smith, Zadie, 6, 9, 89–95, 97, 166, 285n9

Smollett, Tobias, 92–93

Smuts, Barbara, 175

social formalism (Hale), 21–22, 87, 88, 98, 103–4, 135; defined, 263n13

social indexicality (Bourdieu), 21–22, 263n13

Socrates, 169

Sontag, Susan, 290n16

Sophocles, 232–33

Spark, Muriel, 226, 259–60

speaking subject. *See* subject of enunciation

Spinoza, Benedict de, 180

states of affairs: dispersive, 65; ontology of (Armstrong), 86, 114, 167, 221, 301n46

St. Clair, Robert, 238
Stendhal, 22–23, 125
Sterne, Laurence, 92–93
Stoics, 168
Straub, Jean-Marie, 208, 214
subjectivation, 223
subjectivization, 82, 83, 131, 247
subjectivity: multiplicity and, 134; as temporal lag, 191, 199, 213; of the work, 4, 227
subject of enunciation, 34, 119, 155, 163, 171

tact, 51, 94, 96, 98, 99–100, 131–32
Tarr, Béla, 201, 245–48, 249–50, 300n34
terrorism, 171, 185
theater, 226
theory, 32, 38, 132, 155; D. N. Rodowick on, 173
Theory of the Novel (Lukács): abstraction of, 193–94; biographical form, 60–61, 112–13, 176, 206; de Man on, 173–74; entertainment novels, 51, 52, 73–74, 256; experiential quality of, 175, 204–5, 243, 253; historico-philosophical approach of, 44–46; irony, 24–25, 33–34, 248; Lukács's disavowal of, 177; as not a theory of the novel, 72–73, 173–74; and the novel's capacity for thought, 97–100, 173–74; part-whole relations, 51; Pavel on, 23; totality in, 172–73; an "unsurmounted element" in the novel, 237–38, 243, 248, 256–58
Theory of the Novel (Mazzoni), 2
thought: in cinema, 12, 30–31, 192, 202, 206–7, 213–14, 223; deflection of, 185; Deleuze on, 143, 146; and free indirect discourse, 5, 221–22; Frege on the primacy of, 165–67; as ideological, 196–97; instantiated and noninstantiated in the novel, 8, 29, 34, 37, 38, 85, 99, 159, 192, 288n34; Levine on, 182; in literature, 1, 83, 127; as nonsubjective, 222; of the novel, 34, 112, 173–74, 193, 251, 256; and number, 165; without perspective, 141;

representation of, 3, 8, 141, 152, 208. See also ideas; meaning; sense
Thousand Plateaus, A (Deleuze and Guattari), 119, 218–22, 257
time: concrete (lived), 125, 249; instantiation of, 133; as object of representation, 107–8, 124, 227; represented vs. representing, 153; space and, 31, 76, 124, 133, 142. See also chronotope; duration
time-image (Deleuze), 154, 195, 206, 227, 253
Tobler, Adolf, 219, 260, 266n41, 277n14
Tolstoy, Leo, 26, 32, 33, 34
totality, 21, 49, 172–73, 183
Toynton, Evelyn, 267n11
Trilling, Lionel, 179
Truffaut, François, 208, 298n27
Trump, Donald J., 285n9
Tsai Ming-liang, 201
Twain, Mark, 18–19
Two or Three Things I Know About Her (Godard), 211–13, 217, 223–24, 290–91n22
type, 50, 54, 55, 61, 86, 139–40
typicality, 22, 23, 141

Ulysses (Joyce), 52, 78, 224, 294n41
unthinkable, 205–6
Updike, John, 174–75

van Velde, Bram, 29–30, 231, 251–54, 300–301n44, 301n46
ventriloquy, 130, 173–74, 213
"Venus in Two Acts" (Hartman), 293–94n37
Vertov, Dziga, 245
virtual, and actual, relation, 226–27
Vlady, Marina, 224
Vološinov, V. N., 11, 12–13, 20, 125; on free indirect discourse, 35, 37, 218–19, 221–26, 258, 259–60, 277n14; philosophy of language, 115–19, 220–21. See also quasi-direct discourse

Walkowitz, Rebecca, 134–38, 280–81n19
Walser, Robert, 29

Warwick Research Collective (WReC), 282–83n30
Washington Post, 285n9
Watt, Ian, 6, 34, 113–14, 203
Wayward Lives, Beautiful Experiments (Hartman), 47–48, 294n37
Welles, Orson, 195, 244
Wenders, Wim, 202
Wharton, Edith, 88
whatever being (Agamben), 49, 67, 269n24
White Teeth (Smith), 92–94
Whyte, Alistair, 293n30

Winch, Peter, 42, 267n9
Wittgenstein, Ludwig, 41, 42, 295n9
Wood, Michael, 150, 152
Woolf, Virginia, 103, 231, 249
world literature, 81–82, 137; Kelman and, 148–49, 282n30
WReC. *See* Warwick Research Collective
writing, images of, 64–65, 163; bridge as, 74–75, 91, 97, 102, 126, 149, 163, 271n3
writing process, 12, 106–7

Zarzosa, Agustín, 40
Zilcosky, John, 270n41

CPSIA information can be obtained
at www.ICGtesting.com
Printed in the USA
JSHW022250280323
39522JS00001BA/44

9 780231 192972